Switch/Router Architectures

Switch/Router Architectures
Systems with Crossbar Switch Fabrics

James Aweya

CRC Press
Taylor & Francis Group
Boca Raton London New York

CRC Press is an imprint of the
Taylor & Francis Group, an **informa** business

CRC Press
Taylor & Francis Group
6000 Broken Sound Parkway NW, Suite 300
Boca Raton, FL 33487-2742

First issued in paperback 2023

ISBN-13: 978-0-367-40785-8 (hbk)
ISBN-13: 978-1-03-265421-8 (pbk)
ISBN-13: 978-0-367-80904-1 (ebk)

DOI: 10.1201/9780367809041

Publisher's Note
The publisher has gone to great lengths to ensure the quality of this reprint but points out that some imperfections in the original copies may be apparent.

Visit the Taylor & Francis Web site at
www.taylorandfrancis.com

and the CRC Press Web site at
www.crcpress.com

Contents

PART 1   Characteristics of Switch/Routers with Crossbar Switch Fabrics

PART 2   Design Examples and Case Studies

Preface

The continuous growth of the Internet is still creating increasing demands for bandwidth and new services from service providers' networks. The growing reliance on the Internet has also created the demand for value-added services that require faster connectivity, higher quality of service, and more advanced mobile user services. There is little doubt that the rising demand for Internet connectivity and new services will continue to task the performance of network infrastructures and the individual network devices that make those networks. Networks are also under pressure to deliver these advanced services cost-effectively and at reduced operational costs.

Switches, switch/routers, routers, and network devices, in general, have traditionally been based on the following basic interconnect architectures: shared bus, shared memory, ring fabric (using point-to-point interconnects), and the crossbar switch. Shared-bus architectures are simple in design and are easy to implement. They can be constructed from readily available standard commercial products. However, despite these advantages, designers have discovered over the years that shared-bus architectures have practical performance, scalability, and fault tolerance limitations. On the issue of signal integrity, the bus architecture has practical limits on the operating frequency that can be supported, signal propagation delays (or path lengths) that are tolerable, and electrical loading on the signal lines.

The shared bus has serious bus bandwidth utilization limitation because it allows only one data transfer on the bus at a time. On the shared-bus fabric, only one transmission (time-slot) can be carried/propagated on the bus at any given time, which can result in limited throughput, scalability, and low number of network interfaces supported. Although multiple buses can be used to increase the throughput and improve the reliability of bus-based architectures, its inability to scale cost-effectively with higher data rates, number of network interfaces, and bus clock speeds is a serious limitation.

The main disadvantage of a shared-memory architecture is that bandwidth scalability is limited by the memory access speed (bandwidth). The access speeds of memories have a physical limit, and this limit prevents the shared-memory switch architecture from scaling to very high bandwidths and port speeds. Another factor is that the shared-memory bandwidth has to be at least two times the aggregate system port speeds for all the ports to run at full line rate.

Ring architectures overcome the one-at-a-time data-transfer limitations of the shared bus by allowing multiple concurrent data transfers on the ring in order to achieve higher aggregate data throughput. However, high data transfer latencies and ring reliability issues such as single points of failure are major concerns in ring architectures. The ring is susceptible to single-point-of-failures because it supports only one path between any two adjacent nodes. One malfunctioning node or link on the ring can disrupt communication on the entire fabric. The capacity of the ring architectures can be improved by implementing multiple parallel rings.

These rings are usually controlled in a distributed manner, but Medium Access Control (MAC) implementation on the multiple rings can be difficult to realize.

Given the limitations of the other interconnect architectures, designers have long considered the use of crossbar switch fabrics, especially for high-performance, high-capacity systems. Crossbar switch fabrics offer several design benefits over the traditional shared-media fabrics. High-performance crossbar switches can support multiple data transfers over the fabric at the same time and can easily be made nonblocking, avoiding the bandwidth limitations seen in the shared-media fabrics with one-at-a-time data transfer type of operations.

Crossbar switch fabrics have the flexibility of connecting any input to any output, allowing for multiple concurrent data transfers. They can be designed to have relatively higher bandwidth, scalability, and fault tolerance. In addition to its basic architectural advantages, the crossbar switch can be implemented in ASICs and FPGAs. Bigger switches can be constructed from smaller crossbar switch chips. There is an abundance of literature from the commercial sector and academia on how to design crossbar switch fabrics of different types and capabilities. For this reason, a comprehensive list of references will be nearly impossible in this book. More so, crossbar switch fabric design has been a very well-studied area, especially during the days of Asynchronous Transfer Mode (ATM) switch development.

This book discusses the various switch/router architectures that use crossbar switch fabric as their internal interconnects. The book also discusses the main issues involved in the design of these switch/routers that use crossbar switch fabrics. The issues discussed include performance, implementation complexity, and scalability to higher speeds. To enhance reader understanding of switch/routers, the book begins by describing the basics of switch/routers and then the most common crossbar switch fabric-based architectures in today's networks.

After presenting a detailed discussion of centralized versus distributed forwarding architectures, the book discusses the processing considerations that led to the design of distributed forwarding systems using crossbar-based switch fabrics. The discussion includes the hardware and software designs in select but different switch/router architectures, to allow the reader to appreciate the different designs out there and how crossbar-based switch/routers have evolved over the years. The book uses case studies to examine the inner workings of switch/router design in a comprehensive manner with the goal of enhancing reader understanding. The example architectures discussed are selected such that they cover the majority of features found in switch/routers used in today's networks. It is written in a simple style and language to allow readers to easily understand and appreciate the material presented.

Author

James Aweya, PhD, is a chief research scientist at Etisalat British Telecom Innovation Center (EBTIC), Khalifa University, Abu Dhabi, UAE. He has been granted 64 US patents and has published over 54 journal papers, 39 conference papers, and 43 Nortel technical reports. He has authored one book and is a senior member of the Institute of Electrical and Electronics Engineers (IEEE).

Part 1

Characteristics of Switch/Routers with Crossbar Switch Fabrics

1 The Switch/Router

Integrated OSI Layers 2 and 3 Forwarding on a Single Platform

1.1 INTRODUCTION

This chapter introduces switch/routers and the architectures and methods they support to perform multilayer switching. An understanding of multilayer switching is necessary for the reader to better appreciate the various architectures discussed in this book. A switch/router, sometimes referred to as a multilayer switch, is a device that supports the forwarding of packets at both Layers 2 and 3 of the Open Systems Interconnection (OSI) model (Figure 1.1).

The switch/router also supports the relevant Layers 2 and 3 control plane protocols needed to create the forwarding databases used in the forwarding of packets [AWEYA1BK18]. In addition to features for system management and configuration, the switch/router may support quality-of-service (QoS) and security filtering and control mechanisms that use parameters within the Layers 4 to 7 fields of packets being forwarded.

Network devices attached to different virtual local area networks (VLANs) can only communicate with one another through a router (or Layer 3 forwarding device) as illustrated in Figure 1.1. In a Layer 2 network, VLANs can be used to define distinct and separate broadcast domains. Each defined broadcast domain (or VLAN) is the set of devices attached to that domain that can receive Layer 2 broadcast packets (e.g., Ethernet frames) sent from any device within that domain.

Routers are typically used to bound the distinct broadcast domains (VLANs) because routers do not forward broadcast frames—all broadcast traffic within a VLAN is confined to that VLAN and cannot cross any attached router. VLANs are designed to mimic the behavior of legacy shared-medium LAN segments where broadcasts from any one device are seen by all other devices on that LAN segment.

Layer 2 forwarding is relatively simple compared to Layer 3 forwarding [AWEYA1BK18]. To perform Layer 3 forwarding, the switch/router needs a route processor (also referred to as Layer 3 control engine) that runs the routing and management protocols for the system. The routing protocols build and maintain the routing tables required for Layer 3 forwarding. In addition to creating the routing and forwarding databases (tables), the route processor also performs all the non-data transfer housekeeping functions for the system (system configuration,

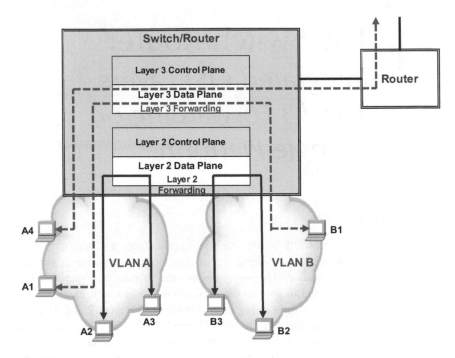

FIGURE 1.1   Layers 2 and 3 Forwarding in the Switch/Router.

monitoring, download of software to other modules, management of QoS and security access control lists (ACL), and other tasks for packet processing).

A switch/router can use either flow-based or network topology-based information for Layer 3 packet forwarding. The advantages and disadvantages of both methods have been discussed in greater detail in [AWEYA1BK18]. Nonetheless, we give a brief overview of these methods later to set the proper context for the discussions that follow in the later chapters.

1.2   FLOW-BASED LAYER 3 FORWARDING

In flow-based Layer 3 forwarding, the switch/router maintains a flow/route cache of the forwarding information of recently processed packets (e.g., destination IP address, next-hop IP node (and its receiving interface MAC address), egress port, and any other relevant forwarding information). To populate the flow/route cache, the switch/router forwards the first packet in any flow to the route processor for software-based processing and forwarding using the route processor's master forwarding table.

After the first packet of the flow is forwarded, the forwarding information used by the route processor is used to populate the flow/route cache so that subsequent packets of the same flow can be forwarded using the simpler and faster flow/route

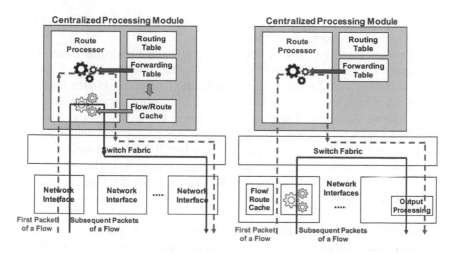

FIGURE 1.2 Layer 3 Forwarding Using Flow-Based Forwarding Table (or Flow/Route Cache).

cache. The basic concepts of flow-based Layer 3 forwarding are illustrated in Figure 1.2.

To enable high-speed Layer 3 packet forwarding, the switch/router typically employs specialized application-specific integrated circuits (ASIC) to perform the forwarding and all the relevant Layers 2 and 3 packet rewrite operations of the forwarded packets. The main Layer 3 (or IP) packet rewrites include updating the time-to-live (TTL) value and recalculating the IP checksum. The basic Layer 2 rewrites (assuming Ethernet is used) include rewriting the source MAC address in the outgoing packet to be that of the egress interface, rewriting the destination MAC address to be that of the receiving interface of the next-hop node, and recalculating the Ethernet checksum.

The Ethernet checksum recalculation is necessary because the source and destination MAC addresses of the packet change as the packet traverses the switch/router when forwarded at Layer 3. The switch/router is required to recalculate the Ethernet checksum as these new MAC addresses are written in the outgoing packet. The packet forwarding may include more rewrites such as adding VLAN tags, updating IP and/or Ethernet packet class-of-service information, and so on.

1.3 NETWORK TOPOLOGY-BASED LAYER 3 FORWARDING

In topology-based forwarding, the route processor runs the routing protocols to create the routing tables. Entries in the routing table can also be created manually as static routes. The most relevant information needed for packet forwarding is distilled from the routing table to generate the more compact forwarding table. The forwarding table contains the same information needed to forward packets as the routing table, the only difference is it contains only the information that can be used directly by a forwarding engine in forwarding packets—it excludes all other information not needed for forwarding.

In topology-based forwarding, the forwarding engine performs Layer 3 forwarding using the Layer 3 forwarding table (also called the forwarding information base (FIB)) and Layer 2 rewrites using information maintained in the adjacency table which is dynamically updated by Layer 2 address discovery protocols such as the Address Resolution Protocol (ARP). Using the Layer 3 forwarding and Layer 2 adjacency tables, the forwarding engine can quickly perform lookups for forwarding information such as a packet's next-hop IP address, egress port, and MAC address of the receiving interface of the next-hop IP node (Figure 1.3).

For topology-based forwarding, the following two main databases are used by the forwarding engine:

- **Layer 3 Forwarding Table**: The forwarding engine performs lookups in a Layer 3 forwarding table for the forwarding information of a packet. Each lookup is performed by extracting the IP destination address of the packet and then making a longest prefix matching (LPM) search in the forwarding table. LPM is more complex than lookups in a flow/route cache and can be time consuming and processing intensive when performed in software. High-speed, high-performance LPM searches are generally done in hardware. Conceptually, the Layer 3 forwarding table is similar to the routing table albeit rather compact and smaller. The forwarding table contains the same forwarding information maintained in the routing table. The routing table is updated (dynamically by the

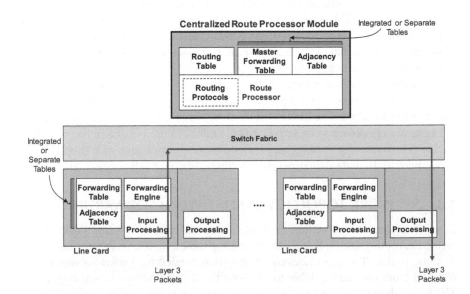

FIGURE 1.3   Layer 3 Forwarding Using Network Topology-Based Forwarding Table.

routing protocols) whenever topology or routing changes occur in the network. The forwarding table is then immediately updated to reflect these changes. The routing table and forwarding table must always be kept synchronized as much as possible. The forwarding table maintains information such as the next-hop IP address information and the corresponding egress port on the switch/router.

- **Adjacency Table**: Two nodes in a network are considered adjacent if they can reach each other over a single Layer 2 protocol hop (e.g., Ethernet, Point-to-Point Protocol (PPP), Asynchronous Transfer Mode (ATM), IEEE 802.11, etc.). The adjacency table is used to maintain Layer 3 address to Layer 2 address mapping. The adjacency table maintains a Layer 2 (e.g., MAC) address for every next-hop IP address in the forwarding table. Before a packet is transmitted out its egress port, the Layer 2 destination address in the outgoing packet is rewritten using the Layer 2 address information read from the adjacency table. This Layer 2 address is that of the receiving interface of the next-hop IP node (the Layer 2 adjacency of the current node). The adjacency table can be integrated into the Layer 3 forwarding table or implemented as a separate table. However, integrating it into the forwarding table allows one lookup to be performed to retrieve all forwarding information including the Layer 2 adjacencies.

The topology-based forwarding model allows the separation (or decoupling) of the control-plane functions (i.e., running routing and control protocols) from the data-plane functions (i.e., forwarding table lookups and packet rewrites). Nevertheless, the control-plane functions (running software in the route processor) are still responsible for creating and maintaining the master forwarding and adjacency tables and then downloading these to the data-plane functions (running in the forwarding engine(s)).

A switch/router may support multiple route processors for redundancy purposes (e.g., primary and secondary route processors running in active-active or active-standby mode). A switch/router may also support multiple forwarding engines running in a distributed manner each using a copy of the master forwarding table maintained by the route processor.

The forwarding engine may not be able to forward all packets it receives. These special packets have to be forwarded to the route processor for further processing. Examples of these special (or exemption) packets are:

- Control packets from routing protocols
- IP packets with IP header options
- IP packets requiring fragmentation
- Packets with IP time-to-live (TTL) expired
- Packets carrying ICMP echo requests (used to ping IP devices)
- IP packets coming from or destined to tunnel interfaces
- Packets requiring encryption, network address translation, etc.

1.4 USING CENTRALIZED OR DISTRIBUTED FORWARDING ENGINES

Packet forwarding can be done using one of two methods, centralized or distributed.

1.4.1 FORWARDING USING A CENTRALIZED FORWARDING ENGINE

In centralized forwarding, a single centralized forwarding engine or a pool of them perform all packet forwarding decisions for all packets received from all network interfaces in the system. In addition to making forwarding decisions, the centralized forwarding engine(s) perform the QoS and security ACL processing and filtering as well as other data-path functions required in the system.

All packets entering the switch/router must pass through the centralized forwarding engine to be processed. Incoming packets are passed from the network interfaces over the switch fabric (which can be a shared-bus, shared-memory or crossbar switch) to the central forwarding engine. Figure 1.4 illustrates the logical architectures of centralized forwarding.

Some centralized forwarding architectures offload some amount of the data-path processing to the line cards or interface modules by allowing them to forward only the packet headers to the centralized forwarding engine [BRYAN93] [CISCCAT6000]. The storage of the packet payloads and some packet rewrite operations are carried out in the line cards. Examples of these kinds of architecture are described in detail in [AWEYA1BK18] and also in *Chapters 4* and *8* of this book.

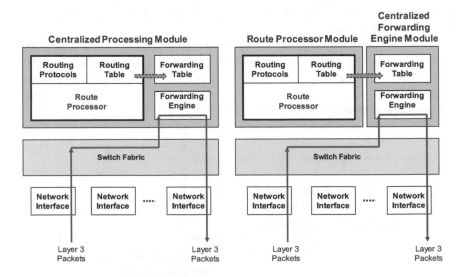

FIGURE 1.4 Centralized Forwarding.

1.4.2 FORWARDING USING DISTRIBUTED FORWARDING ENGINES

In a distributed forwarding architecture, multiple independent forwarding engines are spread out in the system, located typically in the line cards (or network interface modules). This allows the interfaces or line cards to make forwarding decisions independently using their local copies of the forwarding tables downloaded from the route processor (Figure 1.5). In this architecture, the centralized route processor generates the master forwarding table but also ensures that the distributed forwarding tables are kept synchronized to the master table.

The route processor runs the routing protocols to create both the routing table and the master Layer 3 forwarding table. The route processor then copies the contents of its master tables to local forwarding tables used by the distributed forwarding engines located on the line cards. This allows each line card to make forwarding decisions independently without direct assistance from the centralized route processor. An incoming packet is processed by its ingress line card and then transferred directly across the switch fabric to its destination egress line card.

Each line card in the distributed architecture uses its copy of the master for warding table and adjacency table for forwarding packets. Some architectures with local ARP processing capabilities on the line cards may allow the line card to main a local ARP (or adjacency) table which is created and maintained by the local ARP module. Other architectures may relegate all ARP processing to the centralized route processor, which creates all adjacencies for the entire system. Designers who aim to keep the cost and complexity of the line card low (by not

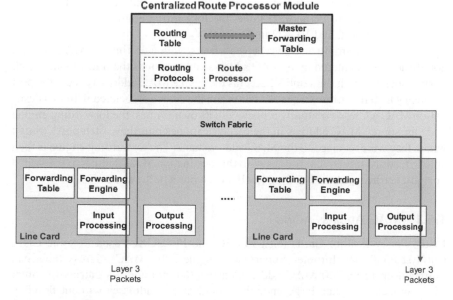

FIGURE 1.5 Distributed Forwarding.

including more processing beyond pure data-path processing) adopt this central-ized ARP processing approach.

High-capacity, high-performance routing systems are generally based on dis-tributed forwarding architectures. The forwarding performance and throughput with distributed forwarding is equal to the aggregate throughput of all the dis-tributed forwarding engines as long as the switch fabric is not a bottleneck. The distributed forwarding architecture also allows each line card to be specifically designed to support its own unique set of local functions and interfaces (encryp-tion, network address translation capabilities, tunneling protocols, different types of Layer 2 protocols and encapsulations, mix of interface types and speeds, etc.). Each line card can be tailor made to meet specific design objectives without being unnecessarily constrained by issues in other system modules.

The Catalyst 6500 with a Supervisor Engine 720 (discussed in *Chapter 8*) supports distributed forwarding using a built-in crossbar switch fabric module and line cards that have an integrated Distributed Forwarding Card (DFC). This Catalyst 6500 switch/router still maintains a centralized forwarding engine (in a module called the Policy Feature Card (PFC)) even when using line cards with DFCs for backward-compatibility with older line cards that do not support the DFC feature.

1.5   BUILDING THE LAYER 2 FORWARDING TABLES

This section describes how the Layer 2 forwarding engine constructs and main-tains the Layer 2 forwarding table (also referred to as the MAC address table). The MAC address table is constructed by reading the source MAC address of arriving Ethernet frames. If the source MAC address and its associated switch port are not listed in the address table, the forwarding engine enters that MAC address, switch port, and VLAN in the table.

When the forwarding engine receives a frame with a destination MAC address not already listed/entered in its MAC address table, it floods the frame to all switch ports associated with the same VLAN (as the source MAC address) except the port through which the frame was received. When the device associated with this desti-nation MAC address eventually replies with its own frames, the forwarding engine adds the source MAC address in the received frames plus the switch port through which they were received to the MAC address table. The forwarding engine is then able to forward subsequent frames with this destination MAC address to the switch port just learned without flooding to all switch ports in the same VLAN.

1.5.1   MAC ADDRESS AGING

In the Policy Feature Cards (e.g., PFC3C and PFC3CXL) used in some Cisco Catalyst 6500 switch/router Supervisor Engines, the MAC address table can maintain up to 96,000 MAC address entries (64,000 address entries for other PFC3 models), a space large enough to hold many addresses without flooding frames belonging to unknown or unlisted MAC address entries. The Layer 2 forwarding engine in the PFC employs a MAC address entry aging mechanism that is driven by a configurable MAC address table aging timer. This aging mechanism is used to delete idle or stale entries in the address table when a MAC address remains inactive for a specified period of time (in seconds). Such inactive entries are removed from the MAC address table and have to be relearned by the Layer 2 forwarding engine when their stations communicate again.

1.5.2 SYNCHRONIZING MAC ADDRESS TABLES IN A DISTRIBUTED FORWARDING ARCHITECTURE

In the distributed Layer 2 forwarding architecture, each distributed Layer 2 engine (on a line card or switching module) learns MAC addresses on its own (by gleaning them from frames sent on its local interfaces). The forwarding engine enters these addresses in a local MAC address table. These MAC address table entries are also appropriately aged using local aging timers. The switch also has to ensure the sharing and synchronization of the MAC address tables learned by the various distributed Layer 2 forwarding engines.

Using, for example, MAC address table synchronization over an out-of-band channel (e.g., the Ethernet Out of Band Channel (EOBC) in the Cisco Catalyst 6500 switch/routers), the switch can ensure the sharing and synchronization of the MAC address tables maintained by the distributed Layer 2 forwarding engines (Figure 1.6). This mechanism eliminates the need for a Layer 2 forwarding engine to flood a frame whose destination MAC address has not been learned and entered in its local MAC address table but is listed and active on another address table. Synchronization (across the EOBC) ensures that all the MAC address tables in the system are consistent and have the same view of the active MAC addresses in the network.

1.5.3 HISTORY OF MAC ADDRESS CHANGES

The Catalyst 6500 switch/routers can be configured to maintain a history (over a period of time) of MAC address changes associated with a particular switch port

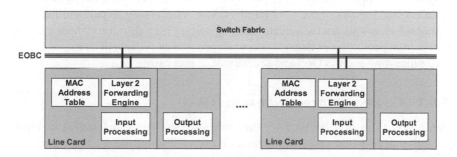

FIGURE 1.6 Synchronizing MAC Address Tables in a Distributed Forwarding Architecture.

(i.e., history of MAC address table entries, removals, and additions for a port). The MAC address change history (i.e., notification of address table changes) can be sent as an SNMP trap notification to a network management or it can be read manually by the network administrator from the SNMP MIB.

1.6   MEMORY ARCHITECTURES FOR STORING FORWARDING DATABASES

Switch/routers use high-speed memories to store the various information required for packet forwarding such as Layer 2 forwarding tables, Layer 3 flow/route caches, Layer 3 forwarding tables, Layer 2 adjacency tables, QoS and security ACL tables, etc. These tables have to be maintained regardless of whether the switch/router operates in a centralized or distributed forwarding mode. However, more tables (and consequently more memory) have to be supported in the distributed forwarding architecture since each line card requires its own set of hardware tables.

The switch/router needs to perform lookups in its QoS and security ACL tables to determine whether a packet with a specific destination IP address is to be dropped (discarded) according to ACL rules defined in the tables. All these tables are implemented in high-speed memories that allow high-performance lookups using search algorithms that are optimized for such memories. This allows high-speed operations that can maintain line-rate performance.

Switch/routers use specialized memory architectures such as Content Addressable Memory (CAM) and Ternary Content Addressable Memory (TCAM) to store the various tables in the system. A switch/router typically uses a CAM for maintaining Layer 2 forwarding tables that can be searched on exact matches such as storing MAC address tables for Layer 2 lookups. A CAM's memory cell can store only two results, 0 (true) or 1 (false). TCAMs are typically used for maintaining Layer 3 forwarding tables that allow searches based on longest prefix matches such as storing IP forwarding tables organized by IP network address prefixes. A TCAM's memory cell provides three results: 0, 1, and "don't care."

Some switch/router architectures such as the Catalyst 6500 with a Supervisor Engine 720 support the ability to perform in parallel, multiple lookups into multiple distinct regions of the CAM and TCAM. This ability to perform multiple parallel lookups allows the switch/router to sustain high data throughput and not suffer from performance degradation when processing packets that require extensive processing such as QoS and security ACL processing.

1.6.1   CONTENT ADDRESSABLE MEMORY (CAM)

A CAM is an associative memory (or associative storage) which allows an input search pattern to be compared against entries of stored data and returns the address of matching data or the matching data itself. A user supplies a data pattern to the CAM and the CAM searches its entire stored content to determine if the presented pattern is stored anywhere in it. If the pattern is found (that is, a successful match or a hit), the CAM returns the storage address of the match or hit or the contents of that storage address.

Switch/routers use CAMs to store Layer 2 forwarding information that include MAC address (and possibly, VLAN ID) to switch port (or network interface) mappings. Search results in the CAM are in binary (0 or 1 operations) and allow a forwarding engine to find exact matches when determining the egress port for a given MAC address (Figure 1.7). For an incoming packet that is being processed for Layer 2 forwarding, the forwarding engine must find an exact match to the packet's destination MAC address and if no match is found, (according to transparent bridging rules) the forwarding engine floods the packet out of all ports in the packet's broadcast domain, that is, its VLAN.

The pattern extracted from the packet and used to perform a lookup in the CAM is called a key. As illustrated in Figure 1.7, the forwarding engine performs the Layer 2 lookup using the destination MAC address and VLAN ID as a search key in the CAM. The steps involved in determining a match and result in the CAM based on a lookup key are summarized as follows:

Step 1: The forwarding engine extracts the key (VLAN ID and destination MAC address) from the packet and feeds it into a hash function that gives an output that is used to search the CAM looking for an exact matching entry.

Step 2: The hash function result identifies a row in the MAC address table. and the key itself (consisting of VLAN and destination MAC address) is compared with entries of the indexed row on all pages simultaneously.

Step 3: The matching entry, if any, provides a result which is, for example, the egress port on the switch to which the packet should be forwarded.

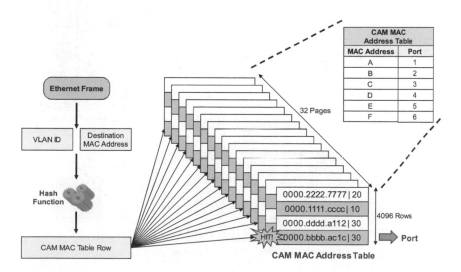

FIGURE 1.7   Lookup in CAM MAC Address Table.

For Layer 2 forwarding tables, CAM maintains forwarding information such as a packet's destination MAC address and egress switch ports.

1.6.2 Ternary Content Addressable Memory (TCAM)

In Layer 3 forwarding, switch/routers and routers do not search for an exact match in the Layer 3 forwarding tables but rather the longest matching network prefix. For example, a forwarding engine that performs a lookup for an IP destination network with a 22-bit (/22) prefix or mask is only concerned with the first 22 bits (i.e., the prefix) of the IP address. In this lookup process, the forwarding engine is not searching for an exact match as done when using a CAM but rather a match on the first 22 bits (prefix) of the packet's IP destination address.

A TCAM is a fully associative memory that can be used to implement a lookup for a data pattern and uses a dedicated comparison circuitry that allows for searches to be done usually within a single clock cycle. The TCAM compares the input search pattern against the stored data and the address of any matching data is returned. The memory cell used in a TCAM stores three states: "1", "0", and "X", where the additional state "X" is referred to as the "don't care" state or "mask". This extra state is used for searches that can match either a "0" or "1" in the input search pattern.

TCAMs are used for searches or lookups that allow both exact and partial matches. Switch/routers and routers typically use TCAMs when performing longest prefix matching in IP network addresses (Figure 1.8). TCAMs allow rapid table lookups and can be used for QoS and security ACL lookups at line speeds.

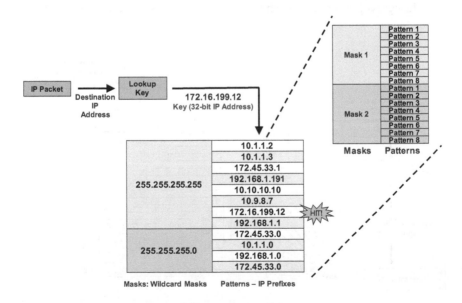

FIGURE 1.8 Lookup in TCAM IP Forwarding Table.

When properly implemented, TCAMs allow the forwarding engine to apply ACLs to packets without degrading significantly the data throughput performance of the system.

The user populates the TCAM holding the forwarding information with a number of entries, each entry with a pattern value, mask value, and an associated result. The stored entries are known, respectively, as value, mask, and result (VMR) entries, and refer simply to the format of entries in the TCAM. The "value" in VMR refers to the data pattern (for example, IP address, TCP or UDP port, DSCP values) presented to the TCAM to be matched. The "mask" refers to the bits associated with the search pattern that should be used in the search (it determines the search prefix in the presented pattern).

The "result" in the VMR refers to the outcome of the search, that is, the result or action that should take place when the search returns a hit for the presented pattern (i.e., value) and mask. For a TCAM used for QoS and security ACLs, the result can take the form of a "permit" or "deny" access to a packet. A result in the case of Layer 3 forwarding table lookup in a TCAM can be a pointer to an entry in the Layer 2 adjacency table that contains the MAC address of the next-hop node and other rewrite information required for a packet. The pointer can be to an entry in a random access memory (RAM) indicating the next-hop IP node and the corresponding egress port on the switch/router.

As illustrated in Figure 1.8, the data structure in the TCAM is segmented into a series of patterns (values) and masks. A specific number of patterns share the same mask by using wildcard-specific fields. To perform a lookup in the TCAM, the forwarding engine checks all entries in parallel which allows faster searches, and the performance can be made independent of the number of TCAM entries. This allows the forwarding engine to perform faster longest prefix match lookups, and to do so with minimal lookup latency.

A TCAM for a switch/router and router can be designed that specifies three different match options that correspond to specific match regions within the TCAM [SIVASUBRA07]. These three match options/regions are defined as follows:

- **Exact-match region**: This region maintains entries for Layer 3 forwarding information such as Layer 2 adjacency addresses for IP next-hop nodes. The entries are MAC addresses for the IP next-hop node interfaces and allow exact searches/matches (that is, given an IP address (key equal to 32 bits), a corresponding MAC address can be found). Other forwarding information such as Layer 2 forwarding tables (MAC addresses and VLAN IDs) and Layer 3 forwarding rewrite information (MAC address rewrite) can be stored in the exact-match regions of the TCAM.
- **Longest-match region**: This region maintains multiple "bins" or groups of Layer 3 address entries organized from the highest to the lowest mask length (i.e., in decreasing order). All address entries within the same bin share the same mask value and pattern value (or key) size. The size of the bins can change dynamically by allowing them to borrow address

entries from neighboring bins **[SIVASUBRA07]**. Layer 3 forwarding tables such as IP unicast prefixes and IP multicast tables can be stored in this region. The search here is, given an IP address (key equal to 32 bits), find the longest matching prefix entry.

- **First-match region**: This region maintains forwarding information that allows lookups that stop after the first matching entry is found. QoS and security ACL entries are examples of applications where the TCAM first-match region can be used.

1.7 PHYSICAL AND LOGICAL INTERFACES ON A SWITCH/ROUTER

An interface on a switch/router can be either a physical interface or a logical (i.e., virtual) interface. Also, an interface can be configured as either a Layer 2 (switch) interface or a Layer 3 (routed) interface. We describe these interfaces in greater detail in this section as well as other interface types such as loopback, tunnel, and port channel interfaces (Figure 1.9 and Figure 1.10). It is important to note that some high-performance network devices implement tunneling and tunnel interfaces locally in the line card forwarding engines and not in the processing intensive software environment of the route processor. The word interface and port are used interchangeably throughout this book.

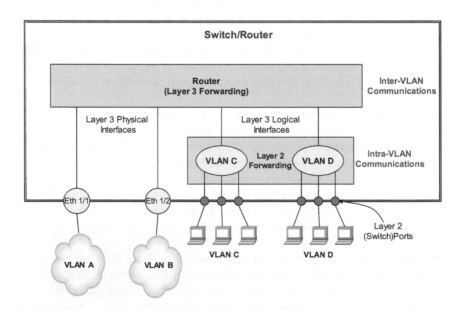

FIGURE 1.9   Logical Layer 3 Forwarding Interfaces in the Switch/Router.

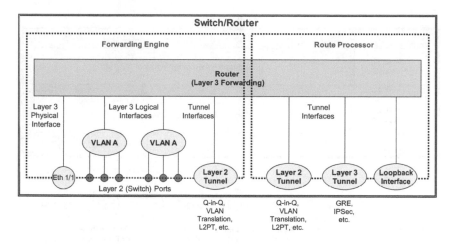

FIGURE 1.10   Layer 2 and 3 Software and Hardware Forwarding Interfaces.

1.7.1 LAYER 2 (SWITCH) INTERFACES

Layer 2 interfaces (also called switch ports or "switchports") are physical interfaces on a Layer 2 switch or switch/router and are directly associated with a Layer 2 protocol and forwarding function on the device. These interfaces have Layer 2 addresses (MAC addresses in the case of Ethernet) and receive Layer 2 frames from other devices. They may also learn Layer 2 addresses in frames received from other stations.

Layer 2 of the Open Systems Interconnection (OSI) reference model (i.e., the Data Link Layer) supports the protocols that control how the Physical Layer (Layer 1) resources are utilized, the operations and sharing of these resources, and how data is structured or formatted before it is placed on the transmission medium (a process called framing). The Layer 2 function of filtering and forwarding framed data (also called Layer 2 packets) in a Layer 2 device is known as bridging.

A physical interface that connects to a Layer 3 protocol and forwarding function (in a routing device) is a physical Layer 3 interface and not a switch port (see discussion later under physical Layer 3 (routed) interfaces). Switch ports are physical ports associated with Layer 2-only functions. These are physical interfaces associated with Layer 2 protocols and forwarding and not Layer 3 routing and forwarding. As illustrated in Figure 1.11, a switch port can either be an access port attached to an end-user device, a trunk port connecting another Layer 2 or 3 device (see also discussion under subinterfaces later), or a port channel or port group (see discussion under port channels later).

1.7.1.1 Access Ports

An access port carries traffic that is sent by only the single VLAN assigned to it. Also, an access port is configured to belong to only a single VLAN and does not mark frames with any identifying tags as they are passed between switches.

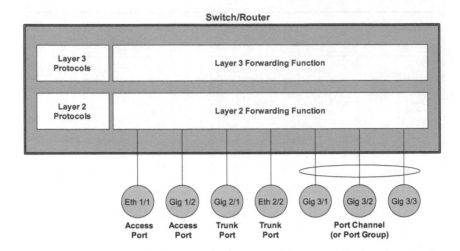

FIGURE 1.11 Layer 2 (Switch) Interfaces.

When creating a VLAN, an access port on the switch/router is assigned to that VLAN. The devices in the VLAN will then be able to communicate through this port to other devices in the same VLAN (assuming the VLAN extends over multiple ports). An access port provides a connection from the switch/router to a corresponding Layer 2 function in another device such as an end-user, server, or another network node such as a router.

Devices within a single VLAN can communicate directly through any of the access ports on a switch on which that VLAN is defined. Communication with other VLANs has to be done through a Layer 3 forwarding device (a router or switch/router), a process known as inter-VLAN routing. This means access ports in different VLANs can only exchange data through a routing device (router or switch/router) or through a routed interface (see discussion later).

1.7.1.2 Access Ports and Tagged Packets

An access port can be defined as a physical port that is assigned to only one VLAN to carry traffic to and from only that one VLAN. In this case, the port receives and sends traffic to and from only the specified VLAN assigned to it in native formats with no Cisco Inter-Switch Link (ISL) or IEEE 802.1Q VLAN tagging required. Unlike a trunk port (discussed later), generally, an access port will not forward packets with identifying tags (either ISL or 802.1Q tags) because a VLAN has been pre-assigned to it. When an access port receives traffic, it assumes that the traffic belongs to the VLAN assigned to it.

However, the way in which an access port treats tagged packets originated by the VLAN that owns the access port depends on the particular switch implementation. It is important to note that the use of the 802.1Q tagging is not limited to VLAN identification only (carried in the 12-bit VLAN ID field) but could include

802.1p class-of-service (CoS) markings to signal to receiving devices the CoS handling requirements of a Layer 2 packet (3-bit Priority Code Point (PCP) and 1-bit Drop Eligible Indicator (DEI)).

So, even though a VLAN could be mapped to a specific access port, dropping in some cases a VLAN tagged packet (solely on the basis that they are tagged) will lead to the loss of important packet information and the ability to signal CoS information even within the owner VLAN and access port. For example, an access port could receive both delay sensitive traffic (such as voice which is 802.1p tagged by the source) and non-delay sensitive traffic (such as email traffic which is untagged) that require the CoS markings to be recognized and adhered to during traffic queuing and scheduling.

For the earlier reasons, in many implementations, if the access port receives a tagged packet for the VLAN assigned to it, the access port will forward the packet (to preserve important information in the tagged packet). The access port behaves in a hybrid mode where it accepts both tagged and untagged traffic. However, if the access port receives a tagged packet that is for another VLAN, it will drop that packet since this requires Layer 3 forwarding (inter-VLAN routing) to get to that VLAN. In this case, even if the source MAC address in the packet was not learned by the Layer 2 forwarding engine and entered in the local MAC address table, the packet is still dropped since the port through which it arrived belongs to another VLAN—the packet arrived on the wrong access port.

1.7.1.3 Trunk Ports

Trunk links operate by passing VLAN information in the form of ISL or 802.1Q tagged packets between the switches attached to the end of the links. Access ports, on the other hand, are mapped to a single VLAN and do not necessarily require any (ISL or 802.1Q) identifying tags on the packets that are passed between the switches. An access port accepts traffic that comes from only its pre-assigned VLAN.

A trunk port, by default, is a member of all the VLANs that are carried in it. The trunk link hauls traffic between the switches for all those member VLANs. To distinguish between the different VLAN traffic flows on the trunk link, a trunk port uses ISL or 802.1Q tags to mark the packets as they pass between the switches. For trunking to work, both sides of the link must be enabled to support either ISL or 802.1Q trunking. For example, if two switches are connected together over a link, the switch ports terminating the link on both switches must be configured to support the same trunking protocol. The two ports must be configured with the same tagging protocol (i.e., ISL or 802.1Q tagging).

An IEEE 802.1Q trunk port can support both tagged and untagged packets simultaneously. An 802.1Q trunk port can be configured to carry a number of VLANs, one of which is a native VLAN that is defined with a specific port VLAN ID and over which all untagged packets' travels are sent on the trunk. The native VLAN (with its trunk port specific VLAN ID) carries all untagged packets and also tagged packets with a NULL VLAN ID. A packet arriving at a trunk port with a VLAN ID equal to its outgoing native VLAN ID is sent untagged. All other packets arriving at the trunk port are sent with a VLAN tag.

The native VLAN ID can be defined on a per-port basis. Trunk Port 1 at one end may define VLAN 1 as its native VLAN while Trunk Port 2 at the other end may define VLAN 2 as its corresponding native VLAN. In this case, if Trunk Port 1 (with native VLAN 1) receives a packet from VLAN 1 and decides to send the packet on the trunk, it will send the packet out on the trunk port untagged. When Trunk Port 2 receives the packet, and it sees that it is untagged, it will associate the packet with its native VLAN which is VLAN 2.

The main features of trunk ports can be summarized as follows:

• Trunk links carry VLAN identification for Layer 2 packets transported between switches.
• IEEE 802.1Q is the standardized method for Ethernet trunking between switches, but Cisco switches also support the proprietary ISL protocol.
• A trunk link must be configured to support the same trunking protocol/mechanism on each end of the link.
• A trunk link can be configured to carry traffic from all VLANs to and from the two switches, but they are generally configured to carry traffic from only limited/specified VLANs.
• GARP VLAN Registration Protocol (GVRP) (defined in IEEE 802.1Q standard) is the standard defined method for registering VLAN membership information between switches. A switch running GVRP can exchange VLAN configuration information with other switches that are GVRP-enabled. Cisco switches also support the proprietary VLAN Trunking Protocol (VTP). Both GVRP and VTP are protocols used to propagate or advertise VLAN configuration information among the connected switches within a domain. VTP, for example, can propagate VLAN information over ISL or 802.1Q trunks.
• Some switches can negotiate the setup of ISL or 802.1Q trunk links. The Dynamic Trunking Protocol (DTP) is a proprietary Cisco protocol that can be used to negotiate ISL or 802.1Q trunking between switch ports on VLAN-aware switches on either ends of a link.

1.7.1.4 Port Channels or Port Groups

A port channel or port group is created when multiple switch ports are bundled together and treated logically as one switch port. A port group is created as a single logical switch port to provide a high-bandwidth connection between two switches or between a switch and a server. A port group also allows balancing of the traffic load across the individual links in the port group. If a link within the port group fails, the traffic carried over the failed link can be distributed and balanced over the remaining active links. Multiple trunk ports (ISL or 802.1Q) can also be grouped into one larger logical (ISL or 802.1Q) trunk port or multiple access ports can be grouped into one larger logical access port.

1.7.2   LAYER 3 (ROUTED) INTERFACES

Layer 3 of the OSI model (i.e., the Network Layer) is primarily responsible for routing Layer 3 packets from their sources across one or more Layer 3 addressed networks or internetworks to their destinations. Thus, Layer 3 interfaces forward routed traffic (IPv4 and IPv6 packets) from one Layer 3 processing entity or device to another. The Layer 3 devices use static or dynamic routing protocols to map out paths to destinations in the interconnected networks. These paths determine where a Layer 3 forwarding entity should forward the Layer 3 (routed) packets for them to get to their intended destinations.

Layer 3 interfaces are used for traditional IP traffic routing as well as for forwarding of Layer 2 traffic going between VLANs, that is, inter-VLAN communication (or routing). Thus, a Layer 3 interface forwards routed traffic only and does not support Layer 2 protocol functions, such as the processing of Spanning Tree Protocol (STP) protocol data units (PDUs).

Other than the Layer 2 interfaces discussed earlier, switch/routers also support Layer 3 interfaces along with Layer 3 routing protocols and forwarding functions. Switch/routers support two types of Layer 3 interfaces: physical and logical. The physical Layer 3 interfaces connect external devices directly to the routing function in the switch/router and allow it to be configured and operate like a traditional router. The logical Layer 3 (routed) interfaces (or VLAN interfaces) connect the different bridging functions (used for forwarding within VLANs) to a Layer 3 routing function in a single switch/router to allow inter-VLAN communication. The logical Layer 3 interface is an interface between a VLAN and the Layer 3 routing function and acts in a manner similar to a physical Layer 3 interface on a router or switch/router.

1.7.2.1   Physical Layer 3 (Routed) Interfaces

A physical Layer 3 (or routed) interface is a physical interface/port that connects to a Layer 3 routing and forwarding function that is responsible for forwarding IPv4 or IPv6 traffic to another device (Figure 1.12). This interface is like the physical port that attaches an external device to a traditional routing device (router). Layer 3 interfaces provide hosts, servers, switch/routers (supporting VLANs), and other routers with physical connectivity to the Layer 3 routing and forwarding function in a switch/router or router.

An IP address must be assigned to a Layer 3 interface to enable routing and communication with other Layer 3 interfaces in the network. The routing protocol and forwarding functions (for example, in a router or IP host) use the assigned IP address to communicate over the interface with other devices. The physical Layer 3 interface is also assigned a MAC address to allow it to connect to a Layer 2 network function (like a VLAN). With this, the routing and forwarding function in a device will communicate through the Layer 3 interface then over the physical Layer 2 port (using the assigned MAC address) to the outside networks.

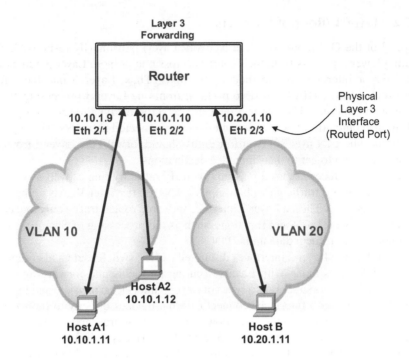

FIGURE 1.12   Inter-VLAN Routing over Physical Layer 3 Interfaces on a Router.

As illustrated in Figure 1.12, inter-VLAN routing takes place when each VLAN (or subnet) is connected to a physical Layer 3 interface (one interface for each VLAN). This arrangement is typically used in networks with small numbers of VLANs and router ports. It is a very simple yet effective method of inter-VLAN routing using the multiple physical interfaces on the Layer 3 forwarding device (router). The router in this scenario provides all the Layer 3 forwarding functionality required for inter-VLAN communication. A major advantage of this approach is that no trunking protocol (such as Cisco ISL or IEEE 802.1Q) is required for trunking of VLAN traffic to a router. The main features of this inter-VLAN routing method are summarized as follows:

- The physical Layer 3 (routed) interfaces on the routing device can be connected straightaway to a VLAN/subnet.
- The physical switch port on the routing device connects directly to a Layer 3 processing and forwarding function.
- The physical switch port on the routing device is not associated or "hard-wired" to a particular VLAN—it can be connected to any VLAN.
- The physical switch port on the routing device behaves like a traditional router interface, it does not support VLAN subinterfaces as discussed later.

- The physical switch port provides a direct Layer 3 path into the routing device for all the devices on the attached VLAN—all of the devices are directly reachable on that single switch port.
- In the case of a switch/router, the physical switch port connects to internal entities that support routing (Layer 3) protocol and bridging (Layer 2) functions.

1.7.2.2 Logical Layer 3 (Routed) Interfaces (VLAN Interfaces or Switch Virtual Interfaces (SVIs))

A VLAN interface or SVI is a virtual or logical Layer 3 (routed) interface that connects a VLAN on a switch/router to a Layer 3 routing and forwarding engine on the same switch/router. Only one SVI must be configured and associated with a VLAN—one SVI per VLAN in the switch/router. An SVI only has to be configured for a VLAN when there is the need to route traffic between VLANs.

An SVI can also be configured to provide connectivity between an IP host and a switch/router through a virtual routing and forwarding (VRF) instance that has not been set up as a management VRF. A management VRF is a type of VRF in a routing device that provides a way of separating out-of-band management traffic from the in-band user data traffic. All non-management VRFs use the main routing table, which is the default routing table for all user data traffic forwarding. However, the management VRF uses a second routing table for forwarding management traffic through the switch/router ports. A switch/router may also create an SVI for a default VLAN (VLAN 1) to allow remote administration of the switch/router.

As illustrated in Figure 1.13, VLANs on Layer 2 switches connect to a Layer 3 routing and forwarding function in a switch/router through logical Layer 3 interfaces or SVIs. The SVIs provide, simply, logical or virtual routing interfaces to allow the VLANs to access the Layer 3 routing and forwarding functions in the switch/router (inter-VLAN routing is required). In the absence of SVIs, the VLANs on Layer 2 switches will require physical Layer 3 (routed) interfaces on a traditional router to perform inter-VLAN routing as illustrated in Figure 1.12 and Figure 1.13 (second figure).

A switch/router provides a single simple platform that can support inter-VLAN routing by integrating the Layer 2 (bridging) and Layer 3 (routing) functions. Inter-VLAN routing is done over the SVIs that connect to the VLANs. An SVI must be configured for each VLAN that will require traffic routing and an IP address must be assigned to that SVI.

To configure logical Layer 3 (routed) interfaces on a switch/router, one can create and configure the VLANs on the connected Layer 2 switches or directly on the switch/router's local Layer 2 (switch) ports. VLAN membership must be assigned to these Layer 2 interfaces, and then IPv4 or IPv6 addresses must be configured for each SVI.

The main features of the logical Layer 3 interfaces or SVIs can be summarized as follows:

- An SVI can be configured for any VLAN that exists on a switch/router.
- An SVI provides a conduit for Layer 3 processing and forwarding of packets from all Layer 2 switch ports associated with that VLAN.

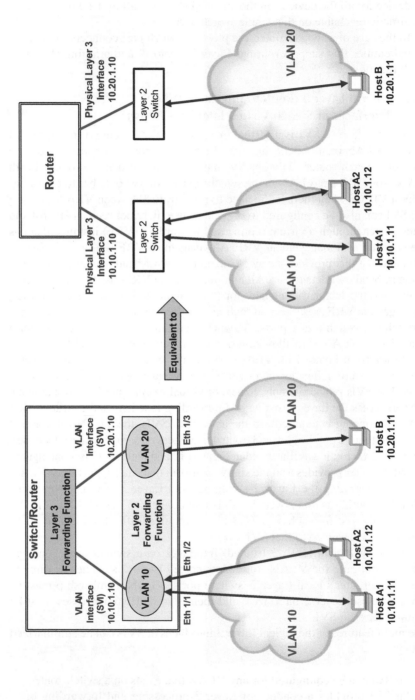

FIGURE 1.13 Inter-VLAN Routing over Logical Layer 3 (Routed) Interfaces in a Single Router.

- Only one VLAN interface or SVI can be mapped to or associated with any given VLAN.
- The main reasons for configuring an SVI are to provide:
  - A default gateway for a VLAN so that it can send traffic for routing to other VLANs
  - Layer 3 (IP) connectivity to Layer 2 switch ports.

1.7.3 SUBINTERFACES

A parent interface such as a physical port or a port channel (see discussion later) can be divided into two or more smaller virtual interfaces, or subinterfaces. Each virtual subinterface created on the parent interface can then be configured, if desired, as a logical Layer 3 interface. For example, a subinterface can be created on the parent interface Ethernet interface 3/1 and designated as Ethernet 3/1.1 where the .1 indicates that is a subinterface of Ethernet interface 3/1.

Subinterfaces can be assigned unique Layer 3 parameters and identifiers such as IP addresses and can be associated with Layer 3 routing and forwarding functions in the routing device. Each subinterface must be assigned a unique IP address and must belong to a different subnet (or VLAN) from the other sub-interfaces on the same parent interface. Generally, a subinterface can be shut down independent of shutting down other subinterfaces on the parent interface. But when the parent interface is shut down, all associated subinterfaces are shut down as well.

Subinterfaces can be created on a parent interface to serve as unique logical Layer 3 interfaces to each VLAN supported by the parent interface as illustrated in Figure 1.14 and Figure 1.15. In this figure, the parent interface serves as a Layer 2 trunk link that connects a Layer 2 switch to a routing device (router or switch/router). Each subinterface can be configured and associated with a VLAN ID using Cisco ISL or IEEE 802.1Q trunking.

In Figure 1.14 and Figure 1.15, the trunk link carries three subinterfaces that interconnect the Layer 2 switch and the router. The parent interface (e1/1 or e2/1 in Figure 1.14) contains three subinterfaces (e 2/1.10, e 2/1.20 and e 2/1.30) that are associated with each of the three VLANs (VLAN 10, VLAN 20, and VLAN 30) carried over the trunk link.

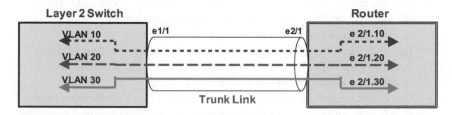

FIGURE 1.14   Trunk Port with Subinterfaces for VLANs.

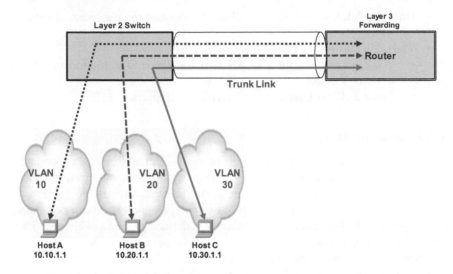

FIGURE 1.15   Inter-VLAN Routing over a Trunk Port with Subinterfaces.

The trunk is a point-to-point link between the Layer 2 switch and the router. The trunk carries traffic from multiple VLANs and allows inter-VLAN communications to be extended across a single link. In Cisco devices, the following two trunking encapsulation methods can be used on Ethernet switch ports:

- Inter-Switch Link (ISL): This is a Cisco-proprietary trunking encapsulation protocol.
- IEEE 802.1Q: This is an industry-standard trunking encapsulation.

A trunk can be configured on a single Ethernet switch port or on a port channel such as an EtherChannel or an IEEE 802.3ad link aggregation group (LAG) (see discussion later). The Ethernet trunk port may support (as in Cisco switches) several trunking modes such as ISL or 802.1Q encapsulation.

An external router using a single trunk to a Layer 2 switch can be used for inter-VLAN routing as explained later:

- A single trunk link to a router can be used and can support either ISL or 802.1Q. ISL, or 802.1Q trunking must be configured on this single physical connection between the Layer 2 switch and router.
- The router can have a separate logical or virtual connection (subinterface) for each VLAN. The same trunk encapsulation protocol must be configured on each subinterface (ISL or 802.1Q).
- This configuration with a router at the end of the trunk performing inter-VLAN routing is referred to as "router on-a-stick", "one-armed-router", "Lollipop" routing, or "one-arm bandit" routing.

The "one-armed-router" method is another (albeit not so efficient) way of implementing inter-VLAN routing. The previous methods of using a physical switch port/interface (routed port) on a router for each VLAN, and using an SVI for each VLAN to pass VLAN traffic to a routing function are more efficient and preferable.

In Cisco switch/routers, for example, one can configure a router on-a-stick as follows:

- Configure subinterfaces on a physical switch port:
  - Identify the physical switch interface on which to configure the subinterface (Type—10/100 Ethernet or Gigabit Ethernet; Slot—the slot number on the switch; Port number—the interface number on the switch):

    ```
    Router(config)#interface FastEthernet slot-
    number/ port-number.subinterface-number
    ```

  - Specify the VLAN encapsulation method (ISL or 802.1Q) to be used:

    ```
    Router(config-subif) #encapsulation dot1Q
    vlan-number
    ```

  - Assign an IP address to the subinterface defined earlier:

    ```
    Router(config-subif)#ip address ip-address
    mask
    ```

1.7.4 LOOPBACK INTERFACES

A loopback interface is a logical interface in a device with a single termination or end-point that is always operational or up as long as the device is operational. Loopback interfaces are always up and functioning, even if other interfaces in the device are down. Because a loopback interface is operational at all times, it does not require a shutdown command to bring it down. A loopback interface is not a physical interface but is designed to emulate a physical interface. A loopback interface is also not a VLAN interface or physical interface like an Ethernet interface on a switch or router.

Many networking devices can support the configuration of multiple loopback interfaces at the same, for example, up to 1024 loopback per device, numbered 0 to 1023. Multiple loopback interfaces can be configured on a router and the IP address assigned to each interface must be unique and not already assigned to any other interface in the system. Also, loopback interfaces are Layer 3 addressable and are treated similarly to physical Layer 3 (routed) interfaces or VLAN interfaces (SVIs) discussed earlier which also have IP addresses assigned to them.

The loopback interface can be used to perform a number of functions, depending on the device and the particular operating system used as discussed later.

1.7.4.1 Local Communications

A loopback interface can be used for internal or local communications in a device. Any information transmitted over a loopback interface is received immediately by the interface. The information terminates in the interface and does not travel beyond it. Most networking devices support a loopback interface to represent an internal loopback facility that allows for local turnaround of transmitted information.

IPv4 specifies the address range 127.0.0.0/8 (127.0.0.1 through 127.255.255.254) for loopback addresses. This allows any information that an entity within the device sends on the loopback address to be addressed directly (turned back) to the same device. The most commonly used IP address for a loopback interface is IPv4 address 127.0.0.1 and IPv6 address ::1. Also, the standard domain name corresponding to the loopback address is "localhost".

The loopback interface in a typical computing device is a special, logical network interface that the device uses to communicate internally with itself. The interface is used mainly for testing, diagnostics, and troubleshooting of processes running internally, for example, to connect servers running locally on the computer.

1.7.4.2 Testing and Performance Analysis

Loopback interfaces can also be used for testing and performance analysis of processes in a device. Because it is an interface with an IP address that is always up, the loopback interface provides a very useful tool for testing within a device. For example, in a routing device, it has become a very useful interface used by designers for rapid and immediate testing of processes within the device.

For instance, the loopback interface can be used for testing internal routing protocol processes in a router (client to/from server communications), allowing it to emulate a network that receives protocol messages from the router. In this role, the loopback interface is simply a logical interface which is used to emulate a physical interface to the router without having to use physical interfaces to the router.

1.7.4.3 Device Identification

Given that the loopback interface (along with its assigned IP address) is an interface that is always up in a device, it can be used as an identifier or part of an identifier that identifies a particular device in a network (e.g., in an OSPF router identifier). The reason why the loopback address is a preferred method for device identification in these circumstances is that it is an address that typically never changes and is always up. Other interface types are generally not stable enough for device identification because they might be removed from the device or their addresses might change due to changes made to addresses in the network topology.

Routing protocol processes on an OSPF router can use a local loopback interface's IP address for identification purposes. By configuring a loopback interface, the OSPF router can use that always-functioning loopback interface address for identification purposes, instead of an IP address that is assigned to a physical port that has the potential of going down. This mainly explains why an IP address of a loopback interface can be used to create a router's OSPF Router ID.

OSPF has a flexible router ID naming process that allows the OSPF routing process in a router to select its Router ID on its own and not be tied to a specifically defined/assigned Router ID as long as the IDs in the OSPF network are distinct and unique. Generally, an OSPF router chooses its Router ID from the list of IP addresses assigned to the interfaces configured and enabled in it. A loopback interface address may be the preferred choice since that interface is always functioning unless the router is specifically shut down. Other than a complete shutdown, interfaces in the router may go down, but the loopback interface is always up.

1.7.4.4 Routing Information Maintenance

A loopback interface in a routing device can be used as an end-point address for routing protocol sessions. Because the loopback interface is always up, it allows routing protocol sessions to stay up and routing protocol messages to be exchanged even if some of the outbound interfaces on the routing device are down. A loopback interface in this case is always functioning and allows, for example, BGP sessions between two neighbor routers to stay up even if one of the outbound interfaces connecting the routers is down. Other uses of a loopback interface are as follows:

- **Loopback Interface as a Filtering Interface**: A router can apply stateless firewall filters to a loopback address to filter packets sent from or destined to the route processor. The loopback interface in this case is a virtual interface (with an IP address) that is internal to the router. This loopback interface is not associated with any physical port in the router and therefore cannot be connected to any external device. It can be used as a filtering interface because it is a software virtual or logical interface that is always placed automatically and in an operational (up) state, as long as the router itself is functioning.
- **Loopback Interface in a MPLS Context**: Commands such as `ping mpls` rely on loopback addresses to operate correctly. MPLS Label Switched Path (LSP) echo request and reply packets are used to test and validate an LSP when troubleshooting with the `ping mpls` command. MPLS LSP ping in [RFC8029] provides a mechanism that can be used for testing LSP connectivity problems. For instance, a network administrator can use MPLS LSP ping to monitor LSPs to detect and possibly isolate problems that occur during MPLS packet forwarding.

1.7.4.4.1 Using Loopback Addresses in MPLS Ping Messages
The Internet Control Message Protocol (ICMP) ping is typically used as part of the diagnosis process when troubleshooting device and link failures in a network. However, LSP failures might not be detected by ICMP ping because ICMP ping packets can be forwarded through the IP layer to the destination even when an

LSP failure occurs. Thus, MPLS LSP ping is more appropriate for testing and detecting LSP failures for the following reasons:

- The TTL value in an MPLS echo request packet is set to 1 and the IPv4 destination address field is set to a 127.0.0.0/8 address and as a result cannot be forwarded through IP.
- Unlike in ICMP ping, in MPLS LSP ping, the Forwarding Equivalence Class (FEC) being examined is not carried in the IP destination address field.

A user can ping a specific LSP by sending MPLS Echo requests carried in MPLS packets over that LSP. The user simply sends an MPLS echo request packet to a target router by specifying the appropriate label stack associated with the LSP to be tested and validated. Sending the MPLS echo request packet with that label stack causes/forces the packet to be forwarded over the specified LSP. The MPLS echo request packet is forwarded to an IP address in the 127.0.0.0/8 (or 127/8) range reserved for loopback addresses (127.0.0.1 being commonly used).

The MPLS label and interface information for constructing and forwarding the echo request packet information as an MPLS packet is no different as done for standard LSP traffic. The main features of MPLS ping are as follows:

- MPLS ping operates through the use of MPLS echo request and MPLS echo reply messages and does not rely on ICMP echo messages. The MPLS echo request/reply messages are sent over UDP/IP with destination port 3503 and forwarded to an IPv4 address in the 127/8 range. The destination IPv4 address in the MPLS request message is specified as a loopback address 127.a.b.c/8 (with a, b, and c taking specific values in the loopback address range).
- The 127.a.b.c/8 loopback address prevents the IP packet with the MPLS echo request message from being forwarded over the IP layer to its destination if there is a breakage in the specific LSP being validated. The sending of the MPLS echo request message cannot be done from a regular IP host or router but can only be initiated from a label switching router. The is because MPLS ping tests connectivity and faults along a particular LSP downstream to an FEC, not to a destination IP address as in ICMP ping.
- The destination FEC specified for MPLS ping could be a global routing prefix or Layer 3 VPN prefix that has labels learned and distributed via the Label Distribution Protocol (LDP). The label switching router performs a lookup in its local Label FIB (LFIB) for the FEC and constructs the label stack corresponding to the specific LSP of interest. The label switching router then builds a special IP/UDP packet, with the source IP address set to the router's assigned IP address.
- The destination UDP port is set to the reserved value of 3503, TTL to 1, and the destination IP address written in the packet is set to one

address chosen from the reserved IP loopback address range 127/8. The label switching router writes, additionally, the special Router Alert IP Option in the IP packet header, which signals to each router on the path to "punt" (i.e., immediately pass) the IP packet up to its route processor. The label switching router also sets the TTL carried in the topmost label to 255 to ensure that testing is done end-to-end.

• The particular combination of information carried in the MPLS ping messages ensure that any router on the travel path of the messages will not attempt to forward the MPLS ping packet via the regular IP routing process once they strip the label stack. Based on the combination of using a destination IP loopback address, the TTL value of 1, and the Router Alert option, this prevents the routers from routing the MPLS ping messages using the traditional IP routing procedure. The use of normal ICMP ping does not prevent IP from forwarding these ping messages to the destination node even if a particular LSP has a breakage.

• When the MPLS ping packet reaches the end of the LSP, the egress MPLS node will process it and generate a response. The receiving egress node examines the contents of the MPLS echo request packet and then transmits an MPLS reply message containing the correct return information. Every router on the path over which the MPLS ping message travels will switch these messages using the normal MPLS label-switching procedure.

• If, for some reason, the MPLS ping packet cannot be label-switched (for example due to a breakage in the LSP), the particular router in question will process the packet and send back an appropriate MPLS echo reply (error-response) message. The MPLS echo reply message will be address to the originator or initiator of the MPLS ping operation, using the source IP address specified in the original MPLS ping messages.

• The MPLS echo reply message contains detailed information describing the reasons behind the LSP breakage.

MPLS traceroute (which is another troubleshooting tool) operates using a sequence of MPLS ping messages, but in this case each ping message carries an increasingly higher TTL value. MPLS traceroute, essentially, probes every router the LSP crosses, and the messages sent from the originator appear like a sequence of MPLS ping operations.

1.7.5 TUNNEL INTERFACES

A number of techniques exists for creating tunnels at Layer 3 (Generic Routing Encapsulation (GRE), IP Security (IPSec), IP over IP, etc.) or at Layer 2 (e.g., IEEE 802.1Q Tunneling (or Q-in-Q tunneling), VLAN translation (or VLAN mapping), Layer 2 Protocol Tunneling (L2PT)). The goal of the discussion here is to describe how these interface types fit within the general architecture of a switch/router rather than to provide a detailed description of the various tunneling techniques. A tunnel has two end-points, the ingress and egress tunnel interfaces.

Tunneling technologies have evolved and advanced to such a point that almost any layer of the OSI model can be tunneled over any layer (same-layer, higher-layer, lower-layer—simply, any-layer tunneling). Tunnels can also be nested with tunnels or carried in other tunnels (Figure 1.16). In this section we describe a few examples of tunneling interfaces, but we limit our discussion only to tunneling over Layer 2 and Layer 3 protocols.

1.7.5.1   Layer 3 Tunnel Interfaces/Ports Examples

An IP packet carrying higher-layer protocol data can be encapsulated in IP itself or any other protocol such as GRE, and then the resulting data transported over an IP tunnel created between two network devices as illustrated in Figure 1.16.

Layer 3 (IP) tunneling comprises the following three main sub-components (see Figure 1.17):

- **Passenger protocol**: This is the client protocol that is to be encapsulated and transported to a destination end-point. With the prevalence of IPv4, it has become the dominant passenger protocol in today's communication services.
- **Carrier protocol**: This is the protocol in which the passenger protocol is encapsulated before being transported. GRE and IP (resulting in IP-in-IP) are examples of common carrier protocols that are used for passenger protocol encapsulation.

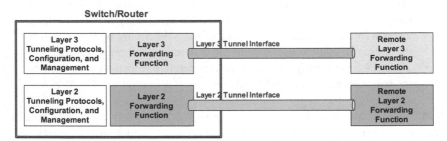

a). Layer 2 and 3 Tunnel Interfaces

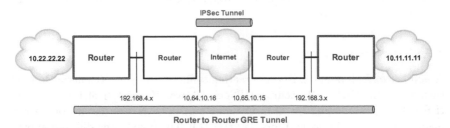

b). GRE Tunnel Example

FIGURE 1.16   Tunnel Interfaces.

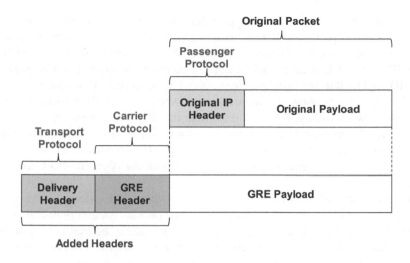

FIGURE 1.17   Generic Routing Encapsulation (GRE) as a Carrier Protocol.

- **Transport protocol**: This is the protocol that is used to transport the carrier protocol (carrying within it the encapsulated (passenger) protocol) to the destination end-point. IPv4 is again the most common transport protocol. While the transport protocol packets are forwarded in the tunnel, the routers along the tunnel path use only the delivery header (that is, the outer header) to route the packets though the network to the egress tunnel interface. As long as the tunnel path is routable, IP packet can be routed through it to the end-point.

1.7.5.1.1   GRE Tunnels

As shown in Figure 1.17, an IP tunnel is created by encapsulating a passenger protocol such as IPv4 within a carrier protocol GRE. The resulting packet made up of the carrier protocol with its encapsulated data is then transmitted over a transport protocol, such as IPv4. The passenger protocol packet is taken in as the GRE payload and a GRE header is added to this payload. A transport protocol header is then added and the resulting packet is transmitted over the tunnel. GRE is multiprotocol and can be used to tunnel any OSI Layer 3 protocol—it can be used as a carrier protocol for a wide variety of passenger protocols.

GRE IPv6 tunnels through an IPv6 network can also be used for transporting packets sourced by other (passenger) protocols like IPv4. Such a tunnel allows the transport of IPv6 packets carrying GRE packets between private networks (running IPv4 addresses) across a public network with globally routable IPv6 addresses. For a point-to-point GRE IPv6 tunnel, the ingress and egress tunnel interfaces require, respectively, a source IPv6 address and a destination IPv6 address. Packets transported across the tunnel are encapsulated with an inner GRE header and an outer IPv6 header similar to Figure 1.17.

A GRE IPv4 tunnel can also support the transport of IPv6 traffic where IPv6 is the passenger protocol, GRE is the carrier protocol, and IPv4 is the transport protocol. The transport protocol can also be IPv6 resulting in an IPv6 over GRE over IPv6 tunnel. Overlay tunneling can be created by encapsulating IPv6 packets in GRE and then in IPv4 packets for transport across a core IPv4 network.

Overlay tunnels allow communication between isolated IPv6 networks over an IPv4 network without the need to upgrade the IPv4 network between them (to IPv6). An overlay tunnel can be setup between two IPv6/IPv4 border networking devices or between an IPv6/IPv4 host and an IPv4/IPv6 border device. In both cases, the two tunnel end-points must support both the IPv6 and IPv4 protocol stacks.

GRE can be used to carry passenger protocols that are IP unicast, multicast, or broadcast, in addition to non-IP protocols. GRE permits routing protocols (such as IPv4, IPv6, OSPF, EIGRP, etc.) and other protocols to be transported across an IP tunnel. However, GRE offers relatively weak security because the basic encryption mechanism it supports allows the key to be carried along with the packet.

1.7.5.1.2 IPSec Tunnels

IPsec, on the other hand, provides a secure method for tunneling data across an IP network. IPsec offers much higher security by providing confidentiality (by means of data encryption, e.g., DES, 3DES, or AES), data source authentication, replay protection, and data integrity assurance (using MD5 or SHA-1 HMACs). The main limitations of IPsec are that it does not support IP multicast or broadcast capabilities, thereby preventing the use of protocols that rely on these services. The use of crypto maps in IPSec does not allow the implementation of routing protocols across the IPSec tunnel.

Also, IPsec was designed to tunnel/transport IP packets only, and has no multi-protocol support—it does not tunnel routing protocols such as OSPF, EIGRP, etc. Before IP packets can be sent through the IPsec tunnel, static routes have to be configured at each IPsec end-point to enable end-to-end communication between the tunnel end-points. The additional configuration overhead required makes this service not scalable when a large number of IPsec tunnels are to be supported.

IPSec can operate either in a tunnel mode or transport mode (Figure 1.18). In the tunnel mode, IPSec encrypts and authenticates the entire IP packet to be transported. IPSec encapsulates the resulting packet into a new IP packet with a new IP header. Essentially, IPSec builds a new IPSec tunnel packet with a new IP header. The tunnel mode is typically used to create VPNs between two networks (e.g., between two border routers), host-to-border router communications (e.g., for remote user access to a corporate network), and host-to-host communications.

In the transport mode, IPSec usually encrypts or authenticates only the payload of the IP packet to be transported. In this case the routing information carried in the IP header is left intact, since the header is not modified or encrypted. The payload of the GRE IP packet is encapsulated by the IPSec headers and

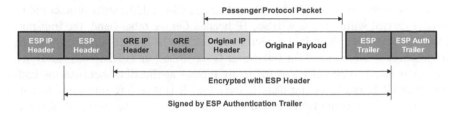

(a) GRE over IPSec Tunnel Mode with Encapsulating Security Payloads (ESP) Header

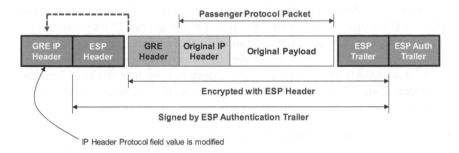

(b) GRE over IPSec Transport Mode with Encapsulating Security Payloads (ESP) Header

FIGURE 1.18   GRE over IPsec Packet Format—Tunnel Mode versus Transport Mode.

trailers. In this mode, the IPSec header reuses the GRE IP header (resulting in 20 bytes less overhead than in the tunnel mode because the GRE IP is omitted) but with a minor modification. The GRE IP header remains intact, except that the IP header protocol field is changed (to 50 for IPSec with ESP header or 51 for IPSec with Authentication header), and the GRE IP header protocol value is saved in the IPSec trailer to be restored when the IPSec packet is decrypted.

As illustrated in Figure 1.18, the GRE IP header is moved and reused at the front of the IPSec packet. By placing the GRE IP header at the front (with minor modifications to the IP header protocol field), IPSec transport mode does not provide protection or encryption to the GRE IP header. In this case, the ESP header is identified in the new IP header with an IP header protocol field value of 50.

Using GRE over IPSec allows IPSec to provide/supplement what GRE alone lacks, which is enhanced security. GRE over IPSec also allows GRE to fill in what IPSec alone lacks. Thus, given that a GRE tunnel can carry routing and multicast traffic, and that IPSec provides higher security, a GRE tunnel can be sent through an IPsec tunnel (GRE over IPsec tunnel) to provide enhanced security for the passenger protocols being transported. In GRE over IPsec tunnel, the original passenger protocol packet is taken in (as the innermost layer) and then the GRE and IP headers are added. Finally, the IPsec headers and trailers are wrapped around the resulting packet for added security. The passenger protocol packet is encapsulated in GRE packet before the encryption process.

The tunnel mode is used when there is the need to additionally protect the IP header carried within the new IPsec IP header. On the other hand, the transport mode is used when there is the need to expose the IP header carried. However, in practice, when the need for GRE over IPsec arises, one often finds the IPSec transport mode to be sufficient for many typical applications because the end-points of GRE and IPsec are usually the same. It is therefore important to note that in such cases, using IPSec tunnel or transport mode makes no big difference, since the original passenger protocol IP header and payload are fully protected as seen in Figure 1.18.

Given that a GRE tunnel provides many features IPSec lacks, using GRE tunnels over IPsec provides the ability to run routing protocols, IP multicast, broadcast, or multiprotocol traffic across a tunnel created between two networks. GRE also enables private addressing to be used in the two networks linked by the tunnel. Without a GRE tunnel protocol, all end devices in both networks will require registered public IP addresses. Using a GRE tunnel to encapsulate the IP packets allows a private address space to be used across the two networks.

1.7.5.2   Layer 2 Tunnel Interfaces/Ports Examples

Q-in-Q tunneling (also called 802.1Q tunneling) and VLAN mapping (also referred to as VLAN translation) allows a service provider to create a Layer 2 Ethernet tunnel that connects two customer sites. A service provider can use these techniques to do the following:

- Bundle/aggregate traffic from different customer VLANs onto a single service (provider) VLAN, or
- Segregate/isolate traffic from different customers' VLAN sent on a single link (for example, in the case where the customers use overlapping VLAN IDs).

Layer 2 Protocol Tunneling (L2PT) is a technique similar to Q-in-Q tunneling and VLAN translation but is used only for transporting of Layer 2 control traffic across the (L2PT) tunnel.

1.7.5.2.1   Q-in-Q Tunneling or 802.1Q Tunneling

Q-in-Q tunneling (or 802.1Q tunneling), standardized in IEEE 802.1ad, is a technique that is used to extend the VLAN space by allowing edge switches in a service provider network to retag IEEE 802.1Q VLAN tagged packets that enter the network. With Q-in-Q tunneling, the edge switch adds a second tag, a service (provider) VLAN tag, to the original customer 802.1Q VLAN tags carried in the packets as they enter the tunnel (Figure 1.19).

Q-in-Q tunneling allows a service provider to assign a service VLAN to each customer without discarding the original customer VLAN IDs tagged to packets as they are transported across the tunnel. All customer tagged packets that enter the Q-in-Q tunnel are tagged with the second tunnel or service VLAN ID before being forwarded across the service provider network.

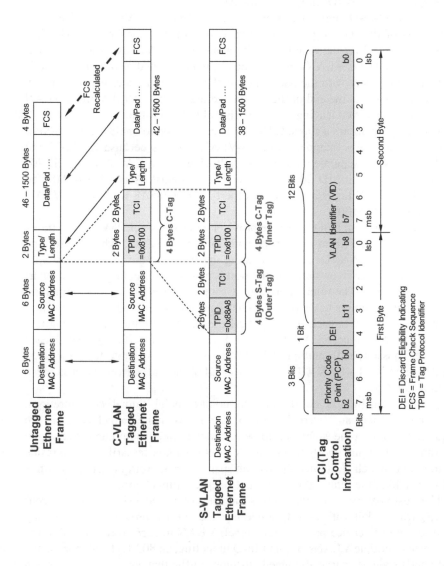

FIGURE 1.19 Untagged and Tagged Ethernet Frames.

To map customer VLANs (C-VLANs) to service provider VLANs (S-VLANs), a VLAN ID translation (or VLAN mapping) mechanism must be configured on the trunk (or tunnel) ports connected to the customer networks. As packets enter a trunk port, they are mapped to (and tagged with) a service provider VLAN ID (S-VLAN ID) based on the ingress trunk port number and the original customer VLAN ID (C-VLAN ID) assigned to the packet.

Thus, in Q-in-Q tunneling, when a packet from a C-VLAN arrives at a trunk port of the service provider network, the VLAN translation mechanism adds another 802.1Q tag identifying the appropriate S-VLAN to the (original) C-VLAN tag. The C-VLAN tag in the packet is not deleted or overridden and is transmitted together with the packet across the service provider network. When the packet arrives at the end of the tunnel and leaves the S-VLAN, the S-VLAN 802.1Q tag is removed leaving only the original C-VLAN tag.

The mapping allows a single C-VLAN to be mapped to one S-VLAN or multiple C-VLANs to be mapped to one S-VLAN. This is because C-VLAN and S-VLAN tags use separate name spaces, allowing both a C-VLAN with ID 201 and an S-VLAN with ID 201, for example, to co-exist. According to 802.1ad standard, S-VLAN tag is assigned an Ethertype of 0x88A8 while the C-VLAN tag is assigned 0x8100.

Using Q-in-Q tunneling, a service provider can use a single S-VLAN to transport traffic coming from customers with multiple VLANs, while preserving the original C-VLAN IDs and segregating the traffic in the different customer VLANs. As discussed earlier, a tunnel port is a port that is configured to support Q-in-Q tunneling. The tunnel ports in the tunnel VLAN are the entry (ingress) and exit (egress) points to the tunnel. When configuring Q-in-Q tunneling, a tunnel port is assigned to each service VLAN dedicated to tunneling, making that service VLAN a tunnel VLAN. In order to keep customer traffic segregated, each customer (possibly with multiple VLANs) is assigned a separate tunnel VLAN, but this one tunnel VLAN will in turn carry all of the traffic from the customer's multiple VLANs.

Q-in-Q tunneling is not limited to point-to-point tunnel configurations. A Q-in-Q tunnel can be configured to support as many tunnel ports as are required to connect the (single) customer's switches and to communicate through the tunnel. The tunnel ports to a tunnel VLAN do not necessarily have to reside on the same switch. A tunnel VLAN can span other network switches and links before reaching the tunnel exit point, that is, egress tunnel port.

The customer switches themselves can be connected using (single-tagged) 802.1Q trunks, but with Q-in-Q tunneling, the service provider switches only need to use one service provider (or tunnel) VLAN to carry traffic from all the customer's multiple VLANs. With Q-in-Q tunneling, an 802.1Q trunk port on the customer's switches carry all tagged customer traffic that enters the edge switch of the service-provider network via a tunnel port. The tunnel port does not remove the received C-VLAN tag from the packet header, instead it adds a S-VLAN tag to the C-VLAN tag. The received customer traffic is then forwarded across the tunnel VLAN to which the tunnel port is assigned.

Similar to SVIs, routed VLAN interfaces (RVIs) can be used with Q-in-Q VLANs. In this case, Layer 3 forwarding (routing) is performed in the service provider network based only on the S-VLAN. The original C-VLAN tag is ignored when a packet leaves the C-VLAN that originates it as well as during the period; it is Layer 3 forwarded across the service provider network. Routed packets within the service provider network retain any S-VLAN tag and these S-VLAN tags are dropped when packets re-enter the customer network.

1.7.5.2.2 VLAN Mapping (or VLAN Translation)

Another method for creating service provider VLANs to carry different customer VLAN traffic is VLAN mapping (or VLAN ID translation) and is performed on trunk ports connected to a customer network. VLAN mapping allows the service provider to map customer VLANs to service-provider VLANs by mapping packets entering the trunk port to a service provider VLAN based on the trunk port number and the original customer VLAN-ID carried in the packet. The C-VLAN tagged packets are mapped to specified S-VLAN tags when they enter the tunnel port and are mapped back to the customer C-VLAN when the packets exit the port.

With VLAN translation, an incoming C-VLAN tag to the service provider network is replaced (overridden) with an S-VLAN tag instead of simply adding the S-VLAN tag to the C-VLAN tag. The C-VLAN tag carried in the incoming packet is therefore lost, which means a single C-VLAN tagged packet becomes untagged when it leaves the S-VLAN (at the egress end of the trunk). Because the C-VLAN tagged is mapped to a S-VLAN tag at the ingress tunnel port, the switches through which the tunnel crosses perform all forwarding operations using S-VLAN information and not C-VLAN information.

If a packet arrives at the ingress of the tunnel and has had a Q-in-Q tunneling tag already applied to it, VLAN translation replaces (overrides) only the outer tag (within Q-in-Q tunneling tag). Then the inner tag (of the original Q-in-Q tunneling tag carried in the packet) is retained and left untouched when the packet leaves the S-VLAN at the egress end of the trunk.

1.7.5.2.3 Layer 2 Protocol Tunneling (L2PT)

Layer 2 protocol tunneling (L2PT) allows a service provider to tunnel Layer 2 protocol data units (PDUs) across the service provider's network to remote switches that are not part of the sender's broadcast domain. L2PT is particularly useful when a customer wants to extend the operations of Layer 2 protocols on a network to include switches that are in remote locations that are connected over a service provider network.

In this scenario, an edge switch placed at the boundary of the service provider network is connected to both the customer network and the tunneling infrastructure. An L2PT tunnel port is created, which is a port on the edge switch through which the customer's Layer 2 PDUs are to be encapsulated and tunneled. Another tunnel port is configured at the egress end so that the tunnel packets can be de-encapsulated as they exit the tunnel for delivery to their destination switches. These L2PT tunnel ports serve, respectively, as the entry (ingress) and exit (egress) points to the tunnel.

Examples of specific Layer 2 protocols PDUs that can be tunneled are PDUs of Spanning Tree Protocol (STP) and variants, Link Layer Discovery Protocol (LLDP) (in IEEE 802.1AB), Generic Attribute Registration Protocol (GARP) VLAN Registration Protocol (GVRP), Multiple MAC Registration Protocol (MMRP), Multiple VLAN Registration Protocol (MVRP), Link Aggregation Control Protocol (LACP), Unidirectional Link Detection (UDLD), 802.1X authentication, etc. The L2PT can be used to tunnel all types of packets whether untagged, tagged, or Q-in-Q tagged.

The ingress L2PT tunnel port encapsulates Layer 2 PDUs and rewrites/changes the PDUs' destination MAC addresses to 01–00–0c-cd-cd-d0 (the predefined multicast tunnel MAC address) before forwarding them onto the L2PT tunnel created in the service provider network. The network devices in the service provider network through which the tunnel crosses handle these encapsulated Layer 2 PDUs as multicast Ethernet packets and forward them to all edge switches for the customer. The egress L2PT tunnel ports at the edge switches receive all the L2PT tunneled PDUs with the same and unique (01–00–0c-cd-cd-d0) destination MAC address.

At the egress L2PT tunnel port, received PDUs are decapsulated and the destination MAC addresses (01–00–0c-cd-cd-d0) are replaced/rewritten with the MAC address of the specific Layer 2 protocol that is being tunneled and the PDUs are then forwarded out of the tunnel to their destination switches. The egress L2PT tunnel ports identify the Layer 2 protocol packet type by carrying out a deeper packet examination after which they replace/rewrite the destination MAC address 01–00–0c-cd-cd-d0 with the appropriate destination MAC address.

The Layer 2 PDUs are transported transparently across the service provider network to the L2PT tunnel egress where the original multicast destination MAC addresses are restored when the Layer 2 PDUs are transmitted. The reconstructed Layer 2 PDUs, in their original state, are sent out to the customer's remote switches. Using L2PT thus ensures that the customer's Layer 2 control PDUs are transported and delivered across the service provider network transparently to the customer's remote sites.

1.7.6 PORT CHANNELS

A port channel is a communication link between two network devices that consists of an aggregation of multiple physical links operating as one single logical or virtual link. Furthermore, a port channel interface is created by aggregating multiple compatible physical Layer 2 (switch) or Layer 3 (routed) interfaces into a channel group to operate as a single logical interface. Simply, a channel group refers to a bundle or group of matching Layer 2 or 3 interfaces on a single switch.

A port channel interface is, therefore, a logical or virtual interface that is made up of a corresponding channel group. The connection of one port channel interface on one switch to a corresponding compatible interface on another switch forms a port channel. Each physical interface on a switch can be in only one port channel at any given time. A user may aggregate up to eight individual active physical interfaces and links to create a port channel as a way of providing increased bandwidth and redundancy in a network.

1.7.6.1 Layer 2 and Layer 3 Port Channels

A Layer 2 port channel can be created by grouping compatible Layer 2 interfaces as illustrated in Figure 1.20. Similarly, a Layer 3 port channel can be created by aggregating compatible Layer 3 interfaces. Once a Layer 3 port channel is created, an IP address can be assigned to each of the port channel interfaces on the Layer 3 devices. Also, a Layer 2 port channel can be configured as either an access link or trunk link as shown in Figure 1.20 (see also discussion on access and trunk ports).

It should be noted that, generally, Layer 2 and Layer 3 interfaces cannot be combined on the same port channel. Also, subinterfaces (as described earlier) can be created on a Layer 3 port channel. A Layer 3 port-channel interface has routed interfaces as channel members and the port channel interface itself may be configured to have subinterfaces.

A single port channel interface can be divided into multiple port channel sub-interfaces where each subinterface represents a logical Layer 3 interface based on an IEEE 802.1Q tagging (VLAN ID) of incoming traffic. Subinterfaces are commonly used in the trunk linking a Layer 2 and Layer 3 device as shown in Figure 1.14 and Figure 1.15. Subinterfaces can also be used to isolate traffic flowing between Layer 3 peers. Here, 802.1Q tags are assigned to each subinterface carrying traffic to a different Virtual Routing and Forwarding (VRF).

While it is understood that subinterfaces can be configured on the virtual or logical interface associated with a port channel, that is, a port channel interface, a number of restrictions may apply:

- A subinterface cannot be configured as a member of a port channel interface.
- A port channel interface should not have as one of its member interfaces a Layer 3 (routed) interface which already has subinterfaces configured on it.
- An interface that is already made a member of a port channel interface should not have subinterfaces configured on it. Any required subinterfaces should be configured on the port channel interface itself since it is considered a single logical interface in its own right.

Subinterfaces that exist on multiple ports of a port channel can be assigned the same VLAN ID, but there should be no bridging between these subinterfaces or between these subinterfaces and any SVIs in the system. Each of these subinterfaces is considered to be in a separate bridge domain.

A user can configure and use port channel interfaces in ways similar to Layer 2 or 3 interfaces as discussed earlier. A port channel interface can be configured

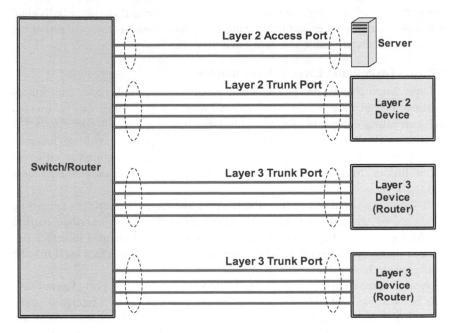

a) Network Devices Using Port Channels

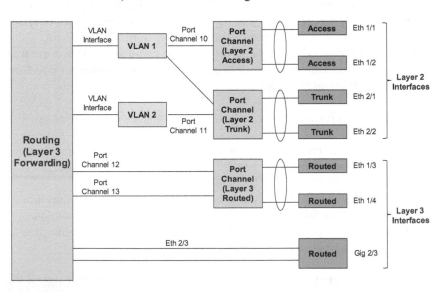

b) Port Channel Examples

FIGURE 1.20   Port Channel Interfaces as Layer 2 or Layer 3 Interfaces.

as a Layer 2 (switch), Layer 3 (routed) interfaces, and as a member of a VLAN. Most of the Layer 2 or 3 interface configuration options are also applicable to port channel interfaces.

Because a port channel is a logical grouping of multiple individual interfaces, any configuration settings that are applied to a port channel interface are also applied to the individual interfaces that make up that port channel. For example, if STP parameters are configured on a port channel, those parameters are also applied to each member interface in the port channel.

1.7.6.1.1   What Is a Bridge Domain?

This section gives a simple explanation of what a bridge domain is. A number of Layer 2 switch ports can be grouped together to create a bridge domain, that is, these ports constitute a set of logical ports that act as a single Layer 2 broadcast domain. These groups of ports share the same flooding, broadcast, filtering, and forwarding characteristics even though they are spread over different switch ports. A bridge domain is simply a single Layer 2 broadcast domain. Similar to a VLAN, a bridge domain can span one or more switch ports on multiple Layer 2 switches.

A bridge domain interface [CISCBDCHP14] (identified by the same index as its bridge domain) is a logical interface that connects one bridge domain through a Layer 3 routing and forwarding function to another bridge domain. The interface allows bidirectional flow of traffic between the bridge domain and the Layer 3 forwarding function. Being a single broadcast domain, one or more VLANs can be carved out of a bridge domain.

1.7.6.2   Load Balancing

Load balancing of traffic can also be performed across the individual physical interfaces of the port channel in order to better utilize the port channel links. Port channels have become an effective way of increasing bandwidth and provide graceful degradation of bandwidth as member link failures occur, thereby increasing network availability. Port channels provide network redundancy by allowing traffic load-balancing across all available active channel member links. If any one of the member links fails, the port channel automatically load-balances traffic across the remaining active member links.

Load balancing of traffic can be done across all operational interfaces/links in a port channel by using a hashing function that hashes specified fields in the packets (such as the addresses) to a numerical value that maps to one of the physical links in the port channel. The load balancing mechanism can select a link in the port channel using one or more of the following packet fields: MAC addresses, IP addresses, and Layer 4 port numbers. When load balancing is configured based on source IP address, the hash function uses the source MAC address of packets to balance the traffic load across the port channel links. The load balancing method used has to ensure efficient distribution of the traffic load (flows) across the port channel links. Flow-based load balancing methods are preferable since they eliminate the need for packet resequencing at the receiving devices.

A port channel (a single logical link) can be created by aggregating bandwidth of up to eight individual physical links. If a member link within the port channel fails, the traffic carried over the failed link is switched to the remaining active member links within the logical link. A port channel is generally designed such that the channel (i.e., the logical interface) stays operationally up as long as at least one of its member physical interfaces is operationally up and is still in the channeling state. In this case, for the port channel to be operationally down, all member interfaces must be operationally down.

1.7.6.3 Dynamic Configuration of Port Channels

The Link Aggregation Control Protocol (LACP) is part of the IEEE 802.3ad standard (now defined in IEEE 802.1AX) and provides mechanisms for creating port channels called link aggregation groups (LAGs). Link aggregation using LACP allows a user to aggregate one or more Ethernet interfaces to form a single logical point-to-point link (or port channel) called a LAG. Two Ethernet switches can automatically establish and maintain LAGs between them using LACP. EtherChannel is a proprietary technology developed by Cisco for creating port-channel or port link aggregation and is primarily used in Cisco switches.

The LAG is also sometimes referred to as a bundle or virtual link. The MAC clients at each end of the LAG (virtual link or bundle) see it as a single logical link. LACP provides mechanisms for automatic determination, configuration, and monitoring of LAG member links. A device that is fully compliant to LACP should be compatible with other peer devices that run the IEEE 802.3ad (or 802.1AX) LACP. LACP allows the switches to automatically bind the LAG member links without requiring the network administrator to manually configure the LAG, thereby eliminating configuration errors.

LACP can be used to configure a port channel with up to 16 interfaces. With this, a maximum of eight interfaces within the port channel can be made active while a maximum of eight interfaces can be in a standby (and inactive) state. A user can configure multiple physical interfaces into a port channel, either statically using manual configuration (static port channel), or dynamically using LACP (dynamic port channel). However, to allow simplified configuration and deployment, a network administrator may set up a port channel using static configuration (by bundling up to eight physical ports) that uses no associated aggregation protocol (such as LACP).

1.8 CHALLENGES

The need to make optimum use of network bandwidth is emphasized by the high tariffs imposed on users and the throughput demands of current high-performance end-user devices. Therefore, the switch/router designer must find ways of optimizing the forwarding of packets in the minimum number of processing cycles in order to fully utilize modern high-speed transmission technology. In addition to high throughput performance, the switch/router or router must provide low system latency when forwarding packets.

Low throughput and excessive latency end up holding up end user applications pending the transfer of data in the network nodes. As packet forwarding performance in the network device increases, the effects of network delay on application performance decreases. This means the architecture and the packet processing speeds in the network devices play an increasingly significant role in determining the overall end-user application performance.

In switch/routers and routers, packet parsing and destination address lookups are two particular data-path operations that constrain the performance of the packet forwarding process. In a switch/router, variable length network prefixes need to be matched in the forwarding table. The most challenging operation is performing the longest prefix matching in the forwarding table, an operation that is the most complex on the data-path. In the Layer 2 forwarding mode, supporting the rapid learning and filtering of MAC addresses is another important requirement that has to properly addressed. To provide consistently high performance, the packet parsing and destination address lookup operations benefit greatly from hardware assistance.

Although the transmission of end-user data is the primary purpose of the network, the network will not function well if it does not handle properly some critical packets such as the network routing protocol control packets. These critical control packets are used by the routing devices in the network to map its topology and to communicate this topological information to routing devices in other networks. Losing end-user data only affects the end-user application performance. If an end-user data packet is lost and is sourced by an application that supports retransmission, the transport protocol can retransmit the packet without significant inconvenience to the application.

However, if an excessive number of routing protocol packets are lost, the routing devices in the network would not be able to create an optimum view of the network topology. The network topology, and hence the optimum paths, frequently change, requiring the routing devices in the network to be quickly informed of these changes. Not properly capturing the network topology can lead to the formation of routing loops in the network and the generation of further wrong control packets describing these non-optimal new paths.

This increased traffic created by the routing loops and wrong paths exacerbates traffic congestion in the network. In the worst case, a positive feedback loop occurs in the overall packet forwarding process, in which there is little useful end-user data being forwarded but only packets circulating but not effectively trying to bring the network back to stability.

As a result, designers place two important design requirements on a switch/router or router. First, the routing device must have the necessary mechanism in place to be able to identify network control packets and direct them to the route processor even under heavy overload conditions, most often even at the expense of forwarding end-user data traffic. Second, the routing device must have adequate processing cycles and be able to process these critical network control packets fast enough to enable the routing tables in the routing devices to converge on a consistent view of the network topology.

As networks continue to grow and scale to very large sizes over wide geographic distances, it is possible that an underperforming routing device in one part of the network could cause incorrect network operations (and topology mapping) in a different region of the network. A routing device must therefore be designed to process all routing protocol traffic, and not export its local incorrect topology information (created due to congestion) to other parts of the network: something akin to placing a "good network citizenship" constraint.

To achieve this, the routing device needs to be equipped with the proper processing and filtering mechanism so that it can operate at line rate. With this, the routing device can receive all traffic at line rate, and extract the routing protocol traffic from the data traffic even under worst-case conditions. In some architectures, careful design of the line card and route processor software can accomplish this. However, as line speeds increase, the parsing and processing of the network control traffic may require hardware assistance. Once the routing protocol traffic has been extracted, the routing device must be provided with adequate processing power to ensure that the network topology view created converges quickly.

Another key requirement of a switch/router is that it should remain manageable even under the worst-case traffic conditions. If the switch/router is being overwhelmed or overloaded with traffic from a malfunctioning node in the network, it might be necessary to shut down the circuit causing the overload. To accomplish this, the switch/router must be able to receive and process the network management packets sent to it despite the overload situation.

The earlier mentioned scenarios are examples of requirements and constraints on the design of a switch/router. The switch/router is required to simultaneously forward Layer 2 and 3 packets, interact with other network devices to maintain a global view of the network topology, and at all times support a number of network management functions. These requirements often demand an architecture with sophisticated hardware and/or software design capable of accommodating the demands imposed by these requirements.

REFERENCES

[AWEYA1BK18]. J. Aweya, *Switch/Router Architectures: Shared-Bus and Shared-Memory Based Systems*, Wiley-IEEE Press, ISBN 9781119486152, 2018.

[BRYAN93]. S. F. Bryant and D. L. A. Brash, "The DECNIS 500/600 Multiprotocol Bridge/Router and Gateway," *Digi. Tech. Jour.*, Vol. 5, No. 1, 1993, pp. 84–98.

[CISCBDCHP14]. Chapter 14: Configuring Bridge Domain Interfaces, Cisco ASR 1000 Series Aggregation Services Routers Software Configuration Guide.

[CISCCAT6000]. Cisco Systems, Catalyst 6000 and 6500 Series Architecture, White Paper, 2001.

[RFC8029]. K. Kompella, G. Swallow, N. Kumar, S. Aldrin, and M. Chen, "Detecting Multi-Protocol Label Switched (MPLS) Data Plane Failures," *IETF RFC 8029*, Mar. 2017.

[SIVASUBRA07]. B. Sivasubramanian, E. Frahim, and R. Froom, "Understanding and Configuring Multilayer Switching," July 6, 2007, Chapter in *Building Cisco Multilayer Switched Networks (BCMSN) (Authorized Self-Study Guide)*, 4th Edition, Cisco Press.

2 Understanding Crossbar Switch Fabrics

2.1 INTRODUCTION

The main challenge in switch fabric design has always been coming out with architectures that achieve high bandwidth and data throughput at a reasonable and acceptable cost-to-bit ratio. The increasing demand for both high-throughput and high-performance systems over the years has also exposed the limitations of shared-media switch fabrics. Switch, switch/router, and router designs have traditionally been based on the basic switch fabrics such as the multi-drop shared bus, multiple parallel buses, shared memory, and point-to-point connections. In multi-drop switch fabrics, the signal driver transmits data that propagates along the medium to more than one receiver. On the other hand, in point-to-point switch fabrics, the signal driver transmits data along a connection to only one receiver.

Multi-drop single or parallel shared-bus switch fabrics were the preferred architecture for networking and computing systems for a number of reasons. They provided higher throughput over relatively short signal lines. Bandwidth and loading on the switch fabric can be increased by adding multiple parallel data lines and/or multiple buses. This allows data throughput in the system to be increased with relative ease.

Even though bus-based fabrics are easy to implement (at normally low cost), the speeds at which they can be clocked in order to preserve data/signal integrity decrease with bus length and loading. Also, power requirements can be prohibitive in a parallel shared-bus system with a large number of devices. For these reasons, shared-bus systems are mostly used, today, in low-bandwidth systems because a data transfer from an input cannot take place on the bus once another is already taking place. Since the signal driver on an input communicates with all receivers on the bus, only one data transfer can take place at a time.

The bus-based switch fabric has physical limits on the maximum bus clock frequency, maximum signal propagation delay that is tolerable, and maximum electrical loading on the bus. The propagation delay limits the physical length of the bus, while electrical loading limits the number of devices that can be connected to the bus.

To address the bandwidth and physical limitations issues of shared-bus architectures, designers turned to the use of multi-port shared-memory systems which became common starting in the late 1980s. These shared-memory architectures allowed the memory to be accessed through different ports simultaneously. However, as the demand for high-bandwidth, high-throughput system grew, it became apparent that shared-memory systems, too, had bandwidth and physical implementation challenges that were not easy to overcome. Such high-performance systems were both difficult and expensive to implement.

In the ring switch fabric architecture, data packets are transmitted on the ring flow in one direction from node to node. Each node on the ring first receives the data and then transmits it to the next node in the ring. The ease of design of ring fabrics and the absence of data bottlenecks make it an attractive option for designers. However, its main disadvantage is that if a single link or channel between any two adjacent nodes on the ring fails, then the entire system fails to function. Multiple ring (typically, dual ring) switch fabrics can be implemented, which can increase the reliability of the overall system should a link or node fail.

In the shared-memory architecture, bandwidth scalability is limited by the memory access speed (bandwidth). There is a physical limit on memory access speed, and this prevents the shared-memory switch architecture from scaling to very high bandwidths and port speeds. Another factor is that the shared-memory bandwidth has to be at least two times the aggregate system port speeds for all the ports to run at full line rate. At very high multigigabit speeds it is very challenging to design the sophisticated controllers required to allocate memory to incoming packets, and implement complex priority queuing, packet scheduling, and packet discard policies required in the system. Furthermore, implementing a redundant switching plane to a shared-memory switch fabric is complex and expensive.

The bandwidth and high-throughput requirements of high-performance systems called for solutions to the limitations of the single or parallel multi-drop shared-bus and shared-memory switch fabrics. Some designers used serial point-to-point connections (arranged in a star or meshed architecture) as switch fabrics, allowing modules in a system to communicate directly with each other. In a mesh architecture, each node has connections to all other nodes in the system. Each node receives and forwards its own traffic, and all nodes appear as equal peers in the system—peer-to-peer system.

This became a popular method for designing switch fabrics because of its ease of design, combined with the higher transmission frequencies that it allowed over the bus-based fabrics. However, the point-to-point systems suffered from scalability and other related issues and were not suitable for large systems including multi-chassis systems.

Over time designers understood that the traditional shared-media switch fabric architectures had many limitations, so they began to turn to crossbar switch fabric architectures. Many would argue that both the present and the future of high-performance switches, switch/routers and routers will be based on crossbar switch fabrics. Crossbar switch fabrics, generally, provide both the bandwidth and design flexibility needed to build high-performance network devices and they offer a degree of scalability and reliability not found in the shared-bus-based and shared-memory systems.

The crossbar switch fabric has become one of the most popular interconnects for building input buffered switches. Crossbar switch fabrics have become the preferred switch fabric architectures for implementing today's high-performance switches, switch/routers and routers. They are reasonably low cost (using ASICs and standard commercial chips, for example), have excellent scalability, and can be designed to be non-blocking.

Crossbar switch fabrics can be used to design architectures that can scale to very high bandwidths. Unlike shared-media switch fabrics which run into band-width bottlenecks due to their centralized resource management feature, a cross-bar switch fabric can be designed to provide full line rate throughput for very large numbers of ports by distributing bandwidth and buffering requirements over multiple internal fabric channels.

Crossbar switch fabrics have become the heart of high-performance switches, switch/routers, and routers, as they offer many advantages. However, these advantages come at a cost, when it comes to adding scalability, redundancy, and hot-swapping of redundant switch fabric modules. Using a crossbar switch fabric may not be the most practical choice for all designs, especially low-speed, low-end switching and routing systems. It is, therefore, incumbent on the designer to con-sider all other switch fabric options and factors before deciding on the most suit-able switch fabric architecture for the particular design.

A comprehensive discussion of crossbar switch fabrics is impossible in this chapter, as many architectures exist, each with its own set of costs and benefits. The discussion here, however, at least introduces the basic design concepts, archi-tectures, and implementation issues.

2.2   THE CROSSBAR SWITCH FABRIC

Up until the late 1990s, most switches, switch/routers, and routers were built based on shared-bus fabrics. Shared-bus architectures provided simple, low cost solutions with sufficient bandwidth as long as the port densities, input data rates, and port utili-zation were relatively low. However, advances in electronic and communication tech-nologies of end systems and the rapid growth of the Internet have created the need for high-bandwidth systems beyond those offered by the shared-bus architectures.

Designers have long used crossbar switch fabric-based systems in telecom-munications (e.g., telephone exchanges, digital cross-connects, multiplexers, switches, etc.) and multi-processing computing systems. These systems were implemented in many different ways depending on design requirements, such as the number of ports, scalability, reliability, and overall system cost. The basic building block in crossbar switch fabric systems is an $M \times N$ (M input by N output) crossbar switch, which allows any one of the M inputs to be spatially connected to any one of the N outputs.

In theory, designers can use a crossbar switch to build a large complete switch-ing system, but in practice, it is difficult to develop a very large system that fully interconnects every input-output pair using one single large (monolithic) cross-bar switch matrix. To build large systems, designers generally use multi-stage switching networks (made up of smaller crossbar switches) that deliver fully non-blocking performance.

Large systems can be developed with a reasonably smaller number of crossbar switch ICs. Mostly using advanced VLSI technologies, designers can now construct

large multistage, multi-chassis non-blocking crossbar switch fabrics using com-
mercially available crossbar switch fabric ICs. Such crossbar switch ICs can be
easily used for the construction of larger practical switch fabrics for switch/routers
ad routers. The switches can also be made "rearrangeable" to allow one switch
fabric connection path to be changed without affecting the other connection paths.

2.2.1 IMPLEMENTING A CROSSBAR SWITCH

The two basic methods for building crossbar switch fabrics using semiconduc-
tor technologies are (i) using N-way multiplexers (Figure 2.1), and (ii) using
crosspoint arrays (Figure 2.2). There are other methods discussed in the vast literature on crossbar switches, but these two are the well-recognized methods used
in practice. In an architecture using N-way multiplexers, a multiplexer is placed at
each output port to select data transmitted from the input ports.

   While this has been the traditional way many designers have built crossbar
switch systems, and is easy to understand, it lacks architectural flexibility (fixed
number of inputs and outputs). Such multiplexer-based architectures are difficult
to implement efficiently in silicon and are difficult to scale up when larger switching systems are required. These designs are not practical for switch fabrics that
are required to carry high port counts.

   In the architectures that use crosspoint arrays (Figure 2.2), a switching element
is placed at each internal fabric input-output intersection, i.e., crosspoint. This
method allows for designs with high-density crosspoint arrays, and has greater
flexibility than the N-way multiplexer-based crossbar switches. This architecture
has greater design flexibility and allows for the construction of large switch fabrics in a cost-effective manner.

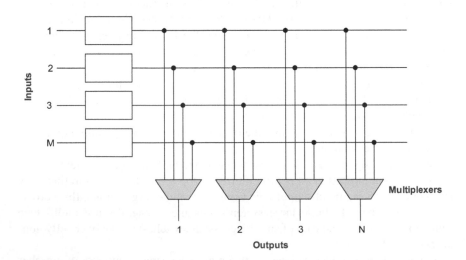

FIGURE 2.1   Designing a Crossbar Switch Fabric Using N-way Multiplexers.

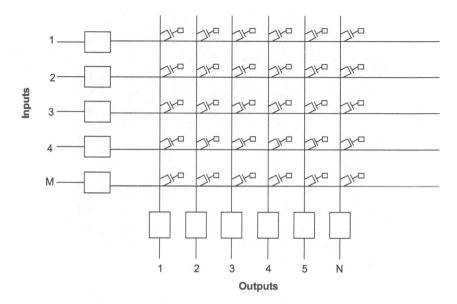

FIGURE 2.2 Designing a Crossbar Switch Fabric Using Switching Elements at Each Crosspoint.

Today the design of crossbar switch fabrics is greatly simplified with the availability of commercial monolithic $M \times N$ matrix size crossbar switch ICs (with crosspoint array elements) already designed with configuration state storage in digital registers. Most of these crossbar ICs can be programmed with serial or parallel data to configure the required input-to-output connections. With these ICs, designers can build cost-effective crossbar switch fabrics using single or multiple crossbar ICs that have excellent performance and reliability.

Designers have long known that it is possible to construct larger switch fabrics from smaller switch elements. However, building a larger crossbar switch fabric this way does not come without its problems, difficulties, and limitations. For example, when the size of a crossbar switch fabric is doubled, the number of basic switch element chips is quadrupled.

Growing a 64 × 64 crossbar switch fabric to a 128 × 128 switch requires four 64 × 64 switch elements (i.e., the naïve approach as illustrated in Figure 2.3). Four 256 × 256 crossbar switch element ICs can be combined to make a 512 × 512 crossbar switch fabric. This method of scaling a switch fabric can quickly become costly and impractical as more, smaller elements are added to build a larger switch fabric.

2.2.2 BUILDING MULTISTAGE SWITCHES

As the demand for bandwidth continues to increase, designers face greater challenges in creating larger switch fabrics with a higher number of input and output

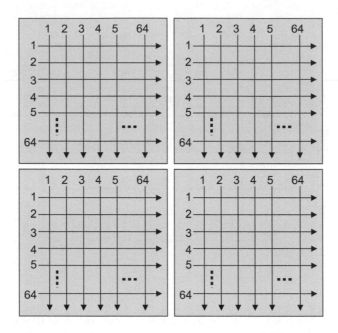

FIGURE 2.3   Naïve Approach for Scaling a Crossbar Switch Fabric.

ports. However, experience has shown that it is not practical to design a very large switch fabric using a single stage crosspoint array device. This difficulty has led designers to develop various techniques to partition the signals in a switch fabric into a manageable set of inputs per module (within the fabric) while at the same preserving the overall throughput and performance of the switch fabric.

Multistage crossbar switch fabrics are commonly used in large high-capacity, high-performance network devices and are an effective way of overcoming the limitations of designing using single chips or boards. Other than providing an effective way of scaling and expanding a switch fabric, a multistage fabric provides several other benefits. Even though they can be built using a number of smaller devices, multistage switch fabrics can be designed to be fully non-blocking, and provide efficient broadcast and multicast features. They can be designed to have effective redundancy, flexible internal routing, and reliability features with no single point of failure in the system. Furthermore, multistage switch fabrics can be designed to be scaled incrementally by allowing one or more modules to be added to the existing system.

Figure 2.4 illustrates a three-stage Clos network [CLOSCH53] which is a well-known example of multistage interconnection of switch fabric modules. Over the years, Clos multistage crossbar switch fabrics have been used in a wide range of telecommunications and networking systems. Designers generally turn to multi-stage interconnects when they need to scale the capacity of a switch fabric beyond the largest feasible single crossbar switch device (IC) available.

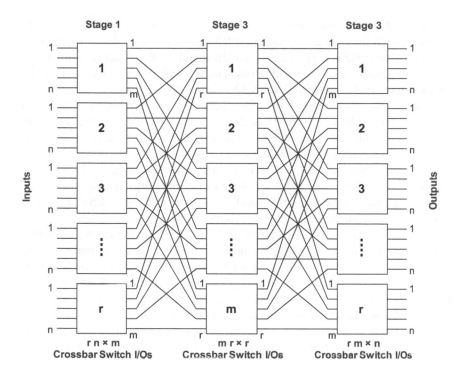

FIGURE 2.4 Three-Stage Clos Network.

The primary advantage of using Clos multistage interconnects is that the number of crosspoints required to construct a crossbar switch can be made far fewer than would be required if the entire switch fabric were constructed as one large single crossbar switch. Clos multistage interconnects can be realized in many different ways, depending on the design constraints and requirements of the system such as the number of input signals, overall system bandwidth, and cost.

A Clos network consists of three stages: ingress stage, middle, and egress stages. Each stage consists of a number of (smaller) crossbar switches (or modules). A signal transmitted on an ingress crossbar switch can be routed through any of the middle stage crossbar switches, to the target egress (destination) crossbar switch. A middle stage crossbar switch module can be used for a new incoming signal if both the path/channel linking the ingress crossbar switch module to the middle stage switch module, and the path/channel linking the middle stage switch module to the egress switch module, are unused or free.

A Clos network can be defined by the following three parameters:

- Each ingress stage crossbar switch module has n inputs.
- Each ingress stage crossbar switch module has m outputs.
- There are r egress stage crossbar switch modules.

There are *n* inputs which feed into each of the *r* ingress stage crossbar switch modules. Each ingress stage crossbar switch has *m* outputs, and each output feeds into one of *m* middle stage crossbar switch modules. Each ingress stage switch module has exactly one connection to each middle stage switch module. There are *r* egress stage switch modules, each with *m* inputs and *n* outputs.

The blocking characteristics of a Clos network are defined by the relative values of *m* and *n*. The Clos network is strict-sense nonblocking if $m \geq 2n-1$. This means a free (unused) input on an ingress crossbar switch fabric module can always be connected to a free output on an egress switch fabric module, without having to rearrange (or reroute) existing calls/signals in the network. The result implies that a Clos network can be designed to be a fully nonblocking switch matrix (without a single point of failure), if *m* and *n* are chosen such that there are multiple paths from each input to each output.

If the values of *m* and *n* are chosen such that $m \geq n$, then the Clos network is rearrangeably nonblocking. This means that a free input on an ingress switch module can always be connected to a free output on an egress switch module, but this can only be done when existing calls are rearranged. Existing calls in the Clos network may have to be rearranged (rerouted) by assigning/transferring them to different middle stage switch modules in the network.

It is possible to construct Clos networks with any odd number of stages greater than 3. For example, when each middle stage crossbar switch module is replaced

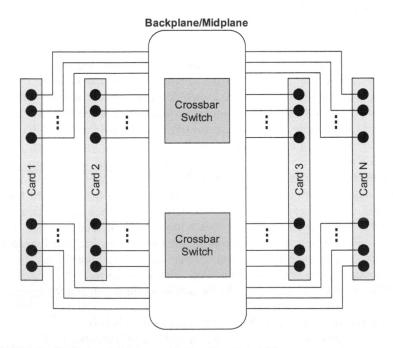

FIGURE 2.5   Backplane/Midplane with Crossbar Switch Elements.

with a 3-stage Clos network, a 5-stage Clos network may be constructed. Using the same process repeatedly, Clos networks with 7, 9, 11 stages and so on, can be constructed.

Today's high-performance systems require backplanes that support high-bandwidth data transfers. Figure 2.5 shows the backplane design which uses configurable digital crossbar switch (DCS) devices. These DCS devices support both programmable connections and buffered input/outputs (I/Os), and are an attractive alternative to conventional backplane designs. The DCS devices generally have good signal delay and skew characteristics that allow for simplified backplane design.

2.2.3 CHALLENGES IN BUILDING LARGER CROSSPOINT ARRAYS

The designer has to make some careful trade-offs when selecting the right crossbar switch technology for a given switch fabric design. There are important design factors to be considered when selecting crossbar switch ICs for large crosspoint arrays and systems. Designers have long understood that arrays larger than 16 × 16 (i.e., 256 connections), that (in many applications) typically use multiple (smaller) crossbar switch ICs, can cause various tolerances and errors present in an individual switch IC to accumulate and worsen [ELECDESG98]. Although the design technology has improved tremendously over the years, and single chip crossbar switches greater than 128 × 128 or even 256 × 256 can be designed, tolerances and errors present in an individual switch IC can accumulate and cause problems in a multi-chip design.

As a first step, the designer can select the largest crossbar switch IC array which offers performance above the desired system specification. This choice can lead to significant savings in product cost and design time, because much of the effort in designing well-performing crossbar switch systems involves creating proper compensation schemes for the system [ELECDESG98]. These compensation schemes are meant to rectify the individual IC device limitations in order to meet overall system specifications. Selecting a larger crossbar switch IC can eliminate significant design effort required for a larger system.

Most designs would require critical performance parameters of the crossbar switch IC to match and be consistent (i.e., not vary excessively) across the switch fabric channels (from one channel to another) as the crossbar switch is programmed to different configurations. Arriving at the right combination of components and board layout that gives the desired performance may involve significant experimentation.

Bandwidth, channel-path delays, crosstalk, dc offsets, and differential gain/phase are typical parameters that may require small adjustments or fine-tuning during the design [ELECDESG98]. It is observed in [ELECDESG98] that the bandwidth will roll off with an increasing number of cascaded devices in a channel, while the differential gain/phase and dc offsets will change as the square root of the number of devices cascades. These critical performance parameters are a direct function of the device specifications, but crosstalk, in particular, can be further made difficult to address by the layout of the printed circuit board used. Crosstalk, in general, will increase as the size of the system increases. Crosstalk is the presence of an undesired/unwanted signal transferred from one channel to another channel.

Crosstalk is a major design challenge in a crossbar switch, because all the inputs and outputs must be constructed to be in close proximity. This means keeping crosstalk to a minimum is critical in crossbar switches. Coupling is the (desirable/intentional or undesirable/accidental) transfer of electrical energy from one circuit segment (i.e., channel in the case of the crossbar switch) to another segment. Crosstalk can be generated from three major sources, mainly due to coupling [ELECDESG98]:

- **Capacitive coupling**: This is the transfer of energy within the crossbar switch system by means of a capacitance that is between circuit nodes. Crosstalk due to capacitive coupling can occur between two or more conductors in the system (for example, two input channels into a crossbar switch IC). The crosstalk resembles capacitive coupling to a resistive load at the input of the crossbar switch IC.
- **Inductive coupling**: In this case a change in current through one channel in the switch fabric induces a voltage across the ends of the other channel through electromagnetic induction. The amount of inductive coupling between the two switch fabric channels is measured by their mutual inductance. Crosstalk can be induced between two conductors in the switch fabric system when large currents are required to drive loads. This crosstalk resembles a transformer with a mutual inductance between the windings that drives a resistive load.
- **Common impedance coupling**: For this coupling to occur, two switch fabric channels must share a common current path with a non-negligible impedance. This coupling occurs when a current passes through the common impedance that is shared by two switch fabric channels.

It becomes more difficult to control crosstalk in all these cases as the signal frequency increases. Some of the well-known techniques used to control crosstalk consist of careful signal routing, component bypassing, and circuit shielding and separation. Some useful suggestions for controlling crosstalk (during the design of a crossbar switch fabric using smaller crossbar switch ICs) are as follows [ELECDESG98]:

- Crosstalk can be minimized by reducing the coupling capacitance of the input circuits. This can be accomplished by using crossbar switch ICs with a power supply or ground pin placed between the signal pins to shield them against crosstalk. Some crossbar switch ICs have this pin as a standard pinout. The power-supply and ground pins should be tied to a large ground plane with a very low return path impedance as best as possible.

- The effects of crosstalk due to inductive coupling can be minimized by increasing the spacing of the conductors and reducing their parallel length. When this cannot be done, or more reduction in crosstalk is required, the magnetic field/flux lines generated by current in the conductors can be reduced by copper shielding. The copper shielding will block the transfer of the magnetic field lines by generating localized eddy currents in the copper shields, thus significantly reducing their (inductive) coupling to other conductors.
- The designer must exercise extreme care to minimize additional crosstalk generated by the circuit board(s). Design issues that must be carefully addressed include shielding, signal routing, supply bypassing, and grounding.
- To have low crosstalk on a circuit board, the signals must be routed, as much as possible, on inner layers with ground planes situated below and above, and in between the signal traces' routing layer. One important consideration is to select a crossbar switch IC with a power-supply or ground pin placed between signal pins to provide shielding up to the entire crossbar switch IC device.
- The designer can lessen the effects of capacitively and inductively induced crosstalk by using multilayer printed circuit boards for the system circuit layout (for example, using a four-layer, printed circuit board layout for signal circuits). With this technique, circuit separation can be realized in a horizontal as well as vertical direction. The designer will also have enough space to route ground planes between signal circuits in order to lower the effective impedance of these traces, as well as to provide shielding. Unused regions in the multilayer layer boards should be filled with ground planes. Thus, on top of having controlled impedances, the input and output traces will also be well shielded.
- Generally, most systems are designed such that their signal paths share a common return path or ground. A signal current through a common return path with a finite (non-negligible) impedance can interact with other signals and produce crosstalk. To avoid this, the designer must ensure that the circuit layout minimizes the signal path ground impedance. This will ensure that the currents in the return path produce coupling that minimally interferes with the (desired) signals. The designer can accomplish this using the common ground planes with the lowest impedance possible.
- Another important source of crosstalk can be the system power supply. When a signal channel is driven by an active device, the resulting current consumed can produce interferences that reflect/transfer back into the power supply. The current in the impedance of the power-supply circuit produces this interference. This means this interference signal can transfer to any channel that shares this power supply as induced crosstalk. To help reduce this interference and crosstalk, the designer can bypass the power supplies by using good high-frequency

capacitors (placed as close as possible to the crossbar switch ICs). A capacitor of 0.01-μF, typically, is a good choice for high-frequency applications.

2.2.4 Designing Today's System Interconnects

Designers of network devices today have a larger number of options available to implement switching systems and interconnects. Yet still, the designer has to make tough decisions on which options and design path to take based on the specific design requirements for the application. The choices made will definitely include consideration of the type of network device to be developed, its features, and performance.

Designers can choose from a variety of implementation methods, ranging from field-programmable gate arrays (FPGAs), application-specific integrated circuits (ASICs), or application-specific standard products (ASSPs). The choice of any one of these implementation methods very often is based on a variety of factors which include overall system bandwidth, scalability, performance, cost, and other systems criteria. The following are some basic criteria used during the design process:

- **Nonblocking**: In current network practice, switch fabrics used in high-performance network equipment are nonblocking. The switch fabric must be nonblocking and have the ability to guarantee the delivery of data from any input to any output.
- **Scalability**: Most enterprise and service provider networks demand network equipment that is designed to be scalable. Such equipment can be expanded simply by adding one or more modules to the system, avoiding the need to completely replace a system with a bigger one. The ability to create larger switch fabrics from smaller switch elements has long been the most practical approach to designing high-capacity, high-performance switching architectures.
- **Performance metrics**: Switch fabric ICs can be described by a number of performance metrics, such as data transfer throughput and clock rate. The specific metrics for an application depend on the design and technology used, but operating frequency and data throughput rate constitute key criteria. Given the wide range of design options in the communication device market, designers must carefully match the switch IC devices with the intended application. Network components operating at very high data rates will require higher-speed devices than components that may be required to handle lower data rates.
- **Signal integrity**: An important characteristic of a switch fabric is that all paths in the fabric must have consistent timing, so that the fabric can have tight clock skew and a high fanout. This allows the designer to simplify the design and increase the switch fabric's reliability.
- **Flexibility**: A design that allows switch fabric ports to be easily configured as inputs, outputs, or bidirectional signals paths provides great

flexibility for designers to easily create switch fabric types with different characteristics. The ability to configure or control each I/O of the fabric with a choice of input-enable, output-enable, and clocking options also provides added flexibility in the design of switch fabrics.

- **Reconfigurability**: The ability to reconfigure switch fabrics on the fly provides designers the flexibility of changing the switch fabric's configuration without the need to replace the switch ICs with newer ones.

As discussed earlier, there are several factors to take into consideration when designing a switch fabric, particularly, a high-capacity multistage switch fabric. Obviously, the most important issue is design complexity. Unlike the traditional parallel shared-media or point-to-point switch fabrics, the multistage crossbar switch fabric requires extensive design efforts that often takes a long time to complete.

A key challenge facing a designer is the complexity associated with the layout of the overall switch fabric. The designer often has to deal with issues of control and overhead requirements in the switch fabric, communication protocol dependencies when transferring data over the fabric, and switch fabric redundancy in case of failure. Additionally, overall system cost may prove prohibitive when implementing a large multistage crossbar switch fabric. Large switch ICs and complex hardware combined with a bigger design team and expensive design tools can easily add up to an unacceptable system cost-to-throughput ratio.

Furthermore, as with any switch fabric and backplane design, a primary concern is signal integrity. The more complicated the switch fabric design, the more challenging it is to control power-supply noise, crosstalk, and reflections. The designer may have to adopt sophisticated routing techniques on the switch fabric boards in order to ensure that the signals pass through a clean, error-free environment.

The continuous growth of the Internet is driving the demand for denser, higher-capacity, higher-performing switch fabrics. Service providers continue to find cost-effective ways to increase port density at the edge of the network, and expand the services they offer to remain competitive. The network devices they deploy must address a number of requirements including:

- High port densities to accommodate continuous customer growth
- High bandwidth and scalability to handle increasing customer demand for data, voice, and video services
- Advanced quality of service (QoS) features to offer new services beyond high-speed packet forwarding and to support new business models
- High availability and redundancy features to ensure reliability and availability of service levels to end users
- Performance-optimized packet forwarding engines that incorporate hardware-based packet processing and forwarding to handle high-volume traffic aggregation
- Advanced security features to ensure continuous uptime in the face of increasingly sophisticated security attacks.

As the demand for more specialized Layer 3 forwarding services grows, service providers generally allocate responsibilities to switch/routers and routers as follows:

- **Low-speed access aggregation routers**: These devices provide individual end users access to the service provider network. The access device works by aggregating end-user traffic into higher speed aggregation devices. These devices tend to support large numbers of relatively low-speed ports connecting to end users.
- **High-speed access aggregation routers**: Similar to low-speed access aggregation devices, these devices provide individual end users with access to the service provider network. These devices tend to have fewer ports than the low-speed access devices but have higher aggregate throughput.
- **Backbone routers**: These devices serve as service provider network and Internet backbone transport. Their focus is on achieving the highest possible data forwarding rates using very high-speed interfaces.

The designers of the switch fabrics used in these categories of devices factor in the responsibilities and role of the device when deciding the capacity, performance, scalability, and reliability of the switch fabric. Table 1 highlights the main differences between access aggregation and backbone routers.

The differences described in the table are not absolute, and there are many router designs that can fulfill either role. However, as service provider network and Internet traffic continue to grow, the demand for access devices that support increased port densities and backbone routers that have greater packet forwarding capacities has become more apparent. Designers have recognized that these requirements are best met when the devices are designed while taking into consideration the specific role they will play in the network.

TABLE 2.1
Comparison of an Access Router versus a Backbone Router

Variable	Access Router	Backbone Router
Packets-Per-Second Forwarding Capacity	Medium to High	Extremely High
Advanced Packet Processing Features	High-touch packet processing with value-added QoS and security services	Minimal or low-touch packet processing with focus on fast packet forwarding
Interface Types	Higher port densities, large number of relatively low-speed ports/interfaces	Lower port densities, modest number of very high-speed ports/interfaces
Traffic Patterns	Predominantly, traffic flow is subscriber-to/from-trunk (also referred to as "north south")	Traffic is from any port/interface to any port/interface

2.3 LOGICAL ARCHITECTURE AND IMPROVING DATA TRANSFER THROUGHPUT

Figure 2.6 shows the logical architecture of a crossbar switch with a traffic scheduler. The $N \times N$ crossbar switch is an example of a space division switch fabric that can physically connect any of its N inputs to any of the N outputs. The switch scheduler manages the setup of the path taken by each packet through the switch fabric from the input port to output port. To set up a path, the switch scheduler closes a series of crosspoints between the input port and the output port. The speed at which these crosspoints are controlled by the scheduler plays a big role in the speed of data transfer through the crossbar switch.

The scheduler is a component that lies in a critical path of the data transfer process and can be a bottleneck in high-speed switches if not properly designed. When packets arrive at the input ports of the switch, the scheduler is responsible for resolving contention for access to the switch fabric and finding a conflict-free match between inputs and outputs. The scheduler decides, in each scheduling interval, which inputs are eligible to send data to which outputs.

Designing schedulers capable of scaling with line speed and/or port count as well as handling integrated unicast and multicast traffic scheduling is challenging

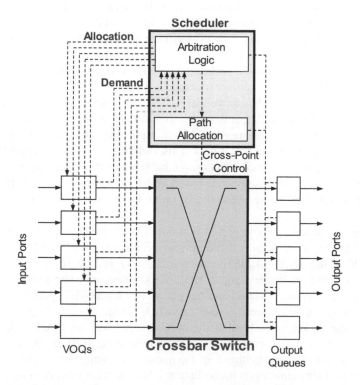

FIGURE 2.6 Logical Architecture of a Crossbar Switch Fabric with Traffic Scheduler.

and is still a subject of active research. Increasing the data transfer rate to very high speeds implies shorter scheduling intervals (i.e., time slots), which means the switch fabric requires simpler and faster, yet efficient scheduling algorithms, especially in systems with a large number of ports.

While a shared bus typically offers several hundred megabits of bandwidth to be shared by all the ports connected to it, a crossbar switch provides a high-speed dedicated path from the input port to the output port. Data is transferred through the switch fabric through dedicated switching elements rather than through a shared medium or resource such as a shared bus or shared memory. Therefore, adding more switching elements and paths in the crossbar switch provides a corresponding linear increase in the crossbar switch's data carrying bandwidth.

Although the $N \times N$ crossbar switch has complexity of $O(N^2)$ internal connections, advances in VLSI technology allow for crossbar switches to be implemented within a single chip for a large N. Crossbar switches have become more cost effective with high scalability, because the complexity is embedded within the switch fabric chip. The scalability of the crossbar switch can be further increased with increase in line speeds and the use of larger pin count packages with reasonable power dissipation.

The cost of a crossbar switch grows at the square rate when multiple chips are naively put together to build a larger switch as illustrated in Figure 2.3. In such cases, multistage switch fabrics, such as those based on Clos networks, are a much more cost-effective solution. Using designs based on Clos networks, large crossbar switch fabrics can be built cost-effectively with excellent scalability and reliability.

In an input buffered switch, packets are queued at the input ports and a scheduler then schedules the packets for transport across the switch fabric to their destination output ports. The basic crossbar switch implemented as an input buffered switch has the fabric running at the input line rate. In this architecture, buffering occurs at the inputs and the speed of the input port memory does not need to be greater than the speed of a single port. This architecture is widely considered to be substantially more scalable than output buffered or shared-memory switches. However, the basic crossbar switch-based architecture presents many technical challenges that need to be overcome in order to provide bandwidth and delay guarantees.

In the case where a single first-in first-out (FIFO) queue is used at each input port, it has long been known that a serious problem referred to as head-of-line (HOL) blocking [KAROLM87] can substantially reduce the switch fabric's achievable data transfer throughput. HOL blocking occurs when a packet queued at the input port is stuck behind another packet that has no clear path to its output port and is still to be switched across the switch fabric.

When the packet at the head of the queue cannot be transferred immediately to its output port, due to contention in the switch fabric itself, or the output port is busy, all other packets behind it in the queue must wait, even if they could be delivered to their output ports immediately. HOL blocking can seriously degrade data transfer throughput in FIFO input queued switches. It has been shown under assumptions of random traffic that an input buffered switch with FIFO queueing can achieve a maximum of only about 58.6% of total throughput [KAROLM87].

In output buffered switches, a packet will immediately be switched across the fabric and placed in its output port queue to be scheduled for transmission on the output link. Output buffered switches do not suffer from the HOL blocking problem, but, to be lossless, they require the output buffer to be fast enough to be able to service all the input ports at full data rates. This requirement calls for very fast memories at the output ports so that the switch can receive and transmit packets from the input ports before the output buffer queues become large and overflow.

Unless for low-end applications (where a switch is designed with low speed ports and/or a small number of ports), the total speed requirements of the output buffer can be difficult to realize even with the faster memory access times available in current memory technologies. An effective method for reducing the effect of HOL blocking is to clock the switch fabric at a speed greater than the input line rates (i.e., increase the speed of the switch fabric by a factor such as two to three times the input line rate).

A 10 Gigabit Ethernet port that supports 15 Gb/s bandwidth to the crossbar switch fabric offers 150% speedup. A fabric speedup enables faster transfer of packets across the switch fabric while minimizing queue build-up at the input ports. Fabric speedup with buffering at the input and output ports provides an effective way of reducing blocking in the systems while at the same time allowing sophisticated traffic management mechanisms to be implemented.

This kind of implementation is also known as a combined input-output queued (CIOQ) switch since packets need to be buffered both before and after the switch fabric. Traffic management mechanisms such as priority queuing, traffic scheduling (weighted round-robin, weighted fair queuing, etc.), priority packet discard, and packet marking/remarking can be easily implemented using the buffering schemes provided.

Switch fabrics used in network devices is a well-studied area and a great deal of studies were carried out during the era of ATM (Asynchronous Transfer Mode) networking [AHMAD89] [TOBAG90]. Various studies have shown that switch fabric speedup makes it possible to achieve data transfer throughput in excess of 99% in switch fabric architectures using CIOQ [CHENJ91] [GUPTA91] [MCKEOWN96AN] [MCKEOWN97] [OIEY89]. Other studies have shown that a CIOQ switch can behave almost identically to an output buffered switch, or one using centralized shared memory [PRABH98].

These studies show that only a moderate switch fabric speedup factor (of at most two) is necessary to approach the data transfer throughput and delay performance of pure output buffered switches [GUERI98]. The studies in [KRISH98] present a crossbar switch fabric arbitration algorithm which is described as work conserving for all traffic patterns and switch sizes for a speedup of only 2. [CHUAN98] and [STOIC98] explain that a CIOQ switch can match the packet latency behavior of an output buffered switch with a speedup of 2. Without dwelling on the specifics of the various studies, the understanding to date is that fabric speedup, CIOQ, and VOQs (see later mention), have helped transformed crossbar switch technologies into vehicles for designing high-capacity, high-performing switch fabrics.

Designers have long recognized that the most effective and primary method of eliminating the HOL blocking is by using queueing structures beyond FIFO at the input ports. Instead of maintaining a single FIFO queue at each input port of the fabric, a separate queue designated to each output port (called a virtual output queue (VOQ)) can be maintained at each input port. The use of VOQs at each port allows packets arriving at a port to be placed into one of several per-output queues at that input port.

As packets arrive at an input port, they are arranged into one of multiple output queues (i.e., VOQs) categorized by output port, and possibly, Class of Service (CoS). The sorting and placement of packets in the VOQs is best done after the Layer 2 or 3 forwarding table lookups (which provide the correct VOQs in which packets should be queued). This means the Layer 2 or 3 forwarding lookup process is best implemented before the VOQs. The use of VOQs requires the destination output port information of packets to be known prior to queuing in the VOQs.

A packet arriving at an input port is placed in a queue associated with its output port so that it is not held up by a packet in front of it. While this queueing structure eliminates the HOL blocking problem, it introduces an extra degree of sophistication that must be introduced in the switch scheduler so that the data transfer throughput over the fabric can be maximized.

This calls for an arbitration algorithm (in the scheduler) to schedule packets between the various inputs (VOQs) and outputs. The data transfer issue and scheduling can be seen to be equivalent to the matching problem for bipartite graphs since there could be contention at the switch fabric's inputs and outputs (see discussion later). The scheduling algorithm is required to match multiple per-output queues (VOQs) at the input ports with the appropriate destination output ports at high speeds to sustain the desired system throughput and to do so in a fair manner.

The goal is to design a scheduling algorithm that configures the crossbar switch fabric during each scheduling cycle and decides which input VOQs will be connected to which output ports. The scheduling algorithm determines which of the input VOQs are served in each scheduling cycle. At the beginning of each scheduling cycle, the scheduler examines the occupancy of the input VOQs and determines a conflict-free match between input VOQs and outputs.

Switch designers do recognize that that an input buffered crossbar switch with VOQs can be designed to provide close to 100% throughput using maximum matching algorithms that have been perfected over the years. The scalability and reliability of crossbar switch architectures have been significantly improved over the years, making these architectures the primary elements in high-capacity and high-performance network devices.

Typically, a high-performance system using a crossbar switch achieves line rate throughput by implementing a combination of the following:

- Using switch fabric speedup as one of several mechanisms for eliminating HOL blocking

- Employing a sophisticated traffic scheduling (or arbitration) algorithm and queuing to eliminate HOL blocking.
- Providing adequate input and output buffering to eliminate the effects of short-term contention and bursty traffic patterns
- Using pipelined arbitration of traffic request into the switch fabric to guarantee full data transfer throughput even for the smallest packet sizes.

Speedup in this case is designed into the switch fabric as an additional measure to improve data transfer throughput in the system. With this, packets are transferred from the input queues to the output queues faster than they arrive at the input ports. Transferring packets faster across the switch fabric not only reduces the time packets wait at the input queues for output ports to become available but also reduces the total port-to-port packet latency in the switch.

An additional advantage of speedup is that it provides more predictable delay and jitter (delay variation) across the switch fabric. By allowing the switch fabric to deliver many more cells within a cell scheduling time, the delay of each cell through the fabric is reduced. A properly selected speedup can guarantee that every cell is immediately transferred across the switch fabric to its destination output port. The combination of an intelligent traffic scheduling algorithm and fabric overspeed enables the crossbar switch to deliver near 100% throughput even under 100% input load distribution randomly and uniformly spread over all output ports.

Typically, the unit of data transfer across the crossbar switch fabric is a fixed-size packet, sometimes referred to as a cell. Designers have understood that fixed-size packets are easier to schedule and queue in the switch fabric than variable-size packets. Arriving packets are segmented into cells before being placed in the VOQs of the switch fabric. These cells are reassembled by the output port before they are transmitted out of the port. Cells can be constructed to be 64, 128, or 256 bytes long (or any suitable length), possibly with an internal cell tag or header, and internal cyclic redundancy check (CRC). The CRC is used as an error-detecting code to allow for errors or accidental changes to the cells to be detected as they cross the switch fabric.

2.4 COMPONENTS OF A PRACTICAL CROSSBAR SWITCH FABRIC SYSTEM

A typical implementation of a crossbar switch fabric system contains the following functional components:

- **Switch Fabric**: The switch fabric, whether single or multistage, carries user data between the various modules attached to its ports (that is, between line cards or between line cards and the route processors). The switch fabric receives scheduling information from a traffic scheduler and system clock information from clock or timing module.

- **Traffic Scheduler**: The scheduler processes requests from the input ports (with VOQs) for access to the switch fabric and specific destination output ports. When the scheduler receives a request from an input port, it determines when to allow access and sets up a path through the switch fabric to the destination output port(s). Requests are sent from the input ports to the scheduler which then grants the requests based on a predefined scheduling algorithm that ensures access priority and fair service to all the input ports. The scheduling algorithm configures the crossbar switch fabric while deciding the order in which packets from the VOQs are served. Once the scheduler issues grants, the crossbar switch fabric is internally configured to map the granted input ports to their requested destination output ports. The crossbar switch fabric is responsible for physically connecting an input port to the requested destination output port or ports (for multicast forwarding), based on the grants issued by the scheduler. Once created, the crossbar switch fabric provides a direct path between each input and the destination output port. In addition to being capable of forwarding unicast packets from multiple input ports to multiple output ports simultaneously, the crossbar switch must also be designed to forward multicast packets from input ports to multiple output ports.
- **System Clock**: The system clock provides timing signals used to synchronize data transfers through the switch fabric from input to output ports. In systems with clock redundancy, two system clocks (i.e., primary and secondary) may be used for system synchronization so that if one clock (i.e., primary) fails, the other clock (i.e., secondary) will take over. The system clock sends timing signals to all modules in the systems including line cards, route processor, and switch fabric modules. The system clock in the switch fabric module generates and distributes a system-wide clock, and if the "cell" is the unit of data transmission across the fabric, it provides the cell time synchronization signaling for the cell-based data transfers. The system clock is generated and distributed to the overall system through timing signal traces in the backplane, and local clock functions are implemented (on the line cards and other modules) to derive timing from the system clock.

In addition to scheduler and clock functionality, the switch fabric system may implement alarm functionality as described in a section later. A crossbar switch in the backplane of a switch, switch/router or router enables each line card module in the device to be connected to every other line card module.

Generally, the size of the switch fabric (and, hence, its data carrying capacity) is related directly to the number of switch fabric modules/planes that are available for data-handling purposes. By installing a second or multiple switch fabric modules/planes in the device, the number of modules/slots or, equivalently, the overall capacity of the system can be increased.

Generally, the switch fabric is implemented as a multi-function module that provides the inter-port switching services, supports as a switch fabric scheduler and controller, provides alarm monitoring facilities for the system (i.e., house-keeping and alarm monitoring functions), and provides onboard power for the switch fabric's own electronic circuitry, as well as power and control functions for the cooling fan trays.

The backplane and the switch fabric both play an important role in interconnecting modules in the system. Line cards and route processors and other system modules are installed (most often from the front of the chassis) and plug into a passive backplane. The backplane is designed to contain serial signal lines (or traces) that interconnect all of the modules to the switch fabric modules, as well as other lines for power and system monitoring/maintenance functions.

For example, a system may be designed with each of its 5 Gb/s chassis slots having up to four 1.25 Gb/s serial line connections, one to each of its four switch fabric cards to provide a total capacity of 5 Gb/s per slot or 10 Gb/s full duplex. Also, a system may have each of its 10 Gb/s chassis slots using four sets of 2.5 Gb/s four serial line connections, providing each slot with a switching capacity of 20 Gb/s full duplex. The system may be designed with its line cards having a fifth serial line that can connect to a redundant system clock and scheduler.

2.5 TRAFFIC SCHEDULING IN THE CROSSBAR SWITCH

A practical crossbar switch eliminates HOL blocking by maintaining multiple VOQs at each input port that send outstanding requests (for data transmission) to a traffic scheduler (Figure 2.7). The scheduler services these requests using a scheduling algorithm that generally provides significant data transfer performance

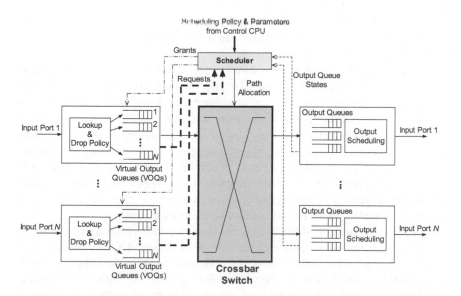

FIGURE 2.7 Crossbar Switch Fabric with Virtual Output Queues (VOQ) and Scheduler.

improvement over the simple FIFO scheduling method. The VOQ-based scheduling algorithms allow packets destined to output ports that are available to bypass packets in front of them which are waiting for busy output ports to become available.

The crossbar switch fabric operates in (scheduling) cycles governed by a system clock and scheduler, and provides a network of paths between the input and output ports based on the requests received. In every cycle, the scheduler examines the requests presented by the input ports, determines which requests should be serviced (issues grants), and sets up connections within the switch fabric to allow for data transfer from the input ports to the output ports.

The scheduling algorithm receives a number of input requests (unicast and multicast) and is required to process all these received requests within a given scheduling interval. The scheduler implements a map of the VOQ's occupancy at each port and determines and sets up the configuration of the internal crosspoint at every cell scheduling time slot. The scheduling algorithm computes the best input-to-output match in that interval that minimizes conflicts and maximizes data throughput.

A properly designed scheduling algorithm along with the input port VOQs enables the crossbar switching fabric to achieve very high levels of data transfer efficiency. This allows the throughput of the crossbar switch fabric to reach up to 100% of the theoretical maximum versus the 58.6% achievable with earlier crossbar switch fabric designs using only single FIFO queuing at the input ports.

Crossbar switch fabrics can be designed to be either internally unbuffered [MCKEOW97IZ] or internally buffered [ABELF03] [NABESH00]. However, both architectures still require VOQs at the input ports to achieve high data transfer performance. The architecture in [ABELF03] uses VOQs at the input port plus combined input- and crosspoint-queued (CICQ) internal structures to enhance the scalability of this input-buffered switch. Unbuffered crossbar switch fabrics are generally less expensive to implement than their buffered counterparts since the designs do not implement internal buffers.

The unbuffered architectures, however, are more difficult to scale due to the centralized nature of the scheduler and its high computational complexity [MCKEOWN95]. Buffered crossbar switch fabrics (and variants) have been developed increasingly over the years since they allow efficient and high-performance distributed scheduling (due to the decoupling of the inputs from outputs). However, the memory storage requirements in the buffered architecture scales quadratically with the number of switch fabric ports. For an $N \times N$ CICQ crossbar switch fabric, N^2 small internal buffers are required. Designers generally face the challenge of developing efficient architectures that maximize system performance and at the same time minimize memory utilization.

The argument in favor of CICQ crossbar switches with VOQs is that a designer can achieve significant reduction in the size of the input VOQs by adding small extra internal buffering in the switch fabric. Given that the size of buffer memory needed at the inputs (VOQs) can be very large (especially for high-speed switches with high port count), significant cost savings in terms of buffering and power consumption can be achieved. The added benefit of reduced complexity of the (distributed) scheduler, resulting in faster and more scalable switch architecture, makes CICQ switches also appealing.

A detailed discussion of scheduling algorithms for input buffered crossbar switches (with VOQs) [MCKEOWN95] is outside the scope of this book. Much of the research and development in this area was carried out when high-speed ATM and IP switches and routers were being developed in academia and the communication industry. This section discusses only briefly the main concepts and features of the commonly used scheduling algorithms in crossbar switches with VOQs. It is important to note that, even though we highlight only the key techniques here, there are many variants developed over the years.

2.5.1 THE SCHEDULING PROBLEM

Let us consider an $N \times N$ crossbar switch fabric (i.e., a switch with N input ports and N output ports). At the start of each scheduling cycle, the scheduler inspects the VOQs and determines a conflict-free match between the N^2 VOQs and the outputs. This scheduling problem can be considered as equivalent to finding a match on a bipartite graph with N vertices [ANDERT93] [MCKEOWN96AN] [TARJANR83].

A bipartite graph, also referred to as a bigraph, is a set of graph vertices (i.e., nodes of a graph) that can be split into two disjoint and independent sets U and V such that no two graph vertices within the same set are connected to each other, but rather every edge (i.e., the line joining any two nodes or vertices) connects a vertex in set U to one in set V. If all nodes in set U are colored red, and all nodes in set V black, then each edge (line) has endpoints of differing colors (red-to-black or black-to-red) as illustrated in Figure 2.8.

The scheduling problem can be interpreted as having requests (i.e., edges) from different input VOQs (i.e., set U) to various outputs (set V) with U and V seen as disjoint and independent vertices in a bipartite graph. In this bigraph there cannot be any edges among the set of VOQs (set U) themselves, nor can there be among the set of outputs (set V) themselves. A maximum matching algorithm tries to maximize the number of connections made (within the switch fabric) in

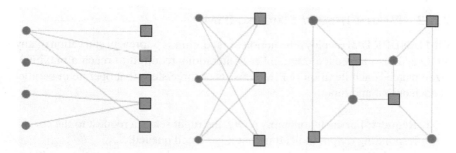

FIGURE 2.8 Example of Bipartite Graphs.

each scheduling interval, with the goal of maximizing the instantaneous allocation of switch fabric bandwidth to the VOQs.

By casting the problem as an equivalent network flow problem [TARJANR83],
one can find the maximum size matching for a bipartite graph. A maximum matching algorithm is an algorithm that finds a match (in the equivalent bipartite graph)
with the maximum size (algorithm called *maxsize*), or weight (*maxweight*). The
maxweight algorithm reduces to *maxsize* if the weight assigned to each of the edges
(lines) in the bigraph is equal to unity. Maximum size matching is also referred to
as maximum cardinality matching or, simply, maximum bipartite matching.

A maximum bipartite matching algorithm attempts to find matches that give
maximum utilization of output ports. Many maximum-size bipartite matching
algorithms have been proposed, and some examples that can guarantee to find a
maximum match are described in [CHIUSSIF93] [HOPCROFT73]. However, the
maxsize can cause indefinite service starvation in some VOQs and, when nonuniform traffic is presented, the algorithm cannot sustain very high data throughput
[MCKEOWN96AN].

These problems arise because the algorithm does not consider the packet backlog in the input VOQs, or the time packets in the VOQs have been waiting to be
served. The *maxsize* matching can lead to unfairness and instability in bandwidth
allocation to the VOQs under nonuniform traffic. Furthermore, maximum bipartite matching algorithms are too complex to implement in hardware and not fast
enough to be of any practical use in high-end, high-performance network devices.

The most common approach to determine a match is to use iterative matching algorithms based on a three-phase request-grant-accept scheme. The typical
three-phase scheme consists of a request phase where inputs send requests to
outputs, a grant phase where outputs resolve request contentions, independently,
by selecting only a single request among multiple received requests to grant, and
finally, an accept phase where inputs resolve grant contentions, independently, by
accepting only one among multiple received grants.

In general, especially for unicast traffic, most scheduling algorithms require
multiple iterations to improve the matching and obtain good performance. Thus,
the three-phase procedure is repeated several times over several scheduling intervals to obtain more optimal matches and thereby high throughput.

2.5.2 PARALLEL ITERATIVE MATCHING (PIM)

PIM [ANDERT93] employs the notion of randomness to prevent starvation of any
VOQ and also to reduce the number of iterations required to reach a maximal-
sized match. Each iteration in PIM consists of three steps that operate in parallel
at each output and input:

1. **Request**: For each nonempty VOQ, the input sends a request to the corresponding output indicating that it has a cell queued.
2. **Grant**: If an unmatched output receives a number of requests (i.e., multiple requests) from its corresponding input VOQs, it selects one randomly
   to grant.

3. **Accept**: If an input receives multiple grants for its VOQs, it selects one randomly to transfer a cell to the corresponding output.

In a maximal-sized match, connections (within the switch fabric) are added incrementally, without having to remove connections made in previous iterations in the matching process. Working based on iterations that consists of these three steps, PIM tries to converge quickly over multiple iterations to a maximal match that is conflict-free. At the beginning of the matching process, all VOQs and outputs are unmatched. PIM considers only those VOQs and outputs that are not matched at the end of an iteration (or scheduling cycle) as eligible for matching in the next iteration.

Since only unmatched VOQs and outputs are considered/eligible (at the beginning of each iteration), this means that PIM only considers connections (within the switch fabric) that were not created in previous iterations. PIM executes the three steps mentioned earlier in each iteration until a maximal match is reached. The algorithm operates in such a way that it does not require coordination among the outputs, making it fast and much simpler to implement than a maximum-sized match.

The operations of PIM can be viewed as finding a match in a $N^2 \times N$ bipartite graph (N^2 VOQs and N outputs), with N independent grant arbiters (one at each output) and N independent accept arbiters (one at each input) making decisions as described in the steps described earlier. The effects of the randomization at the independent output arbiters (that is, each one randomly selects a request among contending requests) is as follows [MCKEOWN95] [MCKEOWN99i]:

- In each iteration, at least ¾ of the remaining possible connections (not made in the previous iteration) will be matched or eliminated on average, and PIM converges to a maximal match in $O(\log N)$ iterations. PIM ensures that eventually transmission requests from all VOQs will be granted, ensuring that none of them suffers service starvation.
- PIM does not require memory or state to be maintained at each iteration (apart from VOQ occupancy) to keep track of which/when connections were made in previous iterations. At the beginning of each iteration or scheduling cycle, the matching process starts, independently of the matches made in previous iterations.

However, the use of randomization in PIM also leads to the following challenges or problems:

- Implementing grant and accept arbiters that must make random selections among the members of a set that is dynamic and time-varying is challenging and expensive (in hardware) especially at high speeds.
- PIM can lead to unfairness in bandwidth allocation between connections when the switch fabric resources are oversubscribed.
- The performance of PIM is poor for a single iteration and throughput is limited to about 63%, for large N, which is only slightly higher than that of a crossbar switch with simple input FIFO queuing.

The main factor that limits the practical use of PIM is that, even though it often converges to a (good) maximal match after several iterations, the time (i.e., scheduling cycles) it takes to converge affects the maximum speed at which the crossbar switch can be operated. The scheduling algorithms discussed later (and their variants) perform better even with just a single iteration and as a result are preferred by switch designers.

2.5.3 Round-Robin Matching (RRM)

The Round-Robin Matching (RRM) algorithm [MCKEOWN95] overcomes the problem of implementation complexity and unfair allocation of switch fabric resources that characterizes the random matching approach (PIM), by granting requests (at the outputs) and accepting grants (at the input VOQs) according to a round-robin priority scheme (Figure 2.9). Assuming an $N \times N$ crossbar switch, the RRM algorithm can be described broadly by the following three steps:

1. **Request**: For each nonempty VOQ, the input sends a request to the corresponding output indicating that it has a cell queued.
2. **Grant**: If an output receives more than one request from its corresponding input VOQs, it selects the next request to be served to be the one next (indicated by a grant pointer value) in its fixed, round-robin schedule. Each input is still notified even if its request was not granted. The output

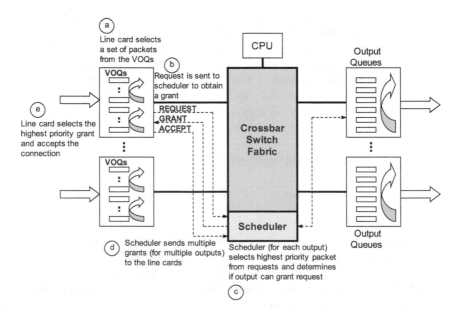

FIGURE 2.9   Packet Scheduling (with RRM) from the VOQs across the Crossbar Switch Fabric.

then moves the pointer to the next priority element of the round-robin schedule that is one location beyond the granted input VOQ.

3. **Accept**: If an input receives multiple grants for its VOQs, it accepts the grant that is next (indicated by an accept pointer value) in its fixed, round-robin schedule. The input then moves the pointer to the next priority element of the round-robin schedule that is one location beyond the accepted output (or equivalently, granted VOQ).

The RRM algorithm comprises two independent sets of round-robin arbiters at the outputs and inputs. Grants are scheduled by a round-robin arbiter at each output and accepts are also scheduled by a round-robin arbiter at each input. Each output arbiter updates its round-robin pointer after every grant and similarly, each input arbiter does so after every accept.

RRM overcomes the complexity and unfairness problems associated with PIM. The round-robin grant and accept arbiters are implemented as priority encoders [MCKEOWN95] [MCKEOWN99i] and are much simpler and faster than PIM. The rotating priority (deterministic round-robin selection) scheduling feature of RRM helps it allocate bandwidth equally and more fairly among requesting input VOQs.

The RRM algorithm has poor performance yielding a maximum throughput of approximately 63% (which is slightly lower than PIM operating over a single iteration) for uniformly distributed random traffic. The reason RRM performs poorly is because the round-robin grant/accept pointers change in lock-step as they are being updated, and the grant/accept pointers get synchronized very quickly, making RRM only able to service very few inputs (VOQs) per cell (scheduling) time. Because the output grant arbiters move in lock-step, only one input (VOQ) is served during each scheduling interval/time.

It is shown in [MCKEOWN95] [MCKEOWN99i] that synchronization of the round-robin grant pointers (at the output arbiters) limits performance of the RRM algorithm with random traffic arrival patterns. These studies also showed that, as the input traffic load to the switch increases, the synchronized output (or grant) arbiters have a tendency to progress in lockstep, and the degree of synchronization of the grant pointers does not change very much, only slightly.

2.5.4 ITERATIVE ROUND-ROBIN MATCHING WITH SLIP (iSLIP)

A variation of the basic RRM algorithm called iSLIP (noniterative and iterative versions) was developed in [MCKEOWN95] [MCKEOWN99i]. The iSLIP algorithm improves upon the RRM algorithm by allowing an output arbiter to update the round-robin pointer not after every grant (whether accepted or not) but only if the corresponding input (VOQ) accepts the grant as described in Step 3 of the RRM algorithm. Thus, the Grant step is modified as:

Grant: If an output receives more than one request from its corresponding input VOQs, it selects the next request to be served to be the one next (indicated by a grant pointer value) in its fixed, round-robin schedule. Each input is still notified even if its request was not granted. The output then moves the pointer to the next priority element of the round-robin schedule that is one location beyond the granted input VOQ if, and only if, the grant is accepted in Step 3.

The iSLIP algorithm reduces the synchronization of the output (grant) arbiters associated with RRM by imposing a condition on how the grant pointers are updated. Except this condition the two algorithms are identical. This minor change (in the way the grant pointers are updated) results in de-synchronization of the output arbiters and very high throughput [MCKEOWN95] [MCKEOWN99i]. Unlike in RRM, the output arbiters in iSLIP move in such a way that they have a tendency to desynchronize with respect to one another.

Studies have showed that a crossbar switch with VOQs and iSLIP can achieve 100% throughput when presented with uniformly distributed traffic (independent identically distributed (i.i.d.) Bernoulli traffic arrivals) [MCKEOWN95] [MCKEOWN99i]. When the traffic presented is nonuniform, iSLIP may not achieve the maximum 100% throughput but operates as a fair scheduling policy that is guaranteed never to starve any VOQ.

Iterative and noniterative versions of the iSLIP algorithm have been developed, as well as modified versions for crossbar switches that carry prioritized traffic in their VOQs [MCKEOWN95] [MCKEOWN99i]. The properties of iSLIP with one iteration are: i) the connection that is just recently made (i.e., accepted grant (or VOQ)) is given lowest priority, ii) no connection (accepted VOQ) is starved, and iii) under heavy offered load, all VOQs to their common output have the same throughput. The performance of iSLIP is further improved when it is operated over multiple iterations, and also results in lower average data transfer latency.

Prioritized iSLIP extends the basic iSLIP to include requests from inputs that want to transfer traffic with multiple priority levels (class- or quality-of-service levels). Using VOQs with priority levels (and possibly with moderate speedup) can make the packet transit delay across the switch fabric more predictable, allowing the system to control delay for delay sensitive traffic such as real-time voice and video traffic. Threshold iSLIP (as an approximation to maximum weight matching (maxweight matching)) and Weighted SLIP (to allocate the throughput to an output according to predefined weights among competing input VOQs) have also been developed in [MCKEOWN95].

An important characteristic of iSLIP is that it is simple to implement in hardware (because of its use of the simple request-grant-accept algorithm and deterministic round- robin arbiters) and can operate at high speed [MCKEOW97IZ]. iSLIP and its variants are simple to implement in hardware [GUPTAPAN99] and have become the most widely implemented form of schedulers for commercial high-speed, high-performance switches, switch/routers and routers with crossbar switch fabrics, and VOQs. The implementation of scheduling algorithms is largely dominated by centralized single-chip solutions which, however, suffer from scalability problems especially when developing very large high-speed crossbar switches [MINKENC06] [SCICCHI07].

2.5.5 Other Considerations in the Design of Schedulers

The designer may supplement the crossbar switch fabric with a scheduler that includes advanced pipelining techniques [GUPTAPAN99]. A scheduler with pipelining capabilities allows the switch fabric to start allocating resources for future scheduling cycles well before data transmission for previous cycles has been completed. Pipelining allows the system to eliminate wasted clock cycles (i.e., dead time), thereby dramatically improving the overall data transfer efficiency of the switch fabric. Adding pipelining to the scheduling mechanism enables high data transfer performance in the crossbar switch fabric and allows it to reach its theoretical maximum throughput.

A pipelining scheme is developed in [GUPTAPAN99] for the ESLIP algorithm used in the Tiny Tera packet switch [MCKEOW97IZ] and Cisco's 12000 GSR router [MCKEOW97WP]. With this pipelining scheme, the scheduler is able to overlap the accept phase (input processing) of one iteration with the request-grant phase (input/output processing) of the next iteration. The scheduler was designed to be clocked at a speed of 175 MHz (approximately 51 ns to complete 3 iterations of the ESLIP algorithm) and with each time slot consisting of 9 clock cycles.

The challenge in the design of a practical scheduler is to come out with one that is not too complex to implement in hardware and can complete scheduling decisions for the input VOQs within each scheduling cycle. The desirable properties of a scheduler for practical high-performance systems are the following [MCKEOWN99i]:

- **Efficiency and Throughput**: A scheduling algorithm that serves as many input VOQs as possible and targets 100% throughput on each input and output while keeping the packet backlog in the VOQs low.
- **Fairness**: An algorithm that does not starve a nonempty VOQ indefinitely or unfairly for a long time.
- **Scheduling Speed**: An algorithm that is fast enough to complete input-output matches within a scheduling interval. The scheduling algorithm must not become the bottleneck, if the switch fabric is to achieve its highest throughput.
- **Ease of Implementation**: An algorithm that is fast but also simple enough and practical to be implemented in hardware. It must not be too complex to be implemented in special-purpose hardware, desirably, within a single chip, or integrated within the crossbar switch chip.

2.6 HANDLING MULTICAST TRAFFIC

A good part of today's network traffic consists of multicast traffic, so a switch fabric must also be capable of handling multicast traffic efficiently. To accomplish this, the switch fabric must be equipped with various mechanisms such as the following:

- Using special hardware or inbuilt capabilities within the switch fabric and line card that perform effective routing and/or replication of multicast packets (desirably on a distributed basis).

- Dedicating separate VOQs on the input ports for multicast traffic so that the flow of unicast traffic is not degraded or impacted adversely. Typically, on the input ports, separate queues and (in some cases, separate) scheduling disciplines are implemented for unicast and multicast traffic.
- Using scheduling mechanisms that handle both multicast and unicast traffic efficiently while recognizing their individual requirements. There is great interest in the design of integrated scheduling algorithms for crossbar switch fabrics that support both unicast and multicast traffic scheduling.

Any port/interface in the system must be able to send both multicast and unicast requests to the scheduler for access through the switch fabric to destination ports/interfaces. When a multicast request is received by the scheduler, it specifies all destination ports/interfaces to which the packets must be forwarded, plus, possibly, the priority of the request. The scheduler, generally, is designed to handle a mix of unicast and multicast requests, while giving precedence to the highest priority requests, whether multicast or unicast.

When an interface/port receives a multicast packet, it sends a multicast request to the scheduler. Once the interface/port receives a grant from the scheduler (which is responsible for configuring the crossbar switch fabric internally to map the granted input ports to their requested destination output ports), the packet is then forwarded across the switch fabric to the output ports. Depending on the switch fabric design, it may be required to make copies (replicates) of the packet and send these to all the destination line cards simultaneously (during the same scheduling (cell) clock cycle). Each destination line card, in turn, may also be required to make additional copies of the multicast packet if it is destined to several local ports/interfaces.

In order to reduce blocking of unicast packets by multicast traffic, the switch fabric design could support within the scheduling framework partial allocation for multicast transmissions in the system. With this the scheduler performs the multicast operation over the switching fabric for all available input and output ports carrying multicast traffic but ensures that unicast traffic is not unfairly locked out. For example, if a destination line card is in the process of receiving a unicast packet from another input port, the multicast transfer (to that line card) can be continued in subsequent allocation cycles.

Switch fabrics that do not properly handle, separate, or prioritize multicast traffic can have cases where high volumes of multicast (and broadcast) traffic can degrade the transfer of unicast traffic. Therefore, intelligent scheduling (and if necessary, proper packet replication mechanisms) to be able to control and efficiently handle and forward multicast traffic has to be inherent in the switch fabric architecture.

To improve fairness and throughput, a crossbar switch fabric needs an intelligent scheduler that supports input buffering with VOQs and unicast and multicast traffic with multiple priority levels. However, the design of efficient unicast and multicast schedulers (whether integrated or separate) remains a challenging research problem and is being investigated actively in the industry and academia.

2.6.1 MULTICAST PACKET REPLICATION

Designers have long recognized that developing crossbar switch fabrics to handle unicast and multicast packets addressed to multiple destination output ports is not an easy task. The simplest approach of sending copies of a packet from its input to each destination independently is not optimal even though it is used in some designs for the sake of design simplicity.

For example, if a specific multicast packet is to be forwarded to eight destination output ports, the packet is duplicated eight times at the input port and forwarded to all eight destination output ports separately. To address this, some switch fabric architectures provide multicast packet replication. Some get around the packet replication issues by allowing an incoming multicast packet to be broadcast to any number of output ports.

The biggest challenge in forwarding multicast packets from an input port across the switch fabric to the designated output ports is multicast packet replication. Network devices that use multicast packet replication generally accomplish this in two stages as illustrated in Figure 2.10 [CISC2TMUL11] [CISCSUP2TA11] [CISCSUP6TA16]. The first stage of the replication process takes place in an

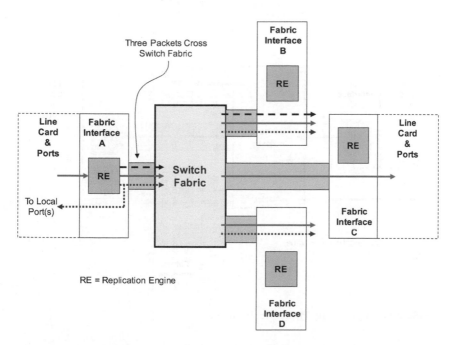

FIGURE 2.10 Ingress and Egress Packet Replication.

ingress line card and handles the branch replications of multicast packets from that line card to multiple destination egress line cards. The second stage is typically carried out by the egress line card and handles the leaf replications of received multicast packets to their individual destination ports/interfaces.

Depending on the switch fabric architecture, the multicast packet replication function can be resource intensive especially when the switch fabric carries heavy multicast traffic. The multicast replication process could cause starvation in CPU processing and memory resources, in addition to contention with unicast packets as they access the switch fabric which is also required to forward the replicated multicast packets.

Architectures that take advantage of the natural multicast properties of the crossbar switch are preferable, although the design of schedulers that can efficiently forward multicast within the fabric is challenging. Such architectures can perform multicast packet (or cell) replication within the crossbar switch fabric by appropriately closing multiple crosspoints simultaneously. This design approach eliminates the need for multicast packet replication in the ingress line card (Figure 2.11). The second-stage packet replication that takes place on the egress line card is still required if it supports multiple ports/interfaces, and can still cause local resource congestion and starvation.

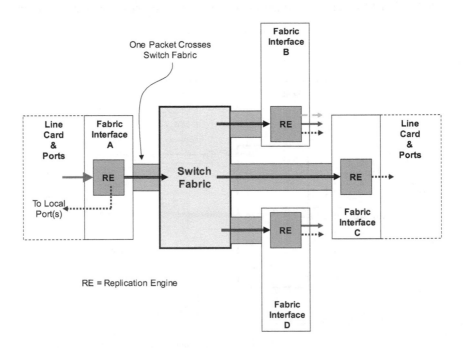

FIGURE 2.11   Egress only Packet Replication.

2.6.2 Multicast Traffic Scheduling

When forwarding multicast traffic over a crossbar switch fabric, a multicast cell (or packet) can be destined to more than one output port, known as the fanout set of the cell (or packet). The fanout set is the set of destination output ports on the switch to which the multicast cell should be forwarded. The fanout of the multicast cell is the number (total count) of the different destination output ports, i.e., the cardinality of (or the number of elements in) the fanout set [HUIJTREN90] [KIMCKLEE90]. A multicast cell has fanout destination j if output port j is a member of the fanout set of the cell. A unicast cell has fanout or cardinality equal to one, and its fanout destination is the single output port on the switch to which the cell must be forwarded.

The queuing structure at the input port in many designs is a combination of unicast and multicast queuing structures. This means that if separate input queues are used for multicast traffic, the number of queues for multicast traffic can vary from just one multicast queue to 2^N-1 queues per input port, where N is the number of output ports in the crossbar switch [MARSANIC01] [MARSANIN01] [PRABH97J].

2.6.2.1 Full versus Partial Multicast Scheduling across the Crossbar Switch Fabric

In each scheduling interval, cells in the input queues contend for access to the switch fabric to reach their destination output ports. The decision on which a (unicast or multicast) cell can be transferred across the switch fabric to its destination output port in each interval is made by the scheduler, which implements a scheduling discipline.

Depending on the input queuing structure and scheduling algorithm used, and subject to output availability, a multicast cell leaving an input may not reach all its destination outputs, (indicated by its fanout set), during one scheduling interval. Full multicast transfer (also referred to as no fanout splitting, total service, or one-shot) refers to the multicast transfer process (over the switch fabric) in which all copies of a multicast cell must be transmitted to their destination output ports in the same scheduling interval (cell time) [PRABH97J].

In this case a multicast cell leaving an input must traverse the crossbar switch fabric only once. For this to work, the cell can be forwarded to its destination output ports if and only if all those outputs are available in that scheduling interval. If any one of the destination outputs is busy, the full multicast transfer cannot happen. The multicast cell loses contention and cannot be forwarded, resulting in its remaining in the input queue. Developing schedulers for full multicast forwarding is a very challenging task and so far, there are no known techniques that do that efficiently.

Partial multicast (also referred to as fanout splitting or partial service), on the other hand, refers to the transfer process where cells might be delivered to their destination output ports over any number of scheduling intervals. A multicast cell in this case is sent to a subset of the fanout set (i.e., destination output ports) in each scheduling cycle. Copies of the multicast cell that were not transferred to their destination (due to output contention) in previous scheduling intervals wait for scheduling opportunities during the next cycles.

At the end of each scheduling cycle for the multicast traffic, the remaining copies of a cell (or equivalently, remaining destination outputs in the fanout set) to be served are referred to as the residue [PRABH97J]. The residue can be defined as the set of fanout destinations that have not yet received a copy of a multicast cell at the end of a scheduling interval. The residue can also be interpreted as the number of copies of a multicast cell still left at the front of its input multicast queue at the end of each scheduling cycle after losing contention for the destination output ports (in the fanout set).

Depending on the scheduling policy used, the residue can be concentrated on just a few input ports or distributed over a large number of input ports. In a concentrating policy, the residue is left on the minimum number of input ports, while in a distributing policy, it is left on the maximum number of input ports. Each scheduling discipline operating with partial multicast transfer has its own specific method of concentrating or distributing the residue among all the contending multicast inputs. To enhance and sustain high throughput and overall switch performance, most multicast schedulers try to send a copy of the multicast cell to the largest available fanout destination outputs in the fanout set.

The flexibility of partial multicast (or fanout splitting) comes with a small increase in scheduler implementation complexity; however, this method provides higher overall switch fabric throughput. It is less challenging to develop schedulers for multicast forwarding with fanout splitting discipline. Most practical schedulers fall into this category and are also easier to implement.

A significant amount of research and work has been done that considers placing a copy (or replication) network before the switch fabric in addition to using a partial multicast transfer (or fanout splitting) discipline. A number of partial multicast scheduling algorithms have been proposed that do not use a replication network but instead the inherent capability of the crossbar switch fabric to deliver multiple copies of a cell from an input to multiple destination output ports [MCKEOWN96PR] [PRABH95] [PRABH96] [PRABH97J].

2.6.2.2   Scheduling in Internally Unbuffered Crossbar Switches

The focus of most of the scheduling algorithms developed over the past two decades has been unbuffered crossbar switches with VOQs. Furthermore, most of the development work focused either on unicast or multicast traffic scheduling but not on combined traffic. Also, the work done on unicast scheduling algorithms is very extensive compared to multicast scheduling.

For multicast traffic, the input queuing structure employed also influences the design of the scheduling algorithm, its implementation complexity, and its overall performance. The input multicast queue structure used obviously affects the scheduling discipline, since the multicast cells that can be selected in each scheduling interval are always a (small) subset of all multicast cells queued at input ports. Essentially, the scheduling algorithm is tailored to work with the specific input multicast queue structure adopted. Several different ways of structuring the input multicast queues can be conceived.

Most integrated scheduling algorithms (mainly, for internally unbuffered crossbar switches) are designed by combining previously designed unicast and multicast algorithms into one unified algorithm [GUPTAPAN99] [MCKEOW97WP]. The input queuing structure considered for these algorithms is also a combination of N unicast VOQs and a smaller number of multicast queues, k, where, $1 < k \ll 2^N - 1$. Most of the practical algorithms developed for commercial products use this approach [MCKEOW97WP].

The type of integrated scheduling algorithm developed depends very much on the input queuing structure used. The design of the input multicast queuing structure is very critical and as a result influences the design of the scheduling algorithm. This has led to the proposal of many different multicast queuing strategies and algorithms over the years. Because the number of input multicast queues is much smaller than the fanout set, a cell placement strategy is required to distribute the incoming cell to the multicast queues.

As discussed later, a cell placement/assignment policy is needed alongside the scheduling algorithm to map incoming multicast traffic to the k input multicast queues, since $1 < k \ll 2^N - 1$ [BIANCO03] [GUPTAS02]. It is assumed that the cells in the input multicast queues each contain an indicator (e.g., a vector or a destination bit map) indicating to which outputs the cell is to be sent. We assume that for each nonempty input queue, the scheduler only examines the first cell (that is, the leading cell) in the queue in each scheduling interval. The multicast scheduling technique proposed in [PRABH97J] uses only one multicast FIFO queue per input port and does not require a cell assignment scheme.

Designers were attracted to these scheduling algorithms with k input multicast queues mainly because of their simplicity, reasonable scalability, low hardware implementation complexity, and the reliance on the intrinsic multicast capabilities of the crossbar switch fabric. These (non-copy network) architectures employ a smaller number of input queues at each input port for multicast traffic which means HOL blocking (within a multicast queue) cannot be avoided for multicast traffic traversing the switch fabric.

The main argument for such simplified queuing structures is that using a separate VOQ for each possible multicast destination output port at each input port would result in a total of $2^N - 1$ VOQs per input port (i.e., multicast VOQs), which is impractical [PRABH97J]. The optimal queuing structure is one that employs $2^N - 1$ different queues at each input [MARSANIC01] [MARSANIN01]. This approach completely avoids the HOL blocking problem but results in scheduling algorithms that are very complex and impractical even for medium-sized crossbar switches.

The main drawback of a many of these multicast scheduling algorithms is that they do not achieve high throughput performance or can be difficult to implement at high speed. This is mainly due to the limited number of input multicast queues used, the performance of the centralized scheduler, and the inefficient use of the inherent internal multicast capabilities of the crossbar fabric switch.

2.6.2.3   Scheduling in Internally Buffered Crossbar Switches

We discussed earlier that a combined input- and crosspoint-queued (CICQ) cross-bar switch with input queuing (i.e., VOQs) can be created by adding small buffers inside the crossbar switch fabric itself (i.e., internally buffered crossbar switch fabric) [ABELF03] [MHAMDL09] [NABESH00]. The addition of internal buffers simplifies the scheduling of traffic through the switch fabric and also makes it possible to implement distributed scheduling.

Unlike the unbuffered crossbar switch fabrics which typically use centralized and a relatively more complex scheduler, a CICQ crossbar switch employs distributed scheduling with one scheduler per input and one scheduler per output. The input and output schedulers are decoupled and can be implemented to operate independently and in parallel, thereby improving the data transfer throughput performance of the overall switch fabric. Most of the work on scheduling in CICQ crossbar switches focused on unicast scheduling algorithms (see [MHAMDL09] and references therein). The work on multicast scheduling, on the other hand, is rather very limited [MHAMDL04] [MHAMDL09] [SUNSHES05].

An integrated unicast and multicast scheduling algorithm for CICQ crossbar switches is proposed in [MHAMDL09] based on using N input VOQs for unicast traffic and k ($1 < k \ll 2^N - 1$) multicast traffic queues at each input port. Most schedulers employ a small number, k, of input multicast queues as the best compromise between using only one input multicast FIFO and the full 2^N-1 number of fanout queue configurations.

However, because k is less than the full optimal number of fanout queues, a cell placement scheme to distribute incoming packets over the k multicast queues is needed as this distribution also affects the scheduler's performance [BIANCO03] [GUPTAS02]. A factor here in the design of the cell placement mechanism is how it prevents cells from being out of sequence as they are transferred to the outputs.

A cell placement/assignment algorithm is proposed in [MHAMDL09] which maps incoming traffic to the k input multicast queues. A round-robin scheduling algorithm (called Multicast and Unicast Round-Robin Scheduling (MURS)) was developed that is capable of scheduling simultaneously unicast and multicast traffic across the CICQ crossbar switch fabric. Arriving variable-size packets are segmented into fixed-size units, cells, before being placed in the input queues of the CICQ switch. At the output ports, cells are reassembled back into packets before being transmitted out of the switch. Time is divided into slots with each time slot equal to a scheduling cycle.

An internally buffered $N \times N$ crossbar fabric contains N^2 distributed crosspoint buffers. If we denote a crosspoint buffer by B, a cell sent from input i and destined to output j is buffered in internal crosspoint buffer B_{ij}. Each input port supports an integrated input scheduler in addition to its input unicast and multicast queues [MHAMDL09]. Each input scheduler examines the cells at the head or front of the eligible queues at that input and selects one cell to be transmitted to a crosspoint buffer.

An input unicast queue (VOQ) is considered eligible (for servicing) if it is not empty and the corresponding crosspoint buffer to the output is not full. An input multicast queue is considered eligible if it is not empty and there is at least one nonfull crosspoint buffer (or equivalently, there is at least one available destination output port). Each output also supports an output scheduler in addition to its output buffers. The output scheduler at output j examines its corresponding crosspoint buffer B_{ij}, $1 \le i \le N$ and selects one cell to be forwarded (for packet reassembly and final processing) at the output port.

The CICQ switch and its scheduler in [MHAMDL09] supports a flow control mechanism that communicates, continuously, the occupancy state of the internal crosspoint buffers to the input schedulers to allow them to throttle their transfers to prevent crosspoint buffer overflow. Obviously, the design of the flow control mechanism and the sizing of the internal crosspoint buffers affects the scheduler's performance.

In each time slot (i.e., scheduling cycle) in the flow control mechanism employed in [MHAMDL09], each input scheduler receives N flow control bits (1 bit for each corresponding crosspoint buffer) from the core of the internally buffered crossbar switch fabric. Each bit (in the N-bit flow control signal) indicates the occupancy status of its corresponding crosspoint buffer (that is, bit value 0 if crosspoint buffer is full, 1 otherwise).

The studies carried out so far on integrated unicast and multicast scheduling algorithms (e.g., [MHAMDL09]) have shown them to have superior performance over their counterpart algorithms proposed for internally unbuffered input queued crossbar switch fabric architectures. Despite the advantages seen in CICQ crossbar switches in regard to addressing the performance, scalability, and scheduling issues faced by the internally unbuffered crossbar switch fabrics, there is relatively less research activity to address the problem of integrated unicast and multicast scheduling in CICQ crossbar switches, particularly at very high link speeds.

2.6.2.4   Special Focus: The ESLIP Scheduling Algorithm

The ESLIP algorithm described in [MCKEOW97WP] and [GUPTAPAN99] is designed to support the integrated scheduling of unicast and multicast traffic and is used in the Tiny Tera packet switch [MCKEOW97IZ] and Cisco's 12000 GSR router [MCKEOW97WP]. ESLIP can be viewed as combining the iSLIP unicast scheduling algorithm [MCKEOWN95] [MCKEOWN99i] with the Multicast Round-Robin Matching (mRRM) multicast scheduling algorithm described in [MCKEOWN96PR] [PRABH95].

The ESLIP algorithm supports input queuing with four (strict) priority levels at the input ports. Each request sent from a unicast and multicast traffic queue at the input may be assigned one of these four different priority values. A higher priority level is given preferential treatment over lower priority values (strict priority), so all requests are prescreened before being sent to the grant arbiter.

A priority filter eliminates all but the highest-priority requests before being passed to the arbiter. To determine the priority value of the requests, the priority filter uses a 2-bit priority value associated with every unicast and multicast request. Each request carries a 4-bit marking with 2 bits used for priority, 1 bit for valid, and 1 bit to indicate a unicast or multicast request. Furthermore, in any given priority, unicast and multicast requests take precedence but in alternate scheduling intervals.

The priority filter takes in a number of requests and outputs the highest priority request. The processing is equivalent to first calculating the highest priority for all valid requests received, and then eliminating all requests that are not of that highest priority value. The priority filter is placed before the grant arbiter, and because it is on the ESLIP scheduler's critical path, it has to be carefully designed [GUPTAPAN99].

ESLIP, although it may not be considered as an optimal algorithm among all the proposed algorithms, is an example of an integrated unicast and multicast scheduling algorithm that has been successfully implemented in commercial products. We discuss this here because of its simplicity and practicality and also as an example algorithm that uses the request-grant-accept mechanisms discussed earlier. The discussion here is also to show a real practical example of a scheduler for a crossbar switch with VOQs that has been implemented in hardware at very high speeds.

The Tiny Tera switch supports 32 input/output ports (i.e., a 32 × 32 switch) each operating at SONET OC-192 (10 Gb/s) line speed. The switch employs a centralized scheduler that schedules traffic across an input-queued crossbar switch fabric. Variable-length packets arriving at the switch are segmented into fixed-size 64 byte data units ("cells"), which are switched across the switch fabric every 51 ns (the scheduling interval).

The Tiny Tera switch employs VOQs to eliminate HOL blocking for unicast traffic and maintains four strict priority classes for each VOQ. The total number of queues supported at each input port is 128 unicast (4 × 32) queues (VOQs) plus 4 multicast queues, resulting in a total of 4,224 queues (32 × 132) across all 32 input ports. In each scheduling interval, an input unicast queue (VOQ) can transmit to at most one output, but a multicast queue can transmit to possibly several outputs. This means, in a scheduling interval, an output can be connected to at most one input queue to receive either unicast or multicast traffic.

In each 51-ns scheduling interval, the centralized scheduler examines the current occupancy of all the input (unicast and multicast) queues and calculates a new scheduling map that can be used to configure the crossbar switch fabric for data transfer. At the beginning of each scheduling interval, ESLIP performs multiple iterations, each consisting of the request-grant-accept three-phase process. After the connections within the crossbar switch have been configured, each input transfers at most one unicast or multicast cell across the switch. Each output, in turn, receives not more than one unicast or multicast cell within the scheduling interval. The crossbar switch fabric replicates (internally) multicast cells when possible and uses fanout-splitting techniques to reduce HOL blocking.

The Cisco 12000 GSR router supports 16 (input/output) ports, with each port operating at 2.4 Gb/s. These 16 ports result in a theoretical maximum aggregate bandwidth of 16 × 2.4 Gb/s = 38.4 Gb/s. The router maintains two types of queues: unicast cells are queued in VOQs, while multicast cells are maintained in separate multicast queues. The crossbar switch fabric is able to perform cell replication internally by closing multiple crosspoints simultaneously. At the beginning of each scheduling interval, a centralized scheduler determines which crosspoints are to be closed to allow data transfer to take place. The Cisco 12000 GSR supports a crossbar switch fabric and uses the ESLIP algorithm to schedule a combined traffic of unicast and multicast cells across the fabric.

To handle multicast traffic, the scheduling algorithm examines the multicast queues at each input and selects which cells are to be transferred in each scheduling interval to their destinations. The algorithm is required to select cells from competing unicast and multicast cells, each cell with its own service priority. The Cisco 12000 GSR supports 4 priority levels in the unicast and multicast queues maintained on its 16 ports. The ESLIP algorithm is designed to schedule unicast and multicast traffic simultaneously, and to provide preferential service to higher priority cells. As discussed earlier, ESLIP is an integrated unicast and multicast scheduling algorithm and is an enhanced version of the unicast iSLIP algorithm.

Similar to iSLIP, all inputs and outputs are considered initially unmatched, and with the algorithm adding more connections with each successive iteration. To determine which connection should be given preferential (priority) treatment, a separate grant pointer for each priority level is maintained by each output. Also, all the outputs share (and collectively maintain) common pointers for multicast traffic. Similarly, a separate accept pointer for each priority level is maintained by each input, and all inputs share (and collectively maintain) common pointers for multicast traffic. The ESLIP algorithm can be described broadly by the following three steps:

1. **Request**: Each input sends a request for each queued unicast cell (plus its service priority) to the output to which it is destined. These requests are from the nonempty queues among the $4 \times N$ unicast queues maintained at each input. The request priority sent to each output belongs to the highest priority cell queued. Similarly, each input sends a prioritized request for each queued multicast cell to every output to which it is destined (i.e., every output in the fanout set).

2. **Grant**: An output must choose only one request among all the requests it receives. Each output examines all the unicast and multicast requests received, keeping only those belonging to the highest priority cells, and discarding the remaining requests. The selected requests are either all unicast, or all multicast. Similar to the grant procedure for iSLIP, if unicast requests at priority k are considered, the output selects the input (unicast queue) that is next (i.e., indicated by a unicast grant pointer value) in a fixed, round-robin schedule. If multicast requests are considered, the output selects the input (multicast queue) that is next (i.e., indicated by a global multicast grant pointer) in a fixed, round-robin schedule. Each input is notified by the output even if its request was not granted.

3. **Accept**: An input accepts only one grant among all the grants it receives. Each input examines all the unicast and multicast grants received,

keeping only those belonging to the highest priority cells, and discarding the remaining grants. If unicast grants at priority level k are considered, the input selects the output that is next (i.e., indicated by a unicast accept pointer value) in a fixed, round-robin schedule. The unicast accept and grant pointers are both incremented similar to iSLIP. If multicast grants are considered, the input selects the output that is next (i.e., indicated by a global multicast accept pointer) in a fixed, round-robin schedule. If this connection is the last one in the fanout set (i.e., it completes the fanout), the global multicast accept and grant pointers and are updated accordingly. To avoid starvation at some input multicast queues, the pointers are only updated after the first iteration.

ESLIP is relatively more complex than iSLIP but has been shown to be simple to implement in hardware [MCKEOW97WP] [GUPTAPAN99]. A scheduler implementing ESLIP consists of output (or grant) arbiters that implement Step 2 of the algorithm, and input (or accept) arbiters that implement Step 3. The ESLIP has the same properties as the iSLIP algorithm which are: it provides high throughput, avoids starvation at the input queues, has fast convergence, and is simple to implement.

2.7 DATA TRANSFER PROCESS OVER THE SWITCH FABRIC

At the heart of many high-capacity, high-performance switch/routers or routers is a multi-gigabit or terabit level crossbar switch fabric that is optimized to provide high-throughput and high-speed switching. The crossbar switch enables high performance switching for the following reasons:

- Communications between line cards across the switch fabric are over internal paths that can operate at very high speeds.
- Multiple transmissions can be supported simultaneously over the switch fabric, increasing the aggregate bandwidth of the system. The switch fabric receives scheduling information and clocking signals from a scheduler and system clock, and performs the switching functions.

This architecture allows multiple line cards including the route processor to transmit and receive data across the switch fabric simultaneously. The scheduler is responsible for selecting which modules can transmit and which ones receive data during any given scheduling cycle. The switch fabric provides a physical path for the system modules to transmit and receive various types of traffic including:

- Data traffic transmitted from line cards including those generated by and destined to the route processor (routing protocol, management, and control traffic)
- The initialization code and configuration data transferred from the route processor to the line cards on system power up

- The forwarding tables and periodic updates from the route processor to the forwarding engines in the line cards and any other distributed forwarding engines
- Statistics and monitoring information from the line cards to the route processor.

The switch fabric is typically designed as an $N \times N$ non-blocking crossbar switch fabric where N denotes the maximum number of line cards that can be supported in the chassis (including the route processor module(s)). This allows each system module to transmit and receive traffic over the fabric simultaneously. In order to have a non-blocking architecture to allow multiple line cards to communicate with other line cards simultaneously, each line card has an N VOQs, one for each possible destination line card, plus one k queue for multicast traffic.

When a packet arrives at an interface/port on a line card, a forwarding table lookup is performed to determine the forwarding instructions for the packet. The lookup provides the forwarding information which generally includes the destination line card, output interface/port on the line card, and appropriate Media Access Control (MAC) address re-write information for the packet.

Before the packet is forwarded through the switch fabric to the destination line card, the packet is segmented into cells. A request is then sent to the traffic scheduler for permission to transmit a cell to the destination line card. Generally, one cell is transmitted every switch fabric scheduling cycle which is pre-configured for the system. The destination line card then re-assembles the transmitted cells into a complete packet, and uses the MAC rewrite information associated with the packet to perform the MAC frame rewrites. After the rewrites, the line card queues the packet on the appropriate output interface/port for transmission to the next hop.

In some designs [CISC12000SF], even if a packet arrives on an input interface on a line card and is destined to another interface on the same line card (or to the same interface in cases where sub-interfaces are used), the packet is still segmented into cells and transmitted over the switch fabric which then switches them back to line card and (sub-) interface itself. In this case the line card does not implement local switching of the cells even when source and destination interfaces are on the same line card.

In other designs [ARISTA7500], packets destined to interfaces on the same line card (with its own local forwarding engine) can be forwarded locally after the forwarding table lookup and do not consume or waste any switch fabric bandwidth resources.

2.8 SYSTEM MONITORING AND CONTROL

Alongside the main crossbar switch fabric, some architectures implement a management bus (MBus) which carries mainly management, control, and monitoring data between modules in the system as illustrated in Figure 2.12 [CISC12000MB] [CISCCAT6500] [FOUNBIG04] [FOUNJET03]. The MBus is sometimes

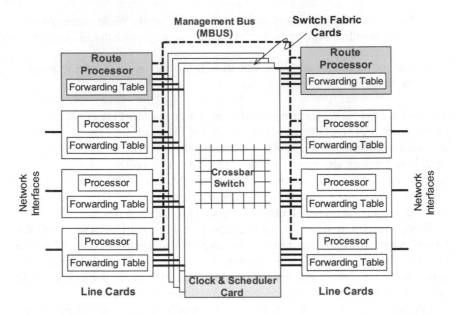

FIGURE 2.12   Crossbar Switch Fabric with a Management Bus.

referred to by other names such as the control bus, maintenance bus, command bus, monitoring bus, etc.

The MBus is typically a low-speed bus (e.g., 1 Mb/s, 10/100 Mb/s, etc.), sometimes with redundancy that interconnects the various modules in the system (route processor, line cards, switch fabric modules, power supplies, cooling fans/blowers, etc.). In this architecture, the route processor (also referred to as the control processor or engine) is the central point of system management and control.

Each module in the system would typically support an MBus interface, which provides an interface to the MBus itself and to the other system modules. Using appropriate software interface tools and commands, instructions and commands can be issued to various modules and processes in the system from the control processor. Commands can be issued to view processes and their status and retrieve statistics from the system modules. Typically, an MBus software agent will be running on the different modules such as the switch fabric module(s) and line cards.

The MBus and the distributed MBus interfaces are used to manage all the non-user data transfer functions of the system. The MBus may consist of two redundant buses that interconnect all the line cards, route processors, switch fabric modules, alarm cards, power supplies, and fan/blower modules. Each of these modules contains an MBus interface that allows the module to communicate through the MBus to the route processor or other modules.

The MBus interface on the different modules may be powered by different sources within the system. The MBus interface on each switch fabric module may be powered individually by, for example, +5 Volts DC supplied by a DC-to-DC converter on each module. Similarly, the MBus interface on each alarm card may be designed to be individually powered by +5 Volts DC supplied by a DC-to-DC converter on each alarm card. A +5 Volts DC may be passed on the chassis backplane to provide power to the MBus interface on the route processor, line cards, fan modules, and the power supply subsystem.

2.8.1 Main MBus Functions

The MBus and MBus interfaces in a switch, switch/router, or router may perform the following functions:

- **Code download**: In the switch/router or router, the route processor can download all or part of the line card operating software and configuration parameters over the MBus. For a higher-capacity MBus, all the downloads can be carried out over that bus. However, for an MBus that is slower than data transfer through the switch fabric, the route processor downloads just enough software code over the MBus to the line cards for them to perform the initial bootup [CISC12000MB]. The line card can then access the switch fabric to complete the download from the route processor.
- **Diagnostics**: To carry out testing and diagnosis of line cards, the route processor can download the diagnostic and testing software image over the MBus to the line card (or other system modules) being tested.
- **Device discovery**: To determine and inventory the type of devices configured in the system (i.e., device configuration), the route processor can use the MBus. The route processor transmits a special message over the MBus to all installed/configured devices requesting them to identify themselves. The devices respond by providing information that includes their chassis slot number, line card type, serial number, component type, etc.
- **Environmental monitoring and alarms**: The MBus interface on each major system module such as line cards, cooling fan/blower modules, and power subsystem monitors the environmental threshold values defined for that module, and then registers that data for transfer across the MBus to the route processor.

  The route processor may be configured to continuously poll the modules and devices in the system over the MBus for temperature, voltage, current, and cooling fan/blower rotational speed values that are out-of-tolerance. If the route processor detects that any of the environment values are out-of-tolerance, it notifies the system/network administrator by logging a message on the system/operator's console and may also raise an alarm with the appropriate alarm severity level on an alarm card or module. This process may require setting alarm lights on a number of light-emitting diodes (LEDs) and/or triggering appropriate alarm card/module relays, activating any external visual or audible alarm devices wired to the alarm card/module.

- **Power-up and power-down control**: The system could be designed such that each MBus interface on a component directly controls the DC-to-DC converters on that component. The MBus interface on the component responds to commands it receives from its onboard non-volatile memory and from the route processor. When the switch/router or router is powered up, all the system MBus interfaces also power up. The MBus interface on the route processor and on the clock and scheduler module immediately turn on their DC-to-DC converters, thereby powering up the respective module. The MBus interface on each line card may wait to power up its corresponding line card until it receives the appropriate command from the route processor.
- **Initial bootup**: On initial load, the route processor can use the MBus to instruct the MBus interfaces on the line cards and switch fabric module(s) to power these modules on. The route processor then downloads a bootstrap image to the line cards across the MBus. The download of field diagnostics software image to the line cards is also done over the MBus. The MBus is also used by the route processor to collect device revision and serial numbers, system environment information (i.e., environmental statistic monitoring), and obtain general system operations and maintenance information. In the case where the system has redundant route processors (primary and secondary), the route processors exchange redundancy messages over the MBus, and also messages which report the results of route processor arbitration.

  The primary route processor periodically restates its mastership status by sending messages through the MBus. The secondary route processor re-enters the arbitration phase whenever it fails to detect the primary route processor's ownership mastership claims for a configurable time period.

Generally, data traffic is never carried across the MBus but instead across the switch fabric. The MBus is used exclusively as an interface for managing and controlling the components within the switch/router or router. The MBus is also used to transport log and debug messages from line cards to the route processor. However, for applications that produce a large number of messages that can overwhelm the MBus (e.g., logging of access control lists (ACL), logging Border Gateway Protocol (BGP) neighbor changes, etc.), log messages can be transferred through the switch fabric using Inter-Process Communication (IPC) messages (between the line cards and route processor). The line cards can be configured to add sequence numbers to transmitted log messages to ensure that the route processor processes the messages sent by either the IPC or the MBus in sequential order.

2.8.2 Alarm Functionality

Switch/routers and routers, particularly high-end ones, provide a comprehensive alarm monitoring functionality for the system. This also provides housekeeping and alarm monitoring functions for the switch fabric and its related components. The alarm functionality provides visual and audible alarm notification of out-of-tolerance values of system environment parameters as well as fault conditions. The alarm facility on the switch/router or router may indicate the following system conditions:

- **LEDs**: LEDs alert the system/network administrator to conditions in the switch/router or router. The determination and designation of what constitutes a Critical, Major, or Minor alarm condition is built into the operating system software running in the route processor. LEDs can be used to provide alarm status for installed components in the system. These LEDs provide a visible indication of the status of line cards, switch fabric, and other components installed in the system. LEDs can be used to indicate the status of the switch fabric, card cage fan tray, and the power supply fan tray. The primary system alarm functions (i.e., the system's primary alarm LEDs) are generally implemented on the switch/router's or router's faceplate. Typically, these LEDs are implemented to correspond to three severity levels of system alarm conditions: Critical, Major, and Minor.
- **General Alarm and MBus status**: These system alarms generally provide for MBus "OK" and "FAIL" indications. The alarm output function related to the MBus operations can consist of a group of LEDs and their associated drivers connected to an alarm MBus interface. As directed by the software on the route processor, the alarm MBus interface can activate specific LEDs. The software which drives these LEDs could be designed to categorize them into, for example, three severity levels of Critical, Major, and Minor. The classification of these severity levels is determined by the operating system software running on the route processor. Each of the three (Critical, Major, and Minor) LEDs can be designed to be dual LEDs (for failure redundancy). The "OK/FAIL" pair of LEDs indicates the status of the alarm MBus facility where "Green" (for "OK") can be used to indicate that the alarm MBus interface is operating properly and "Amber" (for "FAIL") to indicate that the alarm MBus facility has detected an error in itself or with the MBus interface.
- **Fan/blower system fault monitoring**: The status of the cooling fans can be displayed by a number of LEDs. A group of LEDs could include a green "ENABLE" LED, which indicates that the fans are installed and operational, and a red "FAIL" LED, which indicates a fault has been detected on the fan tray installed.
- **AC or DC power source status**: This involves power source monitoring where the alarm facility associated with the MBus is used to monitor the power supply and signals when conditions outside the normal range of operation occur:
  - The monitored voltage is outside the allowable range
  - The monitor current is outside the allowable range

- A fault has occurred in the power source or Power Entry Module (PEM)
- Power source is not being supplied to a system component.
- **DC Power Entry Module (PEM) status**: The PEM can be monitored for the following conditions: operational status, output voltage, and output current.

In high-end, high-performance switch/routers and routers, the line cards, switch fabric modules, and other critical modules such as the cooling fan trays, typically support online insertion and removal (OIR). However, the systems must at all times have one working module installed. Generally, LEDs on the faceplate of the device or a corresponding alarm card display the status of the modules in the system. The device or alarm module faceplate would have a number of LEDs for each of the modules including the switch fabric in the system.

Each pair of LEDs could consist of a "Green" LED indicating "ENABLED" and a "Yellow" (Amber or Red) LED indicating "FAIL". When a "Green" LED is on, then this implies that the module in the corresponding chassis slot is installed and operational. When the LED is off, then this could imply that either the slot is empty or the module installed in the slot is faulty. When a "Yellow" LED is on, then the device (i.e., switch/router or router) has detected a fault on the module in the corresponding slot.

2.9 SCALABILITY

Modern networks are facing increasing challenges of scalability to handle the continuous traffic growth and diverse traffic types. Scalability here refers to the ease with which network device capacities can be increased without significant changes to their architectures. It also refers to the ease with which the size and data carrying capacity of a network can be increased to accommodate more users, traffic, services, and applications without fundamental changes in the network architecture.

In the growing competitive telecommunications market with increasing demand for bandwidth and services, service providers are pressed to improve their profit margins by scaling their networks and service offerings to attract more customers while at the same time reducing or controlling costs. Deploying network devices that have scalable switch fabrics is an effective networking solution to this challenge. Current multistage switch fabrics can be used to design switches, switch/routers, and routers that have distributed architectures and can support bandwidth and service scalability. Such devices can be deployed to boost network performance while maintaining or reducing the cost and complexity of the network.

In high-end, high-performance systems, the designer, generally, wants a switch fabric that can scale from a small system to a large one by adding incrementally smaller fabric components. This allows the user to start with a switch fabric with a small number of components and ports (when the system is initially deployed) and then grow the system as the traffic on the system increases.

The most significant technical limitations on the scalability of the switch, switch/router, or router arise from how easy it is to increase the device's backplane and connectors, and the ease of manufacturability of a complete and reliable system. Designing a system that has high scalability allows for easy system expansion and also decreases cost since the various system components can be implemented without being tightly or rigidly coupled to a single specific system implementation instance.

Network devices (switches, switch/routers, routers) that support scalable switch fabrics provide an efficient and cost-effective way to scale networks with minimal disruption and impact on network operations as the traffic and number of customers grow. The scalability capabilities also provide the ability to harness the higher bandwidth capacities associated with the latest fiber-optic technologies necessary for transporting large volumes of user data.

Designing a system that can support more slots in a single chassis contributes to overall system and consequently network scalability. In the bus-based architectures, the designer will sometimes use an expansion bus to scale up the data carrying capacity of a bus. However, the expansion bus easily becomes a bottleneck because its total throughput determines the aggregate bandwidth and total number of ports that can be added to the system and, generally, the extent to which that bus-based architecture can scale.

A switch, switch/router, or router may provide fabric redundancy that also serves to increase the overall capacity of the switch fabric (through the use of partially or fully redundant switch fabrics). In such architectures, should one switch fabric fail, the redundant fabric assumes complete switching responsibility for the system.

A well-known technique for implementing scalability in crossbar switch fabrics is bit-slicing (Figure 2.13). Bit-slicing is a technique for constructing a single switch fabric system from parallel modules of switch fabrics of smaller bit width, with the goal of increasing the bit width of the overall switch fabric system, that is, to make an arbitrary n-bit wide switch fabric. Each of the parallel component modules of the switch fabric transfers a one-bit field or "slice" of data presented to it. The parallel switch fabric components would then have the capability to transfer the chosen full (n-bit wide) word-length of a particular switch fabric design.

With bit-sliced parallelism, each cell from a VOQ is "striped" across n identical switch fabric planes and the centralized scheduler makes the same scheduling decision for all slices of the cell. However, it is important to note that bit-slicing does not decrease scheduling speed because of the parallelism. Scalability is accomplished in some architectures by a bit-slicing technique that enables, for example, four 1.25 Gb/s channels to form a single 5 Gb/s transmission group through the crossbar switch fabric.

In the typical case, each plane of the crossbar switch digital core in a bit-sliced design is assumed to run at a lower speed. Then to increase the throughput of the overall system, multiple bit-slices are used. The input port signals from each VOQs are first fed to a serial-to-parallel converter and the resulting parallel data are then passed to the multiple bit-slice planes to be switched to their output ports.

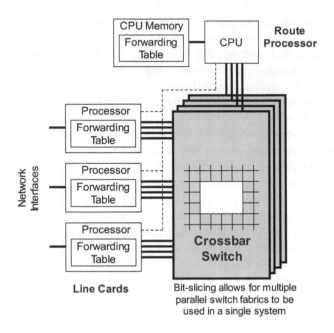

FIGURE 2.13   Crossbar Switch with Bit-Slicing.

After traversing the parallel bit-sliced planes, the outputs are grouped and fed through a parallel-to-serial converter to create a serial bit stream that is sent to the output port.

For example, an 8-plane bit-sliced switch core only needs to run at 250 MHz instead of the 2 GHz required for a single plane system. However, even though a lower clock speed is required, the size of the switch fabric is increased by a factor of 8. The challenge here is designing these parallel switch cores into the crossbar switch chip effectively and efficiently without facing physical design issues such as maintaining signal integrity. Furthermore, increasing the chip size hinders the scalability of the switch particularly for designing multistage switch fabrics. For example, a 128 × 128 or 256 × 256 switch is difficult or even may not be feasible to implement to have multiple bit-slice planes.

In a system with switch fabric plane redundancy, for example, a system with five available switch fabric planes, five parallel 1-bit wide serial data streams can be transferred to and from the line cards across the backplane. The system can be designed such that only four of the data streams are required for data transfer purposes while the fifth stream is used to carry error correction information. When an error occurs on one of the four parallel data streams, this data in error can be recovered through use of the fifth error correcting stream.

In general, using methods other than bit-slicing, the switching capacity of the system can be increased. By adding switch fabric modules to the system, the bandwidth of each line card slot in the system can be increased. The system can be designed such that multiple number (two or more) switch fabric modules can be installed in the system at any given time to provide additional switch fabric capacity.

The switch fabric modules increase the data handling capacity of the system and may also allow any one or all of the additional fabric modules to be removed and replaced at any time (also called hot-swapping) without system operations being disrupted or the system being powered down. In such a design, for the length of time that any switch fabric module is not functional, its data carrying capacity is reduced because a potential data path in the system is unavailable.

2.10 FAULT TOLERANCE

Very often, end users (both enterprise and residential consumers) have a single network connection between their customer premise equipment and the service provider's edge or access router. If the provider's edge device should fail, many end users lose network access until the edge device recovers. In contrast, core or backbone networks comprise network devices that are configured in redundant, mesh configurations, so that traffic can take alternate routes if one network path is disrupted.

However, the industry practice is to use network devices that have in-built redundancy and high-availability features in both the access and core parts of networks to increase overall network service availability. To manage cost, some service providers argue that it is easier to implement many of the system resiliency features in the edge devices first, because redundant network paths are less common in this part of the network than in the core. They argue that since the edge access device represents (in many scenarios) the first hop in an end user's connection and access to the service provider's network, downtime in the edge device makes service delivery much more challenging.

The most effective approach in increasing network availability is reducing the time it takes for network devices (switches, switch/routers, routers, etc.) to recover from failures/outages. Adding to this, it is essential to minimize, as much as possible, the extent to which a failure/outage in a single network device affects the rest of the network. Generally, the following high-availability capabilities and features can be used to enhance the availability of a network. These practices can be used to reduce network and system recovery times thereby eliminating or reducing the need for time-consuming troubleshooting, repairs, maintenance, or complete system reboots if one system module or element fails:

- The use of redundant core or backbone network designs and network operational best practices in combination with high-availability technologies within the network devices.
- Using network devices with redundancy and fail-over features, particularly at the network segments with devices that must deliver the highest levels of availability, as well as network segments that are indispensable to the basic operations of the overall network.

- Using network devices that offer fully redundant switch fabrics to provide maximum availability for mission-critical network segments. For example, a network device may support a number of redundant (i.e., multiple parallel) switch fabric modules (at a minimum, a system with primary and secondary switch fabric modules) that function at a given time as a single entity. In a two-switch fabric design, all interface modules, line cards, forwarding engines, and route processors connect to both switch fabric modules simultaneously via appropriately designed backplane interfaces. Under normal system operation (with the two switch fabrics), the redundant switch fabric module mirrors all configuration parameters and activities of the primary switch fabric module, including routing protocol information and forwarding databases, etc.
- The implementation of a monitoring and management system that queries the health of the switch fabrics for run-time status information, diagnostics, and statistics periodically. In case the primary switch fabric fails, the system software governing their operations will trigger a switchover to the redundant switch fabric module within a very short switchover time, preventing significant service disruption to end users.

Generally, switch/routers and routers that use centralized switch fabrics provide redundant switch fabric cards and fast failover to avoid the centralized fabric from becoming a single point of failure in the system. However, it is very difficult to design a single fabric system to avoid network service glitches during the failover. Some designs use a fully distributed switch fabric which has better failure tolerance than the single fabric system. In these distributed switch fabrics, failures within the fabric can be bypassed by redundant paths and better internal traffic routing, and therefore have a localized impact only.

Crossbar switch fabrics, in simple low-end systems, typically have a (single) centralized architecture. As a result, such systems constitute a single point of failure and are not desirable or suitable for high-end systems. In order to work around this problem without significant complexity, many designs choose to duplicate the crossbar switch fabric so that if one fails, the redundant fabric can be made operational. In a two-fabric implementation, the system can be made active-active (each one carrying not more than half the total system capacity) or active-standby, also referred to as active/passive, (with the active and standby fabrics capable of carrying the expected system load). A system with $N+1$ fabric redundancy can also be made to be active-active or active-standby.

The distributed multistage crossbar switch fabric lends itself to implementations where the relevant portions of the multistage switch fabric can be distributed and built into the line card modules. With this architecture, failures are localized and there is no single point of failure in the switch fabric. If the switch fabric portion in any line card fails, only data transmission in that particular line card is affected, and the rest of the switch fabric continues operating without interruption. However, should one of the middle switches fail, then using (appropriately designed) scheduling and traffic rerouting mechanisms, packets can be redirected to other middle switches until the failed module can be replaced or repaired.

In addition to duplicate data paths, network device hardware can be made more reliable by adding hot-swappable modules, such as dual power supplies, cooling fan trays, alarm functions, etc. For added reliability, all power supplies (AC or DC) in the system can be designed to be load-sharing and hot-swappable. Hot-swapping, sometimes called online insertion and removal (OIR) or power-on servicing, is a feature that permits the removal (or replacement) or addition of modules or cards to a running system without interrupting its power supply, entering commands on a console, or causing other system interfaces or software to shut down.

A crossbar switch architecture may be designed to support clock and scheduler module redundancy. The switch fabric card and its corresponding clock and scheduler module set up the physical data path in the system as well as the clocking signals for the data units (cells) that carry end-user data and control packets between the line cards and route processor.

A second clock and scheduler module in the system provides reference clock and scheduler redundancy. In such a system, the interfaces between the switch fabric and the line cards (and other modules such as the route processor) are monitored constantly and if the system detects a loss of synchronization, it automatically activates the data paths controlled by the redundant clock and scheduler module, and data transfer occurs across the redundant path. The switchover to the redundant clock and scheduler module has to happen within microseconds, with little or no loss of data.

The system and clock and scheduler module can be designed to be removed and replaced, without disrupting normal system operations but only if a redundant (second) clock and scheduler module is installed in the system. One clock and scheduler card must be present and operational in the system at all times to maintain normal system operations.

The switch fabric architecture may consist of three switch fabric cards and two clock and scheduler cards. One clock and scheduler module and the three switch fabric cards constitute the active switch fabric, and the second clock and scheduler module provide redundancy for the four running units. These cards may support hot-swapping or online insertion and removal (OIR), which means that any of these cards can be removed and replaced while the system remains powered up.

Another option for introducing flexibility in system operations and redundancy is using a design based on a midplane chassis architecture. This also allows some line card protection. The midplane architecture can divide the functionality of each line card into two, creating a front and back module or card. Each half-card (front and back card) plugs into a central chassis plane located in the middle. Thus, by adding some degree of line card redundancy in the half-cards, they can be used as standby half-cards that serve as backup to one or more primary half-cards. This allows the network operator to hot-swap a half-card with a standby one without disrupting its other half.

The following methods can be used for internal data protection as transfers occur across the switch fabric and the system as a whole:

- **Checksum**: This is a method used by a receiver to check for data corruption errors and thereby verify the overall integrity of data transmitted to the receiver. The checksum is a value computed over a block of digital data and is often obtained through a series of arithmetic operations defined by a checksum function. The checksum value is computed from the data being transmitted, and then transmitted with the data. Comparing the checksum generated from the received data with the transmitted checksum helps ensure that the received data is genuine and error free.
- **Cyclic Redundancy Check (CRC)**: This is an error-detecting technique in which a sender calculates a CRC or check value (short, fixed-length binary sequence) for a block of data to be transmitted (based on the remainder of a polynomial division of the data block). The sender appends this check value to the data block to form a codeword. The receiver repeats the calculation upon receiving the codeword and, in the event the check values do not match, then the data block contains an error.
- **Frame Check Sequence (FCS)**: The FCS are extra characters (or error-detecting code) added to a frame carrying a block of data transmitted by a sender for error control purposes. The FCS is calculated by the sender based on the data block in the frame and is typically added to the end of the frame. When the frame is received by the recipient, the FCS value is recalculated and compared with the FCS value carried in the frame. If the two FCS values do not match, an error is assumed and the frame can be discarded. FCSs are used in communication protocols such as Ethernet, High-Level Data Link Control (HDLC), Point-to-Point Protocol (PPP), Frame Relay, and other data link layer protocols, where the FCS algorithm is a CRC.
- **Forward Error Correction (FEC)**: FEC is a technique for detecting a limited number of errors that may occur in a block of transmitted data, and often for the receiver to be able correct these errors without the need for the sender to retransmit the data. The sender encodes the block of data with redundant data (an error-correcting code (ECC)) and sends this extra information along with the block of data. This EEC is then used by the receiver to detect and correct for certain type of errors in the data. The design of the EEC determines the maximum number of errors (or errored bits) in the data block that can be corrected by the receiver.
- **Header Error Control (HEC)**: The HEC field within the header of an ATM (Asynchronous Transfer Mode) cell is an 8-bit CRC used to check the validity of the control information in the ATM cell. The receiver checks and corrects for an error in an ATM cell using a CRC-based framing technique. Using the fifth octet in the ATM cell header, the

receiver checks and corrects for an error in the ATM cell header. The CRC-based framing algorithm allows for a single-bit error in the cell header to be corrected or multiple-bit errors to be detected. Switch/ routers and routers that want added data transfer reliability through the switch fabric often employ variations of the earlier HEC concept. The HEC is often used together with any one of the other error-detecting methods described earlier.

A switch, switch/router, and router that is considered a carrier-class design supports, generally, the following features:

- Redundancy in all key system components such as switch fabric, route processor, line cards, power supplies, and cooling fans. This allows the system to minimize service disruption in the event of a failure of any component.
- Hot-swap capability of components such as line cards, switch fabrics, route processors, power supplies, cooling fans, etc. This enables such key components to be removed or added without service disruption.
- Redundancy in switch fabric using a number of parallel switch fabric modules to provide fail-over to backup fabric(s) without service disruption.
- The use of automatic protection switching (APS)/multiplex section protection (MPS) to provide interface redundancy and network resiliency capabilities. Such protection schemes include Ethernet Automatic Protection Switching (EAPS) [RFC3619], Ethernet Protection Switching Ring (EPSR) [EPSRALLTTG] [EPSRALLTWP], Ethernet Ring Protection Switching [ITU-TG.8032], Ethernet Linear Protection Switching [ITU-TG.8031], etc.

Switch/routers and routers with the earlier-mentioned high-availability features can still be used in full mesh networks. A full mesh network is one in which the network nodes are organized in a mesh topology, with each network node connected to every other node via either a virtual or physical path/connection/circuit. A full mesh network offers a great level of network and service delivery redundancy; however, it can be prohibitively expensive to implement. Such topologies are usually reserved for designing network cores or backbones. In practice, such networks are partial mesh topologies but implemented with carrier-class network devices.

2.11   GENERIC SWITCH/ROUTER WITH CROSSBAR SWITCH FABRIC

This section describes how distributed forwarding is implemented in switch/ routers and routers that support crossbar switch fabrics with VOQs (Figure 2.14). Distributed forwarding using network topology based forwarding information is a more scalable form of forwarding intended to address the problems associated with flow/route cache-based forwarding. Here, the forwarding information is

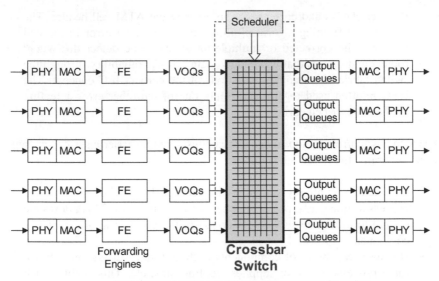

Each network interface card has a packet memory, forwarding table, and an autonomous processor. A copy of the central forwarding table is propagated from the CPU to the network interface cards for local forwarding capabilities.

FIGURE 2.14 Forwarding Engine at Input of Crossbar Switch.

generated from the routing table which is itself maintained by the dynamic routing protocols (OSPF, RIP, BGP, etc.).

With distributed forwarding, the forwarding information (which in some architectures is generated and stored in a simple flow/route cache) is split up and distributed over several forwarding databases in the system. The master forwarding information is stored in forwarding tables maintained by the route processor, and copies of this forwarding information (which are exact replicas of the master information) are distributed and maintained in forwarding tables in slave forwarding processors such as in the line cards (Figure 2.15). The forwarding databases or data structures that hold the most important information required for efficient packet forwarding include:

- **Forwarding Information Base (FIB) or Forwarding Table**: The forwarding engines in the system use an FIB to make IP destination network prefix-based forwarding decisions, generally using longest prefix matching lookups. The content of the FIB, although smaller and more compact, is conceptually similar to the forwarding information held in the routing table (or routing information base (RIB)). The FIB maintains a mirror image of the relevant forwarding information maintained in the routing table, the information that is directly relevant and useful for packet forwarding. When the network experiences topology or routing

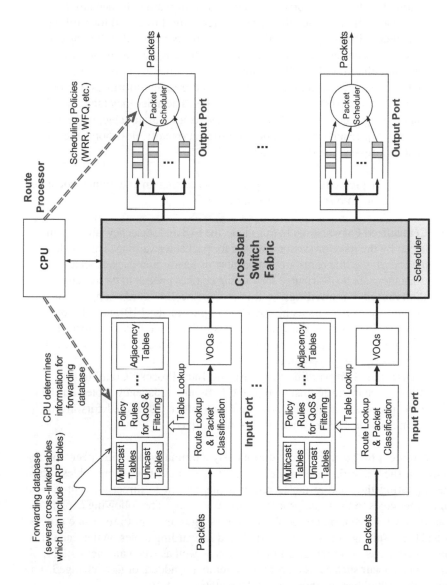

FIGURE 2.15 Components of a Generic Router or Switch/Router.

changes, the routing table is updated, and the FIB is modified accordingly to reflect these changes.

Because both the FIB and routing table hold the same forwarding information, the FIB contains all known network routes and essential information for packet forwarding, thereby eliminating the need for flow/route cache maintenance that is associated with flow-based forwarding.

- **Adjacency Table**: Nodes in the network are considered to be adjacent if they can communicate with each other directly over a single Layer 2 hop. In addition to the FIB, the forwarding engine uses the information in the adjacency tables to rewrite Layer 2 addressing information in outgoing packets to their next-hop IP addresses. The adjacency table, which can be integrated with the FIB or created as a separate table, maintains Layer 2 adjacencies or next-hop addresses (typically, next-hop Ethernet MAC addresses) for all FIB entries.

As discussed in previous chapters, packet forwarding in the switch/router or router can be done in one of two general modes:

- **Centralized Forwarding**: In this mode, the FIB and adjacency tables maintained by the route processor are used for packet forwarding. This mode is used when the line cards are not capable of forwarding packets locally, or when there are no distributed forwarding engines present in the system.
- **Distributed Forwarding**: In this mode, the line cards support local forwarding of packets using identical copies of the FIB and adjacency tables maintained by the route processor. The line cards perform forwarding locally, relieving the main route processor of direct involvement in the forwarding operations.

    Distributed forwarding may use an Inter-Process Communication (IPC) mechanism to ensure that the FIBs and adjacency tables on the route processor and line cards (and any other distributed forwarding engines in the system) are always synchronized.

The route processor has to continuously communicate with peer routing devices in the network to keep the routing tables (and forwarding tables) up to date. Updating the routing tables requires the system to direct all routing and control messages to the route processor for processing. The following explain the process by which routing protocol update messages are sent to the route processor and the resulting update of the distributed forwarding tables on the line cards. The process covers routing table initialization as well as when any network topology changes occur such as when routes are removed, added, or have changed. The process described here is only one implementation example:

1. A packet arrives at a line card and is placed in an input buffer memory on the line card. The forwarding engine reads the Layer 2 and Layer 3 information in the packet to determine how the packet should be

forwarded. The forwarding engine determines that the packet carries routing protocol information and queues a pointer (in the VOQ associated with the route processor) indicating that the packet in buffer memory is destined to the route processor.

2. The line card issues a request to the scheduler indicating that the packet is destined to the route processor. The scheduler issues a grant for the routing protocol packet in the VOQ and the packet is transferred across the crossbar switching fabric to the route processor. The Cisco 12000 Series Internet Router is an example of architecture that transfers routing protocol message over the switch fabric [CISC12000CEF] [CISC12000LC] [CISC12000MD] [CISC12000PS] [CISC12000RP].

   Note: In some architectures that support a special control bus or MBus between the line cards and the route processor, the transfer of routing protocol and other control messages is done over that bus and not through the scheduler and switch fabric [FOUNBIG04] [FOUNJET03].

3. The route processor receives and processes the routing protocol information and updates the routing table. If, for example, the routing information carried in the packet is destined to the interior routing protocol OSPF, the route processor might have to flood link-state advertisement (LSA) information to adjacent routers. The route processor is responsible for generating the packets that carry the LSAs and also for updating the master FIB that it maintains.

4. The route processor then transmits updates to all internal (slave or distributed) FIBs on all the line cards in the system. The FIB updates to the line card FIBs are monitored and checked to ensure that all the slave FIBs and master FIB are synchronized. The master FIB in the route processor is always kept current and this copy synchronized with all line card FIBs. If a new line card is inserted into the chassis (assuming the system supports OIR), the route processor downloads its latest FIB information to the new line card once the card becomes active.

5. The route processor is also notified about Layer 2 adjacencies via the line cards, whenever a new neighbor routing device (i.e., next-hop node) is connected to the system. The route processor can also send out ARP (Address Resolution Protocol) requests to determine the Layer 2 addresses of adjacent routing devices. The line card may also send a notification to the route processor containing new Layer 2 adjacency information such as those over a Point-to-Point Protocol (PPP) link (i.e., send PPP header information). The route processor uses this Layer 2 adjacency information to update its (master) adjacency table and those on the line cards. Each line card uses this Layer 2 information to rewrite the Layer 2 address in each packet as the packet is transmitted from the system. The route processor uses its copy of the adjacency table for initialization purposes when new line cards are added to the system.

Once the line cards have been initialized and properly configured with forwarding information (forwarding tables including adjacency tables), they are ready to forward packets through the switch fabric to their destinations. Using its forwarding information, a line card forwards packets through the system as follows:

1. A packet in transit (that is not a routing protocol or control packet) arrives at a line card and is placed in an input buffer memory on the line card. We assume that the packet is not a routing protocol update, ICMP, or IP packets with options. The forwarding engine determines that the packet contains normal data and not routing protocol or other control data. The Layer 2 address of the packet is examined to determine if it is to be Layer 3 forwarded (i.e., if the destination Layer 2 address of the packet is that of the receiving/ingress interface). If the packet is to be Layer 3 forwarded, the Layer 3 information in the packet is parsed and a lookup is performed in the local FIB table. The forwarding engine determines the forwarding instructions of the packet (next-hop IP node, output port, Layer 2 address rewrite information, etc.) and rewrites, appropriately, the relevant packet fields. Based on the destination output port, the packet (more, appropriately, the pointer to its buffer memory location) is then placed in the appropriate VOQ in the line card.

   Note: If for any reason the packet cannot be forwarded because of lack of sufficient forwarding information after the forwarding table lookup process, the packet can be forwarded to the route processor for further processing. The forwarding engine queues the pointer in the VOQ associated with the route processor indicating that the packet in buffer memory is destined to the route processor.

2. Once the packet's buffer memory pointer is queued in the appropriate VOQ, the line card issues a request to the scheduler for transmission to the output port. The scheduler issues a grant, and the packet is transferred from its buffer memory location across the switch fabric to the destination (egress) line card.

3. The egress line card receives and queues the packet in appropriate output buffers to be transmitted out into the network.

4. The egress line card performs additional processing on the packet, if required, such as QoS tagging/remarking, VLAN tagging, attaching Layer 2 PPP address, etc. If the packet is a multicast packet, the packet is replicated for each port on the egress line card that has a multicast group member.

5. The egress line card then transmits the packet out the network interface when it reaches the front of its output queue.

REFERENCES

[ABELF03]. F. Abel, C. Minkenberg, and R. P. Luijten, "A Four-Terabit Packet Switch Supporting Long Round-Trip Times," *IEEE Micro*, Vol. 23, No. 1, 2003.

[AHMAD89]. H. Ahmadi and W. Denzel, "A Survey of Modern High-Performance Switching Techniques," *IEEE Jour. on Selected Areas in Commun.*, Vol. 7, Sept. 1989, pp. 1091–1103.

[ANDERT93]. T. Anderson, S. Owicki, J. Saxe, and C. Thacker, "High Speed Switch Scheduling for Local Area Networks," *ACM Trans. Comput. Syst.*, Vol. 11, No. 4, Nov. 1993, pp. 319–352.

[ARISTA7500]. Arista 7500 Switch Architecture ('A Day in the Life of a Packet'), Arista Networks, White Paper, Dec. 22, 2016.

[BIANCO03]. A. Bianco, P. Giaccone, E. Leonardi, F. Neri, and C. Piglione, "On the Number of Input Queues to Efficiently Support Multicast Traffic in Input Queued Switches," *Proc. IEEE Workshop on High Performance Switching and Routing (HPSR '03)*, June 2003, pp. 111–116.

[CHENJ91]. J. S. C. Chen and T. E. Stern, "Throughput Analysis, Optimal Buffer Allocation and Traffic Imbalance Study of a Generic Non-Blocking Packet Switch," *IEEE Jour. on Selected Areas in Commun.*, Vol. 9, No. 3, Apr. 1991, pp. 439–449.

[CHIUSSIF93]. F. M. Chiussi and F. A. Tobagi, "Implementation of a Three-Stage Banyan-Based Architecture with Input and Output Buffers for Large Fast Packet Switches," Stanford, CA, Stanford University CSL Technical Report, CSL-93–577, June 1993.

[CHUAN98]. S. Chuang, et al., "Matching Output Queueing with a Combined Input Output Queued Switch," Stanford, CA, Stanford University CSL Technical Report, CSL-TR-98–758, 1998.

[CISC12000CEF]. Understanding Cisco Express Forwarding, Document ID: 47321, Jan. 17, 2006.

[CISC12000LC]. Cisco 12000 Series Internet Router Architecture: Line Card Design, Tech Notes.

[CISC12000MB]. Cisco 12000 Series Internet Router Architecture: Maintenance Bus, Power Supplies and Blowers, and Alarm Cards, Document ID: 47244, Jan. 17, 2006.

[CISC12000MD]. Cisco 12000 Series Internet Router Architecture: Memory Details, Tech Notes.

[CISC12000PS]. Cisco 12000 Series Internet Router Architecture: Packet Switching, Document ID: 47320, July 7, 2005.

[CISC12000RP]. Cisco 12000 Series Internet Router Architecture: Route Processor, Document ID: 47241, July 7, 2005.

[CISC12000SF]. Cisco 12000 Series Internet Router Architecture: Switch Fabric, Document ID: 47240, July 7, 2005.

[CISC2TMUL11]. Building Next-Generation Multicast Networks with Supervisor 2T, Cisco Systems, White Paper, Apr. 13, 2011.

[CISCCAT6500]. Cisco Systems, Cisco Catalyst 6500 Architecture, White Paper, 2007.

[CISCSUP2TA11]. Cisco Catalyst 6500 Supervisor 2T Architecture, Cisco Systems, White Paper, 2011.

[CISCSUP6TA16]. Cisco Catalyst 6500/6800 Supervisor 6T Architecture, Cisco Systems, White Paper, June 2016.

[CLOSCH53]. Charles Clos, "A Study of Non-Blocking Switching Networks," *Bell Sys. Tech. Jour.*, Vol. 32, No. 2, pp. 406–424, Mar. 1953.

[ELECDESG98]. Contributing Author, "Up Close and Personal with High-Speed Crosspoint Switches," *Electronic Design*, Oct 11, 1998.

[EPSRALLTTG]. Feature Overview and Configuration Guide, Ethernet Protection Switched Ring (EPSR), Allied Telesis, Technical Guide.

[EPSRALLTWP]. Ethernet Protection Switched Ring (EPSRing™), Allied Telesis, White Paper.

[FOUNBIG04]. Foundry Networks, BigIron Architecture Brief, White Paper, 2004.

[FOUNJET03]. Foundry Networks, JetCore™ Based Chassis Systems: An Architecture Brief on NetIron, BigIron, and FastIron Systems, White Paper, 2003.

[GUERI98]. R. Guerin and K. N. Sivarajan, "Delay and Throughput Performance of Speedup Input-Queueing Packet Switches," IBM Research report RC20892, Mar. 1998.

[GUPTA91]. A. L. Gupta and N. D. Georganas, "Analysis of a Packet Switch with Input and Output Buffers and Speed Constraints," *Proc. IEEE INFOCOM'91*, Bal Harbour, FL, Apr. 1991, pp. 694–700.

[GUPTAPAN99]. P. Gupta and N. McKeown, "Designing and Implementing a Fast Crossbar Scheduler," *IEEE Micro*, Vol. 19, No. 1, Jan./Feb. 1999, pp. 20–28.

[GUPTAS02]. S. Gupta and A. Aziz, "Multicast Scheduling for Switches with Multiple Input-Queues," *Proc. Ann. IEEE Symp.* High-Performance Interconnects (Hot Interconnects), 2002, pp. 28–33.

[HOPCROFT73]. J. E. Hopcroft and R. M. Karp, "An Algorithm for Maximum Matching in Bipartite Graphs," *Soc Ind Appl Math J. Computation*, Vol. 2, 1973, pp. 225–231.

[HUIJTREN90]. J. Hui and T. Renner, "Queueing Strategies for Multicast Packet Switching," *Proc. IEEE GLOBECOM'90*, 1990, pp. 1431–1437.

[ITU-TG.8031]. Ethernet Linear Protection Switching, ITU-T Recommendation G.8031/Y.1342, Jan. 2015.

[ITU-TG.8032]. Ethernet Ring Protection Switching, G.8032/Y.1344 Recommendation Aug. 2015.

[KAROLM87]. M. Karol, M. Hluchyj, and S. Morgan, "Input Versus Output Queueing on a Space-Division Switch," *IEEE Trans. Communications*, Vol. COM-35, Dec. 1987, pp. 1347–1356.

[KIMCKLEE90]. C. K. Kim and T. T. Lee, "Performance of Call Splitting Algorithms for Multicast Traffic," *Proc. IEEE INFOCOM*, 1990, pp. 348–356.

[KRISH98]. P. Krishha, N. S. Patel, A. Charny, and R. Simcoe, "On the Speedup Required for Work Conserving Crossbar switches," *IWQoS'98*, May 1998.

[MARSANIC01]. M. A. Marsan, A. Bianco, P. Giaccone, E. Leonardi, and F. Neri, "Optimal Multicast Scheduling in Input-Queued Switches," *Proc. IEEE Int'l Conf. Comm. (ICC)*, Helsinki, Finland, June 2001.

[MARSANIN01]. M. A. Marsan, A. Bianco, P. Giaccone, E. Leonardi, and F. Neri, "On the Throughput of Input-Queued Cell-Based Switches with Multicast Traffic," *IEEE INFOCOM'01*, Anchorage, Alaska, Apr. 2001.

[MCKEOWN95]. N. McKeown, "Scheduling Algorithms for Input-Queued Cell Switches," Ph.D. Dissertation, University of California at Berkeley, May 1995.

[MCKEOWN96AN]. N. McKeown, V. Anantharam, and J. Walrand, "Achieving 100% Throughput in an Input-Queued Switch," *Proc. IEEE INFOCOM'96*, 1996, pp. 296–302.

[MCKEOWN96PR]. N. McKeown and B. Prabhakar, "Scheduling Multicast Cells in an Input-Queued Switch," *Proc. IEEE INFOCOM'96*, pp. 271–278.

[MCKEOW97IZ]. N. McKeown, M. Izzard, A. Mekkittikul, W. Ellersick, and M. Horowitz, "The Tiny Tera: A Packet Switch Core," *IEEE Micro*, Jan./Feb. 1997, pp. 26–33.

[MCKEOW97WP]. N. McKeown, Fast Switched Backplane for a Gigabit Switched Router, White Paper, Cisco Systems, San Jose, CA, 1997 (also, *Business Comm. Rev.*, Vol. 27, No. 12, 1997, pp. 1–17).

[MCKEOWN97]. N. McKeown, B. Prabhakar, and M. Zhu, "Matching Output Queueing with Combined Input and Output Queueing," *Proc. 35 Annual Allerton Conf. on Commun.*, Monticello, IL, Oct. 1997.

[MCKEOWN99i]. N. McKeown, "The iSLIP Scheduling Algorithm for Input-Queued Switches," *IEEE/ACM Trans. Networking*, Vol. 7, No. 2, Apr. 1999, pp. 188–201.

[MHAMDL04]. L. Mhamdi and M. Hamdi, "Scheduling Multicast Traffic in Internally Buffered Crossbar Switches," *Proc. IEEE Int'l Conf. Comm. (ICC '04)*, June 2004, pp. 1103–1107.

[MHAMDL09]. L. Mhamdi, "On the Integration of Unicast and Multicast Cell Scheduling in Buffered Crossbar Switches," *IEEE Trans. Parallel and Distributed Syst.*, Vol. 20, No. 6, June 2009, pp. 818–830.

[MINKENC06]. C. Minkenberg, F. Abel, and E. Schiattarella, "Distributed Crossbar Schedulers," *2006 Workshop on High Performance Switching and Routing (HPSR'06)*, Poznan, Poland, June 2006.

[NABESH00]. M. Nabeshima, "Performance Evaluation of Combined Input- and Crosspoint-Queued Switch," *Proc. IEICE Trans. Comm.*, Vol. B83-B, No. 3, Mar. 2000, pp. 737–741.

[OIEY89]. Y. Oie, M. Murata, K. Kubota, and H. Miyahara, "Effect of Speedup in Non-Blocking Packet Switch," *Proc. IEEE ICC'89*, Boston, MA, June 1989, pp. 410–414.

[PRABH95]. B. Prabhakar and N. McKeown, "Designing a Multicast Switch Scheduler," *Proc. of the 33rd Annual Allerton Conf.*, Urbana-Champaign, 1995.

[PRABH96]. B. Prabhakar, N. McKeown, and J. Mairesse, "Tetris Models for Multicast Switches," *Proc. of the 30th Annual Conf. on Information Sciences and Systems*, Princeton, 1996.

[PRABH97J]. B. Prabhakar, N. McKeown, and R. Ahuja, "Multicast Scheduling for Input-Queued Switches," *IEEE Jour. Selected Areas in Comm.*, Vol. 15, No. 5, June 1997, pp. 855–866.

[PRABH98]. B. Prabhakar and N. McKeown, "On the Speedup Required for Combined Input and Output Queued Switching," Stanford University CSL, Technical Report, CSL-TR-97-738, Nov. 1998.

[RFC3619]. S. Shah and M. Yip, "Extreme Networks' Ethernet Automatic Protection Switching (EAPS) Version 1," IETF RFC 3619, Oct. 2003.

[SCICCHI07]. A. Scicchitano, A. Bianco, P. Giaccone, E. Leonardi, and E. Schiattarella, "Distributed Scheduling in Input Queued Switches," *IEEE ICC 2007*, Glasgow, Scotland, June 2007.

[STOIC98]. I. Stoica and H. Abdel-Wahab, "An Efficient Packet Service Algorithm for High Speed ATM Switches," *Jour. Comp. Comm.*, Vol. 21, No. 9, pp. 839–852, July 1998.

[SUNSHES05]. S. Sun, S. He, Y. Zheng, and W. Gao, "Multicast Scheduling in Buffered Crossbar Switches with Multiple Input Queues," *Proc. IEEE Workshop on High Performance Switching and Routing (HPSR '05)*, May 2005, pp. 73–77.

[TARJANR83]. R. E. Tarjan, "Data Structures and Network Algorithms," *Soc. Ind. Appl. Mathematics*, PA, Nov. 1983.

[TOBAG90]. F. Tobagi, "Fast Packet Switch Architectures for Broadband Integrated Services Digital Networks," *Proc. of the IEEE*, Vol. 78, Jan. 1990, pp. 133–178.

3 Introduction to Switch/ Routers with Crossbar Switch Fabrics

3.1 THE CROSSBAR SWITCH FABRIC

Compared to other switch fabric types, non-blocking crossbar-based switch fabrics allow for the design of more scalable, high-capacity platforms and have become the preferred switch fabric for building high-performance, high-end network devices (switches, routers, switch/routers, etc.). The more practical and efficient approach for designing non-blocking crossbar switch fabrics is to use, at each input port, virtual output queues (VOQs) together with an intelligent scheduler that services the VOQs.

As discussed in *Chapter 2*, head-of-line (HOL) blocking occurs when there is a packet at an input port that is to be forwarded to an output port that has transmit bandwidth available but is blocked by another packet ahead of it that is to be forwarded to another port but must wait for bandwidth to become available for it to be transmitted to the particular output port. The approach widely used to prevent HOL blocking without having to use very high-speed and most likely, expensive memories, is to classify the packets at each input port according to their destination output ports and place each class into one of the multiple VOQs.

The network device maintains at each input port a VOQ that is associated with each output port. When a packet is received at an input port, it is placed in the VOQ associated with its destination port. The input port then sends scheduling requests to the scheduler to indicate which input port VOQs have packets that need to be sent to particular output ports in the system. In the case of a switch, router, or switch/router, for example, it is assumed that the destination IP address and output port lookup is performed before placing a packet in its correct VOQ.

The scheduler then makes the decisions required to transmit the packets from the input ports and VOQs to the output ports. The scheduling is typically done with the goal of maximizing the total data throughput and bandwidth allocation fairness within the crossbar switch fabric. The VOQs and scheduler can also be designed to incorporate sophisticated priority queuing, multicasting, and packet discard decisions to enable the crossbar switch fabric to perform QoS functions when handling user traffic with different service requirements.

3.2   ARCHITECTURES WITH CROSSBAR-BASED SWITCH FABRICS AND CENTRALIZED FORWARDING ENGINES

In spite of the scalability and potentially high bandwidth a crossbar switch fabric can provide, some router and switch/router architectures do indeed use crossbar switch fabrics with centralized forwarding engines. These architectures use the crossbar switch fabric mainly to exploit the very high data transfer capabilities such fabrics can provide over the bus-based or shared-memory based switch fabrics. Even though the switch fabric in this case is no more a bottleneck, the overall packet forwarding throughput of the system is still limited by the centralized forwarding engine.

Example Architectures:

- Cisco Catalyst 6500 series switches with Supervisor Engines 1A and 2—Fabric-enabled line cards without a Distributed Forwarding Card (DFC) installed (*Chapter 4*)
- Cisco Catalyst 6500 Series switches with Supervisor Engine 720—Architectures with "Classic" line cards (*Chapter 8*)
- Cisco Catalyst 6500 Series switches with Supervisor Engine 720—Architectures with CEF256 fabric-enabled line cards (optional DFC not installed) (*Chapter 8*)
- Cisco Catalyst 6500 Series switches with Supervisor Engine 720—Architectures with CEF720 line cards (optional DFC not installed) (*Chapter 8*).

As will be seen later, the architecture that best satisfies the scalability and high capacity data transfer requirements of backbone and core networks is the one that employs distributed forwarding engines and crossbar switch fabric with VOQs.

3.2.1   ARCHITECTURES WITH FORWARDING USING A FLOW/ROUTE CACHE IN CENTRALIZED PROCESSOR

This architecture uses a crossbar switch fabric, a route processor, and a centralized forwarding processor that maintains a flow/route cache of frequently seen packets (Figure 3.1). Even with a high throughput crossbar switch fabric, the performance of the device is very much limited by the performance of the centralized forwarding processor.

Other than the type of switch fabric used, this architecture shares the same features as the bus-based architecture with centralized forwarding using the flow/route cache described earlier. A key limitation of this architecture is that it does not fully harness the high forwarding capacity provided by the crossbar switch fabric and thus forwarding throughput is limited by the centralized forwarding processor.

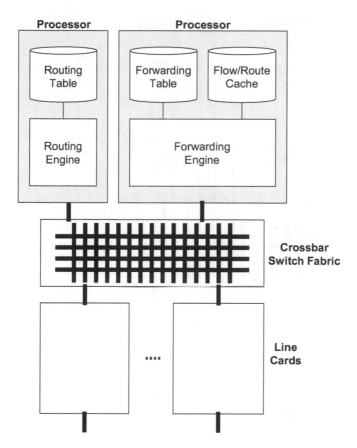

FIGURE 3.1   Architectures with Crossbar-Based Switch Fabrics and Centralized
Forwarding Engines Using Flow Caches.

3.2.2   Architectures with Forwarding Using an Optimized Lookup System in Centralized Processor

In this architecture (Figure 3.2), packets that arrive at the network interfaces
are forwarded over a crossbar switch fabric to a centralized forwarding processor which makes the forwarding decisions (next-hop address, output port(s)) and
then sends them to the appropriate outgoing interface(s). The forwarding engine
may use a smaller optimized topology-based lookup table with corresponding
lookup algorithms for the packet forwarding to fully exploit the capacity of the
forwarding processor. Control and node management software (including routing protocol operation, routing table maintenance, and other control and management protocols such as ICMP, SNMP) are implemented on the route processor.

   This architecture shares the same advantages/disadvantages of the bus-based
architecture with centralized forwarding regardless of the type of forwarding

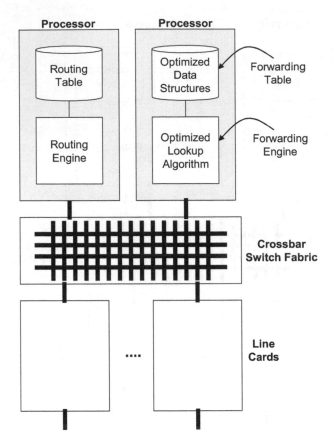

FIGURE 3.2 Architectures with Crossbar-Based Switch Fabrics and Centralized Forwarding Engines Using Optimized Lookup System.

engine used (even if it uses optimized forwarding tables and lookup algorithms). Unfortunately, this architecture, although employing a crossbar switch fabric, can still yield low packet forwarding performance because the central forwarding processor has to process all packets flowing through the device.

Moving packets (or even only packet headers) from an input interface to the centralized forwarding processor and then to outbound interfaces is a time-consuming operation that often causes the crossbar switch fabric to be grossly underutilized. An architecture that distributes forwarding capabilities directly to the line cards has the potential of fully utilizing the capacity of the crossbar switch fabric and provides higher forwarding throughput.

3.3 ARCHITECTURES WITH CROSSBAR-BASED SWITCH FABRICS AND DISTRIBUTED FORWARDING ENGINES

The crossbar switch-based architectures with distributed forwarding engines are much more flexible and optimized to scale to higher forwarding capacities than the shared-bus and shared-memory based architectures. These architectures can scale more efficiently to preserve service providers' equipment investments and to protect against performance degradation as networks grow and users generate more diverse traffic types.

As network traffic grows, this places more demand on the amount of processing power required in the network devices to allow for faster forwarding table lookups and support more advanced QoS and security functions. The newer distributed forwarding system designs have the capabilities to handle packet forwarding at traffic load levels that surpass what a single, centralized, and shared forwarding engine can reliably support.

Example Architectures:

- Avaya P580 and P882 Routing Switch Architecture with 80-Series Media Module (*Chapter 5*)
- Foundry Networks (FastIron, BigIron, NetIron, TurboIron) multilayer switches (*Chapters 6* and *7*)
- Cisco Catalyst 6500 Series Switches with Supervisor Engines 1A and 2—Fabric-only line cards (with embedded DFC) (*Chapter 4*)
- Cisco Catalyst 6500 Series switches with Supervisor Engine 720—Architectures with CEF256 fabric-enabled line cards with optional DFC installed (*Chapter 8*)
- Cisco Catalyst 6500 Series switches with Supervisor Engine 720—Architectures with dCEF256 line cards with integrated DFC (*Chapter 8*)
- Cisco Catalyst 6500 Series switches with Supervisor Engine 720—Architectures with CEF720 line cards with optional DFC installed (**Chapter 8**)
- Cisco Catalyst 6500 Series switches with Supervisor Engines 720—Architectures with dCEF720 line cards with integrated DFC (*Chapter 8*).

3.3.1 Architectures with Forwarding Engine and Flow/Route Cache in Line Cards

This architecture employs a crossbar switch fabric and a flow/route cache in each line card as shown in Figure 3.3. The crossbar switch fabric allows each line card (with its own forwarding engine and flow/route cache) to transmit data directly to any other line card as needed (as long as the flow/cache is properly populated).

Apart from the first packet of a flow, all other packets are transmitted (only once) over the crossbar switch fabric to the destination port or ports (for multicast traffic). Although this architecture allows the line cards to process packets locally some of the time, the overall system throughput is not constrained by the switch fabric as is the case in shared-bus-based architectures.

This architecture shares the same advantages/disadvantages of the bus-based architecture with forwarding engines and flow/route caches in line cards. As with the counterpart bus-based architecture, this architecture has a traffic (or flow) dependent throughput. The route processor can still be a bottleneck when traffic

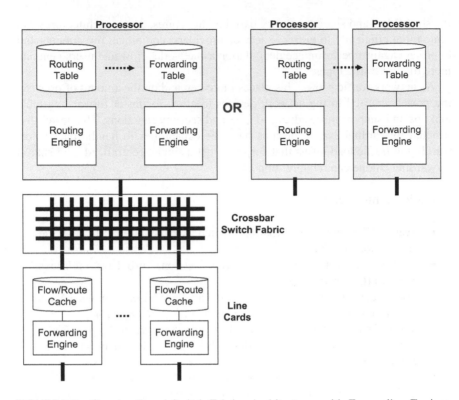

FIGURE 3.3   Crossbar-Based Switch Fabrics Architectures with Forwarding Engines and Flow/Route Cache in Line Cards.

passing through the device consist of mainly short flows where there is a higher percentage of first packets (in the flows). The performance of this architecture can be improved by enhancing each of the line cards with distributed forwarding engines and full (topology-based) forwarding tables.

3.3.2   ARCHITECTURES WITH FULLY DISTRIBUTED FORWARDING ENGINES IN LINE CARDS

In the route processor, a routing table process will be responsible for the calculation of best paths, alternative paths, and the extraction and consolidation of routing information from different routing protocols. In some implementations, the routing table process may interact with the individual routing table of each routing protocol running in the system. All this information will then be merged into a global routing table for the system, where the best path for each destination network is maintained. This routing table information is further distilled into a forwarding table and distributed to the different line cards in the system.

The crossbar switch fabric serves as an effective backplane for interconnecting all modules in the system. It creates dynamic and dedicated connections between all line cards including the route processor and provides fast data switching transmission between them. In this architecture, each input interface on a line card receives a packet that is examined by a local forwarding engine and then forwarded directly to the output interface associated with its destination network (Figure 3.4). Each line card contains both a receive memory and a transmit memory, and each has a high-speed access to the crossbar switch fabric.

An ingress line card receives a packet and performs a forwarding table lookup for the next-hop IP address and its egress interface. During the forwarding process, the IP TTL is decremented and the IP checksum is recomputed. The packet is rewritten with both the outgoing port's MAC address and the next hop's MAC information derived from the forwarding table (and adjacency tables), and the Ethernet checksum recomputed. The Ethernet frame is then forwarded to the appropriate egress interface for transmission to the external network.

In most distributed architectures, if an arriving packet is a control plane or management message, it is punted to the route processor. Examples of packets that are typically punted for processing by the route processor (or in some architectures, a line card's CPU) include:

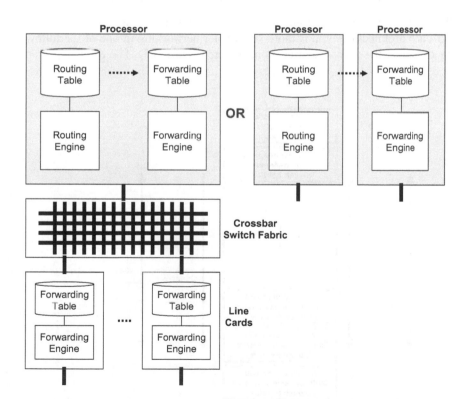

FIGURE 3.4 Crossbar-Based Switch Fabrics Architectures with Fully Distributed Forwarding Engines in Line Cards.

- Control packets from routing protocols such as BGP, OSPF, IS-IS, PIM, IGMP, etc.
- Management packets from protocols such as Telnet, SSH, SNMP, etc.
- Layer 2 packets from protocols such as ARP, LACP PDU, BFD, etc.
- IP packets requiring fragmentation, with the Don't Fragment (DF) bit set
- IP packets with IP Options
- Packets with IP Time-to-live (TTL) expired
- Packets carrying ICMP echo requests (used to ping IP devices).

The architecture with a crossbar switch fabric and distributed forwarding in the line cards is far more efficient than other architectures and provides the system the ability to forward packets with much greater speed, freeing the route processor resources for control and management operations. Ultimately, distributed forwarding in the line cards shortens the entire process of next-hop information lookups and packet processing, resulting in faster transmission of packets transiting the router or switch/router.

3.4 RELATING ARCHITECTURES TO SWITCH/ROUTER TYPES

The switch/router architectures discussed earlier have different characteristics and each architecture type is more suitable for networking in one of the following domains: the access, aggregation, or core (Figure 3.5). The most important

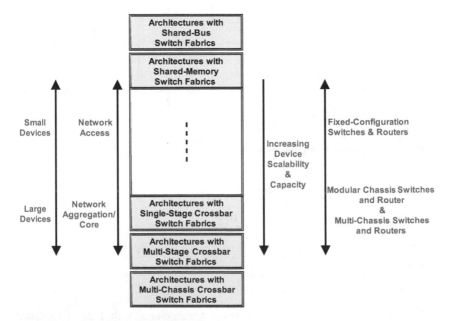

FIGURE 3.5 Relating Architectures to Switch Types.

characteristics that are most commonly associated with an architecture type are device size, form-factor, port density (i.e., the number of ports supported), performance, reliability, and scalability. Small and compact devices tend to adopt bus switch fabrics while the bigger devices are much more flexible and practical to design using crossbar-based switch fabrics. Also, the cost of a switch, generally, depends on its port density, port speeds, packet forwarding rates, overall memory capacity, expansion capacity, and reliability features.

The smaller devices (with a small number of user ports and lower forwarding capacities) which are more suitable at the network access tend to come in fixed configuration platforms. Fixed configuration platforms are designed to have a fixed number of ports and are generally not expandable to include more modules. The switch cannot be expanded to include more features or options beyond those that were originally built into the device. Generally, the features and options available on the device depend on the particular platform and model one purchases. With fixed configuration switches, modules cannot be added or swapped as needed like with modular switches. Vendors typically offer different fixed configuration models of the same switch type that vary in port density and types of ports. The larger devices which are usually employed at the network aggregation and core layers (and have higher forwarding capacities) tend to be based on crossbar switch fabrics and come in the form of modular chassis and multi-chassis platforms.

The port density and features related to scalability and reliability of a switch depend a lot on whether the switch is a fixed configuration or modular platform. The physical packaging including the features and options offered is often referred to as the form factor of the switch (simply referred to as the switch form factor). Vendors offer switch platforms of various types and models with each model differing in terms of physical form factor and configuration, port density, and features/options supported.

Modular chassis are designed to be expandable such that modules can be added to or swapped in the chassis as needed, thereby providing greater flexibility to address the needs of growing and changing networks. Examples of modules that can be added are power supplies, cooling fans, line cards, redundant switch fabrics, router processors, and application-specific modules such as firewall and encryption processors. A network designer provides redundancy in a network to help minimize disruption of services to end users, and the possibility and impact of failures in the network. A common method of providing redundancy is to deploy network equipment with duplicate modules to provide failover services in case one module fails.

To enable networks to scale easily and effectively, network designers typically use modular platforms that are expandable and can be readily upgraded to increase network bandwidth capacity and service capabilities. Network administrators can easily add or swap modules to an existing modular platform to support new features and options without requiring major equipment upgrades. New modules can be integrated in the device (which still acts as one device and not separate devices) resulting in simplified device configuration and management.

Modular architectures are designed to much more easily accommodate redundant components like power supplies, cooling fans, switch fabrics, route processors, and so on.

Vendors typically offer modular switches in different sized chassis that offer different degrees of expansibility, and allow more flexibility in configuration and installation of different and varying numbers of modules. Typically, high-end and high-capability switches are designed as modular switches capable of supporting more features. A key attribute is that they can be expanded and customized to accommodate more features according to network requirements. The crossbar switch fabric-based architectures are more flexible and allow greater scalability and reliability features. When in a modular form factor, they offer greater flexibility for network scalability and growth.

TABLE 3.1

Categories of Architectures Discussed in This Book

	Crossbar-Based Architectures
Architectures with Centralized Forwarding Engines	• Cisco Catalyst 6500 series switches with Supervisor Engines 1A and 2—Fabric-enabled line cards without a Distributed Forwarding Card (DFC) installed • Cisco Catalyst 6500 Series switches with Supervisor Engines 720—Architectures with "Classic" line cards • Cisco Catalyst 6500 Series switches with Supervisor Engines 720—Architectures with CEF256 fabric-enabled line cards (optional DFC not installed) • Cisco Catalyst 6500 Series switches with Supervisor Engines 720—Architectures with CEF720 line cards (optional DFC not installed)
Architectures with Distributed Forwarding Engines	• Avaya P580 and P882 Routing Switch Architecture with 80-Series Media Module • Foundry Networks (FastIron, BigIron, NetIron, TurboIron) multilayer switches • Cisco Catalyst 6500 Series Switches with Supervisor Engines 1A and 2—Fabric-only line cards (with embedded DFC) • Cisco Catalyst 6500 Series switches with Supervisor Engine 720—Architectures with CEF256 fabric-enabled line cards with optional DFC installed • Cisco Catalyst 6500 Series switches with Supervisor Engine 720—Architectures with dCEF256 line cards with integrated DFC • Cisco Catalyst 6500 Series switches with Supervisor Engine 720—Architectures with CEF720 line cards with optional DFC installed • Cisco Catalyst 6500 Series switches with Supervisor Engine 720—Architectures with dCEF720 line cards with integrated DFC

Large networks that support many services and users typically use high-density modular devices in order to better utilize network room and rack space and energy. The use of high-density modular devices reduces or eliminates the need for installing many fixed configuration switches in order to accommodate the number of services and users in the network. Using many fixed configuration devices leads to higher consumption of network closet and rack space and power outlets. Also, the use of many fixed configuration switches requires many additional uplink ports for bandwidth aggregation to and from the core network. Bandwidth aggregation is less of a problem with a single modular switch, because the switch's backplane and uplink ports typically have enough bandwidth capacity to accommodate the devices connected to its ports.

Today, most small form-factor switches employ switch-on-chip (SOC) concepts where the processing and advanced features of the switch are implemented on a single ASIC. This has become standard industry practice for the design of low-cost and low-feature fixed configuration switches. Modular switches also employ SOC in line modules where the SOC is used to implement distributed forwarding concepts and advanced line card features such as encryption and VPN processing.

Most small form-factor switches (typically in fixed configuration format) are based on centralized forwarding designs while large form factor switches typically adopt distributed forwarding concepts. The benefits of using centralized forwarding architectures (in small form-factor switches) include the ability to use lower cost hardware which in turn provides lower design complexity. However, for scalability and deployment in large enterprise core networks, distributed forwarding architectures are more optimal. The access layer of a network usually contains less expensive, lower-performing switches and routers, while the distribution/aggregation and core layers (where a device's packet forwarding rate has a greater impact on overall network performance) use the more expensive, higher-performing devices.

The packet forwarding rate, which defines the number of packets a device can process and transmit per second, is an important consideration when designing and selecting the device. If the forwarding rate of the switch is not adequate enough to handle the target application and traffic, the switch will not be able to handle full wire-speed communication across all of its ports.

Part 2

Design Examples and
Case Studies

4 Cisco Catalyst 6500 Series Switches with Supervisor Engines 1A and 2

4.1 INTRODUCTION

The Catalyst 6500 Series is a high-performance family of switch/routers with advanced features and capabilities beyond those of the Catalyst 6000 Series discussed in [CISCCAT6000]. These switch/routers were designed to meet the growing demand for bandwidth, high-speed packet forwarding, high-availability, and advanced quality of service (QoS) and security services, required in today's enterprise and service provider networks. The Catalyst 6500 Series architecture supports a backplane switching bandwidth of up to 256 Gb/s and Layer 2 and Layer 3 forwarding speeds of over 200 million packets-per-second (Mpps).

The Catalyst 6500 supports both a 32 Gb/s shared switching bus (same type of shared-bus architecture supported in the Catalyst 6000 Series) and a 256 Gb/s crossbar switch fabric module (SFM). The SFM can be installed in Slot 5 in the chassis, and optionally, for redundancy, another SFM can be installed in Slot 6. The SFM provides the Catalyst 6500 with a high-speed internal switching matrix for interconnecting the various system modules. The Catalyst 6000 Series supports only a 32 Gb/s shared switching bus and not an SFM.

The Catalyst 6500 supports a Supervisor Engine module, which implements the control plane and data plane processing functions in the switch (Multilayer Switching Feature Card (MSFC) and Policy feature card (PFC)). The Supervisor Engine options for the Catalyst 6500 include the Supervisor Engine 1A, Supervisor Engine 2, Supervisor Engine 32, Supervisor Engine 720, Supervisor Engine 2T, and Supervisor Engine 6T which are designed to address a wide range of networking requirements of enterprise and service provider networks. This chapter focuses on the architectures of the Catalyst 6500 Series switches with Supervisor Engines 1A and 2 [CISCCAT6000] [CISCSE1A2DS] [MENJUS2003].

The Catalyst 6500 with Supervisor Engines 1A and 2 supports a number of line card types. Adopting the architecture categories broadly used to classify the various designs in *Chapter 3*, the following architectures are covered in this chapter:

- Cisco Catalyst 6500 series switches with Supervisor Engines 1A and 2—Architectures with fabric-enabled line cards without a Distributed Forwarding Card (DFC) installed (see Figure 4.1)

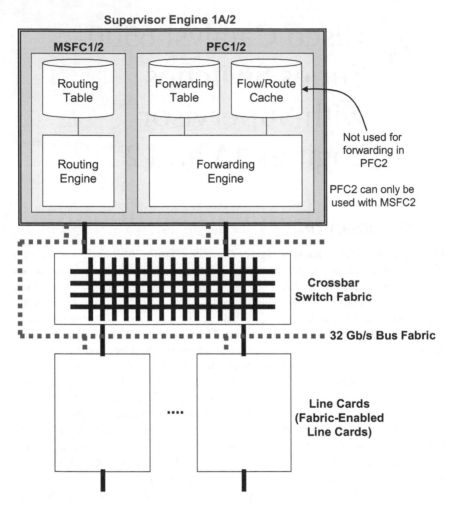

FIGURE 4.1   Architectures with Fabric-Enabled Line Cards without a Distributed Forwarding Card (DFC) Installed.

- Cisco Catalyst 6500 Series Switches with Supervisor Engines 1A and 2—Architectures with fabric-only line cards (with embedded DFC) (see Figure 4.2).

We discuss these architectures in various sections in this chapter including their corresponding packet forwarding operations.

4.2   MAIN ARCHITECTURAL FEATURES OF THE CATALYST 6500 SERIES

The Catalyst 6500 Series supports a 6-slot chassis in the Catalyst 6506, a 9-slot chassis in the Catalyst 6509, a 9-slot NEB chassis in the Catalyst 6509-NEB (in

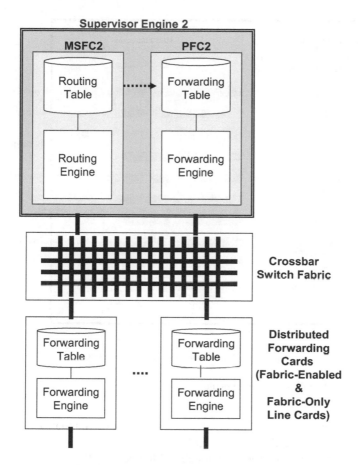

FIGURE 4.2 Architectures with Fabric-Enabled and Fabric-Only Line Cards (with DFCs).

which slots are arranged vertically), a 13-slot chassis in the Catalyst 6513, in addition to other chassis options. These switch/routers also support line cards with a wide range of network interface types with different port densities: 384 10/100 Mb/s Ethernet ports, 192 100Base-FX Ethernet ports, and up to 130 Gigabit Ethernet ports (in the 9-slot chassis options). The 13-slot chassis Catalyst 6500 supports up to 576 10/100 Mb/s Ethernet ports or 192 Gigabit Ethernet ports. The main identifying components on the Catalyst 6506, 6509 and 6513 backplanes are the following:

- **Catalyst 6506 and 6509 (Figure 4.3):**
  - Slot 1 supports the Supervisor Engine
  - Slot 2 supports either a line card or a redundant Supervisor Engine
  - Bus Connectors for the 32 Gb/s Switching Bus: Data Bus (DBus); Results Bus (RBus); Control Bus (CBus) (or Ethernet Out of Band Channel (EOBC))

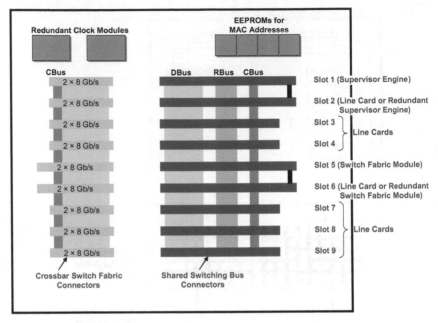

DBus = Data Bus
RBus = Results Bus
CBus = Control Bus also referred to as Ethernet Out of Band Channel (EOBC)

FIGURE 4.3   Catalyst 6509 Backplane.

- Clock module with redundancy (primary and secondary)
- Ethernet MAC Address EEPROMs
- Slot 5 supports the Switch Fabric Module (SFM)
- Slot 6 supports either a line card or a redundant Switch Fabric Module
- All other Slots support line cards
- Bus Connectors for the 256 Gb/s Crossbar Switching Fabric
- **Catalyst 6513 (Figure 4.4):**
  - Slot 1 supports the Supervisor Engine
  - Slot 2 supports either a line card or a redundant Supervisor Engine
  - Bus Connectors for: Data Bus (DBus); Results Bus (RBus); Control Bus (CBus) (or EOBC)
  - Clock module with redundancy (primary and secondary)
  - Ethernet MAC Address EEPROMs
  - Slot 7/8 support either an optional Switch Fabric Module or a line card
  - 2500W/4000W power supply
  - Bus Connectors for the 256 Gb/s Crossbar Switching Fabric
  - Slots 2 to 8 support 1 × 8 Gb/s Fabric Channels
  - Slots 9 to 13 support 2 × 8 Gb/s Fabric Channels.

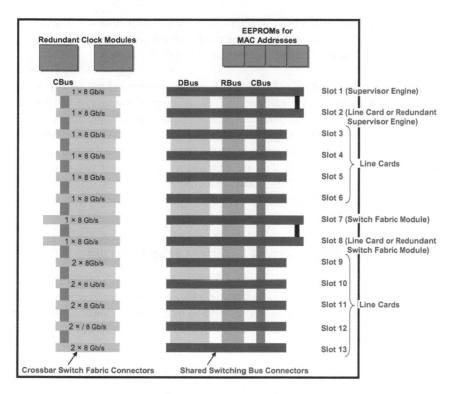

FIGURE 4.4   Catalyst 6513 Backplane.

The line cards can be connected to the Catalyst 6500 via the 32 Gb/s shared switching bus, the 256 Gb/s SFM, or both the shared switching bus and the SFM. To allow for flexibility and to support different switching needs, the following line card versions provide connectivity into the different switch fabrics:

- **Non-Fabric-enabled Line Cards**: These line cards have connectivity to the 32 Gb/s bus *only* and can be used in all chassis options in the Catalyst 6000 and 6500. Both Catalyst 6000 and 6500 support the 32 Gb/s shared bus. The non-fabric-enabled line cards can be installed in any Catalyst 6000 and 6500 chassis type and they are designed to provide design flexibility and investment protection for networks that have already deployed the Catalyst 6000 series switches.
- **Fabric-enabled Line Cards**: These line cards have connectivity to both the 32 Gb/s shared bus and the 256 Gb/s crossbar SFM in the Catalyst 6500 (via two 8 Gb/s full-duplex channels). The Catalyst 6000 Series does not support a crossbar SFM.
- **Fabric-only Line Cards**: These line cards connect only to the 256 Gb/s SFM in the Catalyst 6500 (via two 8 Gb/s full-duplex channels). The

fabric-only line cards provide the highest level of packet forwarding performance. These line cards must be used with the crossbar SFM because
they do not support connectivity to the 32 Gb/s shared bus.

The fabric-enabled or fabric-only line cards are recommended for networks that
require very high bandwidth and packet forwarding performance. All the three
line card types described earlier can interoperate and communicate with each
other, when installed in a Catalyst 6500 (that supports both a 32 Gb/s shared bus
and the SFM). The line cards when installed in the Catalyst 6500 can communicate with each other, even if they are attached to the different switching backplanes. A non-fabric-enabled line card with connectivity to the 32 Gb/s shared
bus in the Catalyst 6500 can interoperate with a fabric-only line card with connectivity to the SFM in the same system.

4.3   CATALYST 6500 SWITCH FABRIC ARCHITECTURE

Figure 4.5 shows a logical layout of the SFM in the Catalyst 6500. The SFM
consists of a 256 Gb/s crossbar switch fabric with packet forwarding rates of over
100 Mpps. The Catalyst 6500 uses the SFM to interconnect fabric-enabled and
fabric-only modules and line cards in the system. The connectors for the SFM

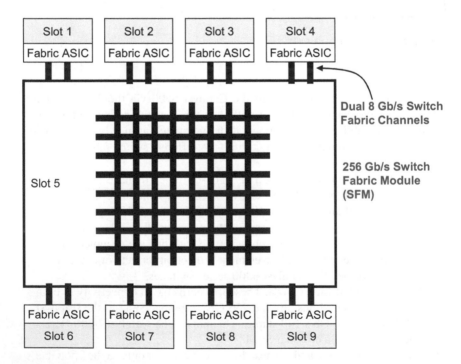

FIGURE 4.5   Catalyst 6500 Switch Fabric Module.

on the Catalyst 6500 are shown in Figure 4.3 and Figure 4.4. The Catalyst 6000 chassis (discussed in [CISCCAT6000]) does not support an SFM and so does not have these crossbar switch fabric connectors on its backplane.

Furthermore, the SFM is supported only in the Catalyst 6500 with a Supervisor Engine 2 (which must be installed in Slot 5). The Supervisor Engine 2 has a much higher packet forwarding rate to better utilize the high bandwidth provided by the SFM. To support switch fabric redundancy, a second (redundant) SFM can be installed in Slot 6. The SFM cannot be used in a Catalyst 6500 with Supervisor Engine 1A because this engine has no provision for the crossbar switch fabric interfaces and connectors.

As illustrated in Figure 4.5, the SFM can be viewed logically as a "switch" with 16 "ports", where the "ports" (channels or connections) connect to the other system modules (e.g., Supervisor Engine) and line cards. The SFM has 16 x 8 Gb/s full-duplex port or connections (i.e., 2 x 16 unidirectional channels) to the system modules. Each slot in the Catalyst 6500 chassis is allocated two crossbar switch "ports", with each port clocked at 8 Gb/s. The total bandwidth is 16 Gb/s per port with one 8 Gb/s channel into the switch fabric and another 8 Gb/s channel out of the fabric.

Figure 4.5 illustrates the SFM and how it provides connectivity to the other modules in the Catalyst 6500 chassis. Slot 5 on a chassis supports the SFM while Slot 6 can be used for a redundant SFM when required. Each module has available two 8 Gb/s full-duplex connections to the SFM. However, depending on the type of line cards installed, the line card can use zero, one, or both of the 8 Gb/s full-duplex connections on the SFM:

- **Connectivity for Fabric-enabled Line Cards**: These line cards have connectivity to both the SFM and 32 Gb/s shared bus. One 8 Gb/s full-duplex connection is provided to the SFM, and a second 8 Gb/s full-duplex connection to the 32 Gb/s shared bus as illustrated in Figure 4.6. Here, the fabric-enabled module has connectivity to one of the ports on the SFM, providing 8 Gb/s full-duplex access into the switch fabric.
- **Connectivity for Fabric-only Line Cards**: These line cards have connectivity only to the SFM via two 8 Gb/s full-duplex connections as shown in Figure 4.7. These line cards do not support direct connectivity to the 32 Gb/s shared bus as in the fabric-enabled cards. The fabric-only line cards connect to the two 8 Gb/s ports on the SFM, providing them with 16 Gb/s of (full-duplex) bandwidth.
- **No Connectivity for Non-fabric-enabled Line Cards**: The non-fabric-enabled line cards have no connectivity to the SFM. They have connectivity only to the 32 Gb/s shared bus.

The Catalyst 6500 SFM employs switch fabric overspeed plus virtual output queuing (VOQ) to overcome the problem of head-of-line (HOL) blocking of packets at the input ports. Switch fabric overspeed is a method where the internal data paths within the crossbar switch fabric are run at a speed higher than the input

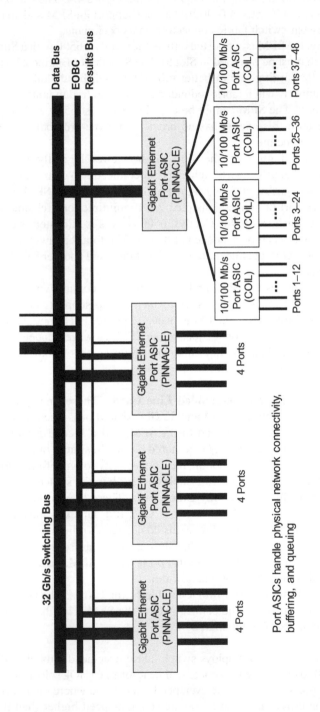

Port ASICs handle physical network connectivity, buffering, and queuing

FIGURE 4.6 Classic Line Card Architecture.

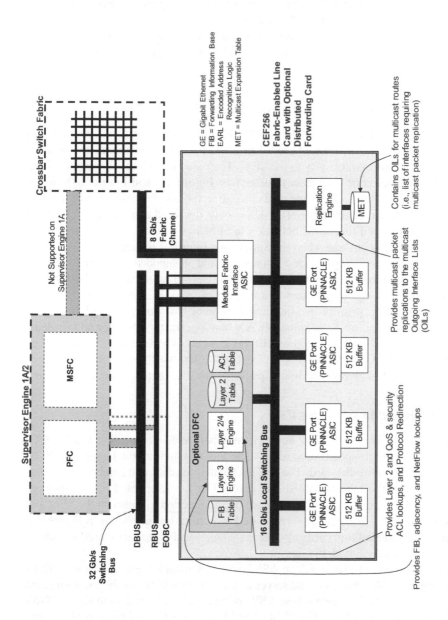

FIGURE 4.7 Catalyst 6500 SFM Fabric-Enabled Line Card with Optional Distributed Forwarding Card (DFC).

speed into the fabric. With this, packets are moved out of the input line card through the switch fabric to the output line card at higher speeds thus avoiding HOL blocking of packets at the input modules.

The Catalyst 6500 SFM implements 3 times overspeed, which means (with each input channel clocked at 8 Gb/s), each internal data path is run or clocked at 24 Gb/s relative to the input line card speed. VOQ together with switch fabric overspeed provides an effective way of avoiding HOL blocking in crossbar switch fabrics.

4.4   CATALYST 6500 LINE CARDS ARCHITECTURES

As discussed earlier, the Catalyst 6500 SFM supports both fabric-enabled and fabric-only line cards. Each of these line cards has fabric interfaces and connectors that provide connectivity to the SFM. They also use a local shared switching bus for internal card level data transfer (see Figure 4.6 and Figure 4.7). When installed in a system, all the line cards including the non-fabric-enabled cards can communicate with each other. The fabric-only line card can communicate with non-fabric-enabled line cards because the SFM has a connection to the 32 Gb/s shared switching bus and when the Supervisor Engine 2 is used.

In addition, the Supervisor Engines 1A and 2 support connectivity to the older Classic (non-fabric-enabled) line cards (see Figure 4.6). The Port ASICs in all of the line card types support a number of features, some of which include packet buffering, priority queuing and port-level QoS, traffic scheduling, congestion avoidance, traffic shaping, VLAN tagging, traffic filtering and broadcast suppression, and link aggregation (EtherChannel). The Classic line cards (e.g., WS-X6416-GBIC 16-Port Gigabit Ethernet modules) use the centralized forwarding engine on PFC for forwarding of packets—no distributed or local forwarding.

4.4.1   FABRIC-ENABLED LINE CARDS

The fabric-enabled line cards support the Distributed Forwarding Card (DFC) which allows high-speed forwarding table lookups and packet forwarding to be done locally within the card. The DFC is a daughter card and can be installed as an add-on in the fabric-enabled line cards. The fabric-enabled line cards (e.g., CEF256 line cards) are designed to have one connection to a port on the SFM and another connection to the 32 Gb/s shared switching bus as shown in Figure 4.7. The fabric-enabled line cards also have a single local (internal) shared switching bus with a bandwidth of 16 Gb/s.

As illustrated in Figure 4.7, an ASIC called Medusa is the main component on the fabric-enabled line card that serves as the interface between the local line card system and the SFM. The Medusa ASIC is the interface between the local 16 Gb/s shared switching bus and the SFM. The Medusa ASIC on fabric-enabled cards (not fabric-only cards) also provides the interface to the main 32 Gb/s shared switching bus as shown in Figure 4.7. The two 16 Gb/s and 32 Gb/s shared switching buses and the SFM are interconnected through this ASIC.

4.4.2 FABRIC-ONLY LINE CARDS

The fabric-only line cards (e.g., dCEF256 line cards) connect to other system modules and line cards only through the SFM over two switch fabric channels as shown in Figure 4.8. As illustrated in this figure, the fabric-only line cards support two local 16 Gb/s shared switching buses. These line cards also support forwarding table lookups and packet forwarding locally using the DFC. The DFC is embedded in the system and is not a daughter card as in the fabric-enabled line cards.

4.5 CATALYST 6500 CONTROL PLANE IMPLEMENTATION AND FORWARDING ENGINES—SUPERVISOR ENGINES

The Catalyst 6500 supports a centralized control plane functionality that is provided by (a daughter card module called) the Multilayer Switch Feature Card (MSFC) on the Supervisor Engine. The packet forwarding (which can exceed 100 Mpps) is handled by the Policy Feature Card (PFC) (also on the Supervisor Engine) and on some line cards that support the DFC.

The Supervisor Engine 1A and Supervisor Engine 2 are the first- and second-generation control engines, respectively, developed for the Catalyst 6000 and 6500 switch/routers. The newer generation Supervisor Engine 720 is described in *Chapter 8* of this book. These different Supervisor Engines were designed for the Catalyst 6500 to address the needs of customers with different networking requirements.

The PFC contains a number of ASICs designed to handle in hardware, Layer 2 and 3 forwarding table lookups and packet forwarding, QoS classification, and access control list (ACL) filtering. However, a route processor (i.e., the MSFC) is required to populate the Layer 3 route/flow cache or forwarding tables used by the PFC's Layer 3 forwarding engine ASIC. If no route processor (MSFC) is installed in the Supervisor Engine, the PFC can perform only limited functions such as Layer 3/4 QoS classification and ACL filtering but not Layer 3 packet forwarding.

In both Supervisor Engines 1A and 2, the MSFC runs the routing protocols and maintains the routing table from which the Layer 3 forwarding tables are generated. The MSFC communicates across an out-of-band bus (Control Bus) to the hardware forwarding ASICs in the PFC or DFC.

4.5.1 SUPERVISOR ENGINE 1A ARCHITECTURE

Supervisor Engine 1A is designed with the following configuration options which range from the basic option with only Layer 2 forwarding, to the full option with full Layer 2 and Layer 3 packet processing and forwarding.

4.5.1.1 Supervisor Engine 1A with Only a PFC1

This configuration option (which is available for both the Catalyst 6000 and 6500) has a Supervisor Engine 1A module with only a PFC1 installed. Here, the PFC1

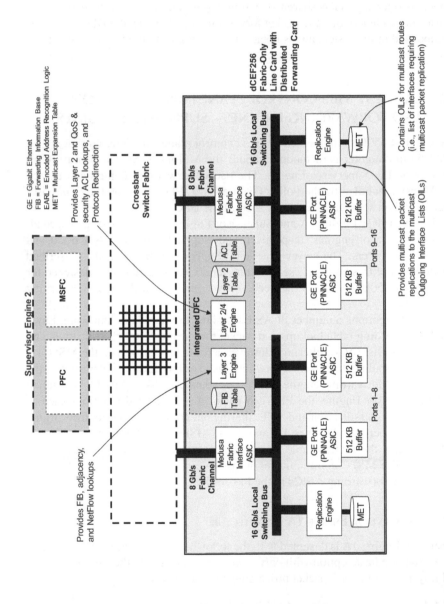

FIGURE 4.8 Catalyst 6500 SFM Fabric-Only Line Card.

supports only basic Layer 3/4 packet classification which allows for QoS classification and queuing and security ACL filtering. The PFC1 does not support Layer 3 packet forwarding because an MSFC is absent to provide route processor functions. Figure 4.9 (ignoring the MSFC-1/MSFC-2 block) shows the architecture of the Supervisor Engine 1A with PFC1.

As illustrated in Figure 4.9, the Supervisor Engine 1A contains the EARL (Encoded Address Recognition Logic) switching system which is a basic Layer 2 forwarding engine. The EARL consults the local Layer 2 forwarding (or MAC address) table to determine the egress VLAN and port of a packet when performing Layer 2 forwarding. The PFC1 also contains a Layer 3 forwarding engine (which does not perform Layer 3 forwarding because an MSFC is not present), flow cache, ACL engine, and ACL table. In the absence of an MSFC, the PFC1 through the ACL engine is responsible for Layer 3/4 QoS classification and security ACL filtering.

The ACL table is maintained in a ternary content addressable memory (TCAM), which structures the ACL information in a format that can be examined efficiently by the ACL engine. The following takes place when a packet arrives at the PFC1 that requires security ACL filtering. While the Layer 2 forwarding engine (in the EARL switching system) determines how to forward the packet based on the information in the Layer 2 forwarding table, the ACL engine at the same time determines if the packet should be denied or permitted into the system. By allowing the Layer 2 forwarding table lookup and ACL table lookup to be performed in parallel, ACLs or QoS classification and processing on arriving traffic does not degrade the packet forwarding performance of the system which is 15 Mpps.

4.5.1.2   Supervisor Engine 1A with a PFC1 and MSFC1/MSFC2

This configuration option supports full Layer 2 and Layer 3 forwarding in the Catalyst 6000 and 6500. The MSFC1 and MSFC2 have similar architectures and differ only in the route processor type, amount of memory supported, and packet forwarding rate. The MSFC1 supports an R5000 200 MHz processor, up to 128 MB memory, and can forward packets in software up to 170 Kpps. The MSFC2 supports an R7000 300 MHz processor, up to 512 MB memory, and can forward packets in software up to 650 Kpps. The Layer 3 packet forwarding rate in the PFC1 hardware stays unchanged at 15 Mpps, and is not dependent on the MSFC type installed.

Figure 4.9 shows the architecture of the Supervisor Engine 1A with PFC1 and MSFC1/2. In this configuration, the Layer 3 forwarding engine on the PFC1 can forward packets at Layer 3, because the MSFC1/2 is present to serve as the route processor in the system. The PFC1 also supports all the other features such as QoS classification and security ACL filtering as described earlier.

The PFC1 and MSFC1/MSFC2 now allow the Catalyst 6500 to perform both Layer 2 and Layer 3 forwarding. The flow cache on the PFC1 is used to Layer 3 forward packet flows through the switch/router. The first packet in a flow is always Layer 3 forwarded by the MSFC1/2, which performs a lookup in its forwarding table to determine the next-hop IP address and outgoing port for the packet.

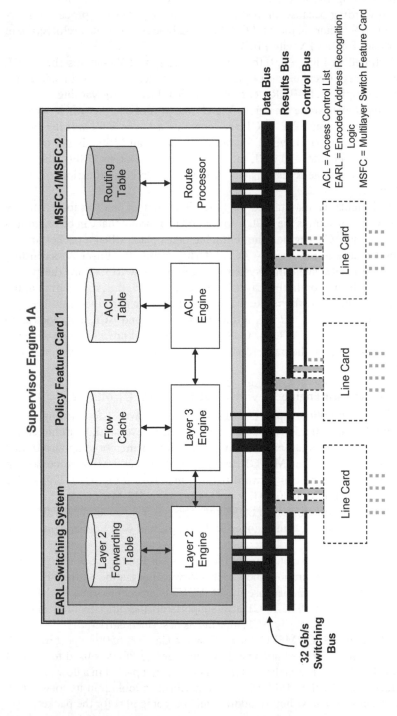

FIGURE 4.9 Supervisor 1 with Policy Feature Card 1 (PFC1) and Multilayer Switch Feature Card (MSFC).

The MSFC1/2 determines the next-hop information and forwards the packet along with its forwarding information back to the Layer 3 forwarding engine in the PFC1. The Layer 3 forwarding engine extracts the forwarding information for the packet and writes this into its flow cache. Subsequent packets belonging to the same flow as the first packet will match the flow cache entry just created and can now be Layer 3 forwarded directly by the PFC1 Layer 3 engine without MSFC1/2 intervention.

The first packet in another newly established flow that does not have an entry in the flow cache maintained by the PFC1 is sent once again to the MSFC1/2 for software processing. The MSFC1/2 performs a lookup using the destination IP address in its forwarding table to determine the next-hop information for the packet. After the MSFC1/2 has forwarded this first packet of the new flow in software, the PFC1 flow cache is then appropriately programmed to forward subsequent packets without MSFC1/2 intervention.

As discussed in the previous chapters, the main limitation of the flow cache-based Layer 3 forwarding method is the processing overhead involved in the initial next-hop information lookup performed in software by the MSFC. Flow cache-based forwarding has an inherent problem in that it relies on the control plane (implemented in software) to forward the first packet of each new flow that enters the switch. The first packet in an IP flow must be passed to the MSFC (route processor) for Layer 3 forwarding. Forwarding via the control plane in the MSFC is sometimes referred to as slow-path forwarding (or process forwarding) while forwarding via the PFC directly is referred to as fast-path forwarding.

In networks that have many short flow connections being established at the same time, the MSFC can easily be overwhelmed with these short flow processing requirements since it has to handle all the first packets of the connections. This problem becomes more acute in enterprise network cores and service provider network environments where many short-term connections can be established at once.

4.5.2 Supervisor Engine 2 Architecture

This section describes the configurations options available for Supervisor Engine 2 for both Catalyst 6000 and 6500. The Supervisor Engine 2 has higher processing and packet forwarding capabilities than the Supervisor Engine 1A.

4.5.2.1 Supervisor Engine 2 with a PFC2

This configuration option has a Supervisor Engine 2 module with only a PFC2 present. In this architecture, as illustrated in Figure 4.10, the functionalities of the EARL switching system are integrated within the PFC2 when compared to the Supervisor Engine 1A with PFC1 only architecture (Figure 4.9). Details of the architecture of the Supervisor Engine 2 are shown in Figure 4.11.

The Layer 2 forwarding engine and ACL engine are merged to create a single Layer 2/4 engine. This combination enhances the QoS classification and security ACL filtering performance capabilities of the system when Layer 2 forwarding is

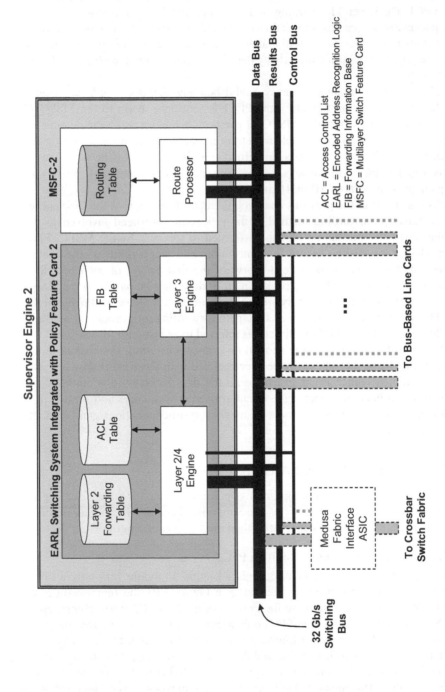

FIGURE 4.10   Supervisor Engine 2 with Policy Feature Card 2 (PFC2) and Multilayer Switch Feature Card (MSFC).

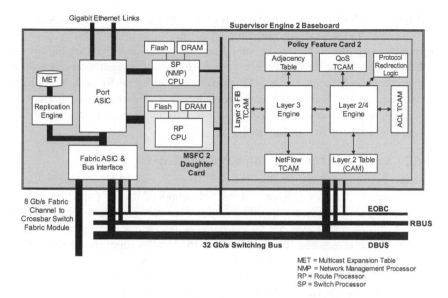

FIGURE 4.11   Supervisor Engine 2 Architecture.

Component	Description
Route Processor	This runs the Layer 3 protocols, maintains Layer 3 routes and state, and generates the forwarding information for download to the forwarding engines
Switch Processor	This runs the Layer 2 protocols, downloads the forwarding tables to the forwarding hardware, and monitors interfaces and environmental status
FIB TCAM	This contains IPv4/IPv6 address prefix entries and their corresponding next-hops and egress ports used for Layer 3 forwarding
Layer 2 CAM	This contains Layer 2 (MAC) address to port mappings used for Layer 2 forwarding
Adjacency Table	This contains IP next-hop to Layer 2 (MAC) address mappings used for rewrites in outgoing packet
QoS TCAM	This contains ACL entries used for QoS processing and filtering
ACL TCAM	This contains ACL entries used for security processing and filtering
NetFlow TCAM	This contains statistics and NetFlow features
Fabric and Bus Interface	This ASIC provides interfaces to the crossbar switch fabric and 32 Gb/s shared switching bus
Multicast Expansion Table (MET)	This contains Outgoing Interface Lists (OILs) requiring multicast packet replication.
Replication Engine	This provides packet replications services for multicast traffic and Switched Port Analyzer (SPAN)
Protocol Redirection Logic	This captures IGMP/MLD packets and redirects them for multicast group membership information to be recorded

being performed. The combined structure with Layer 3/4 QoS classification and ACL filtering supports up to 30 Mpps. The PFC2 and PFC1 have similar functions, and both support Layer 3 classification for QoS classification and security ACL filtering. However, the PFC2 is two times faster than the PFC1 and supports a larger number of ACLs (that are also stored in TCAMs) for QoS and security processing.

Although the Supervisor Engine 2 with PFC2 can Layer 2 forward packets and perform Layer 3/4 QoS classification and ACL filtering at up to 30 Mpps, the system requires an SFM and fabric-enabled line cards to be installed (see Figure 4.7 and Figure 4.8). Since the Supervisor Engine 2 in this configuration has only a PFC2 present (no MSFC), Layer 3 forwarding cannot be performed. The Layer 3 forwarding engine in this case is not used for Layer 3 forwarding, because an MSFC2 (route processor) is not present to generate the necessary routing information needed for the forwarding table.

4.5.2.2 Supervisor Engine 2 with a PFC2 and MSFC2

An MSFC2 is required on the Supervisor Engine 2 with PFC2 to enable Layer 3 forwarding. Supervisor Engine 2 does not support MSFC1 (which can only be used in Supervisor Engine 1A). The Layer 3 forwarding engine on the PFC2 (Figure 4.10) can now Layer 3 forward packets, because a route processor (the MSFC2) is now present in the system. The PFC2 also supports all other features such as QoS classification and ACL filtering. The Supervisor Engine 2 with PFC2/MSFC2 can forward packets at Layer 3 at rates up to 30 Mpps.

The Supervisor Engine 2 with PFC2 and MSFC2 employs a distributed forwarding architecture to perform Layer 3 forwarding where the MSFC2 is responsible for running the routing protocols and generating the appropriate distributed forwarding tables. The MSFC2 does not forward IP packets in transit through the system (except those generated by it (i.e., control plane packets)). Instead, the MSFC2 runs the routing protocols and constructs/maintains a routing table from which a master forwarding table (also known as a Forwarding Information Base (FIB)), is generated.

The FIB contains the same information (but in a more compact form) needed for packet forwarding as the routing table. The Supervisor Engine 2's forwarding engine then uses a highly optimized table lookup algorithm to identify the next hop and outgoing port on the switch/router. The MSFC2 generates the master FIB from the routing table it maintains and also copies this information to the FIB on the PFC2 and any other DFCs in the system. The MSFC2 copies the master FIB directly into the PFC2 and DFC forwarding hardware so that all packet forwarding can be done locally by these forwarding engines and not by the MSFC2.

With the distributed forwarding capability (where packets can be forwarded locally by the PFC2 or DFC (discussed later)), the local Layer 3 forwarding engine has the necessary information to Layer 3 forward all packets, without having to send the first packet associated with a flow to the MSFC (as is the case with flow cache-based forwarding). This distributed forwarding architecture eliminates the problems that flow cache-based forwarding faces when operating in an environment that has a large number of short flow connections being established at the same time.

When a packet arrives at the switch/router it is passed to the Layer 3 forwarding engine in the PFC2 or DFC. The Layer 3 forwarding engine extracts the destination IP address and performs a lookup in its local FIB for the most specific entry (network address prefix) that matches the destination IP address (a lookup process called Longest-Prefix Matching (LPM)). The result of the lookup is the next-hop IP address and egress interface on the switch/router out of which the packet should be forwarded.

The Layer 3 forwarding engine in the PFC2 or DFC also performs a lookup in its adjacency table it maintains for an adjacency (i.e., an adjacent network node) with a destination MAC address associated with the next-hop IP address. The adjacency table can be implemented as a separate table, or the information it holds can be integrated into the FIB to avoid having to make two lookups to retrieve the next-hop forwarding information for a packet. For Ethernet networks, the adjacency table is populated using the Address Resolution Protocol (ARP).

The discovered adjacency information (i.e., Ethernet MAC address) provides the Layer 3 forwarding engine in the PFC2 or DFC with the address that has to be used for rewriting the destination MAC address in the outgoing Ethernet frame. The source MAC address in the outgoing Ethernet frame is rewritten to be that of the MAC address of the egress interface out of which the packet is to be transmitted. Like any interface in an Ethernet network, the egress port also is assigned an Ethernet MAC address which serves as the source MAC address in the outgoing Ethernet frame.

The Layer 3 forwarding engine in the PFC2 or DFC performs the MAC address rewrites in the outgoing Ethernet frame and performs other required forwarding tasks such as TTL decrement, IP checksum, and Ethernet checksum recomputation. The PFC2 or DFC then forwards the packet to the egress interface for transmission to the external network.

4.5.3   SUPPORTING HIGH AVAILABILITY WITH DUAL SUPERVISOR ENGINES

Dual-Supervisor Engine configurations are supported in all the Catalyst 6500 Series chassis (6503, 6506, 6509, 6509-NEB, 6509-NEB-A, and 6513 (6513 is compatible with Supervisor Engine 2 only)) as shown by the extra slots reserved for redundancy in Figure 4.3 and Figure 4.4. The dual-Supervisor Engine configuration also supports the synchronization of system and protocol states between the primary and the redundant (secondary or standby) Supervisor Engines. The goal is to enhance network availability with sub-3-second failover from primary to redundant Supervisor Engine. To maximize network availability, the dual-Supervisor Engine configuration also allows for hot-swapping of the standby Supervisor Engine.

For the system to work properly, both Supervisor Engines in the dual engine configuration must be of the same model and the software image they run must also be the same. This is to ensure that when the active Supervisor Engine fails over to the standby Supervisor Engine, there will not be any glitches and the system can resume normal operation with only a brief downtime during switchover. With no glitches experienced, the user can then proceed to replace the faulty Supervisor Engine.

4.5.4 DISTRIBUTED FORWARDING CARD

The Distributed Forwarding Card (DFC) is a daughter card that can be installed on fabric-enabled line cards to allow them to make Layer 3 forwarding decisions locally without requiring the services of the Layer 3 forwarding engine located on the PFC (in the Supervisor Engine). The DFC daughter card is supported only on fabric-enabled line cards. When installed, an SFM must also be used in the Catalyst 6500 so that it can fully utilize the DFC's capabilities. The fabric-only line card, on the other hand, supports an embedded DFC as shown in Figure 4.8.

In normal operations without a DFC (which achieves 30 Mpps), the Supervisor Engine 2 sends forwarding instructions and control traffic to a line card over (the Control Bus of) the 32 Gb/s shared switching bus. A source line card also sends forwarding requests to the PFC2 on the Supervisor Engine 2 (which has the forwarding engine for the whole system in the absence of a DFC) over the 32 Gb/s switching bus.

The source line card compresses the IP packet header required for the Layer 3 lookup and sends it across the 32 Gb/s shared switching bus so that the PFC2 can perform lookups. The source line card receives the lookup results from the PFC2 (again over 32 Gb/s shared switching bus); however, the complete processed packet is forwarded over the SFM to the destination line card.

When a DFC is used on a line card, the forwarding decision is done locally in the line card without involving the PFC2 on the Supervisor Engine 2. In this case, instead of sending the compressed IP packet headers to the PFC2 on the Supervisor Engine 2, the forwarding lookup is done in the DFC (on the line card). After the lookup, the packet is forwarded directly over the SFM to the destination line card. The distributed forwarding architecture with the centralized Supervisor Engine 2 (with PFC2/MSFC2) and the DFCs on the line cards provides packet forwarding rates of over 100 Mpps.

The DFCs on the line cards allow the Catalyst 6500 with Supervisor Engine 2 to truly support distributed packet forwarding as illustrated in Figure 4.2. The DFC and the PFC2 on the Supervisor Engine 2 are conceptually similar in functionality and design (see Figure 4.12). They share essentially the same packet forwarding components. The DFC does not support a route processor (which runs routing protocols and constructs the routing table); meaning it does not contain an MSFC2. This means that although the forwarding decision is done locally within the DFC in the line card, the route processing is still centralized and handled by the MSFC2 in the Supervisor Engine 2.

The distributed forwarding table used for forwarding in the DFC is still generated centrally at the Supervisor Engine 2 (in the MSFC2) and then downloaded to the forwarding table local to the DFC in the line card (Figure 4.13). This means the master forwarding table maintained by the Supervisor Engine 2 (MSFC2) and the local distributed forwarding tables in the DFCs always have to be synchronized to allow identical forwarding information to be maintained throughout the switch/router.

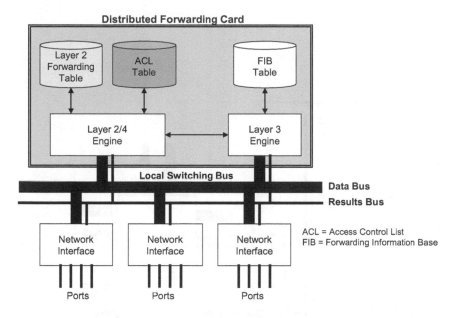

FIGURE 4.12 Distributed Forwarding Card (DFC) Architecture.

This architecture provides the best features of both centralized and distributed processing—centralized system control and management in the Supervisor Engine and distributed high-speed packet forwarding in the DFCs in the line cards. The Catalyst 6500 switch/routers with Supervisor Engine 2 and line cards with DFCs are suitable for the backbone and core layers of very large enterprise and service provider networks where a large number of short flow connections can be established at the same time.

4.5.4.1 Packet Forwarding in the DFC

Figure 4.13 illustrates a Catalyst 6500 switch/router architecture with a Supervisor Engine 2 and a fabric-enabled line card that supports a DFC daughter card. Having similar functions as the PFC, the DFC receives packets directly from its local ports and performs lookup operations using its local forwarding table. The master forwarding table (FIB) for the switch/router is maintained on the Supervisor Engine 2 and is generated from the routing table maintained by the MSFC2. The master forwarding table is copied to the PFC and each DFC in the system.

The local copy of the master forwarding table enables the Layer 3 forwarding engine on each DFC to Layer 3 forward packets locally. When network routing changes occur, they are detected by the routing protocols running in the MSFC2, the routing table and master forwarding table are updated to reflect the changes,

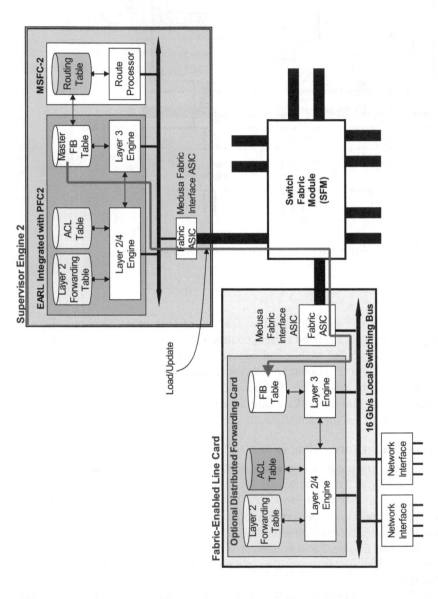

FIGURE 4.13 Multilayer Switch with Supervisor Engine 2 and the Distributed Forwarding Card (DFC).

and the distributed forwarding tables on the PFC and DFCs are immediately updated to mirror the master forwarding table.

Let us assume an Ethernet frame is received on a port on a line card with a DFC and requires forwarding at Layer 3. The Layer 3 forwarding engine on the DFC uses the destination IP address of the packet carried within the Ethernet frame to perform a lookup in the local distributed forwarding table. The lookup produces the next-hop address and egress (i.e., destination) port and the packet is forwarded as follows:

- If the DFC determines that the egress port is a local port within the same line card, the Layer 3 forwarding engine rewrites the MAC addresses in the outgoing Ethernet frame (in addition to other IP forwarding tasks) and forwards the frame out that local egress port.
- If the DFC determines that the egress port is located on another line card located across the SFM, the Layer 3 forwarding engine forwards the packet over the SFM to that line card. The source DFC prepends an internal tag to the packet that identifies the egress port on the destination line card that the frame should be forwarded out of. The tagged packet is forwarded over the SFM to the destination line card, where the local forwarding engine rewrites the MAC addresses in the outgoing frame (in addition to other IP forwarding tasks) and forwards the frame out of the identified egress port.

The earlier forwarding process of packets by the source DFC across the SFM to the destination line card is done without requiring any forwarding intervention by the Layer 3 forwarding engine on PFC2 (in the Supervisor Engine 2).

4.6   PACKET FLOW IN THE CATALYST 6500

In this section, we describe the packet forwarding process in the Catalyst 6500 with the following modules installed:

- SFM and fabric-enabled line cards (without DFCs) with centralized forwarding in the Supervisor Engine 2 (similar to the architecture in Figure 4.1)
- SFM and fabric-only line cards with embedded DFCs that allow for distributed forwarding in the line cards (similar to the architecture in Figure 4.2).

4.6.1   PACKET FLOW IN THE CATALYST 6500 WITH CENTRALIZED FORWARDING

This section describes the packet forwarding process through the Catalyst 6500 with an SFM and fabric-enabled line cards without DFCs [CISCCAT6000]. Figure 4.14 to Figure 4.15 describe the steps involved in the packet forwarding

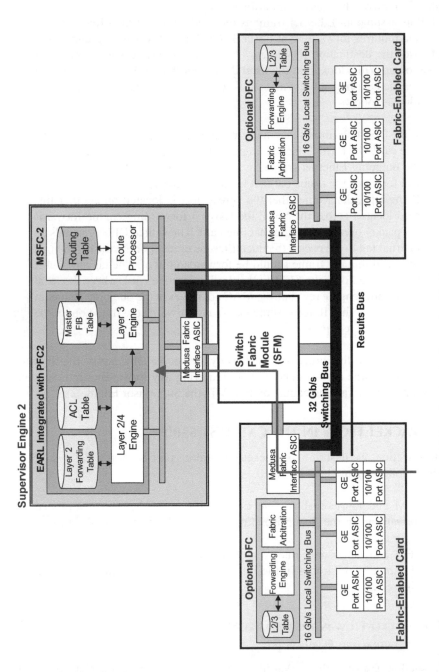

FIGURE 4.14   Step 1: Packet Enters the Switch and Packet Lookup by Supervisor Engine.

process using a routing protocol maintained (or topology-based) forwarding table in the PFC2.

Step 1a (Figure 4.14)—Packet enters the switch/router through a port on a line card:

- A packet enters a port on a line card and is passed to the PINNACLE ASIC on the port, and is temporarily stored in its receive (RX) buffer [CISCCAT6000]. The PINNACLE ASIC provides the functions for Gigabit Ethernet connectivity on a port connected to an Ethernet network.
- The packet is held in the RX buffer while the PINNACLE ASIC arbitrates for access to the local 16 Gb/s shared switching bus on the line card. Each PINNACLE ASIC has a local arbitration mechanism that allows each port to request for access to the 16 Gb/s shared switching bus. The local arbitration mechanism communicates with the central arbitration mechanism on the line card, which then determines when each local arbitration mechanism is allowed to transmit packets on the shared switching bus.
- Upon gaining access to the local 16 Gb/s shared switching bus, the packet is transmitted on the shared bus and all ports on the local bus including the local Medusa ASIC sense the transmission.
- While the packet is being transmitted on the local 16 Gb/s shared switching bus, the packet header information required for the forwarding table lookup process is retrieved by the Medusa ASIC.
- The header information is compressed by the Medusa ASIC, and transmitted across the 32 Gb/s shared switching bus to the PFC2 on the Supervisor Engine.
- As the header information travels along the 32 Gb/s shared switching bus, all the Medusa ASICs on all the other line cards including the Supervisor Engine 2 sense the transmitted information and copy it.

Step 1b (Figure 4.14)—Packet IP destination address lookup performed by Supervisor Engine 2:

- The compressed packet header information sent by the source Medusa ASIC is received by the PFC2 in the Supervisor Engine 2, which contains the Layer 2/4 and 3 forwarding engines and their associated lookup tables. The PFC2 decompresses the header information ready for use.
- The Layer 2/4 forwarding engine in the PFC2 references its Layer 2 forwarding table to determine if Layer 2 forwarding is required. If the packet is destined to a station located in the same VLAN as the source station served by the switch, then Layer 2 forwarding is carried out.

- However, if the Layer 2 destination address in the packet is the MSFC2's registered MAC address (i.e., the MSFC2 is the default gateway), then Layer 3 forwarding is required.
    - If the packet requires Layer 3 forwarding, the IP header information is used by the Layer 3 forwarding engine to perform a lookup in the forwarding table maintained by the PFC2. The PFC2's FIB is an exact copy of the master table maintained by the MSFC2.
    - The Layer 3 forwarding engine uses the packet's destination IP address to perform a lookup in its FIB to determine the next-hop IP address, outbound port, and VLAN of the packet.
- The PFC2 then transmits the discovered forwarding information across the Results Bus, which is sensed once again by all the Medusa ASICs on the line cards. The Medusa ASICs that are not the intended destination flush the packet header information previously sent from their buffers.

Step 2 (Figure 4.15)—Forwarding the packet from the switch/router to the network:

- Following the forwarding table lookup process by the Supervisor Engine 2, the source line card is now informed of the destination of the packet.
- The source line card, through its Medusa ASIC (i.e., the crossbar switch fabric interface), prepends an internal switching tag (which specifies the destination line card) to the packet, and transmits the packet into the SFM.
- The SFM, using the internal switching tag, forwards the frame to the specified destination line card.
- The forwarding information previously transmitted on the Results Bus by the PFC2 indicates to the destination line card the local destination port (or ports in the case of multicast traffic) to forward the packet out of. The forwarding results include the outgoing Ethernet frame MAC address rewrite information, and QoS classifications and queuing instructions for the destination port.
- The destination line card performs on the received packet all the MAC address rewrite operations (plus other IP forwarding operations). The packet is then queued at the destination port according to the QoS instructions, and a traffic scheduler (e.g., Weighted Round-Robin (WRR) scheduler) then schedules the frame out of the port into the network.

4.6.2   PACKET FLOW IN THE CATALYST 6500 WITH DISTRIBUTED FORWARDING

This section describes the packet forwarding process through the Catalyst 6500 with an SFM and fabric-only line cards with embedded DFCs [CISCCAT6000] [CISCSE1A2DS]. The forwarding steps are described in Figure 4.16 to Figure 4.20.

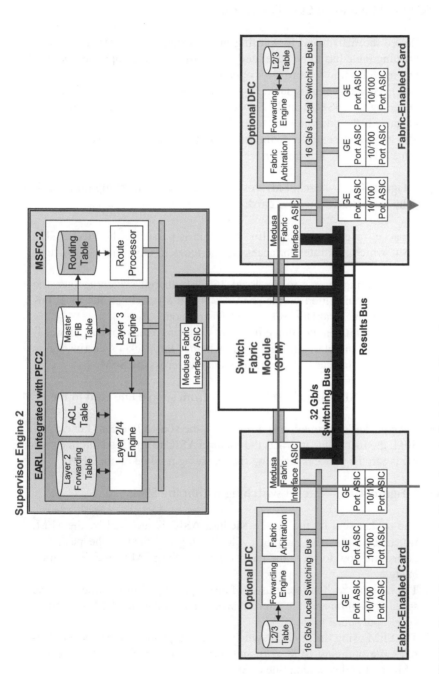

FIGURE 4.15 Step 2: Forwarding the Packet from the Switch to the Network.

Step 1 (Figure 4.16)— The master forwarding table is downloaded from MSFC2 to PFC2 and DFCs in line cards:

*   Before the distributed forwarding process takes place, the master forwarding table has to be generated by the MSFC2 and copied to the system modules that require it for operation.
*   The master forwarding table is generated from the routing table maintained by the MSFC2 on the Supervisor Engine 2. This master forwarding table is then downloaded to the PFC2 and the DFCs on the line cards. The local and centrally maintained master forwarding tables have the same forwarding information.

Step 2 (Figure 4.17)—Packet arrives at a port and forwarding table lookup is done by the DFC in the line card:

*   A packet enters a port on a line card and is passed to the PINNACLE ASIC which arbitrates for access to the local 16 Gb/s shared switching bus.
*   Upon gaining access to the local 16 Gb/s shared switching bus, the packet is transmitted on the shared bus and all ports on the local bus including the local DFC sense the transmission.
*   The local DFC on the source line card performs a lookup in its forwarding table it maintains to determine whether the packet's destination is local to the line card or another destination across the SFM.

Step 3 (Figure 4.18)—Switching the packet from source line card to the SFM:

*   If the packet's destination is not local to the source line card but across the SFM, the local DFC instructs the Medusa ASIC to attach an internal switching tag to the packet specifying the receiving module on the SFM.

Step 4 (Figure 4.19)—Packet switching within the SFM:

*   The packet sent by the source Medusa ASIC is received by the SFM, which examines the internal switching tag attached to the packet to determine how to route the packet through the SFM to the destination module.
*   The crossbar switch fabric uses a fabric speedup of three times the line speed, which means, the internal switching is done at 24 Gb/s for the 8 Gb/s input speed to the SFM.
*   The SFM using the internal switching tag prepended to the packet identifies the outgoing SFM port and forwards the packet to the Medusa ASIC on the destination line card.

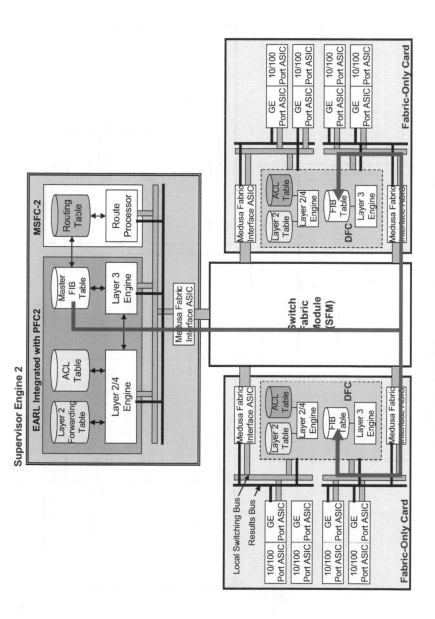

FIGURE 4.16   Step 1: Downloading the Distributed Forwarding Table from MSFC to PFC2, DFC, and Line Cards.

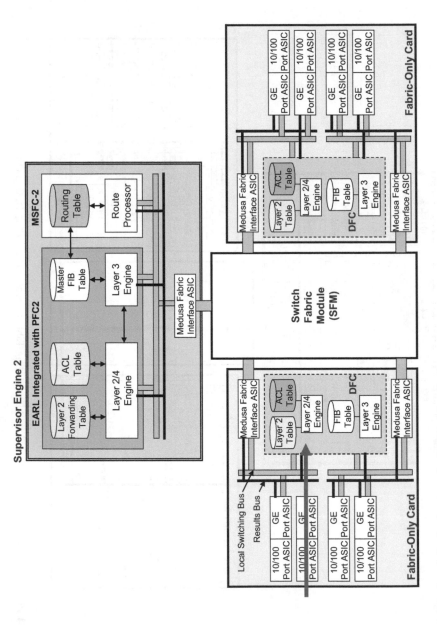

FIGURE 4.17   Step 2: Packet Lookups by DFC in Line Card.

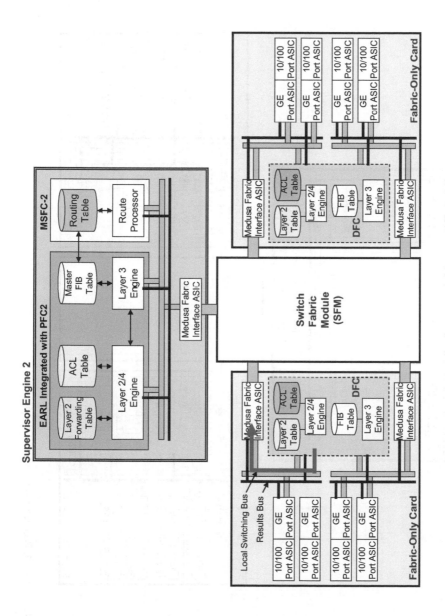

FIGURE 4.18   Step 3: Switching the Packet from Line Card to the SFM.

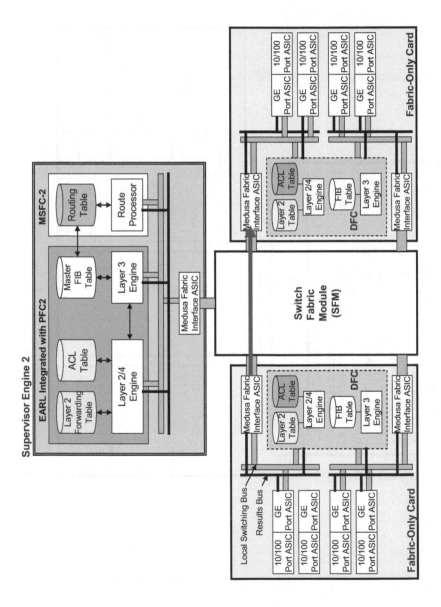

FIGURE 4.19   Step 4: Packet Switching in the SFM.

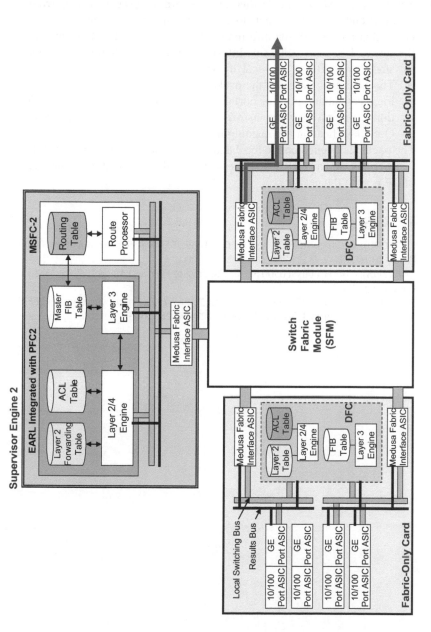

FIGURE 4.20   Step 5: Switching the Frame to the Outbound Port.

Step 5 (Figure 4.20)—Forwarding the packet to the outbound port:

- The Medusa ASIC on the destination line card receives the packet from the SFM and transmits it on its local 16 Gb/s shared switching bus.
- Given that the forwarding information has already been determined by the source line card DFC, this information is transmitted on the Data Bus and Results Bus of the local 16 Gb/s shared switching bus.
  - The Data Bus transmits the packet while the Results Bus specifies the local destination port (or ports in the case of multicast traffic) in addition to other forwarding instructions such as MAC address rewrites and QoS classification and queuing information.
- The packet is queued on the local destination port according to the QoS instructions, and a WRR scheduler is then used to transmit the frame out of the port to the network.

REFERENCES

[CISCCAT6000]. Cisco Systems, Catalyst 6000 and 6500 Series Architecture, White Paper, 2001.
[CISCSE1A2DS]. Cisco Catalyst 6500 Series Supervisor Engine 1A and 2, Cisco Systems, Data Sheet, 2004.
[MENJUS2003]. J. Menga, "Layer 3 Switching," *CCNP Practical Studies: Switching (CCNP Self-Study)* by J. Menga, Ciscopress, Nov. 26, 2003.

5 Avaya P580 and P882 Routing Switch Architecture with 80-Series Media Module

5.1 INTRODUCTION

This chapter describes the architecture of the Avaya P580 and P882 switch/routers with the 80-series media modules [AVAYA80S]. The 80-series media cards are line cards with multilayer switching capabilities. The P580 and P882 are part of the Canjun family of Avaya switches [LUCCAJWP]. The discussion in this chapter presents, in addition, an overview of the Quality of Service (QoS) capabilities of the Avaya 80-series media module.

Based on the architecture categories described in *Chapter 3*, the architecture discussed here falls under "Architectures with Crossbar-Based Switch Fabrics and Distributed Forwarding Engines" (see Figure 5.1).

5.2 BASIC ARCHITECTURE

The P580 switch/router supports a rack-mount chassis with 6 media module slots, while the P882 has a rack-mount chassis with 16 slots. Both models support a wide variety of line card module types with network interfaces that include 10/100BASE-T, 100BASE-FX, Gigabit Ethernet over Copper, Gigabit Ethernet over Fiber, as well as, ATM OC3/OC12 and 10 Gigabit Ethernet. These switch/routers support, in addition, crossbar switch fabrics (with spare crossbar switch fabrics), crossbar switch fabric controllers, power supplies, and cooling fans which can all be configured for N+1 redundancy. Both models can support a maximum port density of 48 10/100BASE-T ports per line card module.

The Avaya P580/P882 switch/routers with 80-series media modules support a switch fabric that can be classified as input/output buffered crossbar switch with fabric speedup to avoid head-of-line (HOL) blocking at the input ports as illustrated in Figure 5.2. Figure 5.3 shows a simplified view of the packet flow through a Gigabit Ethernet port in the Avaya P580/P882 switch/routers. The packet flow through the 10/100 Mb/s Ethernet, ATM, and WAN ports, although slightly different, has the same core processing elements as in the Gigabit Ethernet port.

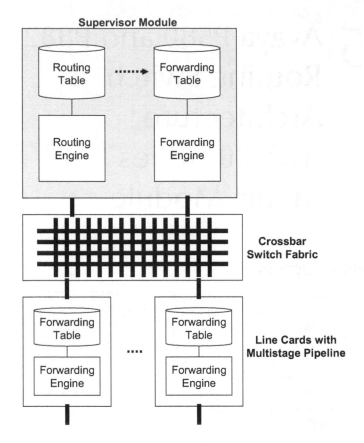

FIGURE 5.1   Architectures with Crossbar-Based Switch Fabrics and Distributed Forwarding Engines.

The Avaya 80-series media module supports packet classification at Layer 1 (otherwise referred to as physical port level classification), Layer 2, Layer 3, and Layer 4. The 80-series modules support queue prioritization and bandwidth management, in addition, to other QoS features. The modules allow for the configuration of a number of QoS capabilities such as the definition of different packet discard behaviors during congestion, traffic shaping (with configurable burst sizes and traffic rates), and buffer allocation (with configurable minimum and maximum sizes), to allow for the control of system resources usage and data transfer latencies.

5.3   DATA FLOW THROUGH THE AVAYA 80-SERIES SWITCH

In the Avaya 80-series architecture, each Gigabit Ethernet port supports a forwarding engine ASIC as shown in Figure 5.2. Each forwarding engine ASIC in turn is responsible for processing traffic from multiple 10/100 Mb/s Ethernet ports. Ethernet frames that arrive at the switch/router port from the network (at

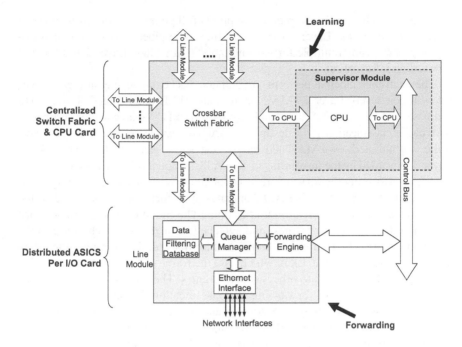

FIGURE 5.2   Basic Architecture of Avaya Canjun Family of Switches.

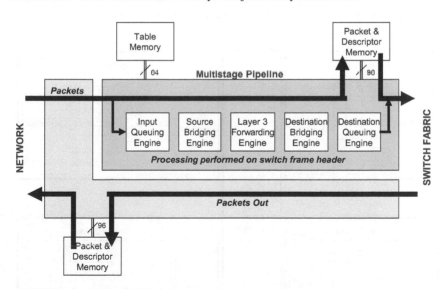

FIGURE 5.3   Gigabit Ethernet Port Architecture.

wire speed of up to 1 Gb/s) are stored by the forwarding engine ASIC in an input buffer.

While an arriving Ethernet frame is being stored, the forwarding engine ASIC examines the frame header using a parallel multistage pipeline as shown in Figure 5.3. The multistage pipeline supports full general feature forwarding at Layer 2, Layer 3, and Layer 2 the second time. The pipeline performs forwarding of packets using multiple forwarding tables that include Layer 2 and Layer 3 forwarding information.

The multistage pipeline performs, in addition, packet processing at Layer 1 (i.e., physical port level), Layer 2 (MAC address and IEEE 802.1Q tags), Layer 3 (IP addresses and DiffServ/ToS tags), and Layer 4 (UDP/TCP source and/or destination port) packet classification. If the destination MAC address of a received Ethernet frame is the switch/router's own MAC address (i.e., the default gateway), then the packet is Layer 3 forwarded by the forwarding engine ASIC, if not, it is Layer 2 forwarded.

After performing the forwarding table lookup to retrieve the forwarding information, the forwarding engine ASIC appends the information about the destination port and traffic classification to the frame. The frame is then assigned to one of eight traffic classes (or queues) and switched through the switch fabric to the destination port. The frame may be marked for discard, for example, filtered by an Access Control List (ACL), in which case the frame is discarded and its buffer reclaimed and reallocated to other arriving frames. The forwarding engine ASIC is capable of making all forwarding and classification decisions at wire speed (i.e., completing forwarding table lookup and packet classification) prior to the frame being completely received into the input buffer [AVAYA80S].

After the frame is fully classified and assigned to one of the eight input queues, it is then forwarded through the switch fabric to one of eight output queues at the destination port (Figure 5.4). The speed of the crossbar switch fabric (i.e.,

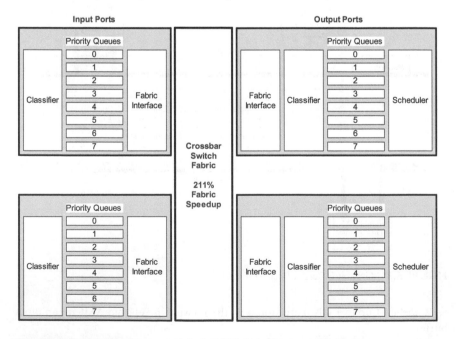

FIGURE 5.4   Priority Queues and Switch Fabric in the Avaya 80-Series.

the fabric speedup) is 211% of the speed of the fastest input port [AVAYA80S]. When crossbar switch fabric contention occurs, packet forwarding is based on the priority of the packet's traffic class (carried in its appended traffic classification information). A multicast frame is sent to multiple output ports in a single cross-bar switch fabric scheduling cycle. This is because the crossbar switch fabric is capable of replicating a packet from one input port to multiple output ports.

A frame queued in one of the eight output queues at a port is transmitted out the port into the network using a variety of scheduling policies. These scheduling policies can be configured through a command line interface (CLI), an internal Web interface of the switch/router, or a policy management system that comes with the switch/router. Traffic in each of the eight queues at a port can be prioritized, and assigned minimum and/or maximum bandwidth.

The traffic in each queue can also be metered, shaped, and marked for Packet Loss Priority (PLP). Generally, the switch/router can be configured to manage traffic to accomplish a wide range of traffic management objectives. When output queue congestion occurs, frames can be dropped using a number of discard policies that include Tail-End Drop or Weighted Random Early Detection (WRED) congestion management mechanisms.

5.4   QUALITY OF SERVICE (QOS) MECHANISMS

The Avaya 80-series family support a number of configuration options that allow for network traffic to be classified at Layers 1 (physical port level), 2, 3, and 4, at line speed. As noted earlier, Layer 1 classification refers to physical port level classification where traffic from different switch/router ports is classified and prioritized. For example, Port 1 may be carrying traffic from a video source or server while Port 2 may be carrying traffic from an email or Web server. Once classified, the arriving packets can be assigned to one of eight traffic queues (classes), each scheduled for transmission by a traffic scheduling mechanism. The various QoS mechanisms supported by the Avaya 80-series switch are described in this section.

5.4.1   CLASSIFICATION PRECEDENCE

As discussed earlier, an arriving Ethernet frame is processed at Layer 1 (physical port level) as part of the classification process, then examined for Layer 2 forwarding (if required), examined for Layer 3 forwarding, and finally processed for Layer 2 forwarding (e.g., VLAN related processing). During the forwarding process of the incoming frame, a number of the processing steps involve explicit classification of the frame (and fields in its payload).

The traffic class information derived from the incoming frame is either in an IEEE 802.1Q or DiffServ/ToS tag in the frame, or classification information derived from a configured or default classification setting such as the setting of the ingress switch/router port or a default Differentiated Services Code Point (DSCP) setting. The switch/router may also use implicit classification where the classification information is derived from certain fields within the frame including its contents. Irrespective of whether the classification is explicit or implicit, the classification process is done stateless, meaning each frame is classified independently of previous or succeeding frames.

The traffic classification precedence for frames flowing through the Avaya 80-series switch/router is presented in Table 1. To determine which of eight traffic queues (classes) a frame will be assigned, the traffic classification is guided by considering entries higher in Table 1 as taking precedence over entries lower in the table.

This classification precedence table can be conceptually viewed in the same light as an IP Longest Prefix Match routing table, in that the highest precedence (i.e., the entry at the top of the table) that matches the classification markers in a frame take precedence and determines which traffic class the frame is assigned. The classification of traffic through the switch/router may consist of the following nine steps (also numbered in Table 1):

- **Classification Steps 1–3**: During traffic classification, IEEE 802.1Q tagging (Classification 2 in Table 1) takes precedence over other tagging mechanisms such as Cisco Inter-Switch Link (ISL) (Classification 1). If the switch/router port, however, is configured to ignore incoming frames with Layer 2 tags, or if the incoming frames are untagged, then the port's configured default priority (Classification 3) takes precedence over any untagged classification and prioritization. ISL is a Cisco proprietary protocol for encapsulating Ethernet frames with their corresponding VLAN information.
- **Classification Steps 4–7**: For classification and prioritization at Layer 2, any Layer 2 prioritization (e.g., based on the Layer 2 source address of frames (Classification 4 and 5)) configured in the ingress Layer 2 forwarding table (MAC address table) takes precedence over any default

---

TABLE 5.1
Classification Precedence Table

Classification	Traffic Class Taken From
9. Layer 3/4 Access List Entry	Layer 3 is Default Priority
8. DSCP Value in IP Header	Priority from DS (DiffServ) Table Lookup
7. Layer 2 Destination Address Max Class	Maximum Allowed Layer 2 outgoing Class
6. Layer 2 Destination Address	Layer 2 Address Table (outgoing)
5. Layer 2 Source Address Max Class	Maximum Allowed Layer 2 incoming Class
4. Layer 2 Source Address	Layer 2 Address Table (incoming)
3. Physical Port Priority Override	Physical Port Default Priority
2. IEEE 802.1Q	IEEE 802.1Q priority
1. Cisco ISL or 3Com Pace Tags	Tag Priority

Source: Note: DiffServ Field Overrides (e.g., remarking) and DiffServ Field Masking omitted in this table (which are used to determine the DSCP used to lookup the priority in the DiffServ Mapping Table only).

port prioritization (Classification 3) or tagged frame prioritization (Classification 2). Egress Layer 2 classification and prioritization in the output Layer 2 forwarding table or address table (Classification 6 and 7) takes precedence over Layer 2 classification and prioritization performed earlier on the frame (if any).

- **Classification Steps 8–9**: Finally, classification and prioritization at Layer 3 (Classification 8 and 9) always takes precedence over Layer 2 (Classification 4 to 7). This holds regardless of what parameters within the packets are used in the Layer 3 classification. This classification case includes the five-tuple Layer 3 parameters (source/destination IP addresses, UDP/TCP protocol, source/destination port numbers) and Layer 4 ACL specifications in the Layer 3/Layer 4 packet flow. For IP routing purposes, the Layer 3/Layer 4 flow filter configured in the switch/router may simply be determined by the Layer 3 destination address used during the IP forwarding table lookup process or the filter may be taken from a Diffserv (DS) override/rewrite designed to override/rewrite all Layer 2 default classifications.

The resulting effect of the earlier classification and prioritization process in the switch/router is that the system can map virtually an infinite number of flows (via per-flow classification) into any one of the eight traffic priorities or classes. These eight traffic priorities or classes are then mapped to eight queues implemented in hardware (ASICs) in the switch.

5.4.2 DiffServ Mapping Table

Each Gigabit Ethernet port, as well as each set of twelve 10 Mb/s Ethernet ports is given its own local forwarding engine ASIC (engine). The forwarding engine ASIC also supports a DiffServ mapping table which it uses to map the result of a DiffServ/ToS field lookup in a packet to one of the eight queues on the forwarding path. The index in the mapping table is the DSCP value which in turn corresponds to a user-configured queue. This allows for mapping packets carrying a specific DSCP value to one queue within the eight priority queues. This mapping mechanism also allows for the PLP of packets to be configured.

A user can configure each forwarding engine ASIC in the switch/router to have different values in its DiffServ mapping table; however, for consistent operation in the switch/router, the management software allows the user to configure one global DiffServ mapping table for the entire switch/router. Once configured, the global mapping table is loaded, at system boot time, to each forwarding engine ASIC in the switch/router.

Any future updates and changes to the global mapping table made (through the user system management interface) is always reflected in each forwarding engine ASIC in the switch/router. The system management software supports a user interface that can be used for setting the entries in the global mapping table. The default PLP setting of each entry is a PLP of 0. By default, the queue mapping in the mapping

TABLE 5.2
Diffserv Mapping Table

DSCP Values	IEEE 802.1p/Q Priority	Default Queue
56–63	7	7
48–55	6	6
40–47	5	5
32–39	4	4
24–31	3	3
16–23	2	2
8–15	1	1
0–7	0	0

table for each DSCP value in a packet is (DSCP÷8); the remainder ignored. Table 2 shows an example DiffServ mapping table for the Avaya 80-series switch/router.

5.4.3 QUEUING AND SCHEDULING

The 80-series line card modules support up to eight input queues and eight output queues at each switch/router port. The queues in the switch/router are implemented in hardware at each port, but queuing policies (or behavior) on a system-wide basis, can be configured via the CLI, built-in Web interface, or system management software interface. The switch/router supports a default queuing behavior (i.e., default configuration); however, in some cases, the user may configure a particular queuing policy to suit the requirements of particular user application or a traffic class.

The switch/router supports two basic queuing policies, Weighted Fair Queuing (WFQ) and Strict Priority, in addition to two more complex queuing policies. In Strict Priority, the highest priority queue (Queue 7) is allowed to transmit all its packets before the next lower queue (Queue 6) is allowed to, and so on. The default configured queuing policy in the 80-series modules is WFQ.

5.4.4 TRAFFIC MANAGEMENT

The Avaya 80-series line card modules have additional traffic management algorithms (implemented on a per queue basis) to improve overall network performance and the QoS of user traffic. These traffic management mechanisms include:

- **Packet discard**: Tail-End Drop or WRED discard policy can be configured per queue
- **Queue size**: Each queue can be configured to have a minimum and maximum size
- **Traffic shaping**: Each queue has mechanisms for metering and controlling traffic flow and traffic burst sizes

A FIFO (First-In First-Out) queue will normally drop packets when the queue becomes full. The packet drops occur, normally, at the "tail-end" of the queue. The WRED traffic discard mechanism, however, can be used to discard packets more intelligently well before the queue gets full. As the queue size builds up, WRED gradually starts to drop a higher percentage of the arriving packets. The goal of WRED is to intelligently discard packets such that the queue size will be virtually stable (yet not filled up completely), and also to avoid TCPs sources from timing out due to excessive packet drops.

The default discard policy for the 80-series modules is Tail-End Drop, and also traffic shaping is disabled. The packet discard behavior (Tail-End Drop or WRED) is configurable on a per queue basis. If Tail-End Drop is enabled in the system, then packet discard occurs only when the queue size reaches its maximum configured limit.

The configured queue size determines the behavior of the Tail-End Drop or WRED discard mechanisms. Queue size also establishes the outer limits of data transfer delay or latency and delay variations (for user traffic that is sensitive to delay variations). The larger the queue size, the more delay and delay variations that can be introduced in traffic flows; however, the more data that can be queued and not lost due to congestion.

In the 80-Series, each queue is assigned a minimum amount of dedicated system memory (implemented on a per-port basis). A common buffer memory pool is implemented for all queues on a port that is used as needed and as the queues grow and shrink. Freed-up memory is returned to the common unused buffer memory pool as queues empty up.

In addition, each queue is configured with a maximum limit on the memory pool it can use. The maximum queue size for the higher priority queues

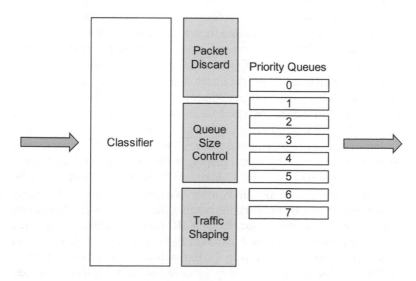

FIGURE 5.5   Traffic Management Mechanisms in the Avaya 80-Series.

is configured to be smaller than that for the lowest (best-effort) queue. This is because high priority traffic tends to be sensitive to delay variations and is better discarded than delivered to the end user late due to network congestion and excessive queuing.

The higher priority queues (Queue 4 to Queue 7 in Table 2) are suitable for traffic sensitive to delay variations, and therefore can be configured with relatively small maximum queue sizes. The default configuration for the Avaya 80-series is relatively small buffer allocations for the high priority queues (4 to 7), which are assumed to be delay-variation sensitive, and relatively large buffer allocations for low priority queues (0 to 3).

The switch/router also supports features that include traffic management algorithms that allow a user to configure bandwidth guarantees and limits, packet discard behaviors, and shaping of traffic exceeding its configured guarantees. The bandwidth guarantees and limits define which packets within a flow conform to or exceed the configured traffic rates and are typically based on the following three parameters:

- **Average Traffic Rate (bits per second)**: The Average Traffic Rate is sometimes referred to as the Committed Information Rate (CIR). This parameter defines the long-term average rate of a flow at a measurement point. Traffic flow that falls below the average rate is deemed conformant and is guaranteed to be forwarded (provided any higher priority traffic on the port under consideration is idle).
- **Normal Burst Size (bytes)**: The Normal Burst Size, also called the Committed Burst Size (CBS), defines how large back-to-back data (that is, traffic burst) can be before the average traffic rate limit is exceeded. Traffic bursts generated up to the Normal Burst Size are guaranteed to be forwarded. The Normal Burst Size is the amount of back-to-back data (in bytes) that can be transmitted from a queue when the traffic is being shaped at the CIR, that is, when the short-term traffic rate from that queue meets or exceeds the CIR. Once the "normal" amount or burst of traffic has been transmitted, the queue stops transmitting data until once again it can send a burst of data without exceeding its CIR.
- **Maximum Burst Size (bytes)**: Maximum Burst Size (or Excess Burst Size (EBS)) defines the maximum amount of back-to-back data (i.e., traffic burst) that can be transmitted before all traffic exceeds the bandwidth guarantee (i.e., the CIR). When shaping at the CIR is applied to a queue, no traffic burst will exceed the Maximum Burst Size without the traffic scheduler having the opportunity to service another queue in the system. Traffic bursts that are between the Normal Burst Size and the Maximum Burst Size are deemed to exceed the CIR, (the guaranteed traffic rate). Traffic sent in excess of the Maximum Burst Size will be forwarded on a best-effort basis and compete for transmission with other best-effort traffic. The Maximum Burst Size is enabled in the switch/router by setting the Maximum Burst Size parameter greater than the Normal Burst

Size. When the Maximum Burst Size is set equal to the Normal Burst Size, then the maximum traffic bursting capability is disabled in the system. The user can control how much data can be transmitted back-to-back at any particular time by appropriately configuring the Normal and Maximum Burst Size parameters. The CIR, CBS, and EBS capabilities for rate and burst limit control can be implemented using the Two-Rate-Three-Color Rate policer [RFC2698] [RFC4115].

5.4.5 IEEE 802.1p/Q and DSCP or ToS Standards in the Avaya 80-Series

This section discusses the implementations of the IEEE 802.1p/Q, DSCP and ToS-related QoS mechanisms in the Avaya 80-series.

5.4.5.1 DiffServ's Per-Hop Behaviors (PHB)

The Avaya 80-series supports all of the DiffServ's PHB as specified in the relevant IETF standards [AVAYA80S]. The PHB supported include the Default PHB, Class Selector (CS) PHBs, Assured Forwarding (AF) PHBs and the Expedited Forwarding (EF) PHBs. The DSCPs for the PHBs are as follows:

- Assured Forwarding PHB consists of 12 DSCP as shown in Figure 5.4
- Expedited Forwarding PHB DSCP: 101110
- Default PHB DSCP: 000000.

In addition to defining the Diffserv field in the IPv4 and IPv6 headers, [RFC2474] also defines the Class Selector code points. These code points are the first three bits (i.e., the leftmost) 3 bits of the DSCP, which also correspond to the IP Precedence field in the old IP ToS field. These code points (xxx000) correspond to the first 3 bits and with the 3 rightmost bits all set to 0. The 3 bits result in 8 Class Selector PHBs. These 8 PHBs are the following 8 code point values (which are mapped to the 8 priority queues in the Avaya 80-series):

- DSCP 000000 (Class Selector 0) maps to Priority 0/Queue 0
- DSCP 001000 (Class Selector 1) maps to Priority 1/Queue 1
- DSCP 010000 (Class Selector 2) maps to Priority 2/Queue 2
- DSCP 011000 (Class Selector 3) maps to Priority 3/Queue 3

	Class 1	Class 2	Class 3	Class 4
Low Drop Precedence	001010	010010	011010	100010
Medium Drop Precedence	001100	010100	011100	100100
High Drop Precedence	001110	010110	011110	100110

FIGURE 5.6 The Assured Forwarding PHB.

- DSCP 100000 (Class Selector 4) maps to Priority 4/Queue 4
- DSCP 101000 (Class Selector 5) maps to Priority 5/Queue 5
- DSCP 110000 (Class Selector 6) maps to Priority 6/Queue 6
- DSCP 111000 (Class Selector 7) maps to Priority 7/Queue 7.

The Default PHB (with DSCP 000000) specifies any traffic that is not mapped to any of the other defined DiffServ PHBs. It maps to Class Selector 0 (in decimal) PHB which has code point 000000. The Class Selector code points 110xxxxx (i.e., Class Selector 6, 48 in decimal) and 111xxxxx (i.e., Class Selector 7, 56 in decimal) maintain the same meaning in IP Precedence (e.g., network control messages, route updates, etc.). These two Class Selectors map to Priority 6/Queue 6 and Priority 7/Queue 7, respectively, in the Avaya 80-series. Class Selectors 001xxxxx (Class Selector 1) through 100xxxxx (Class Selector 4) map well to the Assured Forwarding PHBs. Class Selector 101xxxxx (Class Selector 5) maps to Priority 5/Queue 5.

In the DiffServ field, the bit patterns xxxxx0 are reserved for use by the IETF and are to be used to define future standardized code points similar to the earlier IETF defined code points. Code points in the DiffServ field with bit pattern xxxx11 are reserved for experimental or local use and can be defined in whatever fashion as needed by the user. Code points with bit pattern xxxx01 are also reserved for experimental or local use; however, the IETF may reclaim these code points in the future to define other PHBs if the xxxxx0 code space runs out.

When implementing DiffServ in networks, the IETF RFCs leave the actual DiffServ code point to priority queue mapping in network devices to the user. However, the default configuration in the Avaya 80-series maps the various PHBs to the priority queues as follows [AVAYA80S]:

- Default PHB (000000) maps to Priority 0/Queue 0.
- AF PHB Class 1 (001010, 001100, 001110) maps to Priority 1/Queue 1.
- AF PHB Class 2 (010010, 010100, 010110) maps to Priority 2/Queue 2.
- AF PHB Class 3 (011010, 011100, 011110) maps to Priority 3/Queue 3.
- AF PHB Class 4 (100010, 100100, 100110) maps to Priority 4/Queue 4.
- EF PHB (101110) maps to Priority 5/Queue 5.

Priority 6/Queue 6 and Priority 7/Queue 7 are used for network control traffic such as SNMP, spanning tree, and routing protocols. The PLP is set to 0 for all Class Selector code points (Class Selector 1 to 7) except Class Selector 0. Class Selector 0 maps to Priority 0/Queue 0, which is by default set to 1.

5.4.5.2 Packet Loss Priority (PLP)

The Avaya 80-Series supports two drop precedence settings (binary 1 or 0). It supports a combined medium and high drop precedence with a default drop setting of 1 (which means packet is drop-eligible). For EF PHB, the default PLP setting is 0. For the Default PHB, the default PLP setting is 1, while the code points for Low Drop (i.e., AF 001010, AF 010010, AF 011010, AF 100010) have default PLP settings of 0.

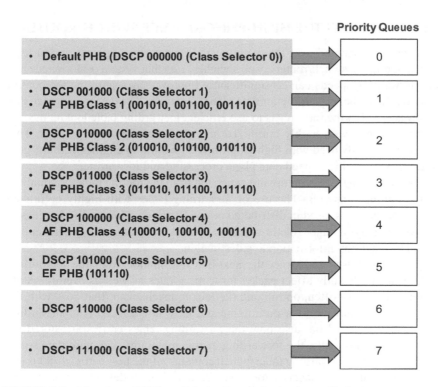

Priority Queues

- Default PHB (DSCP 000000 (Class Selector 0))   ➡ 0
- DSCP 001000 (Class Selector 1)
- AF PHB Class 1 (001010, 001100, 001110)   ➡ 1
- DSCP 010000 (Class Selector 2)
- AF PHB Class 2 (010010, 010100, 010110)   ➡ 2
- DSCP 011000 (Class Selector 3)
- AF PHB Class 3 (011010, 011100, 011110)   ➡ 3
- DSCP 100000 (Class Selector 4)
- AF PHB Class 4 (100010, 100100, 100110)   ➡ 4
- DSCP 101000 (Class Selector 5)
- EF PHB (101110)   ➡ 5
- DSCP 110000 (Class Selector 6)   ➡ 6
- DSCP 111000 (Class Selector 7)   ➡ 7

FIGURE 5.7   Mapping of PHBs to Priority Queues in the Avaya 80-Series.

TABLE 5.3
Recommended Values for IEEE 802.1p/Q, DiffServ Code Points, and Queue Mappings

Traffic Class	DSCP	802.1p/Q Tag	Queue	BW Guarantees?
Network Management	111000	7	7	No
Voice over IP	010100	5	5	Yes
Video Conferencing	010100	5	5	Maybe
One-way Video	000000	0	0	Generally not
Expedited Data	001000	1	1	Perhaps
Best-effort	000000	0	0	No

5.4.5.3   Avaya 80-Series Recommendations for IEEE 802.1p/Q, DSCP Code Point, and Queues

Table 3 gives the recommended DiffServ Code Points, IEEE 802.1p/Q, and priority queue mappings for the major traffic classes and applications along with their bandwidth guarantee requirements.

5.5 DESIGNING THE HIGH-PERFORMANCE SWITCH/ROUTER

It has been recognized over the many years of network equipment design (e.g., switches, routers, switch/routers, web switches, etc.) that system performance and data forwarding speeds can be significantly improved by separating the control functions from the forwarding (or data plane) functions. The design approach that is now adopted in the industry is to use efficient forwarding table lookup mechanisms combined with highly optimized and structured forwarding tables. This approach is mostly used with highly optimized forwarding engines with the goal of achieving very high-speed data plane processing and forwarding.

The forwarding tables in turn are generated from the routing tables maintained by the routing protocols. The use of forwarding tables with highly optimized lookup mechanisms (used in distributed or non-distributed forwarding engines in the system) plays a major role in speeding up a switch/router's or router's ability to find the next-hop information to a destination.

The method used to extract the next-hop information from the forwarding tables can significantly affect packet forwarding rates as well as overall system performance. Very often, optimizing the lookup mechanism (that goes with the forwarding engine) requires optimizing not only how the correct forwarding tables entry is found but also how the forwarding tables entries are stored for later retrieval. Typically, the forwarding engine maintains two main data structures, the Layer 3 forwarding table (which contains all the best paths to all known destinations) and an adjacency (or Layer 2) table (which defines the next-hop's Layer 2 forwarding information, e.g., Ethernet MAC address). In many cases, the adjacency information or table is implemented as part of the forwarding table.

The forwarding engine searches for the best matching (longest prefix matching) entry in the forwarding table to in order to determine the next-hop information required to forward a packet. The forwarding table is conceptually similar to a routing table that is constructed and maintained by the routing protocols. It contains a subset of the forwarding information contained in the routing table that defines the best paths to destinations.

In a typical implementation, when routing or topology changes occur in the network, the routing table is automatically updated (by the routing protocols in the control plane), and the forwarding table also updated to reflects those changes. The forwarding table maintains next-hop address information based on the information in the routing table.

Because there is a direct relationship between forwarding tables entries and routing table entries, the forwarding tables contains essentially all the information needed to forward packets. Performing forwarding operations directly in the forwarding table eliminates the need for maintaining a route/flow cache which requires maintenance as new flows arrive at the system. The preferred approach of using an optimized forwarding engine with a full topology based forwarding table means the system does not have to wait for the first packet in a flow to generate an entry in a route/flow cache to forward packets. This approach allows the system to forward traffic more efficiently.

In addition to the forwarding table, the forwarding engine uses the adjacency tables to preprocess Layer 2 addressing information. The adjacency table maintains Layer 2 next-hop addresses for all forwarding table entries. Two nodes in the network are considered adjacent if one node can reach the other over a single Layer 2 hop. The adjacency table is populated as adjacencies are discovered (via an appropriate protocol such ARP (Address Resolution Protocol) or entered manually).

Each time an adjacency is discovered by a router or switch/router (e.g., ARP), a Layer 2 address for that adjacency node is created and stored in the adjacency table. Once a best route or next-hop entry is found in the forwarding table for the packet, it points to a next-hop IP address and its corresponding adjacency (MAC) address. The Layer 2 address of the adjacency is subsequently used as the destination Layer 2 address in the outgoing Layer 2 frame that encapsulates the outgoing Layer 3 packet.

The source address in the outgoing Layer 2 frame is the Layer 2 address of the port or interface the frame is being forwarded out of. In addition to decrementing the IP time-to-live (TTL) value and recomputing the IP checksum, the Ethernet frame checksum of the outgoing frame also has to be recomputed, given that the source and destination MAC addresses have been rewritten.

There might be several routes/paths to an IP destination address, such as in the case where a router is configured for redundancy and/or simultaneous load balancing over multiple paths. In such a case, for each path, an adjacency (address) is added corresponding to the next-hop interface for that path. This multipath forwarding mechanism can be used for load balancing traffic across the several paths to a particular destination (address). In addition to using adjacencies associated with next-hop interfaces, other types of adjacencies are used to maintain forwarding operations and improve performance when certain exception conditions exist.

Using a forwarding engine directly with a full topology based forwarding table (not a route/flow cache) provides a much more powerful and efficient architecture for the design of networks that aim to deliver improved availability, performance, and scalability. Such networks also enable important services that include:

- Multiprotocol Label Switching (MPLS) with sophisticated network traffic engineering that allows for the creation of services such IP Virtual Private Networks (VPNs)
- Network monitoring and collection tools such as NetFlow and sFlow [RFC3176] that allow for gathering network statistics. sFlow and NetFlow are tools that can be used to generate detailed information on traffic flows in a network to help network operators analyze their traffic patterns and accurately plan network capacity.
- Quality of service (QoS) functions such as traffic policing, traffic shaping, WFQ, WRED and other traffic management mechanisms that help prevent one application (particularly, one generating best-effort traffic) from hogging network bandwidth and starving out other applications (particularly, ones generating real-time traffic).

The approach of using a forwarding engine with both optimized lookup mechanism and topology based forwarding table (referred to as Cisco Express Forwarding (CEF) by Cisco Systems) can be implemented in a distributed architecture where processing tasks are spread across the line cards—distributed forwarding engines (with associated forwarding tables). In the distributed forwarding architecture, the line cards maintain an identical copy of the forwarding table and adjacency information. The line cards perform local forwarding of packets, thus relieving the route processor (control plane) of direct involvement in the forwarding process.

Some distributed forwarding architectures employ shared-memory-based switch fabrics. Others architectures, targeted at higher performance and higher capacity forwarding, use crossbar switch fabrics. Typically, such (distributed forwarding) architectures use some form of inter-process communication (IPC) to ensure synchronization of the forwarding tables and adjacency tables on the line cards to those on the route processor. The system design has to ensure that that there is sufficient memory in the line cards to accommodate the size of the full distributed forwarding tables if it is to be fully equipped and self-sufficient to perform forwarding locally.

IP networks are growing ever larger and are supporting increasingly a higher mix of traffic and sophisticated services. Given this trend, and business' and society's growing reliance on IP network services, the architectures of the switches, routers, and switch/routers (and other network equipment) that make up these networks are evolving accordingly to support the higher bandwidth, low latency (delay), low delay variations, and low data loss required. These requirements have become very important performance metrics by which networks are now judged and are often driven by modern business applications and customer demands.

The design of routers and switch/routers first started with designs that use software-based forwarding. Software-based forwarding was followed by route/flow cache-based packet forwarding, then by the use of forwarding engines operating directly with optimized lookup mechanisms on topology based forwarding tables (in distributed and non-distributed architectures).

The newer forwarding engines and architectures that have emerged over time were designed with the primary goal of isolating packet forwarding functions from control plane functions, thereby improving packet delay variations, stabilizing system performance, and allowing multiple control and forwarding tasks to be run in parallel in a system. Some of these newer designs, all featuring different design philosophies, are discussed in the next chapters of the book.

REFERENCES

[AVAYA80S]. Avaya Communication, Avaya Gigabit LAN Switching—Enhanced QoS for IP Switching, 80-Series Architectural Overview: Robust Quality of Service, White Paper.

[LUCCAJWP]. Performance Optimized Ethernet Switching, Lucent Technologies, Cajun White Paper #1.

[RFC2474]. K. Nichols, S. Blake, F. Baker, and D. Black, "Definition of the Differentiated Services Field (DS Field) in the IPv4 and IPv6 Headers," IETF RFC 2474, Dec. 1998.

[RFC2698]. J. Heinanen and R. Guerin, "A Two Rate Three Color Marker," IETF RFC 2698, Sept. 1999.

[RFC3176]. InMon Corporation's sFlow: A Method for Monitoring Traffic in Switched and Routed Networks.

[RFC4115]. O. Aboul-Magd and S. Rabie, "A Differentiated Service Two-Rate, Three-Color Marker with Efficient Handling of in-Profile Traffic," IETF RFC 4115, July 2005.

6 Foundry Networks Multilayer Switches with IronCore™ Network Interface Module

6.1 INTRODUCTION

This chapter describes the switch/router architectures developed by Foundry Networks based on the company's second-generation chipset. This second-generation application-specific integrated circuit (ASIC), developed for Layer 2 and 3 forwarding, was referred to as the IronCore™ chipset [FOUNBIG04]. The JetCore™ chipset [FOUNJET03], described in the next chapter, was the third generation of Foundry Networks ASIC for Layer 2 and 3 networking products.

The IronCore™ chipset was designed to consolidate a wide variety of Layer 2 and 3 forwarding functions into a single chipset and also to allow the switch/routers to support higher port densities beyond what the older chipsets allowed. In addition, the IronCore™ chipset supported newer networking features and allowed more packet forwarding functions to be performed in hardware.

The Foundry Networks switch/routers that used these chipsets consist of the FastIron™, BigIron™, NetIron™, and TurboIron™ family of switch/routers. These devices were designed based on the IronCore and Jetcore networking chipsets and share essentially the same hardware components but are each configured with different processor capabilities to perform different functions in a network. The newer lines of Foundry switch/routers used the newer JetCore architecture which allowed them to deliver additional networking features to the end user.

According to the architecture categories outlined in *Chapter 3*, the multilayer switches designed based on the IronCore architecture fall under "Architectures with Crossbar-based Switch Fabrics and Distributed Forwarding Engines with Flow/Route Caches" (see Figure 6.1).

6.2 SWITCH CHASSIS OVERVIEW

The Foundry switch/routers include the following devices:

- FastIron: This series of switch/routers targets Layer 2/Layer 3 forwarding in enterprise networks.

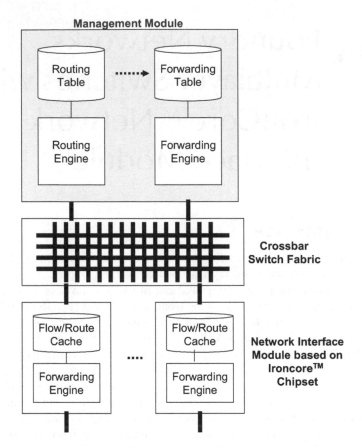

FIGURE 6.1 Architectures with Crossbar-based Switch Fabrics and Distributed Forwarding Engines with Flow/Route Caches—Network Interface Modules with IronCore™ Chipset.

- BigIron: This series of switch/routers targets Layer 2/Layer 3 forwarding in data centers and server farms as well as large campus networks.
- NetIron: This series of switch/routers targets Layer 2/Layer 3 and MPLS forwarding in service providers, and wide area network backbones.
- TurboIron: This series of switch/routers has the same Layer 2/Layer 3 forwarding capabilities as NetIron, except that it differs in the type of network interfaces supported. TurboIron supports Gigabit Ethernet interfaces on all ports.

The earlier systems come in three chassis configurations:

- 4-slot chassis—4 payload slots, hot-swappable network interface modules, redundant management modules with high-availability failover, hot-swappable redundant power supplies (total of 2 power supply modules), temperature sensors to allow for chassis temperature monitoring

- 8-slot chassis—8 payload slots, hot-swappable network interface modules, redundant management modules with high-availability failover, hot-swappable redundant power supplies (total of 4 power supply modules), temperature sensors to allow for chassis temperature monitoring
- 15-slot chassis—15 payload slots, hot-swappable network interface modules, redundant management modules with high-availability failover, hot-swappable fan tray, hot-swappable redundant power supplies (N+1 redundancy), temperature sensors to allow for chassis temperature monitoring.

All of the earlier switch/routers are based on a distributed forwarding architecture. The systems employ the Foundry chipsets to provide wire-speed, higher capacity non-blocking packet forwarding with very low data forwarding latencies. To allow for high-speed forwarding, the packet forwarding functions are distributed to the network interface modules to allow them to forward packets locally. Each network interface module supports locally a forwarding engine, buffers for priority queuing, and a local (internal) switch fabric.

This architecture equips the switch/router with an efficient mechanism to forward packets in a non-blocking fashion directly between the individual network interface modules. The interface modules employ high-bandwidth components— shared memory, shared-memory switch fabric, crossbar switch fabric interface, packet classifier, etc.—which are capable of handling traffic from all the physical ports on the module.

The BigIron series of switch/routers, for example, consists of the BigIron 4000 with a 4-slot chassis, the BigIron 8000 with an 8-slot chassis, and BigIron 15000 with a 15-slot chassis. In a chassis that is fully populated with line cards and other necessary operational components, the BigIron 4000, BigIron 8000, BigIron 15000 chassis delivers 128 Gb/s, 256 Gb/s, and 480 Gb/s, respectively, of total switching capacity.

6.3   CHASSIS CROSSBAR SWITCH FABRIC

At the core of all the Foundry switch/routers is a main chassis crossbar switch fabric. The chassis crossbar switch fabric allows the switch/router to provide high-speed non-blocking data transfer between the network interface modules in the system. The chassis crossbar switch fabric for the 8-slot BigIron 8000 switch/router is illustrated in Figure 6.2. The 4- and 15-slot chassis have a similar architecture but each with different numbers of slot, internal paths, and overall switch fabric bandwidth.

The chassis crossbar switch fabric allows connectivity from each network interface in a slot to every other interface module (slot) in the chassis. As illustrated in Figure 6.2, the crossbar switch fabric provides fully meshed connectivity to all slots which allows for parallel packet flows between the network interface modules. This allows for multiple parallel or simultaneous data flows between the network interface modules without any one module having to arbitrate for a switch fabric path for data transfers, or path allocation to be controlled by a

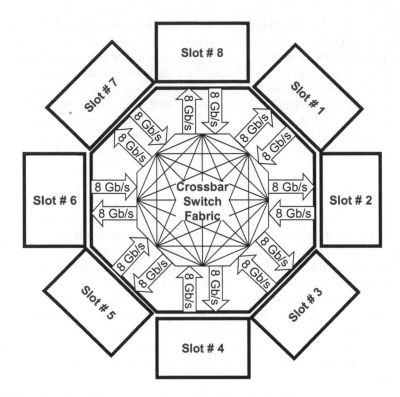

FIGURE 6.2   Chassis Crossbar Switch Fabric for an 8-Slot Chassis.

single control mechanism. This architecture effectively avoids blocking within the switch fabric.

Another benefit of employing a crossbar switch fabric is that there is no need to deliberately reserve points or paths within the switch fabric to accommodate specific functions such as a system control or management module (which can also reduce the overall bandwidth of a switch fabric). This flexibility allows for control and management modules to be inserted into any available chassis slot without the need to have a chassis slot allocation plan pre-determined.

The crossbar switch fabric of the Foundry switch/router is provisioned with enough bandwidth to serve all interface module slots without any blocking when all modules are active simultaneously and operating at full line speed. As illustrated in Figure 6.2, the switch fabric allocates to each interface slot an 8 Gb/s transmit channel, and 8 Gb/s receive channel. The chassis crossbar switch fabric has full duplex 8 Gb/s bandwidth to each interface module slot.

The switch/router supports multiple quality of service (QoS) queues on each interface module and within the crossbar switch fabric to ensure that prioritized traffic flows from the source module to their destinations without incurring blocking and data loss (caused by lower priority traffic). The use of the traditional single first-in first-out (FIFO) queuing approach at the input ports of the crossbar switch always results in head-of-line (HOL) blocking.

To avoid HOL blocking, packets at the input side of the crossbar switch fabric are queued in separate queues according to their destination network interface modules (or slots). This technique is known as Virtual Output Queuing (VOQ) and has become an effective and practical way of eliminating HOL blocking in switch fabrics that use single FIFO queues at their input ports.

HOL blocking occurs when a single FIFO queue is used at the input ports of a switch fabric. HOL blocking occurs when a packet in the input FIFO queue has a clear path (i.e., channel and bandwidth available) to its destination but cannot be sent there because a packet ahead of it (i.e., at the front of the queue) has not yet been forwarded to its destination. This results in the packet at the front of the queue (still waiting to be forwarded to its destination) blocking the other packets behind it, regardless of whether they have clear paths to their destinations during that scheduling time cycle.

HOL blocking significantly reduces the overall data transfer throughput of the switch fabric even if the switch fabric has ample bandwidth available for the offered traffic load. Even when subjected to traffic with Bernoulli arrivals, HOL blocking can reduce the throughput of a switch fabric to 59% [KAROLM92]. VOQ eliminates HOQ blocking, and when used with intelligent scheduling algorithms, could boost switch fabric data transfer throughput to 100% of the switch fabric bandwidth [MCKEOWN96].

With VOQ, the crossbar switch fabric supports multiple queues at its input port, each queue holding packets for a given output end of the fabric. This eliminates HOL blocking because a packet at the front of a VOQ queue that cannot be forwarded to its destination during a scheduling time cycle (maybe because there is not yet a clear path to that destination), would not block other packets in the other VOQ queues that have clear paths to their destinations.

6.4   IRONCORE™ NETWORK INTERFACE MODULE ARCHITECTURE

This section describes the high-level architecture of the network interface modules based on the second generation IronCore chipset [FOUNBIG04]. Figure 6.3 shows the overall switch/router architecture using the IronCore chipset. The architecture of the network interface module and management port subsystem of the IronCore chipset is shown in Figure 6.4.

The discussion here is centered around the BigIron switch/router but equally applicable to the other Foundry switch/routers. The BigIron architecture supports the high-speed crossbar switch fabric described earlier and illustrated in Figure 6.2. The switch/router architecture employs the IronCore ASICs on each interface module which also supports 32 Gb/s of local switching bandwidth. The interface module connects to the crossbar switch fabric via 8 Gb/s full-duplex data channels.

This section also provides the component level descriptions of the network interface module, the shared-memory local switch fabric used within each network

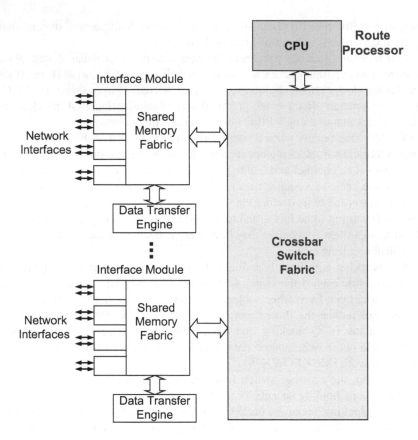

FIGURE 6.3 Multilayer Switch Architecture Using the IronCore™ Chipset (2nd Generation Chipset).

interface, and the main crossbar switch backplane at the core of the switch/router. The discussion at the end of the chapter includes a description of the processes involved in forwarding a packet as it transits the BigIron switch/router.

6.4.1 NETWORK INTERFACE MODULE COMPONENTS

6.4.1.1 Physical Ports

The physical ports as depicted in Figure 6.4 provide the required connectivity between the network interface module on the switch/router and end user systems and other external network devices. The architecture supports a range of features such as auto sensing, half-/full-duplex ports, 10BASE-T Ethernet, 100 Mb/s Ethernet (100BASE-TX, 100BASE-FX), and Gigabit Ethernet (1000BASE-SX, 1000BASE-LX, 1000BASE-LX10) connectivity, as well as OC-3/12/48 Packet over SONET (POS) and OC-3 ATM interface modules.

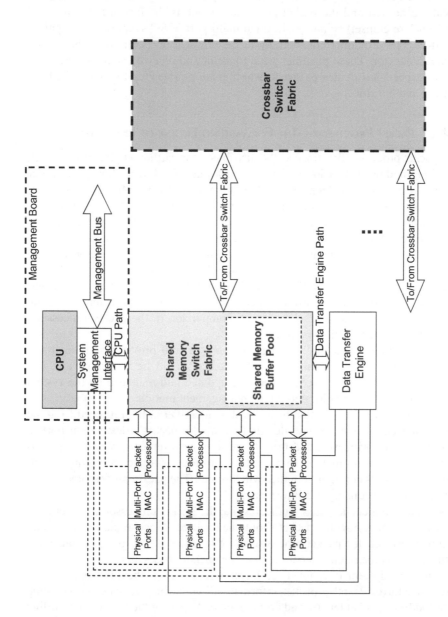

FIGURE 6.4 Architecture of the Network Interface Module and Management Port Subsystem of the IronCore™ Chipset (2nd Generation Chipset).

6.4.1.2 Multi-Port MAC

The multi-port Media Access Controller (MAC) provides the connectivity between a group of physical ports (eight ports for 10/100 Mb/s and two for Gigabit Ethernet) and the packet processor (which is the forwarding engine of the IronCore chipset) (Figure 6.4). Each multi-port MAC supports two separate pipelines, one providing connectivity to the physical ports and the other to the packet processor. These pipelines have transmit and receive channels that allow for wire speed full-duplex packet forwarding at line rates (up to 4 Gb/s) for both Layer 2 and 3 traffic.

6.4.2 PACKET PROCESSOR—THE FORWARDING ENGINE OF IRONCORE

The packet processor functions as the distributed forwarding engine of a network interface module. It provides a forwarding a rate of 1.488 million packets per second (Mpps) per Gigabit port, and 148,800 pps per 10/100 Mb/s Ethernet port. The packet processor receives packets from the multi-port MAC, and examines their Layers 2, 3, and 4 fields to determine how they should be forwarded. It supports one pipeline (with transmit and receive interfaces) to the multi-port MAC and another to the switch fabric, each supporting full-duplex line rate operations.

The switch/router supports a port or system-level (i.e., system-wide) configuration that specifies how deep (Layers 2, 3, 4, etc.) the packet processor examines each packet during the forwarding process. The information extracted during the packet examination is used to perform a comparison in the packet processor's forwarding cache (i.e., flow/route cache).

A forwarding cache "hit" (or matched comparison) provides additional forwarding information regarding how the packet should be processed and forwarded. The forwarding cache entries are updated and managed by the system management entity/CPU located on the management module.

The forwarding information or forwarding identifier (FID) retrieved from the forwarding cache may include details such as the packet's destination port(s), classification/prioritization and priority queuing requirements, VLAN information, multicast group membership, port monitoring (or mirroring) requirement, and other features configured in the switch/router. The packet processor will then forward the packet using this information.

A forwarding cache "miss" indicates that the packet processor does not have information about how the packet should be handled. A cache miss results in an FID that instructs the packet processor to forward the packet to the management entity/CPU (on the management module) for further processing.

When the system is enabled for Layer 3 forwarding, the FID may contain additional Layer 2 and 3 packet information, which may include the next-hop MAC address, packet length, and protocol type. As part of the Layer 3 forwarding process, the packet processor also performs standard IP forwarding processing which includes rewriting the next-hop MAC address into the destination MAC address field of the outgoing Ethernet frame, rewriting the MAC address of the switch/router's egress port into the source MAC address field of the outgoing frame, decrementing the IP time-to-live (TTL), and recalculating the IP header and Ethernet frame checksums.

When the system is enabled for Layer 4 processing, the FID may include information that defines flow classification, which may include inspection of the packet's source IP address, destination IP address, transport protocol type (UDP or TCP), and source and destination port numbers.

6.4.3 ROUTE PROCESSOR COMPONENTS

6.4.3.1 System Management Module/Board— The Route Processor Module

The route processor including system control and management functions is provided in the Foundry switch/router by one or two (separate) management modules added to the chassis. The management module provides the platform on which all the control plane functions, management tools, and interfaces required for system configuration and control are implemented.

A major benefit of employing a crossbar switch fabric is the ability to provide full non-blocking connectivity to all the network interface modules in the switch/router including the management module (which on its own can support up to 8 Gb/s ports or 16 10/100 Mb/s Ethernet ports locally). The ports supported locally on the management module further increase the overall port density of the switch/router and also provide connectivity to end user systems and other network devices. Figure 6.4 shows the sub-components of the management module. The management module has a design similar to a network interface module except it supports the management CPU and system management interface.

6.4.3.2 System Management Interface/CPU

The system management interface (Figure 6.4) provides connectivity to a CPU which serves as the central control engine of the switch/router. This control engine runs the routing protocols, maintains various tables such as the routing table, master Layer 2 and Layer 3 forwarding tables, Layer 4 flow information, port and system-level master configuration tables, and all FID registers for the switch/router. The control engine also supports various control and management functions such as SNMP, ICMP, ARP, IGMP, RSTP, etc.

IP packets or any other packets requiring additional processing (such as routing protocol messages, IP packets with options, SNMP, ICMP, ARP, IGMP, etc.), are sent to the CPU on the management module. The packets sent to the CPU are stored in the shared memory and are identified by their shared-memory identifier (SMID). The CPU is able to access these packets in the shared memory (using their SMID) through the system management interface (Figure 6.4). This interface provides a dedicated connection (i.e., the CPU path) into the shared-memory switch fabric as shown in Figure 6.4.

Each packet processor in a network interface module communicates with the management module through a management bus which in turn has connectivity to the system management interface (Figure 6.4). FIDs that are updated by the management module, for packets that required additional processing by the CPU, are sent back to the forwarding cache of the originating packet processor through the management bus.

The system management interface, with connectivity to both the packet processors and shared memory, also provides the hardware control interface for the CPU. The management module also provides the configuration, initialization, and control information needed to manage all the packet processors (i.e., forwarding engines) in the switch/router.

6.4.3.3 CPU Path and Data Transfer Engine Path

The CPU Path provides the connectivity between the shared-memory switch fabric and the system management interface (and the CPU it supports) (Figure 6.4). The Data Transfer Engine Path provides connectivity between the data transfer engine and shared-memory switch fabric. Packets stored in the shared-memory buffer pool that require further processing are tagged with FIDs that indicate they should be sent to the CPU. Through the CPU Path, the CPU uses the SMIDs to access these special and exception packets in their shared-memory locations.

6.4.3.4 Management Bus

The management bus (Figure 6.4) is a 2.5 Gb/s bus that provides connectivity between all the packet processors (on the network interface modules) and the management module. The management bus connects to the system management interface which in turn connects to the CPU.

The management bus is used to transfer the information needed for system initialization, configuration, and control to the network interface modules. It also carries updated FIDs for packets that required further processing by the CPU, back to the forwarding cache of the packet processor.

6.4.4 SHARED MEMORY AND SWITCH FABRIC INTERFACE COMPONENTS

6.4.4.1 Shared-Memory Switch Fabric and Buffer Pool

As illustrated in Figure 6.4, each network interface module supports a shared-memory buffer pool and a shared-memory switch fabric ASIC that provides 64 Gb/s (i.e., a 512-bit wide data path clocked at 133 MHz) of total full-duplex bandwidth for local packet storage and forwarding. The actual one-way bandwidth through the shared-memory switch fabric is 32 Gb/s, which is half the total bandwidth. The total rate of 64 Gb/s represents the bandwidth into and out of the shared memory because packets traverse the switch fabric in both directions.

The system is configured in such a way that all the ports and packet processors on a network interface module have equal access to the shared-memory switch fabric and memory buffer pool (for packet writes and reads). The IronCore chipset also supports queue size control mechanisms that ensure that a single port on the network interface module does not consume all or an unfair amount of the memory resources.

6.4.4.2   Data Transfer Engine

Each packet stored in the shared-memory pool of the shared-memory switch fabric is assigned a shared-memory identifier (SMID). Using the packet's SMID and forwarding instructions contained in each FID, the shared-memory switch fabric ASIC controls packet transfers (i.e., writes and reads) in and out of the shared-memory buffer pool.

The data transfer engine (Figure 6.4) uses the FID to provide the basic functions required in forwarding a unicast, multicast, or broadcast packet to the destination ports from a single location in memory. To facilitate local co-ordination and association of FID information when the packet processors perform packet writes and reads, the data transfer engine has connectivity to every packet processor on a given network interface module through a separate control data path (Figure 6.4).

6.4.4.3   Crossbar Backplane Connection—Module Connection to Crossbar Switch Fabric

As illustrated in Figure 6.2, an 8 Gb/s full-duplex backplane interface provides the connection between each network interface module and the crossbar switch fabric (which allows for point-to-point parallel data transfers between the interface modules). The chassis architecture provides an 8 Gb/s channel from each slot into the switch fabric, and another 8 Gb/s channel out of the switch fabric to each slot. The backplane itself supports (in one or more parallel planes) data paths, timing distribution paths, low-voltage distribution paths, and grounding paths.

6.4.4.4   Multiple Destination Output Priority Queues

Figure 6.5 illustrates the priority queuing architecture in a network interface module in Slot 1 of the 4-slot BigIron 4000 switch/router based on the IronCore chipset. This simplified illustration describes only the priority queues in the shared-memory switch fabric on an ingress network interface module. Figure 6.5 also shows the 8 Gb/s channel or connection from the network interface module to the main chassis crossbar switch fabric (used to interconnect all modules in the switch/router).

Each ingress network interface module has a set of priority queues with each set associated with a specific egress module. There are four priority output queues assigned per destination port on the chassis. This means each destination port on the chassis is assigned four priority queues on an ingress module. A destination port can be either a local physical port on the same ingress module or a port on other modules in the switch/router.

Figure 6.5 shows only the four priority queues on ingress module 1 in a 4-slot BigIron 4000 chassis. The figure shows the priority queues for the other three modules in slots 2, 3 and 4. The figure omits the four priority queues for the physical ports local to the ingress module. It should be noted that in the architecture, high priority packets, identified by their FIDs, are always served before low priority packets (also appropriately identified).

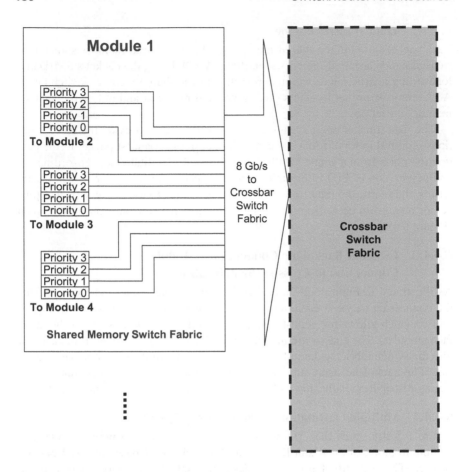

FIGURE 6.5   Illustrating a Module in Slot 1 of BigIron 4000.

A single BigIron 8000 network interface module could be provisioned to support up to 124 individual priority queues. For example, a 24-port 10/100 Mb/s Ethernet network interface module supports 96 priority queues (that is, 24 ports x 4 queues). The 96 priority queues are for the other 23 ports local to the module itself (i.e., $23 \times 4 = 92$ queues), plus 1 set for the management module CPU (i.e., 4 queues), plus 28 priority queues for the 7 other network interface modules in the remaining 7 slots.

6.4.4.5   Multiple Input Source Buffers per Output Port

Figure 6.6 shows a partial view of the crossbar switch fabric of a 4-slot BigIron 4000 switch/router. This partial view shows only a subsection of the output side of the crossbar switch fabric with the 8 Gb/s output connection to network interface module 1. This subsection of the crossbar switch fabric shows three paths or channels to their respective switch fabric buffers. The three switch fabric

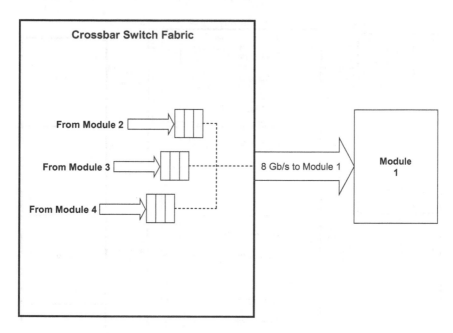

FIGURE 6.6   Per Source Input Queuing in BigIron 4000.

buffers in turn are connected to the 8 Gb/s output channel to network interface module 1.

The switch fabric buffers are serviced by a round-robin scheduler which transfers packets directly from each buffer once every scheduling cycle to the output port. The round-robin scheme allows each ingress network interface module a chance to transfer a packet to its intended destination and ensures that no one module hogs an output port.

6.5   BIGIRON 4000 COMPLETE CROSSBAR SWITCH SYSTEM

Figure 6.7 illustrates the crossbar switch fabric architecture in a BigIron 4000 switch/router with all 4 slots fully populated. Omitted in the diagram (to reduce its complexity), are the four priority queues for the physical ports local to each (ingress) network interface module. The figure shows the four network interface modules with their output priority queues sourcing the 8 Gb/s channel from each slot into the crossbar switch fabric.

Figure 6.7 also shows the input buffers (holding the virtual output queues (VOQs)) of the crossbar switch fabric. The crossbar switch with the VOQs provide fully meshed interconnectivity to the slots, allowing multiple parallel packet flows between the network interface modules. The four 8 Gb/s channels out of the switch fabric to each network interface module are shown as well.

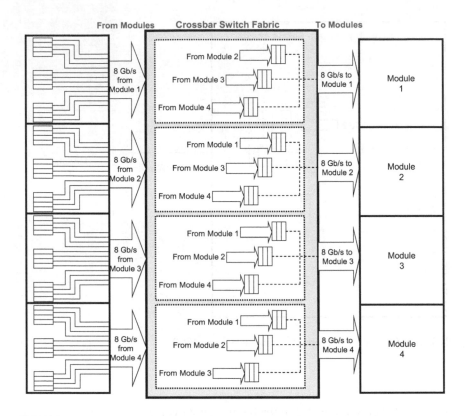

FIGURE 6.7 BigIron 4000 Crossbar Switch Fabric Architecture Overview.

6.6 PACKET PROCESSING OVERVIEW

The (BigIron) switch/router can be configured as a Layer 2 and Layer 3 device and to also use Layer 4 and upper level protocol information for packet forwarding. Each packet processor (forwarding engine) examines a packet for forwarding as soon as up to the first 64 bytes of the packet is received. For packet forwarding, the packet processor reads from a forwarding cache a forwarding identifier (FID), which contains the instructions for forwarding the packet based on the capabilities and feature set configured for the port and switch/router.

The packet processor receives a packet from the multi-port MAC and while it inspects the first 64 bytes of the packet, the packet is transferred into a shared-memory buffer location that is marked (pointed to) with a location identifier (the SMID). The SMID, and not the actual packet itself, is stored in one of the four priority queues as directed by the instructions in the FID. The scheduling and forwarding of a packet (from its queue to the destination port) is based on the instructions in its FID. Only when the packet's SMID moves to the front of its queue is the packet transferred to its destination output port.

The processed packet is forwarded to either one (or more) of the local physical ports on the same network interface module, or over the crossbar switch fabric (via the module's 8 Gb/s full-duplex switch fabric connection) to another interface module. With distributed forwarding engines assigned to all the network interface modules, all modules are able to process and forward packets independent of each other. This means that a module can forward packets to its local ports and to other modules/ports across the crossbar switch fabric, and at the same time receive packets from other modules simultaneously.

6.6.1 ROLE OF THE DATA TRANSFER ENGINE AND PACKET FLOW FOR UNICAST AND MULTICAST TRAFFIC

The packet processor receives a packet from the multi-port MAC, examines it, and performs a look-up operation in its forwarding cache. A successful cache look-up produces an FID which contains the forwarding instructions for the packet. An unsuccessful cache look-up provides an FID that indicates that the packet should be forwarded to the CPU for further processing. The information carried in the FID (and not the packet itself) dictates how all forwarding, including filtering operations in the packet processor, are carried out.

After the forwarding cache lookup at the ingress network interface module, the packet, along with its FID header, are transferred into the shared-memory switch fabric. The data transfer engine reads the FID and places the packet in a shared buffer memory location pointed to by an SMID. Using the forwarding information provided by the FID, the data transfer engine transfers the SMID into one of four priority queues designated for the destination port (unicast traffic) or ports (multicast and broadcast traffic).

As packets (i.e., the SMIDs) are scheduled, the SMID eventually reaches the front of its queue, and the data transfer engine transfers the packet from its location in the shared buffer memory to the shared-memory switching fabric for delivery to the appropriate destination port(s). The destination port(s) can be other ports on the same module ("local FID"), remote ports on a different module ("remote FID"), or the management module CPU for further processing ("CPU FID").

When the packet's destination port is another port on the same module (i.e., a local FID), the data transfer engine transfers the packet from its shared-memory location to the packet processor associated with that destination port. For a CPU FID, the data transfer engine delivers the packet to the CPU on the management module. The packet transfer process in this case is similar to that of a remote FID (discussed later).

For a CPU or remote FID, the data transfer engine uses the SMID of a packet to locate and move it from its shared-memory location into the crossbar switch fabric (since it is the entity that provides connectivity to the other modules). When the packet arrives at the destination module, the local data transfer engine reads the packet's FID while the packet itself is written into a new shared-memory location (pointed to by a new SMID).

Using the new SMID, the data transfer engine transfers the packet from its new shared-memory location to be processed finally by the packet processor associated with the destination port. The final processing steps at the destination module are similar to the processing steps involved in handling a packet with a local FID.

During packet forwarding, packets have to be transferred in and out of the shared-memory buffer on a network interface module through its shared-memory switch fabric. This means the shared-memory switch fabric has to be provisioned with enough bandwidth to avoid its becoming the processing bottleneck on the network interface module.

To create a shared-memory switch fabric on each network interface module that is truly non-blocking, each module is provided with 32 Gb/s of internal one-way bandwidth (i.e., 64 Gb/s full-duplex). This bandwidth is more than two times the total bandwidth of the 8-port Gigabit Ethernet network interface module (i.e., 8 Gb/s in total).

6.6.1.1   Forwarding Unicast Traffic

Using the information carried in the FID of a packet, the data transfer engine queues the packet's SMID in the appropriate priority queue. The packet is held in the shared-memory buffer until its SMID moves to the front of its priority queue. Upon reaching the head of the queue, the SMID triggers the data transfer engine to transfer the packet to a local destination port (local FID), the management module CPU (CPU FID), or the crossbar switch fabric for delivery to a destination module (remote FID).

Upon reaching the destination module (for a remote FID), the data transfer engine reads the packet's FID, writes the packet into a new shared memory, and passes the new SMID to the packet processor associated with the destination port. Again using the FID, the destination packet processor transfers the packet out of the destination module's shared-memory buffer pool and delivers it to the correct local destination port. Once the packet is delivered to the port, the data transfer engine clears (flushes) the packet from the shared-memory buffer.

6.6.1.2   Forwarding Multicast Traffic

In the case of multicast traffic forwarding, the FID of a multicast packet identifies all members of the multicast group and their corresponding switch/router destination ports to which the packet should be forwarded. The members of the multicast group can exist on multiple modules, and if this is the case, the data transfer engine places one SMID (per destination module) into the appropriate output priority queue for each target multicast destination module.

Thereafter, the processing steps are the same as described earlier for unicast traffic with some minor differences. The packet is held in the ingress module shared-memory buffer pool until its SMID reaches the front of its priority queue, upon which the data transfer engine is triggered to transfer the packet to a local destination port on the same module, and/or the crossbar switch fabric to other modules.

The ingress network interface module sends only one copy of the multicast packet to each destination module, meaning if multicast group members exist on four modules, four copies (one per module) of the packet will be transferred through the crossbar switch fabric to those modules. Only when all the four destination modules have received their copy of the multicast packet will the ingress module clear the packet from its shared-memory switch fabric.

The system employs a multicast packet counter (based on the number of destination modules (not ports) associated with the multicast group members) to maintain count of multicast packets transferred. The multicast packet counter is decremented by one whenever a module receives a copy of the multicast packet, and when the packet counter reaches zero (indicating all target destination modules have received their copy of the multicast packet), the ingress network interface module clears the packet from its shared-memory switch fabric.

Upon reaching the destination module, the data transfer engine reads the multicast packet's FID to identify the specific port (or ports) that is a member of the multicast group. The packet is placed in the destination module's shared-memory buffer pool (pointed to by a new SMID) while the local data transfer engine transfers the new SMID to the destination packet processor.

Using the packet's FID, the destination packet processor transfers the packet to the destination port associated with the multicast group. Once the multicast packet is transferred out of the port, the data transfer engine flushes the packet from shared-memory buffer pool.

In the case where there are multiple ports on a destination network interface module belonging to the particular multicast group, the data transfer engine initializes a multicast packet counter with a value equal to the number of ports on the module involved in the multicast group. The destination packet processor copies the multicast packet from the module's shared-memory buffer pool (pointed to by the new SMID) and decrements the packet counter for each packet copy transferred to a port.

The multicast packet counter decrements to zero when all target destination ports in the multicast group have received a copy of the multicast packet from the destination module's local shared-memory buffer pool. Once all ports in the multicast group have been served, the data transfer engine flushes the packet from the shared memory.

6.7   IMPORTANT ATTRIBUTES OF THE SHARED-MEMORY BASED IRONCORE ARCHITECTURE

The IronCore based switch/router architectures (which employ a shared-memory switch fabric plus a main chassis crossbar switch) have the following important attributes [FOUNBIG04]:

- **Protection from Head-of-line (HOL) Blocking**: The switch/router architecture employs multiple input side buffers with multiple priority queues per output port to avoid HOL blocking conditions.
- **Low Latency**: The switch/router architecture provides low latency data transfer because the shared-memory switch fabric copies an arriving packet into the shared-memory buffer pool only once (with the packet's

memory location pointed to by an SMID). Other architectures will copy a packet from one memory buffer location to another or from an input memory buffer to an output memory buffer, creating unnecessary memory and processing resource consumption, which leads to system bandwidth wastage and increased data transfer latency.

- **Multicast Capabilities**: The architecture supports effectively multicast and broadcast packet forwarding because multiple destination ports on a network interface module belonging to a multicast group can read a multicast packet from a single shared-memory location. This architecture eliminates the need to make multiple copies of a multicast or broadcast packet to the destination ports belonging to the multicast group. This approach reduces significantly the time and resources required to forward multicast traffic.

REFERENCES

[FOUNBIG04]. Foundry Networks, BigIron Architecture Brief, White Paper, 2004.
[FOUNJET03]. Foundry Networks, JetCore™ Based Chassis Systems: An Architecture Brief on NetIron, BigIron, and FastIron Systems, White Paper, 2003.
[KAROLM92]. M. Karol, K. Eng, and H. Obara, "Improving the Performance of Input Queued ATM Packet Switches," *Proc. IEEE INFOCOM'92*, 1992, pp. 110–115.
[MCKEOWN96]. N. McKeown, A. Mekkittikul, V. Anantharam, and J. Walrand, "Achieving 100% Throughput in an Input-Queued Switch," *IEEE Trans. on Comm.*, Vol. 47, No 8, 1999, pp. 1260–1267.

7 Foundry Networks Multilayer Switches with JetCore™ Network Interface Module

7.1 INTRODUCTION

This chapter describes the JetCore™ chipset developed by Foundry Networks for switch/router designs. Designed as the third-generation chipset, JetCore™ [FOUNJET03] was developed to consolidate all the networking functions of the IronCore™ chipset (described in the previous chapter) in addition to some new functions into a smaller number of ASICs.

This allowed switch/routers based on the JetCore chipset to provide higher port densities, reduced implementation costs, and a higher number of network functionalities. JetCore was designed to combine the functions supported in seven of the older IronCore ASICs into one ASIC. The newer lines of the Foundry switch/routers were based on this third generation JetCore chipset.

According to the architecture categories described in *Chapter 3*, the Foundry Networks switch/routers based on the JetCore architecture fall under "Architectures with Crossbar-based Switch Fabrics and Fully Distributed Forwarding Engines" (see Figure 7.1). JetCore supports line speed packet forwarding locally on the network interface module hardware, without requiring the first packet of a flow to be sent to the management module for forwarding [FOUNJET03].

7.2 JETCORE™ NETWORK INTERFACE MODULE ARCHITECTURE

The IronCore chipset supports a shared-memory switch fabric that is at the core of the switching and forwarding functions in each network interface module (see *Chapter 6*). The JetCore chipset, on the other hand, supports a module crossbar switch fabric as the main switching backplane in each network interface module as illustrated in Figure 7.2 and Figure 7.3. As shown in these figures, groups of network ports (24 10/100 Mb/s Ethernet ports or 4 Gigabit Ethernet ports) are assigned their own hardware switching logic plus a shared-memory switch fabric, which, together, connect to the module crossbar switch fabric.

All the module crossbar switch fabrics in the system in turn connect to the central chassis crossbar switch fabric. This arrangement allows switch/routers that use the JetCore interface modules to be more scalable and have higher port

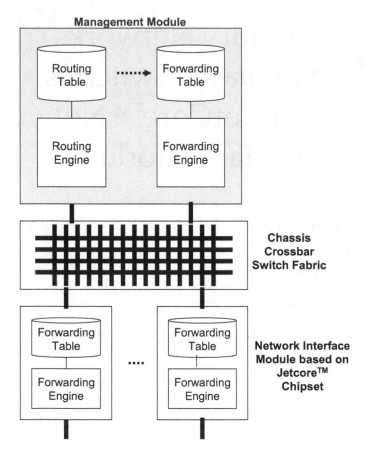

FIGURE 7.1   Architectures with Crossbar-based Switch Fabrics and Fully Distributed
Forwarding Engines—Network Interface Modules with JetCore™ Chipset.

density. These features were achievable due to the way the functional components
in the JetCore chipset are implemented in ASICs.

The single ASIC on which the module crossbar switch fabric is implemented
is called the Backplane Interface Adapter (BIA). The port group switching logic
with its corresponding shared-memory switch fabric (excluding the Content
Addressable Memory (CAM) and Parameter Random Access Memory (PRAM)),
and shared memory (see Figure 7.3) are implemented on a single ASIC called the
Integrated Port Controller (IPC) for 10/100 Mb/s Ethernet ports, or the Integrated
Gigabit Controller (IGC) for Gigabit Ethernet ports [FOUNJET03].

The components of the network interface modules based on the JetCore chipset are described next. The main features of the port group switching logic and
shared-memory switch fabric (Figure 7.3) are also described later.

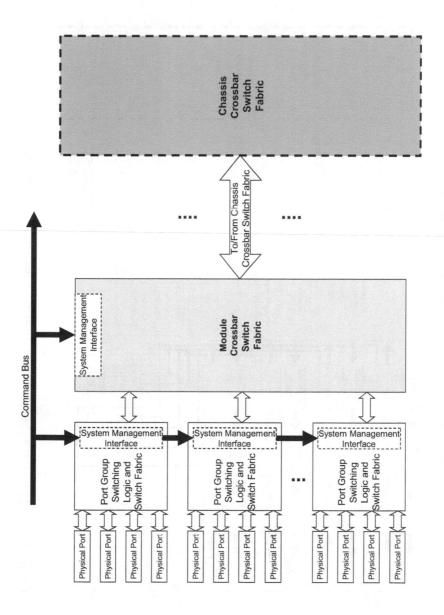

FIGURE 7.2   Architecture of the Network Interface Module of the JetCore™ Chipset (3rd Generation Chipset).

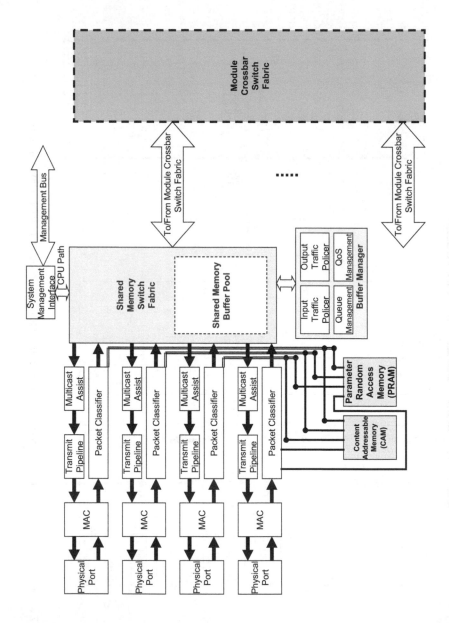

FIGURE 7.3 Detailed View of the Port Group Switching Logic and Switch Fabric of the JetCore™ Chipset.

7.2.1 NETWORK INTERFACE COMPONENTS

7.2.1.1 Physical Ports

The physical ports (Figure 7.2 and Figure 7.3) provide the interfaces through which end user systems or other network devices are connected to the JetCore based switch/router. The ports options include 10/100 Mb/s Ethernet, Gigabit Ethernet, 10 Gigabit Ethernet as well as Packet over SONET (POS) and ATM. The Ethernet interfaces support auto sensing, half, or full duplex capabilities where appropriate.

7.2.1.2 Media Access Controller (MAC)

The MAC provides connectivity between the physical port and the packet classifier (which is the forwarding engine of the JetCore based switch/router). The MAC is responsible for prepending/removing Ethernet frame preamble, Start Frame Delimiter (SFD), padding, addressing of Ethernet frames, appending/checking Frame Check Sequence (FCS), auto-negotiation, and other Link Layer protocol functions.

7.2.2 JetCore FORWARDING ENGINE COMPONENTS

7.2.2.1 Packet Classifier—The Forwarding Engine of JetCore

The packet classifier (Figure 7.3) is the local distributed forwarding engine of a network interface port and connects to both the MAC and the shared-memory switch fabric of a port group logic. It is responsible for receiving incoming packets from the MAC, parsing and examining them at Layers 2, 3, and 4, determining how the packets should be forwarded.

Each port group is given a Content Addressable Memory (CAM) and Parameter Random Access Memory (PRAM) to allow for packet forwarding to be done locally. All packet classifiers in the port group interface to both the CAM and the PRAM. A packet classifier performs a lookup in the CAM using the information extracted from the packet headers.

The packet classifier also consults the PRAM, which holds the forwarding information that specifies how a packet should be forwarded when a CAM lookup produces a match. Basically, the packet classifier is the local forwarding engine responsible for making the packet forwarding decisions in the network interface module, and hence, it is the most important packet forwarding component to the distributed forwarding architecture discussed here.

The packet classifier performs packet processing and forwarding table lookups in the CAM and PRAM. The result of a lookup is a forwarding identifier (FID) that specifies the destination port(s) for the processed packet (in the case of Layer 3 forwarding, the next-hop IP address and packet rewrite information).

After processing the packet, the packet classifier attaches an internal switching or routing header to the packet. This internal switching tag is an optimized internal header that specifies to the switch/router hardware components and switch fabrics how the packet should be handled and routed until it reaches its destination port(s). The FID is formatted and carried as part of this internal switching tag.

The packet classifier is also designed to support applications such as Extended RMON (XRMON) and sFlow (RFC 3176) traffic sampling and monitoring. The packet classifier has extra capabilities that allow it to randomly sample packets out of a stream of packets passing through it (1 in N sampling) and mark them as packets to be copied (or mirrored) to the system management module (the route processor module). This packet sampling function is a key requirement for most traffic monitoring tools such XRMON and sFlow.

An XRMON or sFlow software agent running on the management module will then examine the sampled packets, extract the relevant flow information (possibly including some statistics), and send that along with extracted portions of the headers of the sampled packet to an external XRMON or sFlow collector station. The parameters of the algorithm used by the packet classifier to randomly select the packets can be controlled by the Foundry Networks switch/router operating system, and are configurable and tunable by the network administrator.

Within the packet classifier module itself, packet processing is performed in a pipeline which consists of smaller processing sub-modules. This is done in order to support wire speed performance and forwarding. A brief description of the most important sub-modules of the packet classifier is given later.

7.2.2.1.1 Programmable Lookup Processor (PLP)

The PLP is a sub-component within the packet classifier and is responsible for examining the fields in packets and extracting the relevant (Layers 2, 3, and 4) information used to perform a comparison in the CAM. The sub-module that actually performs the comparison in the CAM using the extracted information is the CAM lookup handler (discussed later).

The PLP is actually a small, very high-speed RISC microprocessor built into the packet classifier as a sub-module. The PLP (running a simple program provided by the operating system) is capable of examining packet fields at line speed and extracting the relevant information (to be stored in the PLP registers) that is then used to make the comparison in the CAM.

The PLP is a very important programmable sub-module in the packet classifier that allows the system to be flexible enough (in terms of packet parsing and examination) to accommodate future packet switching/forwarding features [FOUNJET03]. This is because packet technologies are always evolving with new protocols and packet encapsulations developed. Even new functions for switching and forwarding packets continue to evolve to address emerging network applications and customer needs.

The idea is, should new packet parsing, examination, and lookup features be required (i.e., beyond the features currently implemented in the PLP), the PLP's internal program could be enhanced or modified to accommodate the new features. The goal is to allow the PLP's program to be modified through an operating system upgrade rather than having to make changes to the existing hardware and ASICs in the system [FOUNJET03].

7.2.2.1.2   CAM Lookup Handler

The PLP extracts the relevant information from the packet fields and stores this in the PLP registers. The PLP then exports the information in its registers to another module (the CAM lookup handler) to be used to perform the comparison in the CAM. The CAM lookup handler immediately takes a copy of the contents of the PLP registers, thereby freeing the PLP to process another packet. The CAM lookup handler then proceeds to perform the CAM comparison using the register contents. This process forms part of the pipelined process in the packet classifier mentioned earlier.

The CAM lookup handler takes the PLP register contents and makes a comparison in the CAM, looking for a match. CAM lookups can be performed using packet field information such as the Ethernet destination and/or source MAC address (DA/SA), IP destination and/or source address, transport protocol type (TCP/UDP), transport protocol destination and/or source port, etc. The result of a successful CAM lookup (a "hit") is an index into the PRAM, that is, an index that can be used to retrieve information from the PRAM.

The PRAM contains information on the destination port(s) and how the packet should be handled along the forwarding path until it reaches its destination port(s). The index retrieved from the CAM is used by the PRAM lookup handler (discussed later) which actually performs the search in the PRAM.

7.2.2.1.3   Parameter Random Access Memory (PRAM) Lookup Handler

The PRAM lookup task is part of the pipelined packet processing. The index obtained from the CAM by the CAM lookup handler is passed to the PRAM handler to be used to retrieve information from the PRAM. The output of the PRAM indicates which switch/router ports the packet should be forwarded to and the necessary QoS related operations to be performed on the packet (priority queuing, packet drop policies, priority marking/remarking, etc.).

As part of the pipelined processing, while the PRAM lookup handler is performing the lookup, the PLP and the CAM lookup handler are freed to process other packets. This allows the packet classifier to maintain wire speed packet processing performance even when parsing and examining packets with more extensive fields, and performing complicated lookups [FOUNJET03]. The result of the PRAM lookup is information about the packet's outbound port, priority queue, packet drop setting, Ethernet MAC address rewrite information, VLAN, IP Precedence and DSCP marks/remarks, and other information required to complete the packet forwarding process.

7.2.2.2   Content Addressable Memory (CAM)

The first portion of the lookup information returned to the packet classifier (by the CAM lookup handler) is maintained in the CAM (Figure 7.3). The information in the CAM provides an index (the first portion) to further forwarding information stored in the PRAM. The PRAM's contents (the second portion) make up the actual information used by the packet classifier to forward a packet to its destination ports. The information used to perform the lookup in the CAM is based on a number of fields parsed from the packet.

The packet classifier extracts certain fields in the arriving packet (such as destination MAC address, destination IP address, etc.) and passes this to the high-speed CAM lookup handler to perform a lookup in the CAM. If a matching entry is found in the CAM, an index is returned showing a location in the PRAM where the forwarding information for the packet is stored.

JetCore uses ternary CAMs (TCAMs), which allow for the creation of CAM entries having "don't care" bits. This results in a more efficient utilization of CAM space. With a larger CAM size than the IronCore architecture, JetCore offers better forwarding table and switch/router scalability and higher forwarding performance [FOUNJET03].

7.2.2.3   Parameter Random Access Memory (PRAM)

The PRAM is a high-speed memory that maintains the actual forwarding information (linked to the index returned from the CAM search) that indicates to the packet classifier how a particular packet should be forwarded. As mentioned earlier, the PRAM handler takes the index returned by the CAM lookup and performs a lookup in the PRAM that returns to the packet classifier instructions on how the packet should be handled.

This information includes the destination port or ports, MAC address of the next-hop, VLAN ID, priority queue, packet drop setting, packet priority value remarking/marking, etc. The forwarding information obtained from the PRAM (by the PRAM handler) is used to construct the internal routing header (tag) that is prepended to the packet before it is dispatched on its way to the destination port(s). This forwarding information (carried in the internal routing tag) is used by other system modules to determine how to forward the packet to the destination port(s) and what packet rewrites have to be performed.

7.2.2.4   VLAN Multicast Assist Module

In the (normal) case where a unicast/multicast packet needs to be sent out a given destination port to only one VLAN (normal operations), the JetCore hardware is capable of writing the appropriate VLAN ID to the unicast/multicast packet before it is transmitted out the port. However, when a multicast packet needs to be transmitted out a given destination port multiple times, each time with a different VLAN ID (for instance, the switch/router is a one-armed router to different IP subnets attached to that port), the hardware-based VLAN multicast assist module handles the required packet replication and VLAN tagging functionality [FOUNJET03]. The VLAN multicast assist module carries out its functions on the transmit side of the port group switching logic (Figure 7.3).

To carry out the packet replication and VLAN tagging functions, each VLAN multicast assist module maintains a VLAN multicast counter in addition to a VLAN multicast map. The counter and multicast map are user programmable via configuration tools in the operating system. With these, the VLAN multicast assist module can locally and independently replicate (and VLAN-tag) multicast packets multiple times up to the maximum number (of

VLANs attached to the port) initialized in the VLAN multicast counter. Each multicast packet replicated is tagged with a new VLAN ID as specified by the VLAN multicast map.

7.2.2.5 Transmit Pipeline

The transmit pipeline connects the VLAN multicast assist module to the MAC on the transmit side of the port group logic (Figure 7.3). This is the module actually responsible for writing the VLAN ID specified by the VLAN multicast map into the packet before it is sent out the destination port. The transmit pipeline works under the control of the VLAN multicast assist module which provides it with the correct data for VLAN ID insertion. This pipeline allows for the forwarding, replication and tagging of a multicast packet to multiple VLANs (attached to the same port) to be performed in hardware without loss in packet forwarding performance [FOUNJET03].

The transmit pipeline is also responsible for performing the required IP packet operations (i.e., IP TTL decrement, IP header checksum recomputation, source and destination MAC address rewrites, Ethernet frame checksums recomputation) before the packet is transmitted out the destination port. Also, before the packet is sent to the MAC of the destination port, the transmit pipeline strips the internal routing header (i.e., the internal switching tag).

7.2.3   MEMORY COMPONENTS OF THE PORT GROUP SWITCHING LOGIC AND SWITCH FABRIC

7.2.3.1 Shared-Memory Switch Fabric

The shared-memory switch fabric is a core component of the port group logic and connects to the module crossbar switch fabric. It handles the movement of packets to and from the port group logic's embedded high-speed shared memory. As illustrated in Figure 7.3, the shared-memory switch fabric interfaces with the buffer manager, module crossbar switch fabric, packet classifier (i.e., the forwarding engine of JetCore), and the VLAN multicast assist module.

When the packet classifier passes a packet that has been processed to the shared-memory switch fabric, it places the packet in a free location in the shared-memory pool. When the packet is stored, the shared-memory switch fabric provides to the buffer manager the following information:

- A pointer or buffer number which indicates the location of the packet in the shared memory
- Forwarding Identifier (FID) which indicates the destination port(s) and other forwarding information for the packet
- Packet priority which indicates the priority queue the packet should be assigned to on its way to the output port
- A "result" that indicates whether a copy of the packet should be sent to the management module (i.e., route processor module).

The earlier information helps the buffer manager maintain a detail profile of the packet in addition to its location in the shared memory. The information is also used to manage the shared-memory buffer space in order to reserve memory for other incoming packets, determine the destination port(s) of the packet, and determine the priority queue the packet should be assigned to.

Working with instructions provided by the buffer manager, the shared-memory switch fabric also reads the packets stored in the shared memory and transfers them to their correct destination ports according to the instructions provided by the buffer manager.

7.2.3.2   Buffer Manager

The buffer manager (Figure 7.3) is the component in the port group logic that manages the buffer space in the shared-memory pool as packets are stored. Other functions performed by the buffer manager are as follows:

- Managing the per port priority queues where packets are placed based on their assigned priority
- Managing the QoS mechanisms working on the queues, as well as ensuring that each packet is assigned the correct priority queue. The JetCore based switch/router architecture supports 4 priority queues per port. Packets are processed and classified into these 4 priority queues and scheduled using either strict priority or weighted fair queuing (WFQ) scheduling
- Handling traffic policing for inbound packets (at the ingress side of the port group)
- Handling traffic policing for outbound packets (at the egress side of the port group)

As soon as the buffer manager is provided the pointer or buffer number of the shared-memory location of a new packet, the buffer manager places the buffer number in the appropriate priority queue based on the packet's destination port and priority setting. As packets are scheduled, a packet's pointer reaches the front of its priority queue, and the buffer manager indicates to the shared-memory switch fabric the correct shared-memory location to retrieve the packet (using the pointer or buffer number), and which destination port(s) to forward it to.

The buffer manager is also responsible for performing in-hardware traffic policing (rate limiting) for both inbound and outbound traffic [FOUNJET03]. Unlike other router or switch/router architectures with centralized traffic processing and forwarding, a JetCore based switch/router does not have to forward (inbound or outbound) packets to a central processing module where traffic policing is typically carried out in software. The JetCore based network interface module (i.e., port group logic) is designed to perform both inbound and outbound traffic policing locally in hardware without any help from any other system module [FOUNJET03].

7.2.3.3   Shared-Memory Buffer Pool

After the packet classifier performs the forwarding table lookup for packets to determine their destination ports and priority, they are sent to the shared-memory buffer pool which then provides the temporary storage space needed for the packets. The packets are held here until it is time to forward them out to their destination ports. The priority queuing and forwarding of a packet is based on its priority and the status of the port priority queue it was assigned to. The port group logic relies on a high-speed shared memory to implement these functionalities.

Packets can be written into and read from the shared memory at speeds equal to the sum of all the line speeds of all the physical ports within the port group plus the speed of the connection to the module crossbar switch fabric. This capability allows the JetCore based switch/router to provide a true wire speed non-blocking packet forwarding architecture.

7.2.4   ROUTE PROCESSOR COMPONENTS

The Layer 2/3 control plane and system management functions are provided by a management module (i.e., route processor module) that occupies a slot in the chassis. This module provides the system operating software that includes the necessary management tools needed for system control and management.

The management module is designed such that it can be plugged into any slot in the chassis just like any other network interface module [FOUNJET03]. The management module has connectivity to the chassis crossbar switch fabric which made it possible for some versions to be designed to have physical ports on them to interface to end user devices. This provides another way to increase the port density and versatility of the switch/router.

7.2.4.1   Command Bus

As illustrated in Figure 7.2, a 2.1 Gb/s command bus, dedicated mainly for system management and control, connects the management module to all the network interface modules (including their packet classifiers) and the module crossbar switch fabrics in the switch/router. This bus carries information required for chassis management, configuration, and control from the management module to the various system modules.

7.2.4.2   System Management Interface

The system management interface shown in Figure 7.2 connects the port group logic (with its internal shared-memory switch fabric and memory pool) and the module crossbar switch fabric to the 2.1 Gb/s command bus. Operating via the command bus, the management module (i.e., the route processor module) is able to initialize, configure, control, and update any of the port group logics in the switch/router (Layer 2/3/4 forwarding information updates, FIDs, etc.).

The system management interface also allows the management module to collect a wide range of packet forwarding statistics from the port groups and the network interface modules. As shown in Figure 7.2 and Figure 7.3, each of the components on a network interface module (port group logic and module crossbar switch fabric) has a system management interface built into it that connects the particular component to the 2.1 Gb/s command bus.

7.2.5 MODULE CROSSBAR SWITCH FABRIC

The module crossbar switch fabric provides connectivity (for high-speed packet forwarding) between the port group logics attached to it and the other port groups attached to the main chassis crossbar switch fabric. As shown in Figure 7.2 and Figure 7.3, each port group in a network interface module supports a local embedded shared-memory switch fabric.

When the packet classifier forwards a packet that has a destination on another port on the same network interface module but the port is in a different port group, the module crossbar switch fabric provides the connectivity. On the inbound port group logic, once the pointer or buffer number of the packet reaches the front of its assigned priority queue (associated with the destination port in a different port group), the packet is forwarded to the module crossbar switch fabric, which then transfers it to the destination port group.

7.2.5.1 Backplane Connectivity

The module crossbar switch fabric provides an additional function which is to interface with the backplane (i.e., main chassis crossbar switch fabric) slot. An aggregator placed adjacent to the module crossbar switch fabric (on the same chip) handles the necessary word length conversion to allow for interfacing with the backplane.

The module crossbar switch fabric provides the bandwidth required to handle all the port group logics connected to it, in addition to the backplane (or chassis crossbar switch fabric) slot when operating at full data speeds. To provide non-blocking performance (i.e., to avoid head-of-line blocking), the module crossbar switch fabric employs virtual output queuing (VOQ) on the ingress of the switch fabric.

7.2.5.2 Replication of Multicast Packets

When a multicast packet is sent from the backplane slot (i.e., the chassis crossbar switch fabric), and if it happens that the packet has destinations on more than one port group (as indicated by its FID), the module crossbar switch fabric provides the necessary multicast packet replication, sending one copy of the packet to each destination port group. At the port group level, if the multicast packet is destined to more than one physical port, then the shared-memory switch fabric handles any further packet replication.

In the case where the bandwidth to a port group is oversubscribed (i.e., temporarily overloaded with too much traffic), the module crossbar switch fabric supports local buffering to handle the offered traffic [FOUNJET03]. When the port group bandwidth is not oversubscribed, packets are forwarded on the fly to their destination port group(s) without buffering. However, in the case where a port group is temporarily overloaded with packets, the packets are held temporarily in the local buffers until the port group asserts the "Ready" signal again (to receive more packets). One benefit of this feature is that packet loss for unicasts is significantly reduced.

Another benefit is that the system is able to provide non-blocking and expedited forwarding of multicast packets. Let us assume, for example, that a multicast packet is received from the backplane (chassis crossbar switch fabric) and destined to ports in port groups 2, 5, and 6, and port group 5 is momentarily unable to accept arriving packets.

The module crossbar switch fabric in this case sends the multicast packet to port groups 2 and 6, and buffers a copy of the packet to be forwarded to port group 5 at a later time. This means that the forwarding of a multicast packet would not be blocked (thereby blocking other packets following it), nor unnecessarily delayed due to a port group belonging to a multicast group temporarily not being able to receive packets.

7.2.6 MULTIPLE DESTINATION OUTPUT PRIORITY QUEUES

Similar to the IronCore chipset, the JetCore architecture supports four priority queues per destination port and per destination module. The architecture implements, specifically, the following priority levels:

- Four output priority queues per physical port within the same port group logic
- Four output priority queues per each of the other port groups on the chassis
- Four output queues per each of the other module crossbar switch fabrics on the chassis.

Figure 7.4 illustrates the output priority queues on port group 1 of a network interface module in slot 1 of a 4-slot switch/router chassis. The figure shows the priority queues provided for the other local physical ports, as well as the other module crossbar switch fabrics in the chassis.

The JetCore based switch/router supports the ability to prioritize arriving packets based on IEEE 802.1p, IP Precedence, and DSCP bits. The system can be configured to use strict prioritization or weighted fair queuing (with configurable weights) scheduling on the priority queues. This feature allows the network administrator to configure the traffic management mechanisms to meet the requirements of the applications and services using the switch/router.

In addition, JetCore architecture allows for rewriting IEEE 802.1p, IP Precedence, or DSCP priority bits in hardware after the packet classifier performs the forwarding table lookup. This feature allows for the application of tailor-made policies to traffic management within a network. With these features network managers can mark up or mark down priorities of traffic flows based on the current

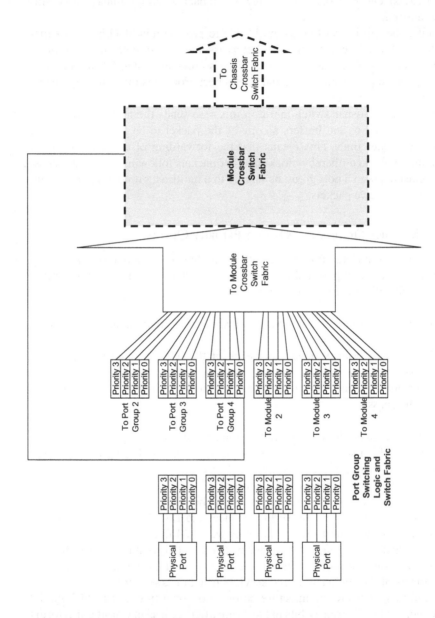

FIGURE 7.4 Diagram Illustrating Port Group 1 of an Interface in Slot 1 of a 4 Port Chassis Using the JetCore™ Chipset—Four Priorities per Destination.

needs of applications and services, and the available network resources. Network managers could also implement these features at the network edge devices to offer different service levels to users.

7.3   OTHER JETCORE FEATURES

The JetCore architecture supports other features in addition to those discussed elsewhere in this chapter. The chipset supports the following additional features [FOUNJET03]:

- **Hardware-Based Traffic Policing**: The JetCore architecture supports a hardware token bucket-based system for traffic policing. This system allocates a specified number of tokens to use within a given interval (1 ms) to a traffic flow being policed, with the possibility of carrying over unused tokens to the next interval(s). The architecture allows traffic policing to be performed at the interface level without any assistance from any other (centralized) traffic policy module or the management module. Performing traffic policing in a distributed manner and in hardware allows for the system to have scalable traffic policing capabilities without impacting packet forwarding performance, since traffic flows are not policed by a centralized module.
- **Access Control Limits (ACLs) and Wire Speed Policy-Based Routing**: The JetCore architecture supports in-hardware, packet filtering (using ACLs), and line rate policy-based routing directly in the network interface modules, without requiring that the first packet of a flow be sent to the management module for processing. This makes the architecture more capable of handling network environments with very bursty traffic that require policy-based routing and application of specific ACLs and access policies.
- **Traffic Monitoring via XRMON and sFlow**: The JetCore architecture supports random packet sampling and monitoring via capabilities implemented in the packet classifier. This allows the JetCore based switch/router to support scalable traffic monitoring and statistics collection (XRMON and sFlow), which in turn can be used for traffic pattern analysis and network capacity planning. The ASICs based traffic monitoring capabilities allows the switch/router architecture to be scalable up to 10 Gigabit Ethernet line speeds without packet forwarding performance penalties [FOUNJET03].
- **Jumbo Frame Support**: The JetCore based architecture supports Jumbo frames of up to 14,336-byte frames. In high performance computing (HPC) applications (e.g., using supercomputing and large clusters for simulation, modeling, seismic tomography, and computational fluid dynamics), for example, very large volumes of data are exchanged between processors, and processor interrupts are very costly. Using Jumbo frames during data exchanges allows for much higher processor

and overall system throughput and performance. With Jumbo frames, the processors in the HPC system receive and send large amounts of data and do not have to be interrupted as often as they would be when smaller normal sized Ethernet frames are exchanged. In most practical applications, the hosts and network nodes send Jumbo frames with frame size of up to 9,000 bytes [FOUNJET03].

7.4 PACKET PROCESSING OVERVIEW

This section describes the packet flow through the JetCore based switch/router from an ingress port to egress port.

7.4.1 PACKET FLOW FOR UNICAST AND MULTICAST TRAFFIC

A physical port receives a packet and passes it to the MAC to perform its functions as described earlier. The packet is then passed to the packet classifier (the forwarding engine) that receives and reads the relevant packet fields and performs lookups in the CAM and PRAM to determine the forwarding information (that includes the forwarding identifier (FID), packet's priority, VLAN, and other information) required to forward the packet to its destination port(s).

The packet classifier encodes the forwarding information into an internal routing header (internal switching tag) that is prepended to the packet. In the event the lookup produces no match in the CAM, the packet classifier forwards the packet to the management module (route processor module) for further processing. The management module will process and forward this packet and at the same time create appropriate CAM and PRAM entries that will then allow the packet classifier to forward subsequent packets associated with the packet to the same destination.

The packet classifier then passes the packet to the shared-memory switch fabric which places it in the high-speed shared-memory buffer pool, and provides the buffer manager with the packet's FID, priority, pointer to the shared-memory location (i.e., buffer number), and an indicator if a copy of the packet should be sent to the management module.

The buffer manager, which manages the priority queues maintained in the shared memory (Figure 7.4), queues the buffer number (pointer) of the packet in the appropriate priority queue(s) associated with the destination port(s). As packets (buffer numbers) are scheduled, the buffer number reaches the front of its priority queue and the buffer manager signals the shared-memory switch fabric to extract the packet from its shared-memory location and transfer it to the destination port(s).

The packet's destination could be a physical port in the same port group; a port on another port group on the same module crossbar switch; or a port on another module crossbar switch fabric, a mirror port (i.e., a traffic monitoring port), or the management module. After the packet is successfully transferred to its destination(s), the buffer manager then clears the packet from its shared-memory location.

7.4.1.1 Forwarding Unicast Traffic to Destination Port(s) on a Different Module Crossbar Switch Fabric

Using the information in the packet's FID and its priority, the buffer manager queues the buffer number in its priority queue (Figure 7.4). The packet is held in the shared-memory buffer pool until its buffer number moves to the front of its priority queue.

Upon reaching the head of its queue, the buffer manager informs the shared-memory switch fabric to transfer the packet to the destination module crossbar switch fabric. The shared-memory switch fabric transfers the packet to the module crossbar switch fabric, which then forwards the packet to the chassis crossbar switch fabric.

The packet is transferred through the chassis crossbar switch fabric to the destination module crossbar switch fabric, which in turn delivers it to the destination port group's shared-memory switch fabric. The packet is then placed in the destination port group's shared-memory buffer pool, and the buffer manager is provided its shared-memory buffer number.

Using again the packet's FID and priority, the buffer manager queues the packet's buffer number in a priority queue for the destination port. As packets (buffer numbers) are scheduled, the packet's buffer number moves to the front of its priority queue, and the buffer manager signals the shared-memory switch fabric to transfer the packet to the destination port. The buffer manager then clears the packet from its shared-memory location.

7.4.1.2 Forwarding Multicast Traffic to Destination Port(s) on Different Module Crossbar Switch Fabric(s)

In the case of multicast traffic forwarding, the FID specifies all the outgoing ports on the chassis that have members in the multicast group. If multicast group members exist on ports on multiple module crossbar switch fabrics, the buffer manager queues the buffer number (only once) in the appropriate output priority queue for each destination module crossbar switch fabric as illustrated in Figure 7.4.

The forwarding process then follows that described earlier for unicast traffic with minor differences. The packet is held in the shared-memory buffer pool until its buffer number moves to the front of its priority queue, which signals the buffer manager to inform the shared-memory switch fabric to transfer the packet to its destination module crossbar switch fabric.

The system transfers only one copy of the multicast packet to each destination module crossbar switch fabric and not one packet per destination physical port. This means that if multicast members exist on four destination module crossbar switch fabrics, then four copies (one per module) of the multicast packet are sent through the chassis crossbar switch fabric. Only when all of the four destination module crossbar switch fabrics have received their copy of the multicast packet does the ingress port group logic on ingress module crossbar switch fabric clear the packet from its shared-memory buffer pool.

To accomplish this, the system employs a packet counter based on the number of destinations (i.e., local destination port group ports, remote destination port groups, and remote destination module crossbar switch fabrics). When the packet counter decrements to zero (indicating that all destinations have received their copy of the multicast packet), the ingress port group logic on the ingress module crossbar switch fabric deletes the packet from its shared-memory location.

Upon reaching the destination module crossbar switch fabric, the multicast packet is forwarded to its destination port group(s). In the case where the multicast packet has destination ports that are in more than one port group, the destination module crossbar switch fabric replicates the multicast packet, sending one copy of the packet to each destination port group.

Within the destination port group, the multicast packet is stored in the local shared-memory buffer pool the port group supports. Using the packet's FID, the buffer manager queues the packet's buffer number in the appropriate destination port queue or queues (i.e., in the case where the destination port group has more than one multicast member port). When the buffer number moves to the front of its queue, the buffer manager signals its shared-memory switch fabric to forward the packet to the destination port.

A packet counter is used to ensure that all multicast member physical ports located on the destination port group receive their copies of the received multicast packet. The packet counter is initialized to a value equal to the total number of multicast member destination ports (in the port group). The counter is decremented by one whenever a copy of the multicast packet is forwarded out one of the multicast member destination ports. The packet counter decrements to zero when the last destination port (in the multicast group) receives the packet, at which point the buffer manager clears the multicast packet from its local shared-memory location.

The multicast packet replication is carried out in a hierarchical manner in order to keep the packet replication to a minimum at the module and chassis crossbar switch fabric level. The multicast packet forwarding takes place as follows, depending on the destination of the multicast packet:

- If the multicast packet is to be sent to destination ports in the same (local) port group, then only one copy of the packet is sent to each local port.
- If the multicast packet is to be sent to a destination port(s) on another (remote) port group(s) on the same module crossbar switch fabric, then only one copy of the packet is sent to each one of the other port groups.
- If the multicast packet is to be sent to a destination port(s) on another (remote) module crossbar switch fabric(s), only one copy of the packet is sent across the chassis crossbar switch fabric to each module crossbar switch fabric.

At the destination port group, the multicast packet is buffered and its buffer number queued (as described earlier) until it moves to the front of its queue. The destination shared-memory switch fabric then transfers the packet from its shared-memory location and passes it to the local VLAN multicast assist module and its connected transmit pipeline located at the destination port.

The VLAN multicast assist module and transmit pipeline then perform the processing required for VLAN attachment, after which the internal switch header is detached from the packet. The packet is then sent to the MAC which performs the required transmit operations (which includes FCS (Frame Check Sequence) calculation and attachment), after which the packet is transferred to the physical port for transmission to the external network.

7.5 FOUNDRY IRONWARE™ SOFTWARE ARCHITECTURE

Figure 7.5 shows a high-level view of the Foundry IronWare operating system used by all the Foundry switch/routers and not only those based on the IronCore chipset [FOUNJET03]. The diagram shows the major components and illustrates the relationship between the component rather than a protocol stack.

- **Kernel**: The kernel runs in the route processor (management module) and is responsible for managing the system hardware and software resources, and providing an interface to the hardware for initialization, monitoring, programming, etc.
- **Layer 2/3/MPLS Forwarding Tables and ACLs**: These forwarding tables are generated from the routing protocols running in the route processor and are stored in the CAM and PRAM. The information stored in the CAM and PRAM include, among other information, the Layer 2 (MAC) address table (for Layer 2 forwarding), the IP forwarding table, IP cache, and ACLs.

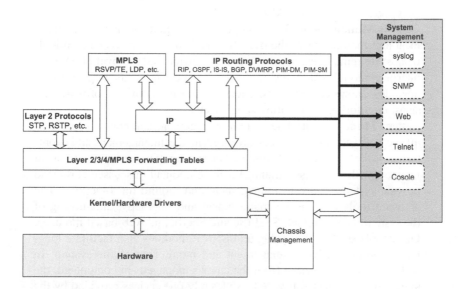

FIGURE 7.5   Foundry Networks IronWare™ Software Architecture.

- **Layer 2 Protocols**: The route processor supports several Layer 2 protocols such as Spanning Tree Protocol (STP), Rapid STP (RSTP in IEEE 802.1w), etc. These protocols determine the active loop-free Layer 2 network topology of a LAN, and control the logical blocking and unblocking of the Layer 2 switch ports in the LAN, as well as the aging or flushing of the MAC address table entries in case of host station movements and LAN topology changes.

- **IP**: This component represents the actual IP stack in the route processor, which is used by the other TCP/IP protocols including the routing and management protocols.

- **IP Routing Protocols**: These include the unicast and multicast routing protocols supported by the route processor and include protocols such as RIP, OSPF, IS-IS, BGP, DVMRP, PIM-DM, and PIM-SM. Each of these protocols uses services from the IP component and participates in the generation of the Layer 3 forwarding tables maintained in the CAM and PRAM. Each routing protocol (i.e., RIP, OSPF, IS-IS) maintains its own routing table, and only the best routes (i.e., those with the lowest Administrative Distance) out of all routes to a particular destination are included in the Layer 3 forwarding table.

- **MPLS**: This component represents the MPLS protocols such as LDP (Label Distribution Protocol) and RSVP-TE (Resource Reservation Protocol—Traffic Engineering). These MPLS signaling protocols use services from the IP component (for transporting protocol information to peer nodes). The MPLS protocols generate the Layer 3 and MPLS forwarding tables that represent the current Layer 3 network topology. The MPLS protocols generate the MPLS label forwarding entries that are programmed in the CAM and PRAM.

- **Chassis Management**: This component is responsible for the management and monitoring of the overall switch/router. This includes initializing system modules, monitoring the insertion and removal of network interface modules and the management module, managing software upgrades on system modules, checking and maintaining software versions, monitoring temperature sensors, etc.

- **System Management**: The system management component represents all the software modules that are used in the management and monitoring of the overall switch/router. The system management component interacts with the chassis management component (discussed earlier) to provide system hardware management and monitoring functions. The software tools used in the management and interactive monitoring of the system include telnet, SSH (Secure Shell), and web-based modules. Other tools such as the syslog and SNMP modules also facilitate long-term (non-interactive) management and monitoring of the system. In addition to using services from the chassis management component, the system management software modules rely on services provided by the kernel.

7.6   SWITCHING AND ROUTING ARCHITECTURE

The Foundry Network switch/routers shared the same core hardware components but are configured with different processors and packet forwarding capabilities to serve different networking roles [FOUNJET03]:

- The FastIron switch/router is designed to be positioned in front of a traditional router, as a front-end device to the router, to off-load and forward routing traffic at wire speed. In the network, the FastIron switch/router serves as a front-end processor; however, the router is not aware of the FastIron switch/router's presence, and the other networking devices operate as if they are communicating directly with the router. The FastIron switch/router is conceptually a "virtual router", a front-end processor that off-loads up to 80% of the traffic sent to a router [FOUNJET03]. The FastIron switch/router is transparent to the other downstream network devices. These devices are aware of only the router the FastIron switch/router is attached to. The FastIron switch/router learns about IP forwarding addresses (to create its own forwarding table) on the fly by monitoring ICMP route discovery protocols and broadcast traffic [FOUNJET03].
- BigIron, NetIron, and TurboIron switch/routers all perform standard Layer 2 and Layer 3 (IP) forwarding concurrently on a single platform. Routers and hosts in a network see any one of these devices as just another router (Layer 3 device), while switches (Layer 2 devices) view it as either a switch (Layer 2 devices) or a router (Layer 3 devices), depending on the type of forwarding being performed. These switch/routers support unicast routing protocols such as IP, RIP, and OSPF, and multicast protocols such as IGMP, DMRP, and PIM-SM [FOUNJET03].

The FastIron switch/router is typically used in a network to relieve existing router bottlenecks, while the BigIron, NetIron, and TurboIron switch/routers are designed as backbone or core routers for campus, enterprise, and service provider networks.

7.6.1   FOUNDRY SWITCHING AND ROUTING ARCHITECTURE

Figure 7.6 shows a high-level view of the Foundry Networks integrated switching and routing architecture [FOUNJET03]. The FastIron, BigIron, NetIron, and TurboIron switch/routers are all based on this architecture.

- The top portion of Figure 7.6 shows the network ports. These ports are auto-sensing and auto-negotiating 10/100 Mb/s Ethernet ports (over copper or fiber), or Gigabit Ethernet ports in the case of the TurboIron switch/router, which also supports an additional 100 Mb/s or Gigabit Ethernet fiber expansion ports.

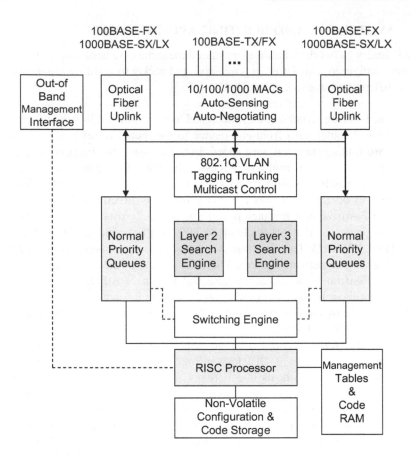

FIGURE 7.6 Foundry Switching and Routing Architecture.

- The Layer 2 and Layer 3 forwarding (search) engines are presented in the middle of Figure 7.6. These are flanked by the normal priority queues, which in turn are connected together by a high-speed switch fabric (i.e., the switching engine).
- The bottom portion of Figure 7.6 represents the route processor functions which are connected to memory resources (management tables and code RAM, and non-volatile configuration and code storage). This portion of the diagram maintains the control and management functions—all the Layer 3 routing protocol functions such as RIP and OSPF are supported here.

The condition under which a switch/router would perform Layer 2 or Layer 3 forwarding depends on the VLAN or subnet membership of the end stations. Traffic between end stations that belongs to the same VLAN or subnet is forwarded at Layer 2, while traffic from stations belonging to different VLANs or subnets is Layer 3 forwarded.

7.6.2 PACKET HANDLING MECHANISMS IN THE MULTILAYER SWITCH

Like in routers, IP forwarding in the Foundry switch/routers involves a number of primary functions. The switch/router first must learn about the network topology and locate adjacent routers and other Layer 3 devices. The process also involves learning about directly connected IP host addresses. The switch/router runs a number of routing protocols to discover the network topology and the Layer 3 peer devices. Static routes can also be (manually) configured by the network administrator.

When a packet is received, the switch/router performs a high-speed IP destination address lookup in its Layer 3 forwarding table, and then immediately forwards the traffic after performing IP TTL decrement, IP checksum update, source (egress port) and destination (next-hop) MAC address rewrite, and Ethernet frame checksum update. The Layer 3 forwarding table is generated from the routing tables maintained by the routing protocols.

Figure 7.7 shows the main mechanisms involved in packet forwarding in the Foundry switch/routers. The first task is for the switch/router to determine whether an arriving packet should be forwarded by Layer 2 or Layer 3 forwarding (or search) engine. If the packet has a destination MAC address that is the switch/router's MAC address, then the packet requires Layer 3 forwarding to reach its destination, and, therefore, should be processed by the Layer 3 forwarding engine.

Otherwise, the packet requires Layer 2 forwarding and the Layer 2 forwarding engine performs a lookup in its Layer 2 (or MAC) address cache and forwards the packet to the appropriate output port. All the necessary Layer 2 forwarding functions like MAC address learning, packet flooding, and filtering are performed by the Layer 2 forwarding engine.

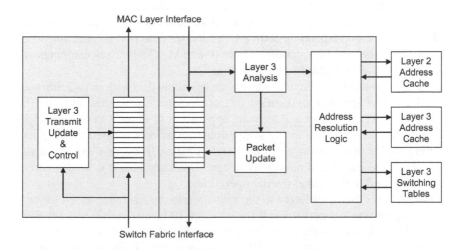

FIGURE 7.7   Packet Forwarding Mechanisms of the Foundry Switching and Routing Architecture.

If the packet requires Layer 3 forwarding (and depending on the type of switch/ router architecture), the Layer 3 forwarding engine may perform a destination address lookup in its Layer 3 address cache for the next-hop information. The Layer 3 address cache maps a destination IP address to IP next-hop address and egress port (and next-hop MAC address). All of the Foundry's switch/routers have a cache that maps Layer 3 to Layer 2 addresses.

The contents of the Layer 3 address cache are compiled automatically by gleaning MAC addresses and their corresponding IP addresses contained in packets streaming in the normal traffic flow in the network [FOUNJET03]. The Layer 3 forwarding engine performs a lookup in this Layer 3 address cache first (using the packet's destination IP address) and when it finds the corresponding IP next-hop MAC address (and egress port), it then quickly performs the standard IP header and Ethernet frame update and rewrite operations and forwards the packet through the outbound port. All these functions are performed in the IronCore and JetCore ASICs at wire speed and form the core of the Foundry Networks Layer 3 forwarding.

7.6.3 FastIron Multilayer Switch Architecture

When deployed in a network, the FastIron switch/router automatically discovers routers and other Layer 3 forwarding devices in two ways [FOUNJET03]. First, the FastIron switch/router transmits ICMP router discovery requests that cause routers and Layer 3 devices to respond to advertise their presence. Secondly, the FastIron switch/router monitors network traffic for ICMP, as well as RIP, OSPF, and IGRP messages. The information gleaned from these two methods provides the FastIron switch/router a view of the local routers and Layer 3 networks operating as neighbors.

Once the routers and Layer 3 peers are discovered, the FastIron switch/router monitors host station traffic to learn about the host addresses attached to it. The FastIron switch/router inspects the source MAC addresses in the packet headers and maps to the corresponding source IP addresses (and port of attachment) of sending and receiving host stations. These IP and MAC addresses mappings are then stored in Layer 3 address tables (Figure 7.8).

These hardware-based Layer 3 address caches allow the FastIron switch/router to perform wire speed IP destination address lookups, as opposed to using the traditional slower processor and software approaches of Layer 3 lookups and forwarding. As packets arrive at the switch/router, a hardware-based Layer 3 forwarding engine immediately performs the destination IP address lookup (in the Layer 3 address cache) and maps it to an egress port and next-hop MAC address that can be used in the packet rewrite operations.

The packet is then transferred to the next stage in the hardware-based Layer 3 forwarding engine that performs all the standard IP header update and Ethernet frame MAC address rewrite operations, after which the packet is forwarded out the outbound port. A packet whose IP destination address is found in the Layer 3 address cache is simply forwarded by standard Layer 3 processing and forwarding using the full (network topology-based) Layer 3 forwarding (address) table.

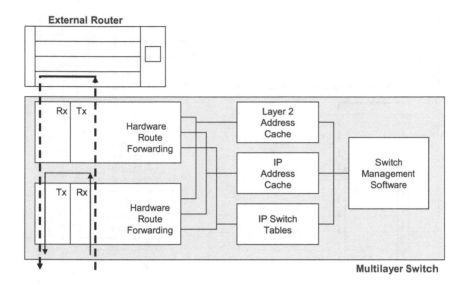

FIGURE 7.8   FastIron™ Multilayer Switch Architecture and Packet Forwarding.

If the Layer 3 forwarding engine in the FastIron switch/router cannot find a corresponding destination IP address for a packet in its Layer 3 address cache, then the switch/router will forward the packet to the (relatively more sophisticated) IP router that it front-ends (Figure 7.8). This situation may arise because the IP destination of the packet does not often transmit or receive traffic through this front-end FastIron switch/router and as a result its Layer 3 address cache does not contain an entry for that destination.

7.6.4   BigIron, NetIron, and TurboIron Multilayer Switch Architecture

If the Layer 3 forwarding engine cannot find a corresponding IP address for an arriving packet in its Layer 3 address cache, the BigIron, NetIron, or TurboIron switch/router, on the other hand, will call on its full Layer 3 forwarding functions and Layer 3 forwarding table on the management processor to Layer 3 forward the packet (Figure 7.9).

The forwarding engine (based on the Foundry Networks IronCore or JetCore chipsets) located on each line interface module has a local shared-memory switch fabric. All packets, whether Layer 2 or Layer 3 forwarded, pass through this switch fabric at wire speed [FOUNJET03]. Priority queuing of packets in the shared-memory buffer pool is coordinated with the Layer 2 and 3 forwarding engines to help regulate traffic rates on a per-port basis. Individual end users and applications, devices, and VLANs can be classified and assigned to normal or high priority queues, with bandwidth allocated to the priority queues by user

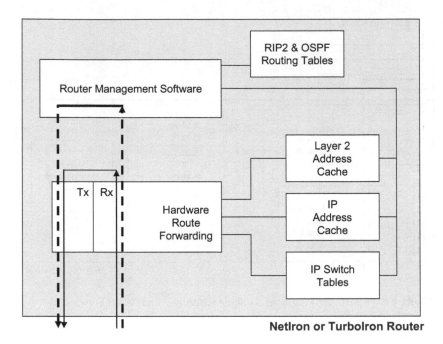

FIGURE 7.9   BigIron™, NetIron™ or TurboIron™ Multilayer Switch Architecture and Packet Forwarding.

configurable scheduling algorithms, and with each queue managed by appropriate congestion management mechanisms (e.g., Weighted Random Early Detection (WRED)).

REFERENCE

[FOUNJET03]. Foundry Networks, JetCore™ Based Chassis Systems: An Architecture Brief on NetIron, BigIron, and FastIron Systems, White Paper, 2003.

8 Cisco Catalyst 6500 Series Switches with Supervisor Engine 720

8.1 INTRODUCTION

In the newer Supervisor Engine 720 (unlike the older Supervisor Engines 1A, 2, and 32), the crossbar switch fabric is built into the Supervisor Engine 720 baseboard itself, which makes the need for a standalone switch fabric module (that will take up a separate chassis slot) no longer necessary. The new integrated crossbar switch fabric on the Supervisor Engine 720 has an overall bandwidth of 720 Gb/s, much higher than the previous standalone switch fabric module which has a capacity of 256 Gb/s. The newer versions of the Supervisor Engine 720, that is, Supervisor Engine 720–3B and Supervisor Engine 720–3BXL, also support the same switch fabric bandwidth of 720 Gb/s. The "720" in the name "Supervisor Engine 720" refers to the 720 Gb/s integrated crossbar switch fabric.

The Catalyst 6500 with Supervisor Engine 720 can be fitted with a wide range of line card types. Adopting the architecture categories broadly used to classify the various designs in *Chapter 3*, the following architectures are covered in this chapter:

- Architectures with Crossbar-Based Switch Fabrics and Centralized Forwarding Engines (see Figure 8.1):
  - Catalyst 6500 Series switches with Supervisor Engines 720— Architectures with "Classic" line cards
  - Catalyst 6500 Series switches with Supervisor Engines 720— Architectures with CEF256 fabric-enabled line cards (optional Distributed Forwarding Card (DFC) not installed)
  - Catalyst 6500 Series switches with Supervisor Engines 720— Architectures with CEF720 line cards (optional DFC not installed)
- Architectures with Crossbar-Based Switch Fabrics and Distributed Forwarding Engines (see Figure 8.2):
  - Catalyst 6500 Series switches with Supervisor Engines 720— Architectures with CEF256 fabric-enabled line cards with optional DFC installed
  - Catalyst 6500 Series switches with Supervisor Engines 720— Architectures with dCEF256 line cards with integrated DFC
  - Catalyst 6500 Series switches with Supervisor Engines 720— Architectures with CEF720 line cards with optional DFC not installed

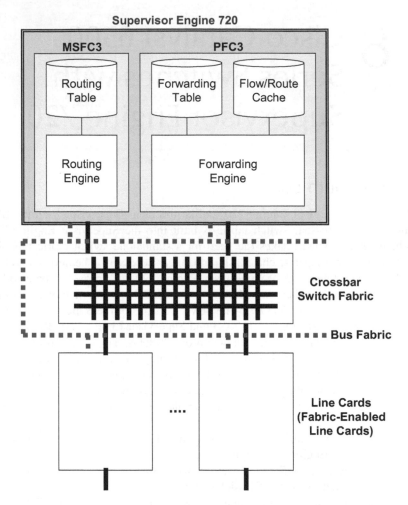

FIGURE 8.1 Architectures with Crossbar-Based Switch Fabrics and Centralized Forwarding Engines (Fabric-Enabled Line Cards without a Distributed Forwarding Card (DFC) Installed).

- • Catalyst 6500 Series switches with Supervisor Engines 720— Architectures with dCEF720 line cards with integrated DFC
- • Architectures with Crossbar-Based Switch Fabrics and Forwarding Engines and Flow Cache in Line Cards (see Figure 8.3):
  - • Catalyst 6500 Series switches with Supervisor Engines 720— Architectures with aCEF line cards (forwarding with flow cache in line cards).

These architectures are discussed in various sections in this chapter, including their corresponding packet forwarding operations.

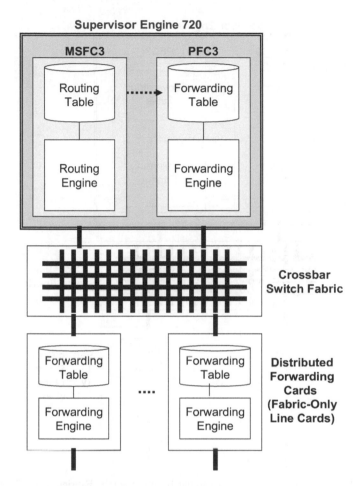

FIGURE 8.2 Architectures with Crossbar-Based Switch Fabrics and Distributed Forwarding Engines Architectures (Fabric-Only Line Cards (with Embedded DFC)).

8.2 CISCO CATALYST 6500 BACKPLANE

The Catalyst 6500 with Supervisor Engine 720 has packet forwarding performance of up to 400 million packets-per-second (Mpps), and supports a wider range of chassis options with slot capacities ranging from 3 to 13 slots. The chassis options all support redundant supervisor engines in addition to redundant power supplies. This Catalyst 6500 family of switches is comprised of the Catalyst 6503, 6506, 6509, 6509-NEBS, 6509-NEBS-A, and 6513 switches. The newer "E" series chassis (Catalyst 6503-E, 6504-E, 6506-E, and 6509-E switches) are designed to deliver a higher power output over the switch backplane as well as a higher power to each line card slot.

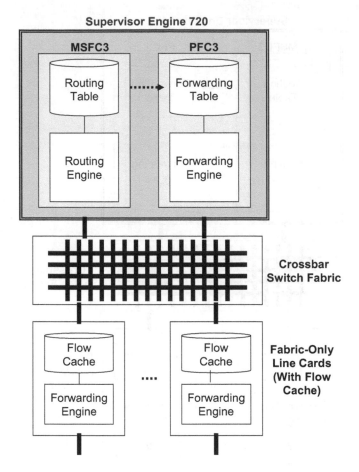

FIGURE 8.3   Architectures with Crossbar-Based Switch Fabrics and Forwarding
Engines and Flow Cache in Line Cards (Fabric-Only Line Cards with
Accelerated Cisco Express Forwarding).

In each Cisco Catalyst 6500 chassis option, the crossbar switch fabric supports
(in a slightly different configuration) a number of fabric channels (or discrete
paths into the switch fabric) to each line card slot (see [CISCCAT6500] which
details each chassis fabric layout). Figure 8.4 illustrates the backplane architecture and line card connector layout in the Cisco Catalyst 6509-E chassis.

8.3   CISCO CATALYST 6500 CROSSBAR SWITCH FABRIC

The integrated 720 Gb/s crossbar switch fabric on the Supervisor Engine 720
clocks each fabric channel at either 8 Gb/s or 20 Gb/s. This allows the crossbar
switch fabric to support connectivity to both the older version fabric line cards
at 8 Gb/s per fabric channel (see fabric-enabled and fabric-only line cards in

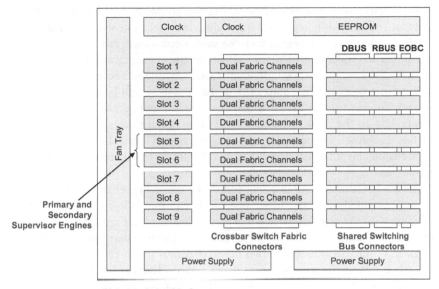

Slots 1 to 4 plus 6 to 9:
• Classic line cards slots
• Single fabric channel line card slots
• Dual fabric channel line card slots

FIGURE 8.4   Cisco Catalyst 6509-E Backplane.

Chapter 4), and the newer version fabric line cards at 20 Gb/s per fabric channel
(see discussion later). In addition, the Supervisor Engine 720 also supports connectivity to the Classic (non-fabric-enabled) line cards.

These features and capabilities allow the Supervisor Engine 720 to provide
full backward compatibility for all earlier generation line cards. A major benefit
of this dual clocking capability of the integrated 720 Gb/s crossbar switch fabric
is that the customer is able to preserve investment in earlier generation line cards
that support 8 Gb/s connections into the crossbar switch fabric.

The clocking speed that the switch fabric selects for a fabric channel is deter-
mined/selected by the line card type the channel connects to (i.e., the CEF256,
dCEF256, CEF720, or dCEF720 line cards). When the CEF256 and dCEF256
line cards are installed, they cause the crossbar switch fabric to clock the connecting fabric channels at 8 Gb/s. The CEF720 and dCEF720 line cards, on the
other hand, will cause the switch fabric to clock the connecting fabric channels at
20 Gb/s. The fabric channels will each independently auto-sync (auto-clock) to 8
Gb/s or 20 Gb/s depending on the type of line card supported. The CEF256 line
cards are described in *Chapter 4*.

The crossbar switch fabric can support, at the same time, fabric channels to
different line cards clocked at different speeds. This feature allows the Supervisor
Engine 720 to, for instance, support a single fabric channel to a CEF256 line card
at 8 Gb/s, and two fabric channels to a CEF720 line card at 2 × 20 Gb/s. As will be

discussed later, the Supervisor Engine 720 crossbar switch fabric is able to deliver bandwidth of 40 Gb/s (via two separate fabric channels) to each line card slot.

The crossbar switch fabric in both the standalone switch fabric module (SFM) used in earlier supervisor engines and in the Supervisor Engine 720, 720–3B, and 720–3BXL supports 18 individual fabric channels. These fabric channels are divided among the line card slots in the chassis. In all but the 13-slot chassis, each line card slot is assigned two channels (in and out) of the switch fabric (Figure 8.5). In the 3-, 4-, 6-, and 9-slot chassis, each line card slot is allocated two fabric channels connecting to the crossbar switch fabric. In the 9-slot chassis fabric channel layout illustrated in Figure 8.5, Slot 5 is assigned to the Supervisor Engine 720.

The Cisco Catalyst 6513 does not follow the two-fabric channels per line card slot assignment described earlier. Instead, it has the following fabric channel assignment for the crossbar switch fabric. As illustrated in Figure 8.6, each slot in Slots 1 to 8 is assigned a single fabric channel to the crossbar switch, while each slot in Slots 9 to 13 is assigned two fabric channels to the crossbar switch. The dual fabric (channel) line cards (see discussion on line card types later) cannot be installed in slots 1 through 8 because these slots support only a single fabric channel to the crossbar switch fabric.

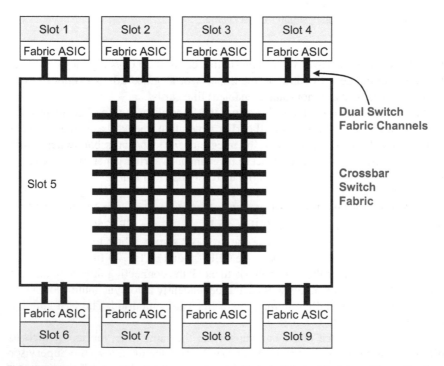

FIGURE 8.5 Fabric Channel Layout for the Switch Fabric Module—Cisco Catalyst 6509 Crossbar Switch Fabric.

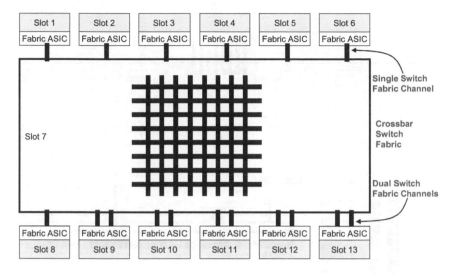

FIGURE 8.6   Fabric Channel Layout for the Switch Fabric Module—Cisco Catalyst 6513 Crossbar Switch Fabric.

The 720 Gb/s crossbar switch fabric architecture employs a combination of per output port buffering at every input port (virtual output queuing (VOQ)) and fabric over-speed (fabric speedup or overspeed) to overcome any potential congestion and head-of-line (HOL) blocking conditions. Fabric Overspeed is a technique used to accelerate packet switching through the switch fabric in order to minimize the impact of congestion. Overspeed refers to the clocking of the internal switch fabric paths at a speed higher than the speed of channels leading into the crossbar switch fabric.

For the Supervisor Engine 720 switch fabric, where the external fabric channels are clocked at 20 Gb/s, the internal paths are clocked at 60 Gb/s, resulting in three times overspeed. Buffering and queues are also employed internally within the crossbar switch fabric to handle any temporary periods of congestion.

8.4   SUPERVISOR ENGINE 720

The Supervisor Engine 720 [CISC6500DSSE] [CISCGOLD04] is a newer generation Supervisor Engine beyond the older Supervisor Engines 1A and 2 (*Chapter 4*) and Supervisor Engine 32 [CISCSUPENG32]. All the Supervisor Engines options (720, 720–3B, and 720–3BXL) have the 720 Gb/s crossbar switch fabric integrated onto the supervisor engine module itself, support a connection to the 32 Gb/s (Classic) shared switching bus, and have another single 20 Gb/s connection to the onboard crossbar switch fabric (Figure 8.7). Furthermore, all Supervisor Engine 720 options support centralized packet forwarding rates of up to 30 Mpps (i.e., forwarding performed by centralized forwarding engines in the Supervisor Engine) and distributed packet forwarding rates up to 400 Mpps (i.e., forwarding performed by forwarding engines in the line cards).

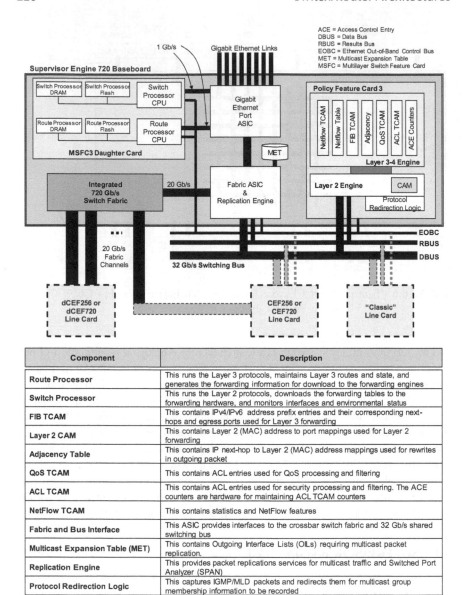

FIGURE 8.7   Supervisor Engine 720 Baseboard Architecture.

Supervisor Engines 720, 720–3B, and 720–3BXL all support a Policy Feature Card 3 (PFC3) and Multilayer Switch Feature Card 3 (MSFC3), in addition to the 720 Gb/s crossbar switch fabric, all into a single module. In these supervisor engines, the PFC3 and MSFC3 are no longer supported as optional components as in Supervisor Engines 1A and 2 (see *Chapter 4*). The Supervisor Engine 720 employs a 600 MHz CPU as the switch processor and a 600 MHz CPU as the route processor (Figure 8.7).

The Supervisor Engine 720 also provides a number of feature enhancements and capabilities beyond Supervisor Engines 1A and 2, which include the following:

- Hardware-based forwarding of MPLS and IPv6 packets
- Hardware assisted processing of Network Address Translation (NAT) and Generic Routing Encapsulation (GRE) traffic
- Integrated crossbar switch fabric channel bandwidth increased to 2 × 20 Gb/s, which is higher than the 2 × 8 Gb/s in the standalone Switch Fabric Module (SFM) employed with the older Supervisor Engines 1A and 2
- Maximum packet forwarding rate of 400 Mpps which is almost two times that of the Supervisor Engine 2 with SFM installed.

The Supervisor Engine 720 has a significantly higher number of slots available for line cards compared to the previous engines. For example, in a non-redundant Catalyst 6509 chassis (Figure 8.4 and Figure 8.5) with nine slots, the Supervisor Engine 720 consumes only a single slot, leaving eight slots for line cards. In comparison, a Supervisor Engine 2 with a standalone SFM installed in a chassis consumes two slots, leaving only seven slots for line cards.

In a configuration with supervisor engine redundancy, the two Supervisor Engine 720 engines required will take up only two slots. In the corresponding configuration, the two Supervisor Engine 2 modules and redundant SFMs will take up four slots. In the Catalyst 6506, 6509, and 6513, the primary Supervisor Engine 720 sits in Slot 5, while the redundant Supervisor 720 sits in Slot 6.

In the default configuration, a Supervisor Engine 720 will automatically detect the multicast packet replication mode based on the line card types installed in the system. If all line cards in the chassis are capable of egress replication of multicast packets, the system will enter into egress replication mode. If the supervisor engine detects that the line cards installed are not capable of egress replication, the system automatically changes the replication mode to ingress replication.

The system administrator can override the earlier configuration with appropriate commands so that the system continues to operate in egress replication mode even if there are fabric-enabled line cards installed that do not support egress replication of multicast packets. If egress replication mode is forcefully configured in a system that has fabric-enabled modules (that are not capable of egress replication), then the user must make sure that these line cards are not sending out or receiving multicast traffic. The user can also configure the system to operate only in ingress replication mode.

8.4.1 MULTILAYER SWITCH FEATURE CARD 3 (MSFC3)

The MSFC3 handles the control plane functions in addition to other management tasks in the Cisco Catalyst 6500 with Supervisor Engine 720 which include running the routing protocols, generating and maintaining the routing table, implementing access control, handling flow initiation, and other services not found in the PFC or line card hardware. The packet forwarding performance of the control plane (which is implemented in software) depends very much on the type and number of processes running on the MSFC3. The MSFC3 supports a maximum packet forwarding rate of 500 Kpps.

The MSFC3 fits into the Supervisor Engine 720 in the form of a daughter card as illustrated in Figure 8.7. The MSFC3 contains the Route Processor CPU which performs a number of functions, including running the routing protocols and ICMP, performing address resolution functions to map IP addresses to Layer 2 addresses, initializing and managing the switched virtual interfaces (SVIs), and running and configuration of the Cisco IOS Software. The Switch Processor CPU (which is also located on the daughter board (see Figure 8.7)), on the other hand, is primarily responsible for running the Layer 2 protocols such as Spanning Tree Protocol (STP), VLAN Trunking protocol, IEEE 802.1AB Link Layer Discovery Protocol (LLDP), etc.

The MSFC3 maintains the routing tables and generates the main (master) forwarding table but does not actively handle the forwarding of normal user packets—a function reserved for the PFC3 and Distributed Forwarding Cards (DFCs). The MSFC3 communicates with its routing peers to determine the network topology and build the routing tables. From the routing tables, the MSFC3 generates the forwarding table and copies this to the PFC3 and any DFCs present in the chassis.

8.4.2 POLICY FEATURE CARD 3 (PFC3)

The PFC3, which is also a daughter card on the Supervisor Engine 720 baseboard (Figure 8.7), provides complementary services to the MSFC3. The PFC3 contains the "heavy lifting" hardware functions (in the form of specialized ASICs) that are used to forward packets at Layer 2 and Layer 3, process QoS and security ACLs, and generate NetFlow statistics. The PFC3 is not optional as in the Supervisor Engines 1A and 2 but rather a standard feature in the Supervisor Engine 720. It provides centralized packet forwarding of up to 30 Mpps. As illustrated in Figure 8.7, the PFC3 supports a Layer 2 engine and Layer 3 forwarding engine each performing different functions.

The PFC3 Layer 2 forwarding engine is responsible for a number of functions of which the major ones include the following:

- Performing Layer 2 MAC address table lookups into the CAM table (Figure 8.7) holding the Layer 2 addresses (in the PFC3)
- Examining arriving packet headers to determine if a forwarding decision has to be made at Layer 2 or Layer 3
- If a Layer 3 forwarding operation is required, the packet is forwarded to the Layer 3 forwarding engine (in the PFC3) for further processing.

The PFC3 Layer 3 forwarding engine is responsible for a number of functions some of which include the following:

- Implementing the hardware-based forwarding logic that allows for the high-speed forwarding of IPv4, IPv6 and MPLS packets, in addition to supporting a unique Ethernet MAC address for each Layer 3 VLAN interface (or SVI)
- Supporting QoS mechanisms that allow for packet classification using ACLs, marking/rewriting QoS tags in packets, policing and shaping of traffic, and NetFlow statistics collection
- Communicating with neighboring nodes and performing address resolution functions in order to maintain adjacency entries and statistics required for packet forwarding
- Supporting security ACLs and mechanisms that can be used to check against incoming packets as part of a security policy, in addition to maintaining security ACL counters.

The processing capabilities of the PFC3 have also been enhanced beyond the features in PFC2 used in Supervisor Engine 2, and allow for the processing of the following in hardware: IPv6 ACLs, IPv6 tunneling, multi-path unicast reverse path forwarding check (uRPF), NAT and Port Address Translation (PAT), Bi-Direction Protocol Independent Multicast (BIDIR-PIM), user based rate limiting (UBRL), egress policing of traffic, etc.

The PFC3 hardware options all support hardware-based DoS rate limiters for control plane protection. DoS attacks can compromise the performance or even stop the operations of the Supervisor Engine, thus making the protection of the Supervisor Engine from these types of attacks more paramount in today's networks. The Supervisor Engine 720 rate limiting mechanisms protect against both unicast and multicast DoS traffic attacks. Reference [CISCCAT6500] describes the traffic types that the Supervisor Engine 720 will apply rate limiters to if that traffic exceeds a configured threshold.

8.5   SUPERVISOR ENGINE 720–3B

The Supervisor Engine 720–3B was developed as a newer iteration to the Supervisor Engine 720. It has a similar architecture to the Supervisor Engine 720 and they both share the same integrated 720 Gb/s crossbar switch fabric and backplane connection designs used. The Supervisor Engine 720–3B, however, employs a newer PFC3B which allows the engine to support a higher number of features and capabilities.

The following are some of the features that distinguish the Supervisor Engine 720–3B from the older Supervisor Engine 720: Ethernet over MPLS (EoMPLS) traffic processing, increased storage for ACL labels from 512 to 4096, support of security ACL hit counters, matching of IEEE 802.1Q class of service (CoS) and VLAN in ACLs, application of Layer 2 ACLs to IPv4 traffic, application of QoS policies on tunnel interfaces, support of up to 256K multicast routes in PIM sparse mode, increased storage of NetFlow entries in the NetFlow table, etc.

8.5.1   POLICY FEATURE CARD 3B (PFC3B)

A number of enhancements were added to the PFC3 with the introduction of the newer PFC3B. The PFC3B enhances the PFC3 by adding a number of new hardware-based functions, in addition to increasing the number of flow entries that can be maintained in the NetFlow table. One of the most noticeable enhancements is the hardware forwarding of MPLS tagged packets, which enables any Ethernet based line card to process locally (i.e., receive and forward) MPLS tagged packets as well as support Ethernet over MPLS.

As discussed earlier under the Supervisor Engine 720–3B section, the PFC3B also supports a number of new QoS capabilities, which include the ability to apply QoS policies on tunnel interfaces, the support of a higher number of ACL labels of up to 4096, and matching ACLs to CoS and VLAN values on incoming packets. The PFC3B is designed as an upgradeable option to the PFC3 which allows a Supervisor Engine 720 to be upgraded to a Supervisor Engine 720–3B simply by installing a PFC3B (see discussion later).

8.6   SUPERVISOR ENGINE 720–3BXL

The Supervisor Engine 720–3BXL and Supervisor Engine 720–3B are designed to be functionally identical except that the Supervisor Engine 720–3BXL has a higher storage capacity for routes and NetFlow entries. The upgraded Supervisor Engine 720–3BXL supports a storage capacity of up to 1 million routes in its forwarding tables and 256K entries in the NetFlow tables it maintains.

8.6.1   POLICY FEATURE CARD 3BXL (PFC3BXL)

The PFC3BXL and PFC3B are also functionally identical except the PFC3BXL supports up to 1 million routes in its forwarding tables and 256K entries in the NetFlow tables. The PFC3BXL also supports a higher number of multicast routes of up to 256K multicast routes (an increase from the effective maximum of 64K entries in PFC3 and PFC3B) when the Supervisor Engine 720 is running in PIM-SM. Similar to the PFC3B, the PFC3BXL is also designed as an upgradeable option which allows a Supervisor Engine 720 to be upgraded to a Supervisor Engine 720–3BXL when installed.

8.7   PACKET FORWARDING IN SUPERVISOR ENGINES 720, 720–3B, AND 720–3BXL

Similar to Supervisor Engine 32, Supervisor Engines 720, 720–3B, and 720–3BXL all utilize a forwarding architecture based on network topology derived forwarding tables and optimized lookup algorithms (called Cisco Express Forwarding (CEF) by Cisco) to forward packets. These supervisor engines can forward Layer 2 and 3 packets up to 30 Mpps when using centralized forwarding, and up to 400 Mpps when using distributed forwarding.

In the flow cash-based forwarding architecture, a line card would send the initial or first packet of a flow to the Supervisor Engine, where the packet is processed and forwarded using the master forwarding table maintained there. The forwarding result obtained from the Supervisor Engine is then transferred and stored in a local flow cache on the line card where the flow entered the switch. The ingress line card would then make any subsequent forwarding decisions for packets associated with the flow using the information stored in the local flow cache.

The distributed forwarding architecture allows the control plane functions (running in the MSFC3) to interact with peer routing functions running in other Layer 3 devices and routers to build a picture of the network topology. From this topology information which is stored in routing tables maintained in the MSFC3, the MSFC3 generates a Forwarding Information Base (FIB) that is transferred to the PFC3/3B/3BXL (and any installed DFCs in the system).

In the PFC3/3B/3BXL (and DFC), the FIB is programmed into hardware TCAM. With the local FIB, the PFC3/3B/3BXL (and DFCs) has full a picture of the network topology at all times and can make local forwarding decisions on incoming packets. Whenever the network topology changes, the master FIB is modified and copied to the PFC3/3B/3BXL (and DFCs) keeping them informed of the current network topology at all times.

8.8 CATALYST 6500 LINE CARDS SUPPORTED BY SUPERVISOR ENGINE 720

The Catalyst 6500 with Supervisor 720/720–3B/720–3BXL supports line card types—Classic, CEF256, CEF720, dCEF256, and dCEF720. All of these line card types, when installed in the same chassis, can interoperate and communicate with each other. This section described the CEF720, dCEF256, and dCEF720. The Classic and CEF256 are discussed in detail in *Chapter 4* and [CISCCAT6500].

The CEF256 fabric-enabled line cards connect to both the 32 Gb/s shared switching bus and the SFM (that is, 256 Gb/s fabric in Supervisor Engine 2 or 720 Gb/s fabric in Supervisor Engine 720). These line cards use an optional DFC on the line card or the centralized forwarding engine on PFC for forwarding of packets. When performing central lookup in the PFC, the line card transfers only packet headers on the 32 Gb/s shared switching bus, but the packet payload is always sent over the switch fabric.

The Cisco Catalyst 6500 Supervisor Engine 720/720–3B/720–3BXL has a distributed architecture and is designed such that not all forwarding operations have to be performed on the Supervisor Engine. The line cards are designed with a range of forwarding functions (implemented in on-board ASICs) to support high-speed forwarding of packets locally:

- Per-port receive and transmit buffering
- Input virtual output queuing (VOQ) and scheduling to eliminate head-of-line (HOL) blocking

- Per-port QoS classification that allows for CoS priority bits to be examined and rewritten/modified
- Congestion management of individual line card and Supervisor Engine queues using algorithms such as Weighted Random Early Discard (WRED)
- Scheduling of queues using Strict Priority and Weighted Round-Robin (WRR) algorithms.

Line cards with both DFCs and dual crossbar switch fabric channels have two packet replication engines (one connected to each fabric channel). Each replication engine handles packet forwarding and replication to and from the line card interfaces associated with the crossbar switch fabric channel it is connected to. A replication engine considers the line card interfaces connected to its crossbar switch fabric channel as local.

The network administrator can disable redundant replication of multicast packets across the crossbar switch fabric channel by manually instructing any of the two replication engines (on a line card) to forward packets only to its local interfaces in particular. When this mode of operation is enabled, the multicast expansion table (MET) aligned with each replication engine will be populated with the local Layer 3 interfaces only. This mode of operation prevents replication for interfaces that are not local to the replication engine (non-local interfaces) and also increases overall packet replication and forwarding performance.

Local egress packet replication is also supported on a line card when the following software configurable options are enabled: IPv4 egress packet replication is configured, dual switch fabric channel DFC-equipped line cards are used, and when Layer 3 routed interfaces (that are not part of a switch port channel) are used.

8.8.1 DCEF256 LINE CARD ARCHITECTURE

A dCEF256 line card supports two 8 Gb/s fabric channels to the crossbar switch fabric as well as two local 16 Gb/s shared switching buses to which the line card ports are connected as shown in Figure 8.8. These line cards require the crossbar switch fabric to communicate with the Supervisor Engine and other line cards. Unlike the CEF256 line cards ([CISCCAT6500]), the dCEF256 line card has no connection to the 32 Gb/s shared switching bus.

As shown in Figure 8.8, the fabric ASICs in the dCEF256 line card serve as the only interfaces between the local ports on the line card, and other modules and ports located across the crossbar switch fabric. An example of a dCEF256 line card is the WS-X6816-GBIC line card. The WS-X6816-GBIC supports 2 x 8 Gb/s fabric channels and 16 GBIC based Gigabit Ethernet ports. The Port ASICs (in all line card types) support packet buffering, priority queuing and port-level QoS, traffic scheduling, congestion avoidance, traffic shaping, VLAN tagging, traffic filtering and broadcast suppression, and link aggregation (EtherChannel).

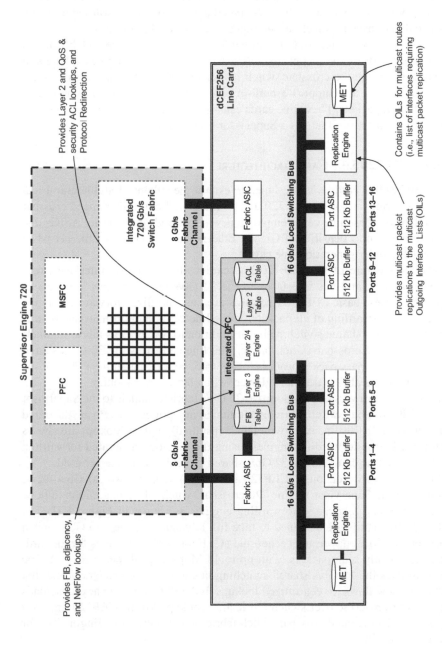

FIGURE 8.8 Dual Fabric Cisco Express Forwarding Line Card Architecture (dCEF256 Line Card).

As illustrated in Figure 8.8, one 16 Gb/s shared bus serves one group of 8 Gigabit Ethernet ports on the WS-X6816-GBIC line card and the second 16 Gb/s shared bus serves the remaining group of 8 ports. Packets that are to be forwarded between ports on a particular 16 Gb/s shared bus are locally forwarded over that bus and do not have to travel outside that shared bus or the line card.

However, packets that are to be forwarded from a port on one 16 Gb/s shared bus to other ports on the second 16 Gb/s shared bus on the same line card are still forwarded through the crossbar switch fabric. The dCEF256 line cards connect to the SFM only and support a built-in or integrated DFC which allows local forwarding of packets. These line cards can also be upgraded to support a DFC3a when used in a chassis that has a Supervisor Engine 720.

8.8.2 CEF720 LINE CARD ARCHITECTURE

The CEF720 line cards were designed to exploit the enhanced architectural features of the Supervisor Engine 720 and its integrated but higher-speed crossbar switch fabric. These line cards employ a new set of high-performing ASICs that support higher port densities of Gigabit Ethernet and 10 Gigabit Ethernet when compared to older generation line cards.

The architecture of the CEF720 line card with only fabric interfaces, replication engines, and bus interfaces to the 32 Gb/s switching bus is shown in Figure 8.9. These basic CEF720 line cards use the centralized forwarding engine on PFC3 for forwarding of all packets. These line cards support internal connections to a 32 Gb/s shared switching bus in addition to two 20 Gb/s fabric channels to the integrated crossbar switch fabric. The line card uses the 32 Gb/s shared switching bus to pass packet headers for centralized lookups in the PFC, but the packet payload is always transferred over switch fabric after lookup.

Some line card versions support two 20 Gb/s fabric channels to the Supervisor Engine 720 crossbar switch fabric in addition to an optional DFC3a as illustrated in Figure 8.10. In this line card (with DFC3 installed), ingress lookups are always performed by the forwarding engines (using the topology generated forwarding tables) on the line card and the 32 Gb/s shared switching bus is never used.

Other line card versions (aCEF720 line cards) support two 20 Gb/s fabric channels to the Supervisor Engine 720 crossbar switch fabric in addition to flow/ route caches and associated forwarding engines as shown in Figure 8.11. The aCEF720 line cards are designed to take full advantage of the 720 Gb/s switch fabric but use local flow/route caches and aCEF forwarding engines for forwarding of frequently seen packets (with up to 48 Mpps at peak performance). The line card uses the 32 Gb/s shared switching bus to pass the headers of the first packets of new flows for centralized lookups in the PFC, but the packet payloads are always transferred over switch fabric after lookup. All the CEF720 line card types use the integrated crossbar switch fabric on the Supervisor Engine 720 for packet forwarding.

As illustrated in Figure 8.9 to Figure 8.11, the CEF720 line cards employ a new fabric (interface) ASIC which integrates support for multicast packet replication.

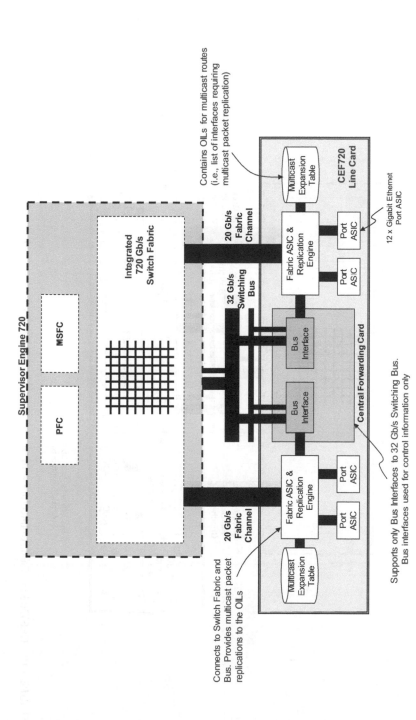

FIGURE 8.9 CEF720 Line Card Architecture with Only Fabric Interfaces, Replication Engines, and 32 Gb/s Switching Bus Interfaces—WS-X6700 Series Modules.

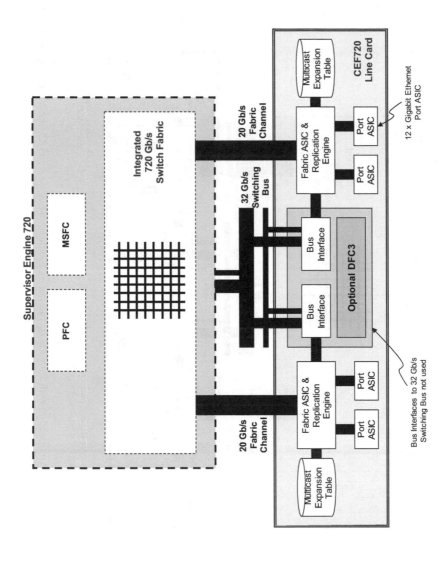

FIGURE 8.10 CEF720 Line Card Architecture with Optional DFC3 — WS-X6800 Series Modules.

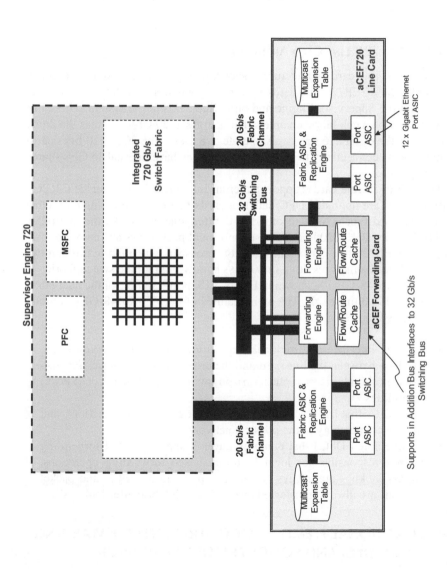

FIGURE 8.11 CEF720 Line Card Architecture with Flow/Route Cache-Based Forwarding Engine (or aCEF720 Line Card).

Multicast packet replication was implemented in a separate ASIC in earlier generation line cards. Some line card versions have a single port ASIC that supports twelve local Gigabit Ethernet ports. Other line card versions have two port ASICs each supporting two 10 Gigabit Ethernet ports. As stated earlier, an optional DFC3 can be used with these line cards to provide local processing and forwarding of packets.

8.8.3 DCEF720 LINE CARD ARCHITECTURE

The dCEF720 line card architecture is shown in Figure 8.12. Like the dCEF256 line cards, the dCEF720 line cards require a crossbar switch fabric to communicate with the Supervisor Engine and other line cards in the system. These line cards have two switch fabric channels that operate at 20 Gb/s whereas the fabric channels in the dCEF256 line cards operate at 8 Gb/s. The dCEF720 lines cards do not support connectivity to a 32 Gb/s nor do they have internal 16 Gb/s shared switching bus(es).

The dCEF720 line cards support either an integrated DFC3C or DFC3CXL, both of which are upgraded DFC daughter cards that can also be fitted on other newer line card types. As with other DFC fitted line cards like the dCEF256, the DFC on the dCEF720 line cards support local packet forwarding of up to 48 Mpps. A dCEF720 line card connects to the crossbar switch fabric through two 20 Gb/s fabric channels resulting in 40 Gb/s bandwidth into the switch fabric.

The WS-X6748-GE-TX, shown in Figure 8.13, is an example of the dual fabric channel dCEF720 line cards. The main features of the WS-X6748-GE-TX architecture are as follows:

- A fabric interface and multicast replication engine that serves as the interface between the line card and the crossbar switch fabric, and also provides the multicast replication and switched port analyzer (SPAN) capabilities
- Port ASICs that have hardware processing logic and port functions, and provide connectivity to the physical network
- An integrated DFC3 that contains Layer 2 and Layer 3–4 forwarding engines responsible for local hardware-based forwarding operations. Ingress lookups are always performed on the local DFC3, and packet payloads are always transferred over the switch fabric after lookups.

8.9 FUNCTIONAL ELEMENTS OF DISTRIBUTED FORWARDING CARD (DFC) AND POLICY FEATURE CARD (PFC)

As discussed earlier, the Distributed Forwarding Card (DFC) can be used on selected line card types to support forwarding of packets locally within the line card without having to send them to the forwarding engines in the Supervisor Engine. The DFC employs the same Layer 2 and Layer 3 forwarding ASICs as those used on the PFC. Figure 8.14 shows the common architecture employed in

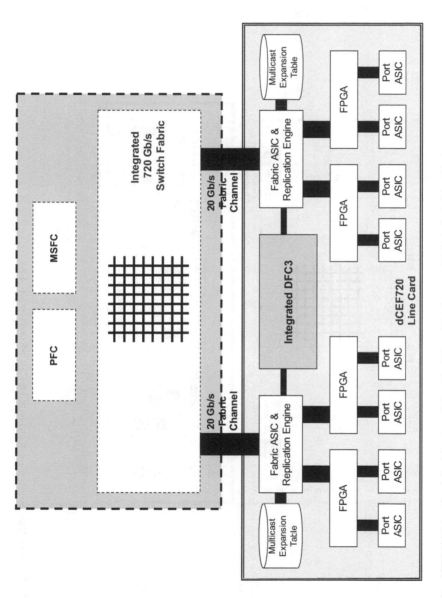

FIGURE 8.12   dCEF720 Line Card Architecture (Line Card Does Not Support 32 Gb/s Switching Bus).

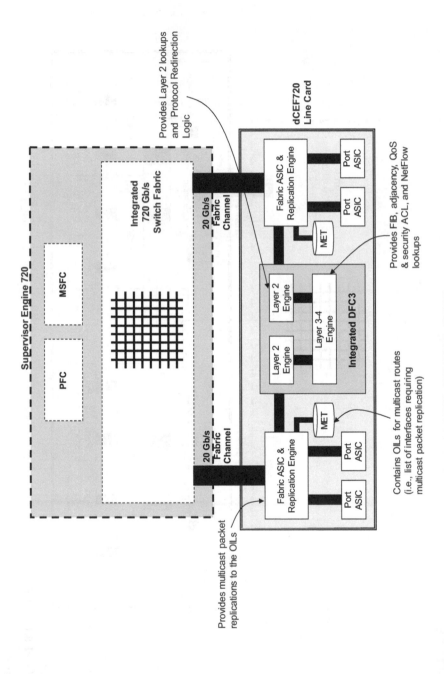

FIGURE 8.13 Example Dual Fabric Line Card with DFC3 (WS-X6748-GE-TX).

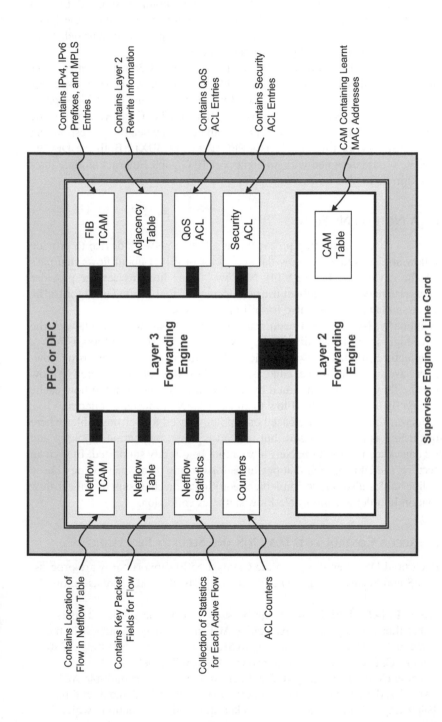

FIGURE 8.14 Policy Feature Card (PFC3) and Distributed Forwarding Card Functional Elements.

the DFC and the PFC. The DFC and PFC both also maintain the same ACLs used for QoS and security processing in the system. These features allow the DFC, when forwarding a packet locally in the line card, to process in parallel, local security and QoS policies configured in the system.

The CEF256 or CEF720 line cards can also use the DFC3a when a Supervisor Engine 720 is installed in the system. The DFC3a comes in two versions—one for the CEF256 and another for the CEF720. Both the DFC3a and the PFC3 support only hardware-based forwarding of IPv4 and IPv6 traffic. Other versions of the DFC are the DFC3B and DFC3BXL. These can be used when the corresponding PFC on the Supervisor Engine 720 is a PFC3B or PFC3BXL. Both the DFC3C and DFC3CXL are designed with an eight port 10 Gigabit Ethernet module integrated within them.

8.9.1 A NOTE ON NETFLOW

NetFlow is a Cisco networking protocol that allows a network device to provide traffic flow statistics to a NetFlow data collector or server about flows that pass through the device (see Figure 8.14). Netflow is used in many service provider and enterprise networks to collect traffic information that is often used for traffic monitoring and analysis, and also for billing purposes.

Traditionally, NetFlow had been implemented in routers; however, with the advent of high-speed forwarding at Layers 2, 3, and beyond, NetFlow is now a common feature in other network devices. A router or switch/router using flow-based forwarding, for example, can easily be adapted to accommodate NetFlow because the flow entries maintained by the forwarding engine in the flow cache can be directly exported by NetFlow to an external NetFlow data collector.

In a forwarding architecture based on topology based forwarding tables where the forwarding is not flow-based, but instead is based on routing topology and Layer 2 adjacency information, NetFlow cannot be directly supported. In such an architecture, the DFC or PFC that performs forwarding using the topology based forwarding tables also has to implement additional mechanisms to collect flow information in order to support NetFlow statistics collection.

8.9.2 ACCESS CONTROL LISTS FOR QOS AND SECURITY PROCESSING

The PFCs (and DFCs) employed in the Catalyst 6500 support hardware processing of QoS and Security ACLs. The two major parts of an ACL are as follows:

- **ACL Label**: Multiple ACLs can be supported in the system. This is a label that is assigned to a particular ACL to uniquely identify it in the system. The PFC3 can support up to 512 unique labels while the PFC3B and PFC3BXL can both support up to 4096 ACL labels.
- **Access Control Entries (ACEs)**: Each ACL can support multiple ACEs. An ACE defines a matching condition based on Layer 2 and 3 (and possibly Layer 4) information in a packet along with an "action" which is

either to permit (i.e., forward) or deny (i.e., drop) the packet. The PFC3 can support up to 32,000 ACEs which can exist across the 512 ACL labels. In the PFC3B and PFC3BXL the 32,000 ACEs can exist across the 4096 ACL labels.

As stated earlier, the PFCs (and DFCs) employ TCAMs to enable fast lookup of ACL entries. A mask is applied to the TCAM to determine where an ACL entry can be stored. The mask indicates which of the address bits in the TCAM are to be checked and which bits are to be ignored. The PFC3 supports up to 512 masks (which corresponds to 512 ACL labels) while the PFC3B/PFC3BXL supports 4096 masks. The system uses one mask per ACL label.

The same mask is used by the TCAM to determine where in TCAM memory the ACE is to be stored. The actual number of ACEs stored in the system varies depending on the number of masks (or corresponding to the number of ACL labels) used by the system. When the system uses a single mask, then the TCAM can store a maximum of 32,000 ACE entries. However, when the system uses more than one mask, then a reduced number of ACE entries can be stored in the TCAM.

The system performs ACLs lookups in the TCAM in parallel to Layer 2 and 3 forwarding table lookups. By performing lookups in hardware, the PFC does not experience performance degradation when processing of ACLs is enabled. The system also allows any ACL that is configured in the PFCs to be also mirrored in any existing DFC. The DFC can then perform ACLs searches using its local TCAM memory when carrying out local forwarding of packets. The DFC3 maintains up to 4096 ACL labels (corresponding to 4096 masks) and up to 32,000 ACEs.

8.9.3 DISTRIBUTED FORWARDING OPERATIONS IN CATALYST 6500 WITH PFC OR DFC

This section describes the forwarding process in a Catalyst 6500 with a PFC (or DFC) in the system. The PFC33/3B/3BXL receives a copy of the main FIB from the MSFC3 and uses this as a local FIB or forwarding table. This local forwarding table is implemented using a TCAM which is designed for very high-speed forwarding information lookups.

The PFC2, PFC3, and DFCs can maintain up to 256,000 entries in the FIB. Even though the PFCs and DFCs use topology based forwarding tables to forward packets, a flow entry is still created for each new flow entering the system. However, the flow entries are used by the NetFlow process to collect statistics as illustrated in Figure 8.14.

When a packet enters the PFC2/3, a lookup is performed in the forwarding table using a longest match prefix lookup. The main forwarding table is generated from network topology and allows for any network topology changes to be updated immediately by the MSFC3. This forwarding method is more resilient to topology changes than the flow cache-based forwarding method.

In parallel to examining the FIB, the PFC3 also examines the QoS and security ACL tables to determine if any QoS and/or security policies have been defined for the flow to which the packet belongs. The PFC3 extracts this ACL information to determine if the packet is to be forwarded or dropped. The information may also indicate if any classification or policing is to be applied to the packet. After performing the required action (i.e., forward or drop), the NetFlow statistics and counters (Figure 8.14) are updated for the flow. The PFC3 then examines the adjacency table (Figure 8.14) to determine the rewrite information required to modify packet headers to enable it to be forwarded to the next-hop.

8.10 PACKET FLOW IN THE CATALYST 6500 WITH SUPERVISOR ENGINE 720

This section describes the processing steps involved in forwarding a packet through the Cisco Catalyst 6500 with Supervisor Engine 720. We describe here the processing steps involved in centralized and distributed forwarding. We also discuss briefly the flow cache-based packet forwarding method referred to as Accelerated Cisco Express Forwarding (aCEF) [CISC6500DS04] [CISC6500DSSE].

8.10.1 CENTRALIZED FORWARDING

Using the CEF256 line card as an example, we describe the steps involved in performing a centralized forwarding through the Catalyst 6500. The corresponding markings of the processing steps are shown in Figure 8.15.

Step 1: Packet enters an input port on a CEF256 line card from the network:

- A packet enters the line card through the port ASIC from the network and is handed over to the fabric ASIC on the line card.

Step 2: Fabric ASIC on line card arbitrates for access to 32 Gb/s shared switching bus:

- The line card fabric ASIC arbitrates for access to the 32 Gb/s shared switching bus to enable it to transmit the packet header to the Supervisor Engine 720.
- If the 32 Gb/s shared bus is idle, the central arbitration mechanism in the fabric ASIC on the Supervisor Engine 32 will grant access to the bus (by forwarding a grant or permit message to the local arbitration mechanism in the line card's fabric ASIC indicating that it is allowed to transmit).
- When the fabric ASIC on the ingress line card receives the grant message from the central arbitration mechanism on the Supervisor Engine 720, it transmits only the packet header without the data payload over the 32 Gb/s shared switching bus to the fabric ASIC on the Supervisor Engine 720.

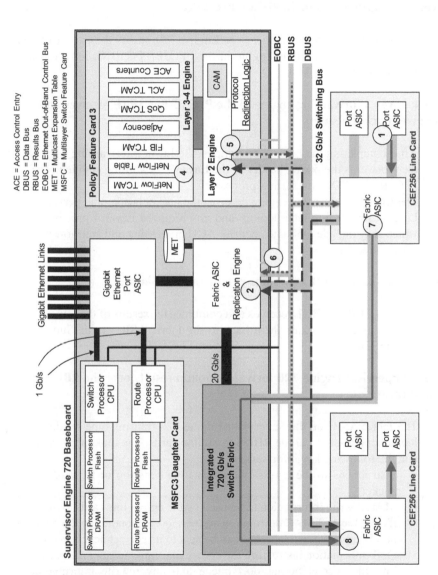

FIGURE 8.15 Packet Flow: Centralized Forwarding.

- Given that the 32 Gb/s shared bus is a shared medium, all other line cards connected to this shared bus will see the transmitted header.

Step 3: Supervisor Engine 720 receives packet header and forwards it to Layer 2 forwarding engine in PFC3B/PFC3BXL:

- The fabric ASIC on the Supervisor Engine 720 passes the packet header to the Layer 2 forwarding engine in the PFC3B/PFC3BXL for a Layer 2 forwarding table lookup.

Step 4: Layer 3 forwarding engine in the PFC3B/PFC3BXL receives and processes packet header:

- After completing the Layer 2 operations, the Layer 2 forwarding engine then forwards the packet header to the Layer 3 forwarding engine in the PFC3B/PFC3BXL for further processing.
- The Layer 3 forwarding engine receives the packet header and performs Layer 3 forwarding table lookup and any required Layer 4 processing which may include QoS and security ACL processing and NetFlow statistic collection.

Step 5: PFC3B/PFC3BXL combines results of all lookups:

- The PFC3B/PFC3BXL receives and combines the results of the Layer 2/3/4 processing and forwards them back to the fabric ASIC on the Supervisor Engine 720.

Step 6: Supervisor Engine 720 forwards lookup results over the RBUS to all line cards:

- The fabric ASIC on the Supervisor Engine 720 transmits the result of the lookup operations over the RBUS to all line cards. The lookup results contain the following key information:
  - Instructions to the egress line cards to either drop or forward the packet
  - MAC rewrite information to be used by the egress line cards to modify the Layer 2 MAC destination address (corresponding to the next-hop IP address) so the packet can be sent to its correct next-hop node
  - QoS information instructing the egress line cards to store the packet into the correct output port queue and any rewrite information needed for modifying outgoing DSCP values.

Step 7: Ingress line card receives results of lookup operations:

- As soon as the ingress line card receives the lookup results, it transmits the packet data payload over the crossbar switch fabric to the destination line card. The payload is not transmitted over the 32 Gb/s shared switching bus.

Step 8: Destination line card receives data payload from the crossbar switch fabric:

- The fabric ASIC on the destination line card receives the packet data payload from the crossbar switch and combines this with its corresponding packet header received earlier on over the 32 Gb/s shared switching bus.
- The combined packet is further processed (IP TTL, IP checksum, MAC address rewrite, Ethernet checksum) and then forwarded out the destination port.
- QoS information instructing the destination line card to store the packet into the correct output port queue and any rewrite information needed for modifying outgoing DSCP values is also processed at this point.

8.10.2 DISTRIBUTED FORWARDING

In distributed forwarding, the forwarding engines located on the line cards make forwarding decisions locally without the need to send packets to the PFC for forwarding. The DFCs use the same hardware forwarding engines as the central PFC, and can forward packets between two local ports, directly or across the crossbar switch fabric to other ports, without involving the Supervisor Engine. Each line card with a DFC has a dedicated forwarding engine complete with a fully populated and maintained forwarding table.

The central PFC located on the Supervisor Engine and the DFC located on the line cards are populated with the same forwarding table generated by the MSFC before any end user traffic is processed in the switch. When a packet arrives at a line card, its DFC examines the packet and accesses the information in the forwarding table (Layer 2, Layer 3, ACLs, and QoS) to make a local forwarding decision for that packet.

The local forwarding engine manages all forwarding on that line card. As discussed earlier, the Supervisor Engine 720 can also support line cards without DFCs such as the CEF256 line cards discussed earlier. With the DFCs being able to make all the forwarding decisions locally, the central PFC can dedicate more of its forwarding resources to line cards in the chassis not equipped with a DFC.

The following main features allow the system to support distributed forwarding:

- The MSFC runs the routing protocols to create the routing tables. The MSFC then generates the forwarding table from the routing table and distributes it to the DFC-enabled line cards:
  - The earlier feature eliminates the Supervisor Engine from the forwarding path for user traffic.
  - This feature also frees the Supervisor Engine so that it can focus on running routing and management protocols, supporting network services such as security, QoS, etc.

We describe the steps involved in distributed forwarding through a Catalyst 6500 with a CEF720 line card with a local DFC on the ingress. The discussion

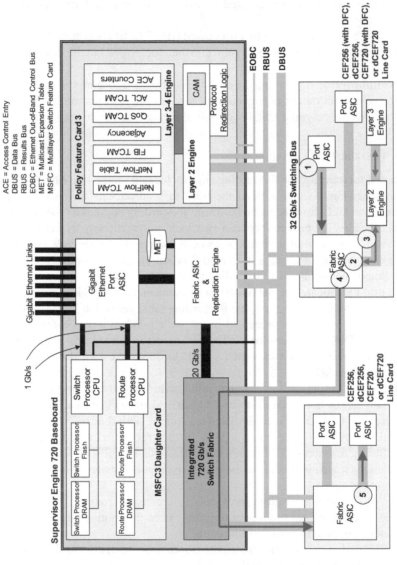

FIGURE 8.16   Packet Flow: Distributed Forwarding.

applies to other DFC-enabled line cards. The processing steps are also marked in Figure 8.16.

Step 1: Packet enters an input port on a CEF720 line card from the network:

- A packet enters the line card through the port ASIC from the network and is handed over to the fabric ASIC on the line card.

Step 2: Line card fabric ASIC sends packet header to local DFC:

- The line card fabric ASIC extracts the packet headers from the packet and sends it to the local DFC for processing.

Step 3: DFC processes the packet header:

- The DFC performs a Layer 2 and, if required, a Layer 3 forwarding table lookup to determine how to forward the packet.
- In addition to the earlier lookup operations, the DFC performs a lookup in the QoS and security ACLs tables to determine if there are any QoS or security policies that have to be applied to the packet being processed.
- The DFC assembles the results of the lookup operations and forwards them back to the line card fabric ASIC.

Step 4: Line card ASIC forwards packet to a local port or to the crossbar switch fabric module (SFM):

- If the destination port is a local port on the line card, the line card fabric ASIC forwards the packet to the destination port ASIC.
- If the destination port is on another line card, the DFC indicates to the SFM the exit SFM port (i.e., the line card) and destinations ports, by prepending a tag on the packet carrying this information.
- The tag is used by the line card fabric ASIC to forward the packet over the crossbar switch fabric to the destination line card and port.

Step 5: SFM uses tag to switch packet to destination line card:

- The ingress SFM port receives the tagged packet from the line card fabric ASIC and examines the tag in order to make a switching decision across the SFM.
- The ingress SFM port determines the exit SFM port on the SFM (i.e., the line card) and the SFM switches the packet to the specified line card.
- The destination line card receives the packet from the SFM and transmits it on its local bus.

- The packet is queued, with any required QoS and security policies applied, and the packet is transmitted out the line card through the target exit port ASIC.

8.10.3   FLOW CACHE-BASED PACKET FORWARDING— ACCELERATED CISCO EXPRESS FORWARDING (aCEF)

The Accelerated Cisco Express Forwarding (aCEF) method is a flow-based forwarding approach that uses two forwarding engines operating in a master-slave fashion to forward packets [CISC6500DS04] [CISC6500DSSE]. The aCEF forwarding method uses a central forwarding engine located on the PFC3 on the Supervisor Engine 720s and a scaled-down flow-based forwarding engine located on the line card (see Figure 8.11).

The central forwarding engine on the PFC3 makes the initial forwarding decision for the first packet of a flow, and the forwarding results are passed to the flow-based forwarding engine on the line card. The line card forwarding engine stores the result which it then uses to make forwarding decisions for subsequent packet of the same flow locally. aCEF has the following main features:

- Similar to the centralized forwarding discussed earlier, the central PFC3 is populated with the forwarding table generated by the MSFC3 before any end user traffic is processed.
- When a packet arrives on an aCEF720 line card, the forwarding engine on the line card examines the packet, and if it finds that no specific forwarding information exists for the packet in its flow cache, it forwards the packet to the central PFC3 for further processing.
- The PFC3 receives the packet and makes a forwarding decision for the packet (Layer 2, Layer 3, QoS and security ACLs, QoS marking, NetFlow, etc.).
- The PFC3 processes the packet and then passes the forwarding results to the aCEF forwarding engine on the line card. The forwarding engine stores the results in its flow cache which it then uses to make forwarding decisions for subsequent packets of the same flow. The central PFC3 processes any packets that the aCEF line card forwarding engine cannot process.

Details of the forwarding process in the Supervisor Engine 720 with aCEF70 line cards are given in Figure 8.17 and Figure 8.18.

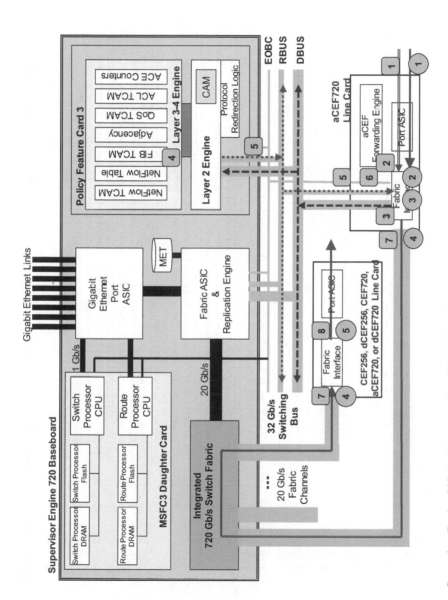

FIGURE 8.17 Supervisor Engine 720 Architecture with aCEF720 Line Cards—Unicast Flow/Route Cache-Based Forwarding.

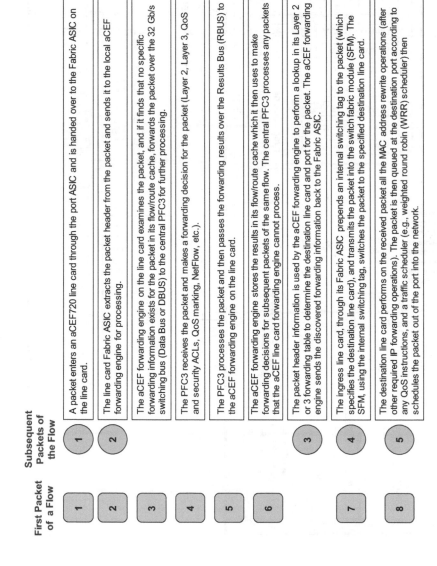

First Packet of a Flow

Subsequent Packets of the Flow

First Packet	Subsequent	Description
1	1	A packet enters an aCEF720 line card through the port ASIC and is handed over to the Fabric ASIC on the line card.
2	2	The line card Fabric ASIC extracts the packet header from the packet and sends it to the local aCEF forwarding engine for processing.
3		The aCEF forwarding engine on the line card examines the packet, and if it finds that no specific forwarding information exists for the packet in its flow/route cache, forwards the packet over the 32 Gb/s switching bus (Data Bus or DBUS) to the central PFC3 for further processing.
4		The PFC3 receives the packet and makes a forwarding decision for the packet (Layer 2, Layer 3, QoS and security ACLs, QoS marking, NetFlow, etc.).
5		The PFC3 processes the packet and then passes the forwarding results over the Results Bus (RBUS) to the aCEF forwarding engine on the line card.
6		The aCEF forwarding engine stores the results in its flow/route cache which it then uses to make forwarding decisions for subsequent packets of the same flow. The central PFC3 processes any packets that the aCEF line card forwarding engine cannot process.
	3	The packet header information is used by the aCEF forwarding engine to perform a lookup in its Layer 2 or 3 forwarding table to determine the destination line card and port for the packet. The aCEF forwarding engine sends the discovered forwarding information back to the Fabric ASIC.
7	4	The ingress line card, through its Fabric ASIC prepends an internal switching tag to the packet (which specifies the destination line card), and transmits the packet into the switch fabric module (SFM). The SFM, using the internal switching tag, switches the packet to the specified destination line card.
8	5	The destination line card performs on the received packet all the MAC address rewrite operations (after other required IP forwarding operations). The packet is then queued at the destination port according to any QoS instructions, and a traffic scheduler (e.g., weighted round robin (WRR) scheduler) then schedules the packet out of the port into the network.

FIGURE 8.18 Supervisor Engine 720 with aCEF720 Line Cards—Unicast Flow/Route Cache-Based Packet Forwarding Processing Steps.

REFERENCES

[CISC6500DS04]. Cisco Catalyst 6500 Series Switch, Cisco Systems, Data Sheet, 2004.

[CISC6500DSSE]. Cisco Catalyst 6500 Series Supervisor Engine 720, Cisco Systems, Data Sheet, 2003.

[CISCCAT6500]. Cisco Systems, Cisco Catalyst 6500 Architecture, White Paper, 2007.

[CISCGOLD04]. Generic Online Diagnostics on the Cisco Catalyst 6500 Series Switch, Cisco Systems, White Paper, 2004.

[CISCSUPENG32]. Cisco Catalyst 6500 Supervisor Engine 32 Architecture, Cisco Systems, White Paper, 2006.

9 Multicast Routing and Multicast Forwarding Information Base (MFIB) Architecture

9.1 INTRODUCTION

Dynamic routing protocols facilitate the dissemination of network reachability information and allow routers to exchange updated routing information when topology and link cost changes occur in the network. The main responsibility of a dynamic routing protocol includes the discovery of directly attached and remote hosts and networks, exchange of routing updates to maintain up-to-date routing information in routers, calculation of best paths to network destinations, and the determination of new best paths if the existing paths are no longer available or reachable.

To perform the earlier functions, each router runs dynamic routing protocols which are essentially a set of processes that execute specialized algorithms and allow protocol messages to be sent and received to facilitate the exchange of routing information. Through this, each router populates its routing table with the best paths that lead to each known network destination. Unlike the discussions in the previous chapters which focused mainly on switch/router architectures running unicast routing protocols, the discussion in this chapter focuses on multicast routing protocols and their related databases.

The multicast forwarding mechanisms discussed in this chapter are based on the Cisco Catalyst 6500 Series of switch/routers. The Catalyst 6500 family of switch/routers supports a wide range of multicast forwarding features which makes this discussion representative of the main multicast forwarding features found in the typical switch/router in the market. This case study allows the reader to appreciate better the kind of multicast forwarding features the typical switch/router would support.

IP multicast is a very powerful and useful packet forwarding model which allows for the efficient distribution of data from an IP source to multiple IP receivers simultaneously. This capability opens a wide range of opportunities for data forwarding and services which may be otherwise too inefficient and cost-prohibitive with generic unicast or broadcast data transfer.

A wide variety of users, such as the traditional multimedia broadcast service providers, financial market operators, network service providers, and transportation authorities, use multicast forwarding to enhance their operations and also offer new services. IP multicast, however, is relatively more complex than unicast, and requires in many cases specialized protocols, software management and monitoring tools, and hardware capabilities.

IPv4 multicasting with multilayer (Layer 2/Layer 3) packet forwarding capabilities was first introduced in the Catalyst 6500 family of switch/routers in the early 2000's [CISC2TMUL11]. This multilayer switching/forwarding feature was unique and innovative at that time when many new IP multicast specific functions were developed in software and implemented in routers and switch/routers. As the years progressed, developers created entirely new ways to translate the forwarding methods based on software-based standards protocols such as PIM (Protocol Independent Multicast) and IGMP (Internet Group Management Protocol) into combined hardware- and software-based functions. In the Cisco routing architectures, this Layer2/Layer3 (combined hardware- and software-based) multicast capability became known as the Cisco Multicast Multi-Layer Switching (MMLS) infrastructure.

As many other Cisco packet forwarding devices (routers and switch/routers) began to implement hardware-based IP unicast and multicast forwarding features, it became clear that a single, uniform IP multicast hardware infrastructure beyond the MMLS was necessary for the many Cisco switch/router platforms developed. This led to the development of the newer Multicast Forwarding Information Base (MFIB) infrastructure which is platform-independent and works over a wider range of routing devices [CISC2TMUL11] [CISCMFIB11] [CISCUNDERIPMUL].

The MFIB used in present day routing devices (from a majority of vendors) with multicast forwarding requirements are designed to logically separate the multicast control plane from the multicast data plane, while at the same time allowing the use of high-speed hardware-based forwarding architectures that do not rely on platform-specific forwarding information. This chapter describes the MFIB architecture used in the Cisco switch/routers which also reflects the architecture used in switch/routers from a majority of vendors.

9.2 BENEFITS OF THE MFIB ARCHITECTURE

The MFIB architecture [CISCMFIB11] [CISCUNDERIPMUL] provides a modular system design that allows the separation of the multicast control plane functions (responsible for running protocols such as PIM and IGMP) from the multicast forwarding plane functions (which uses the routing entries for data forwarding). The multicast routing protocols are responsible for generating a multicast routing information base (MRIB) which serves as a repository for all multicast traffic routes. The multicast routing information in the MRIB is extracted and used to construct the MFIB which structures the routing entries in a format that is more tailored and efficient for use in actual multicast packets forwarding.

Through the separation of the control and forwarding planes, the use of hardware forwarding engines, and route processors that support the software-intensive control plane, the MFIB architecture is able to simplify greatly multicast router design and operations. This architecture also eliminates the need for multicast route cache maintenance normally associated with flow caching schemes (such as multicast fast switching) which are less efficient [CISCMFIB11] [CISCUNDERIPMUL].

9.3 PROTOCOL-INDEPENDENT MULTICAST (PIM)

PIM is called "protocol independent" because it does not have its own built-in topology discovery mechanisms, but instead uses routing information provided by whichever unicast routing protocols already exist in the router to perform the multicast forwarding functions. By not depending on any specific unicast routing protocol, a unicast routing protocol such as EIGRP, OSPF, BGP, and static routes can be used to populate the router's unicast routing table, which PIM then uses for the reverse path forwarding (RPF) functions. PIM uses the idea that the unicast routing tables in PIM Routers in the routing domain should converge to contain routes to network destinations that are loop-free.

Multicast routers using PIM do not exchange (send and receive) routing updates and do not build and maintain their own independent and complete multicast routing tables like Distance Vector Multicast Routing Protocol (DVMRP). Unlike other unicast and older multicast routing protocols, PIM routers do not propagate at all any type of multicast routes (and do not build their own multicast routing tables) but instead use the unicast routing table created and maintained by any existing unicast routing protocol for the RPF functions (see RPF discussion later). PIM still requires network reachability information but that is supplied by a unicast routing protocol. However, the key benefit here is PIM does not depend on a specific unicast routing protocol.

PIM is the dominant multicast routing protocol in use in enterprise networks, service provider networks, and the Internet today. Actually, PIM is a family of multicast routing protocols consisting of the following protocols: PIM Dense Mode (PIM-DM) [RFC3973], PIM Sparse Mode (PIM-SM) [RFC7761], PIM Source-Specific Multicast (PIM-SSM) [RFC4607], and Bidirectional PIM (BIDIR-PIM) [RFC5015]. Each of these sub-protocols is optimized for a different multicast networking environment—one-to-many communication, many-to-many communication, distribution of multicast traffic data over a LAN, enterprise network, service provider network, or the Internet.

PIM also has two versions, PIMv1 [RFC2117] and PIMv2 [RFC4601] [RFC7761], which are not directly compatible although routers may implement both versions, and can also coexist on the same network (on the same router and even on the same router interface). It is important to note that PIMv1 and PIMv2 here mean forms or versions of PIM-SM which was the first PIM mode developed (see [RFC2117]), well before the other PIM types were created (PIM-DM

[RFC3973] was standardized in January 2005). The main difference between PIMv1 and PIMv2 is that they have different message formats but the meaning of the messages is the same and routers processes these PIM messages the same way.

PIMv1 messages are sent in IGMP packets, while PIMv2 has its own packet structure and is assigned the IP protocol number of 103 and is encapsulated directly over IP similar to TCP, UDP, IGMP, ICMP, OSPF, EIGRP, etc. Some PIMv2 implementations provide interoperability and transition between PIMv1 and PIMv2. Such a PIMv2 implementation can recognize PIMv1 messages and allow a router interface to automatically downgrade itself to PIMv1.

Even though PIMv1 and PIMv2 have different message formats, their having the same message meaning and processing allows a router to easily mix PIMv1 and PIMv2 interfaces. However, to avoid interoperability problems, it is recommended that all routers attached to an IP subnet such as a shared Layer 2 network use the same PIM version. PIMv1 (or equivalently, PIM-SMv1) is now considered obsolete and PIMv2 (or PIM-SMv2) is now the recommended standard. The PIM-SM discussion here focuses only on PIMv2 [RFC7761].

9.4 TYPES OF MULTICAST TABLE ENTRIES

A multicast table route entry consists of a destination group IP address (G) and an optional source IP address (S). Also, two primary types of multicast routes carry multicast traffic flow—(Source, Group) (or (S, G)) routes and (*, G) routes. The wildcard symbol * represents any source address sending traffic to a multicast group G. The (S, G) route carries traffic from a source (IP address of the multicast source (S)) to a multicast group (destination IP address of the multicast group (G)). The (*, G) route carries traffic from a PIM Rendezvous Point to all receivers of a multicast group (IP destination address of the multicast group). Note that only PIM-SM and BIDIR-PIM use (*, G) routes to send traffic to multicast groups.

This section summarizes the types of multicast table entries supported by the typical multicast router:

- **(*, G)**: These are shared multicast distribution tree entries used by PIM-SM and BIDIR-PIM.
- **(S, G)**: These are source-based multicast distribution tree entries used by PIM-DM, PIM-SM and PIM-SSM.
- **(*, G/mask)**: These are shared multicast distribution tree entries used by the BIDIR-PIM in the Cisco MFIB and are described in **[CISC2TMUL11] [CISCMFIB11]**.

PIM routers monitor and keep a record of the multicast forwarding state for their incoming (upstream) and outgoing (downstream) interfaces for each multicast group. The states are the (*, G) or (S, G) entries described earlier and are the information the multicast router keeps and uses for forwarding multicast packets. The earlier multicast protocols and their related multicast table entries are explained in appropriate sections following sections.

9.4.1   MULTICAST TABLE CONTEXT

Multicast tables can be further defined by the following contexts:

- **IPv4 addresses**: A multicast table can be in the IPv4 address family context.
- **IPv6 addresses**: A multicast table can be in the IPv6 address family context.
- **VRF (Virtual Routing and Forwarding) Instances**: A multicast table can be used in the Layer 3 VPN context.
- **Global**: A multicast table can be used in a global non-VRF context.

9.5   TYPES OF MULTICAST TABLES

The main multicast tables used by a routing device are as follows:

- **Multicast Route (Mroute) Table**: This table maintains (S, G) and (*, G) multicast states on the router including the PIM mode used, incoming (upstream) router interfaces, and outgoing (downstream) router interfaces.
- **Multicast Routing Information Base (MRIB)**: The MRIB is a multicast-based network topology table (map) derived from an existing unicast routing table in the multicast router. In PIM-SM, a router uses the MRIB to decide where to send PIM-SM Join/Prune messages. The MRIB also stores routing metrics for destination addresses. The router uses these routing metrics when sending and processing PIM-SM Assert messages. The MRIB maintains (S, G), (*, G), and (*, G/mask) (simply denoted as (*, G/m)) route entries that are processed to generate entries that are then populated in the MFIB. The (*, G/m) entries are used in [CISC2TMUL11] [CISCMFIB11] to describe a multicast group range (not a single group address but a range of group addresses) present in a multicast router's local group-to-Rendezvous Point mapping cache.
- **Multicast Forwarding Information Base (MFIB)**: This table maintains (S, G), (*, G), and (*, G/m) route entries plus the router interfaces and next-hop routers used for actual multicast packet forwarding.
- **IPv4 Multicast Forwarding Cache (or Multicast Flow/Route Cache)**: The multicast forwarding cache maintains the individual multicast routes which consist of (S, G) or (*, G) group entries used for forwarding subsequent packets of a multicast flow after the first packet has been forwarded via the router processor in software. These multicast flow cache entries are dynamically created from receiver join state information and first packet lookup results provided by the route processor.

The discussion later presents some protocol-specific tables that are used for multicast routing and forwarding.

9.5.1 IGMP CACHE

In IP multicast routing, any given multicast traffic from an IP source is associated with a multicast group (of receivers) which is identified by a specific IP multicast address. Multicast routing is done in such a way that only multicast group members receive the multicast traffic and not nonmembers. Multicast group membership protocols such as IGMP and Multicast Listener Discovery (MLD) protocol allow a multicast router to discover when a host on a directly attached VLAN or subnet wants to receive a particular multicast traffic (that is, wants to join a particular multicast group).

Multicast group memberships are managed using IGMP (in IPv4 networks) and MLD (in IPv6 networks). Both IGMP and MLD are protocols used to manage multicast group memberships. IGMP and MLD have evolved over the years and have several versions that can be used by network hosts and multicast routers: IGMPv1 [RFC1112], IGMP2 [RFC2236], IGMPv3 [RFC3376] [RFC4604], MLDv1 [RFC2710], and MLDv2 [RFC3810] [RFC4604]. When compared to IGMPv1, IGMPv2 adds the ability for a host to signal its desire to leave a multicast group. Also, when compared to IGMPv2, IGMPv3 adds support for Source-Specific Multicast (SSM). MLDv1 (based on IGMPv2) provides, among other features, the ability of an IPv6 router to discover the presence of multicast listeners (or receivers). MLDv2 (based on IGMPv3) provides, among other features, the ability of a multicast listener to specify a source IPv6 address when sending a PIM Join message.

IPv4 hosts use IGMP to join, maintain, and leave multicast groups while multicast routers use IGMP to establish, maintain, and remove multicast groups and group members on their outgoing interfaces. An IPv4 host uses IGMP (e.g., IGMPv2) to inform an immediately neighboring multicast router that it is interested in receiving a particular multicast traffic. IGMPv2 supports the following messages [RFC2236]: Membership Query (Type = 0x11), IGMPv2 Membership Report (Type = 0x16), and Leave Group (Type = 0x17). A host registers and joins a multicast group (expressing its interest in multicast traffic), by sending an IGMPv2 Report message to the neighbor upstream multicast router.

A multicast router uses IGMP to learn/discover on each of its local attached networks (VLANs or subnets) which multicast groups have members. The multicast router then adds any discovered multicast group to the list of multicast groups on its attached networks (VLANs) that should be forwarded a particular multicast traffic. The multicast router does not maintain state information about the individual hosts (in the group) that should be sent the multicast traffic or their identities. Generally, an IPv4 multicast router uses an IGMP cache to maintain its local IGMP multicast memberships (groups with active members). The information obtained from IGMP allows the router to maintain a list of the multicast group memberships on each of its outgoing interfaces—active group membership on a per-interface basis. An IPv6 routing device uses an MLD cache to maintain its local multicast group memberships.

A host sends an IGMPv2 Leave message to the multicast router when it no longer wants to receive a particular multicast traffic. When the multicast router receives this message, it sends an IGMPv2 Query message to the local VLAN/subnet to determine if there are any group members remaining. The router sends the Query message to all hosts in the VLAN or subnet using the "All-Hosts" multicast address 224.0.0.1.

If any group member responds, the router continues to send the particular multicast traffic to the group. If no response is received, the router removes that multicast group from its IGMP cache table and stops forwarding traffic to the multicast group. A router considers a multicast group membership to be active on an interface if it receives an IGMP request expressing interest in the multicast group traffic from at least one receiver on the interface.

9.5.2   REVERSE-PATH FORWARDING (RPF) TABLE

A multicast router uses unicast routing information (in a table referred to as the RPF table) to build a logical multicast distribution tree on the reverse path from the multicast receivers toward the multicast traffic source. The multicast router can use an existing unicast forwarding table maintained by the unicast routing protocols for RPF checks, or a dedicated forwarded table created solely for RPF checks. The multicast routers then forward multicast packets from the source to the receivers along the multicast distribution tree while ensuring loop-free forwarding of the packets. Forwarding loops particularly degrade network performance because packets can be replicated each time they pass through the forwarding loop.

RPF is a key component of multicast packet forwarding and enables multicast routers to correctly forward multicast traffic from the source down the distribution tree to interested receivers (without creating forwarding loops). The multicast routers receive packets and then perform RPF checks using the existing unicast forwarding information to determine if the packets are coming in through the correct upstream interface and not through a downstream interface leading toward multicast receivers. Each multicast router along the multicast distribution tree consults an RPF table for every RPF check performed on multicast packets.

A multicast router will forward a multicast packet only if it is received on the interface on the nearest/shortest path leading back to the multicast source (referred to as the RPF interface). This means the router will forward a multicast packet only if it is received on the interface that is nearest or on the shortest path (as defined by the unicast routing protocol) to the multicast packet source (which can be the content source (S) or a Rendezvous Point (*)):

- When a router receives a multicast packet from a source (S) with unicast IP source address IP_Addr_Source through one of its interfaces IF_G1, it checks whether IF_G1 is the interface the router itself would use to reach IP_Addr_Source. The Router will only forward the multicast packet if IF_G1 is the interface the router would use to reach IP_Addr_Source.

The router does not forward multicast packets that fail the RPF check. The RPF checks performed by the routers ensure that the multicast distribution tree is loop-free.

9.5.3   PIM DENSE MODE (PIM-DM) TABLE ENTRIES

PIM-DM [RFC3973] uses the unicast routing table in the router and a flood-and-prune mechanism to build a source-based (shortest-path) multicast distribution tree for sending traffic to multicast subscribers. To create the source-based distribution tree and to ensure that there are no routing loops when multicast packets are being forwarded among PIM routers that wish to receive these packets, PIM-DM uses RPF. Each PIM-DM router in the network creates an (S, G) entry (for each multicast stream) in its PIM-DM forwarding table after a successful RPF check. Through the flood and prune mechanism, PIM-DM routers in a multicast domain are able to receive multicast streams and at the same time accumulate multicast state information. Other than the source (S) and multicast group (G) addresses, the state information that is used to build the multicast forwarding table includes the associated incoming and outgoing router interfaces.

PIM-DM is less sophisticated than PIM-SM and operates on the simple assumption that when a multicast source starts sending traffic, all or most of the downstream routers and hosts want to receive that traffic. PIM-DM initially floods traffic from a source throughout the network while hoping that PIM-DM routers that do not have any downstream neighbor routers or hosts will send back PIM Prune messages to stop the unwanted traffic.

PIM-DM is, therefore, seen to use a data push model where data is delivered toward the downstream nodes and receivers without waiting for the receivers to explicitly request the data. PIM-DM floods a multicast stream periodically and also uses flooding to refresh state information, such as the source IP address (S) and multicast group (G) information. Each PIM-DM router that receives a multicast packet will forward it, but only after performing the required RPF check to ensure that the packet arrived on the upstream interface leading back to the source.

If a router has no interested receivers for a multicast stream, it sends a PIM Prune message to the upstream router to stop sending the traffic. The upstream router, upon receiving a Prune message and modifying its state information, will then stop flooding subsequent multicast packets to this router on the pruned branch. If all the interfaces of a PIM-DM router are pruned, the router itself will also be pruned from the source-based distribution tree.

So, unlike PIM-SM which only forwards a particular multicast traffic when requested (via an explicit PIM Join request), a PIM-DM router always floods any new multicast data that it receives from an interface to all other interfaces and only stops flooding that data on a given interface/link if it is explicitly informed to stop (i.e., upon receiving a PIM Prune message sent by the downstream PIM-DM router). This makes PIM-DM more ideal or suitable and efficient for environments where there is at least one active receiver on every VLAN/subnet in the network, or where there are many hosts in the overall network subscribing to the multicast traffic (with few or no prunes occurring). In these environments, the expectation is that most of the PIM routers will receive and then forward all the multicast packets sent to them.

It should be noted that PIM-DM supports only source-based multicast trees (S, G) entries) and does not build shared distribution trees using Rendezvous Points as in PIM-SM (see later). For each multicast group, PIM-SM explicitly constructs unidirectional shared multicast distribution trees that are rooted at a Rendezvous Point. PIM-SM also uses RPF to ensure loop-free forwarding of multicast packets. PIM-DM, on the other hand, implicitly constructs a source-based (shortest-path) tree for each multicast group by flooding multicast traffic throughout the routing domain, then uses PIM Prune messages to prune back branches of the tree that have no receivers present.

A multicast source in a PIM-SM domain announces its existence to one or more Rendezvous Points, and a receiver sends request to a Rendezvous Point to initiate the reception of multicast traffic. A receiver must send an explicit PIM-SM Join message to a Rendezvous Point to receive multicast data. Also, all routers in a PIM-SM domain must be provided the multicast group-to-Rendezvous Point mapping. The Rendezvous Point is the only router that needs to be notified of all active multicast sources in a PIM-SM domain while the other PIM-SM routers just need to know how to reach the correct Rendezvous Point for a given multicast group.

9.5.4   PIM Sparse Mode (PIM-SM) Table Entries

PIM-SM [RFC4601] [RFC7761] tries to remedy some of the deficiencies of PIM-DM by operating on the principle that having a small number of hosts in a network interested in receiving a multicast stream does not justify flooding that traffic in the entire network. PIM-SM operates on the assumption that receivers for any particular multicast stream are sparsely distributed throughout the PIM domain. So, PIM-SM operates to limit multicast traffic such that only those routers interested in receiving traffic sent to a particular multicast group will receive that traffic.

Thus, unlike PIM-DM, PIM-SM uses a data pull model where multicast traffic is delivered only to downstream routers with receivers that have explicitly requested the data. Routers with downstream or directly attached members belonging to a given multicast group are required to send explicit PIM-SM Join messages to be able to join that particular PIM-SM multicast distribution tree. PIM-SM routers use PIM Join and Prune messages to join and leave a particular multicast group or, equivalently, a multicast distribution tree.

A router will not receive multicast traffic addressed to the multicast group if it does not become part of the multicast distribution tree for that group. In contrast, PIM-DM assumes the presence of downstream multicast group members and proceeds to forward multicast traffic on the downstream links until explicit PIM-DM Prune messages are received. As discussed earlier, the default forwarding behavior of PIM-DM is to forward/flood multicast traffic, unless requested not to, while the default forwarding behavior of PIM-SM is to block (or not to forward) multicast traffic unless it is explicitly requested.

9.5.4.1 Concept of Rendezvous Point

In PIM-SM, a router does not know the source IP address of a multicast stream if that source is not currently forwarding traffic through it. As a result, PIM-SM routers need a way to determine the source IP addresses of multicast streams for which they have received requests from downstream group members. To address this problem, PIM-SM supports the concept of Rendezvous Points which are specific PIM-SM routers that receive notification of all available multicast streams destined to their respective multicast groups. The Rendezvous Point is responsible for receiving notifications/registrations from all multicast sources wishing to send traffic to their respective multicast groups in the multicast routing domain.

9.5.4.1.1 Rendezvous Point Discovery

The use of Rendezvous Points in turn requires that PIM-SM also provide a way for routers to determine the identities of the Rendezvous Points in the domain. Thus, PIM-SM introduced the concept of a Bootstrap Router (BSR) which is a device that knows the identity of each Rendezvous Point in the network and in turn advertises this information to all other PIM-SM routers. The BSR maintains a list of Rendezvous Point candidates in the PIM-SM domain and also specifies all the multicast groups associated with each Rendezvous Point.

The main function of the BSR is to manage the collection of Rendezvous Points in the PIM-SM domain and allow a group of receivers interested in a specific multicast stream (multicast group) to find the source of that stream. Another function of the BSR is to select a Rendezvous Point set from BSR Rendezvous Point candidates and to broadcast the Rendezvous Point set to all PIM-SM routers in the domain. The Rendezvous Point candidates send their candidate advertisements directly to the elected BSR in the PIM-SM domain. The elected BSR then transmits BSR messages (carried within PIM messages) containing Rendezvous Point set information out on all its interfaces to all routers. The BSR messages are flooded/forwarded hop-by-hop to all PIM-SM routers in the domain.

Other than a BSR, other Rendezvous Point (RP) discovery mechanisms include Static configuration (or Static RP), Automatic RP (or Auto-RP), Anycast RP, and Embedded RP [CISC3750GUIDE] [CISCPIMGUIDE] [JUNMULTGUID]. Also, PIM-SM provides a registration mechanism to allow Rendezvous Points to be notified of new multicast streams. A router (having learned the source IP address of a multicast stream from the Rendezvous Point), can then accesses that multicast stream via a direct path to the traffic source (using a source-based distribution tree).

9.5.4.1.2 Role and Benefits of Rendezvous Points

A Rendezvous Point is a device that serves as a "meet place" (i.e., information exchange point) for multicast group members and sources, and where the receivers can access the multicast data sent from the sources. Each multicast group must be mapped to a single active Rendezvous Point. A PIM router can serve as a Rendezvous Point for more than one multicast group. However, only one Rendezvous Point address can be used for a particular multicast group at any given time within a PIM domain. Each receiver interested in joining a multicast group contacts its directly attached PIM-SM router, which in turn sends an explicit PIM-SM Join message to the group's Rendezvous Point to enable it to join the multicast distribution tree.

The use of a Rendezvous Point in a PIM-SM domain reduces the amount of state information non-Rendezvous Point routers have to maintain. Also, this removes the need to flood information about active multicast sources in the PIM-SM domain to non-Rendezvous Point routers. The explicit PIM Join mechanism used in PIM-SM also prevents unwanted multicast traffic from flooding all the network links in the PIM-SM domain.

9.5.4.1.3 PIM-SM Designated Router

Each network segment (subnet) in the network must have one PIM Designated Router. The Designated Router on the subnet in which a source resides, creates a (unicast) tunnel for the multicast stream to the Rendezvous Point which also informs the Rendezvous Point that the stream is available. This multicast model requires the PIM-SM routers to maintain some knowledge of the list of Rendezvous Points in the network prior to the arrival of any multicast traffic data. In contrast, PIM-DM does not use Rendezvous Points or define any state for a multicast group until the first data packet arrives at the routers.

9.5.4.2 PIM-SM Router Architecture

Figure 9.1 shows a high-level architecture of a PIM-SM router. The Tree Information Base (TIB) maintains the collection of states at a particular PIM-SM router. A PIM-SM router stores in the TIB the state of all multicast distribution trees it is part of. The PIM-SM router creates the TIB by receiving PIM-SM Join/ Prune and Assert messages, as well as IGMP/MLD information gathered from its locally attached hosts.

9.5.4.3 Sending Multicast Data

A multicast source has no idea which routers and host (if any) will receive the traffic it generates so it simply sends out the data. It is up to the routers in the network to receive the traffic and forward it to where it needs to go. It is the responsibility of the router closest to the multicast source, also referred to as the first-hop router (or Designated Router), to ensure that a copy of a given multicast stream gets to the Rendezvous Point. So, like all PIM-SM routers in the network, the Designated Router learns the multicast group-to-Rendezvous Point mapping from the BSR. With that mapping, the Designated Router knows the IP address of the Rendezvous Point to which it can forward any given multicast stream.

A multicast traffic source announces its existence in a PIM-SM domain through PIM-SM Register messages sent by the source's Designated Router to the

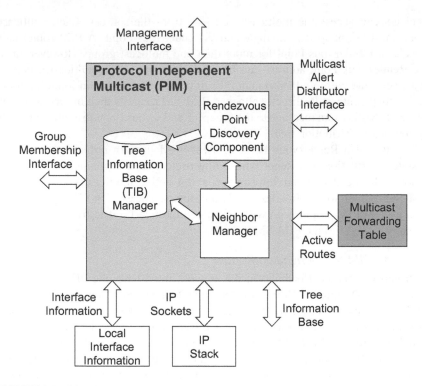

FIGURE 9.1   PIM-SM Router High-Level Architecture.

Rendezvous Point. The Designated Router cannot forward the multicast stream
to the Rendezvous Point via multicast since the routers between the Designated
Router and the Rendezvous Point will not know how to forward the packets.
Instead, the Designated Router (registers the stream with the Rendezvous Point)
by creating a unicast tunnel and encapsulating the multicast packets in PIM-SM
Register messages. The Register messages each carry a unicast header, and are
forwarded over the tunnel to the Rendezvous Point. Thus, the Designated Router
registers the multicast source by sending these unicast packets to the Rendezvous
Point.

Once the Rendezvous Point starts receiving the given multicast stream via the
Register message in the unicast tunnel, it can proceed in one of the following two
ways:

1. If the Rendezvous Point has received requests for this particular multicast stream, it will de-encapsulate the received packets, and forward
   them out the interface(s) on which the explicit PIM-SM Join requests
   were received. At the same time, the Rendezvous Point will send its
   own PIM Join request messages upstream toward the multicast source,
   to establish a shortest-path tree (SPT) so that the stream can be delivered

via multicast. The Rendezvous Point adds a new multicast source in its PIM table to keep track of sources and their distribution trees. Once the source's Designated Router receives the Join message, and starts sending the stream via multicast through the newly created (S, G) route, the Rendezvous Point will request (via a PIM-SM Register-Stop message) that the Designated Router stop sending the stream in unicast PIM-SM Register packets over the tunnel.

2. If the Rendezvous Point has no currently active receivers for the multicast stream, it will simply signal the source's Designated Router to stop sending any further register packets for the multicast stream.

The Rendezvous Point adds an interface to its multicast routing table only when it receives PIM Join messages from downstream routers over that interface, or when a directly connected multicast group member is on the interface. The Rendezvous Point also keeps track of multicast groups on all of its interfaces.

It should be emphasized that the multicast source simply sends multicast packets and it is the source's Designated Router that registers and then handles all subsequent data transfers to the Rendezvous Point. The Rendezvous Point then sends PIM Join messages to the Designated Router of the multicast source to bypass the use of the unicast registration tunnel. A receiver's Designated Router, on the other hand, indirectly interacts with a particular multicast source only when it receives data packets on the shared distribution tree from that source through the Rendezvous Point.

9.5.4.4 Receiving Multicast Data

When a receiver sends an explicit PIM Join request to a multicast group, this also triggers an RPF check. The receiver's Designated Router sends a (*, G) PIM Join message toward the Rendezvous Point. The Join message is forwarded hop-by-hop upstream through the RPF interface of each router (hop) until it reaches the Rendezvous Point. The (*, G) PIM Join message is eventually received by the Rendezvous Point which adds the receiving interface to the outgoing interface list (OIL) for the multicast group.

The OIL is an entry in the forwarding state of the Rendezvous-Point Tree (RPT) just created for the receiver and the receiving interface. The RPT created connects the receiver with the Rendezvous Point and remains in effect, even if no active multicast sources are sending traffic to the Rendezvous Point. The Rendezvous Point starts sending multicast packets downstream along the created RPT to the receiver's Designated Router for delivery to all receivers interested in the multicast stream.

9.5.4.4.1 SPT Switchover

When the receiver's Designated Router receives the first multicast packet from the RPT, it sends a PIM Join message to the source's Designated Router in order to establish a direct SPT to the source. This is because, once the receiver's Designated Router receives the first multicast packet, it will see the source IP address of the multicast source.

At that point, the receiver's Designated Router can take the opportunity to send a PIM Join message directly to the source, rather than receive the multicast stream via the Rendezvous Point. When this PIM Join message is received by the source's Designated Router, it starts forwarding the multicast traffic along the newly created SPT.

9.5.4.4.2   Benefits of SPT Switchover

Once a receiver gets multicast traffic from a source via the Rendezvous Point, the receiver's Designated Router can optionally stop receiving traffic from the Rendezvous Point through the RPT (*, G) if it determines that the new source-based (S, G) SPT is shorter or the optimal path to the multicast source. The receiver's Designated Router migrates to the (S, G) SPT if that path is shorter than through the RPT for that particular multicast group. The receiver can then get the rest of the multicast data directly from the source. The transition of PIM-SM from a shared-based tree (centered at a Rendezvous Point) to a source-based distribution tree is a major feature of PIM-SM. This feature prevents sources and receivers from overloading the Rendezvous Point or the network links that make up the RPTs.

When the receiver's Designated Router starts receiving multicast packets directly from the source through the SPT, it sends a PIM Prune message to the Rendezvous Point instructing it to stop sending packets through the RPT. The Rendezvous Point stops sending multicast packets along the RPT to the receiver's Designated Router, and, in turn, sends a PIM Prune message on the RPT leading to the source's Designated Router instructing it to stop sending multicast packet to the Rendezvous Point on the RPT.

9.5.4.4.3   Optimizing Network Resources at a Rendezvous
Point without Active Receivers

In the case where the Rendezvous Point receives a PIM Register message from an active multicast source but there are no receivers in the PIM-SM domain interested in that traffic, it will still create an entry for that active source in its PIM table. However, after entering the active source in the PIM table, the Rendezvous Point will send a PIM Register-Stop message to the source's Designated Router. This feature is to reduce network resources utilization based on the idea that the Rendezvous Point is aware of the active source's existence but does not need traffic from the source at the moment.

9.5.4.5   PIM Assert Mechanism

When there are multiple PIM routers attached to a common shared network segment, it is possible that any of these routers could receive duplicate multicast traffic sent to the network segment. Any of these routers could receive copies of the same multicast packets sent by the source to the network segment, but it will be very inefficient for multiple routers to forward the same packets onto the shared network segment. This could potentially cause the attached routers to forward multiple copies of all the multicast traffic from the source toward the receiver.

The duplicate traffic also leads to a waste of network bandwidth and processing resources in the network nodes.

To stop the attached routers from duplicating multicast traffic onto the shared segment, the routers will elect a single forwarder for that network segment. Since PIM does not have an inbuilt routing protocol that can be used to compute best paths on which to send packets, it uses a special mechanism called the PIM Assert mechanism to detect and stop the attached routers from duplicating multicast traffic onto a shared segment [RFC7761].

It is important to note that this mechanism does not prevent the routers from duplicating multicast traffic. Instead, the duplication of multicast traffic serves as a trigger for the routers to activate the Asset mechanism to elect a single forwarder for the shared network segment. The elected PIM forwarder is responsible for forwarding multicast traffic to the downstream receivers while the Assert losers will prune their connected interfaces to the shared network segment and stop forwarding traffic to the multicast group.

When the attached PIM routers detect duplicate packets on the shared network segment (on their Outgoing Interface Lists (OILs)), they trigger/initiate the election of a single router to forward the multicast packets by each issuing PIM Assert messages. The PIM Assert mechanism instructs a router that when it receives a multicast packet from a particular source or Rendezvous Pont on an interface that is already listed in its own OIL for the same (S, G) pair, it must send a PIM Assert message. The Assert messages sent by the PIM routers (in order to elect the PIM forwarder for the network segment) also contain the routing metric of the unicast route leading to the multicast source, the Administrative Distance associated with the unicast routing protocol used to discover the route, the associated multicast source (S), and group (G).

9.5.4.6 Electing the PIM Forwarder—PIM Assert Winner

Two or more PIM routers on a shared network segment may have different routing information about how to reach a particular multicast source or Rendezvous Point. These routers could each send a join message to two different PIM routers closer to the source for a shortest path tree (SPT) or the Rendezvous Point for a Rendezvous-Point Tree (RPT). This situation can potentially cause the PIM routers to forward multiple copies of all multicast traffic (from the source or Rendezvous Point) toward the downstream receivers.

The routers send and receive the PIM Assert messages and elect the PIM forwarder using the following rules:

1. If one router lies on an SPT and the others are on an RPT, the router on the SPT is considered to have the shortest path to the multicast source, and wins the PIM Assert election. If all routers are either on an SPT or RPT, then the following rules apply:
2. The router sending a PIM Assert message that has the lowest Administrative Distance is elected the forwarder.
3. If the Administrative Distances in all the Assert messages are equal, then the message with the best unicast routing metric (shortest path)

is used to break the tie and the associated sending PIM router will be
elected the PIM forwarder.

   a. For example, if both routers lie on the RPT, the router with the short-
     est path to the Rendezvous Point (i.e., the lowest routing metric to the
     Rendezvous Point) wins the PIM Assert.

   b. If both routers lie on the SPT, then the router with the shortest path to
     the multicast source (the lowest routing metric to the source's Desig-
     nated Router) wins the PIM Assert.

4. If the unicast routing metrics in all the Assert messages are the same, the
   router with the highest IP address will be elected the PIM Forwarder.

The PIM router that wins the Assert election effectively eliminates multicast traffic duplication and is responsible for forwarding multicast packets to the shared
network segment. The PIM forwarder will act as the local Designated Router for
any IGMP members on that segment. The downstream routers on the network
segment also receive the PIM Assert messages, and send all their join messages
to the elected PIM forwarder.

With the election of the PIM forwarder, there will be no more duplication of
multicast traffic on a shared segment—there are no more multiple routers on a
shared segment that can send multicast traffic to the same (S, G) or (*, G) group.

9.5.5   PIM Sparse-Dense Mode

Typically, only one of the PIM protocols (PIM-SM, PIM-DM, PIM-SSM or
BIDIR-PIM) is used throughout a single multicast domain at a given time.
However, it is possible to use a combination of the different PIM modes on
the same network, router, or interface. A multicast router employing PIM
Sparse-Dense mode is one example of combining different PIM modes on
the same network, router, or interface [CISC3750GUIDE] [CISCPIMGUIDE]
[JUNMULTGUID]. This is possible because a PIM mode (the particular method
of distributing traffic from a multicast source) is effectively tied to a multicast
group—it is not possible for a single multicast group to operate in more than
one mode at the same time. A multicast group itself has an IP multicast group
address that must be unique for the particular traffic sent to it, and network scoping limits are used to enforce the division between actual or potential multicast
group address overlaps.

PIM Sparse-Dense mode allows a PIM router interface to operate either in
the Sparse mode or Dense mode, but the selected mode has to be the same as
the mode of the multicast group connected to the interface. That is, the Sparse
or Dense mode is a property of a multicast group, and not a router interface.
Thus, the context of the PIM mode used (Sparse or Dense) applies to the multicast groups for which the PIM router is a member. So, with PIM Sparse-Dense
mode, a multicast group that is in Dense is not mapped to a Rendezvous Point,
but, instead, receives packets by means of PIM-DM rules. A group that is in the
Sparse mode is mapped to a Rendezvous Point, and receives packets by means

of PIM-SM rules. PIM Sparse-Dense mode is useful in PIM domains that implement the Auto-RP feature for PIM-SM.

9.5.5.1 Auto-RP

For the correct operation of a PIM-SM domain, all PIM-SM routers within the domain must be able to correctly map a particular multicast group to the same Rendezvous Point. Recall from the discussion earlier that a multicast group must be mapped to a single active Rendezvous Point. Auto-RP (which has not been standardized in any IETF RFC) provides a more dynamic way of assigning Rendezvous Points in a PIM domain. When an Auto-RP is configured in a PIM router, the router learns the addresses of Rendezvous Points in the domain automatically.

However, when using Static RP, it is important to (manually) ensure that the Rendezvous Point address for any given multicast group is consistent across all PIM-SM routers in the domain. Using a static configuration for Rendezvous Point assignment (Static RP) is simple and convenient; however, if the Static RP becomes unreachable or unavailable, there is no automatic failover mechanism available to bring in another Rendezvous Point.

Auto-RP is one of the mechanisms a PIM-SM router can use to learn the set of multicast group-to-Rendezvous Points mappings in a PIM-SM domain [CISC3750GUIDE] [CISCPIMGUIDE] [JUNMULTGUID]. Auto-RP distributes information to PIM routers in the domain describing which Rendezvous Point address must be used for a set of multicast groups. Auto-RP not only eliminates inconsistencies in group-to-Rendezvous Point assignment across routers, it enables scalability in PIM networks, and provides automatic failover. The Auto-RP function automatically distributes the mapping information to PIM-SM routers. Auto-RP also simplifies the use of multiple Rendezvous Points for serving different multicast group address ranges, and allows a PIM-SM domain to employ multiple Rendezvous Points to act as backups to each other.

Auto-RP designates one router to act as the Auto-RP mapping agent. Also, the Auto-RP function uses PIM-DM to advertise control traffic. A key benefit of PIM Sparse-Dense mode is that it allows Auto-RP information to be distributed in PIM-DM mode yet allows the multicast traffic to be sent to multicast groups in the PIM-SM mode. Potential Rendezvous Points announce their presence to the Auto-RP mapping agent, and the Auto-RP mapping agent is responsible for resolving any conflicts that arise. The following describe how Auto-RP works:

- One PIM-SM router must be designated as the Auto-RP mapping agent, which receives announce messages from the Rendezvous Points and arbitrates conflicts among them.
- Auto-RP mapping agents themselves join the Rendezvous Point announce group (with the well-known multicast group address 224.0.1.39). All candidate Rendezvous Points periodically advertise their presence using this Rendezvous Point announce group address. The Auto-RP mapping agent listens to announce messages from all Rendezvous Point

candidates and determines which of the candidates will be used for each multicast group.

- The Auto-RP mapping agent then uses PIM-DM flooding to distribute the multicast group-to-RP mappings to all other PIM-SM routers. Using a Rendezvous Point discovery message, the Auto-RP mapping agent advertises the Rendezvous Point and its associated multicast groups to all PIM-SM routers in the domain. This enables all the PIM-SM routers to automatically discover which Rendezvous Point to use for the multicast groups they are supporting.
- All PIM-SM routers join the Rendezvous Point discovery group (with the well-known multicast group address 224.0.1.40), which allows them to receive all multicast group-to-Rendezvous Point mapping information distributed by the Auto-RP mapping agent. All PIM-SM routers receive and store the group-to-Rendezvous Point mappings in their private or local cache.
- Auto-RP announce and discovery messages provide mapping information to each PIM-SM router (i.e., IP addresses of the Rendezvous Point candidates, multicast groups, etc.) which is vital to the PIM-SM operations in the domain.

Auto-RP uses multicast flooding of control messages to announce the presence of potential Rendezvous Point candidates and to discover the elected Rendezvous Points in the PIM domain. Multicast flooding is done using PIM-DM procedures, where the multicast group address 224.0.1.39 is used as the destination address for announce messages, and the group address 224.0.1.40 as the destination address for discovery messages. This means the announce group (224.0.1.39) and the discovery group (224.0.1.40) for the Auto-RP function must be configured explicitly as PIM-DM multicast groups.

The key benefits of Auto-RP are summarized as follows:

- **Easier Administration of Rendezvous Point Assignment**: Using Auto-RP, all PIM-SM routers automatically learn the Rendezvous Point information in the PIM domain, thereby making it easier to update and administer Rendezvous Point information across all routers. This eliminates the need for separate configuration on every PIM-SM router (except on candidate Rendezvous Points and Auto-RP mapping agents). Any change to the Rendezvous Point designation must be configured only on the PIM-SM routers that are Rendezvous Points (Auto-RP mapping agents) and not on the other routers.
- **Eliminates Inconsistencies in Multicast Group-to-Rendezvous Points Mapping**: Auto-RP avoids the inconsistencies that can occur in manual Rendezvous Point configurations which can cause network connectivity problems. Another advantage of Auto-RP is that it allows the scoping of Rendezvous Point addresses within a PIM domain and this can be achieved by defining specific TTL (time-to-live) values allowed for the Auto-RP advertisements.

- **Rendezvous Point Failover**: Auto-RP provides also an important failover feature where multiple PIM routers can be configured as Rendezvous Point candidates. The use of Auto-RP allows back-up Rendezvous Points to be configured providing a Rendezvous Point failover mechanism. In the event the elected Rendezvous Point fails, one of the other preconfigured Rendezvous Point candidates takes over the Rendezvous Point functions. The failover capability is controlled by the Auto-RP mapping agent.

9.5.5.2 Using PIM Sparse-Dense with Auto-RP

The Auto-RP mapping agent uses PIM-DM to send the multicast group-to-Rendezvous Point mapping information to other PIM routers in the domain. The specific multicast groups used are 224.0.1.39 for announce messages and 224.0.1.40 for discovery. PIM-DM is necessary to make Auto-RP to work, which in turn is needed to make PIM-SM mode in PIM Sparse Dense work—meaning PIM Sparse-Dense mode works in a PIM domain that uses Auto-RP.

As stated earlier, a PIM router interface configured to use PIM Sparse-Dense mode settles in either the Sparse mode or Dense mode of operation, depending on which mode the connected multicast group is set to operate. If the multicast group is set to operate with a known Rendezvous Point, then the interface settles in the Sparse mode. If the multicast group has no known Rendezvous Point, then by default the interface settles in the Dense mode and multicast traffic will be flooded over the interface [CISC3750GUIDE] [CISCPIMGUIDE].

When the router interface enters the Dense mode, it is added to the outgoing interface list (OIL) of the multicast routing table when any one of the following conditions is true [CISC3750GUIDE] [CISCPIMGUIDE]:

- Multicast group members exist on the interface.
- There exist PIM neighbors and the multicast group has not been pruned.

When an interface enters the Sparse mode, it is added to the OIL of the multicast routing table when any one of the following conditions is true:

- Group members exist on the interface.
- A PIM neighbor has received an explicit PIM-SM Join message on the interface.

9.5.6 MULTICAST SOURCE DISCOVERY PROTOCOL (MSDP) CACHE

MSDP [RFC3618] [RFC4611], which typically runs on the same router acting as the PIM-SM Rendezvous Point, is used to interconnect multiple multicast routing domains. Similar to the way BGP peers establish adjacencies in a network, each MSDP router sets up adjacencies with other MSDP peers both internal and external to its routing domain. Each MSDP router informs its MSDP peers about active multicast sources within its multicast routing domain.

The Rendezvous Point of a multicast routing domain can use MSDP to announce sources that have traffic to send to a multicast group. Recall that a Rendezvous Point (receives PIM-SM Join messages and) knows about the receivers that are in its local domain. Also, by design, each standard PIM-SM domain has its own Rendezvous Points and does not need to depend on Rendezvous Points in other PIM-SM domains. However, MSDP allows Rendezvous Points in different PIM-SM domains to learn about multicast sources that have data to send to a multicast group.

Thus, MSDP enables a Rendezvous Points in a PIM-SM domain to share information about active sources with Rendezvous Points in other domains. When a Rendezvous Point in another domains learns about active sources (in other domains), it can pass on that source list information to its local receivers and multicast traffic can then be forwarded between the different PIM-SM domains. In the case where all receivers and multicast sources are located in the same PIM-SM domain, MSDP is not useful. This means MSDP is only used to discover active multicast sources in other PIM-SM domains.

A PIM-SM Rendezvous Point running MSDP, that is, an MSDP router, in a multicast routing domain maintains peering relationships with MSDP peers in other multicast domains. The MSDP peers establish their peering relationship over a TCP connection (using the well-known TCP port number 639) which is used primarily to exchange a list of sources sending traffic to multicast groups. The MSDP peer having the higher IP address waits in LISTEN state for the other MSDP peer with the lower IP address to establish a TCP connection to it.

When an MSDP router (which is typically a PIM-SM Rendezvous Point supporting MSDP as alluded to earlier) detects an active source, it sends explicit PIM-SM Join messages to the active source. Also, when an MSDP router discovers a new local source, it transmits Source-Active TLV (type, length, and values) messages to its MSDP peers. An MSDP peer receives information about all active sources in other PIM-SM domains (discovered through the exchange of Source-Active TLV messages) and maintains that in its local MSDP cache table. The receiving MSDP peer then uses the source lists to establish a path to the multicast sources. If there are receivers in the multicast routing domain that are interested in the multicast sources, the normal PIM-SM source-tree building mechanism (discussed earlier earlier) is used to deliver the multicast data to the receivers.

9.5.6.1 MSDP Peer-RPF Checks

When an MSDP peer receives a Source-Active TLV, it performs a peer-RPF (peer-Reverse-Path-Forwarding) check (which is different from a regular multicast RPF check) to make sure that the sending MSDP peer lies on the path leading back to the originating Rendezvous Point (i.e., originating MSDP peer) [CISCMSDP12.4T]. If the sender is not on that path, the receiving MSDP peer rejects and drops the Source-Active TLV. The MSDP peer-RPF check is not the same as the RPF checks performed by standard (non-MSDP) multicast routers and is used to ensure loop-free forwarding of Source-Active messages.

9.5.7 PIM SOURCE SPECIFIC MULTICAST (PIM-SSM) TABLE ENTRIES

PIM-SSM [RFC4607] is derived from PIM-SM [RFC4601] [RFC7761] and uses IGMPv3 [RFC3376] [RFC4604] to determine how and which IP receivers should be sent multicast traffic directly from a multicast source. IGMPv3 supports source filtering which is a feature that PIM-SSM requires. PIM-SSM uses a subset of the PIM-SM functionality to create a source-based distribution tree (shortest path tree (SPT)) between the source and the receiver but constructs the SPT without the involvement of a Rendezvous Point.

In PIM-SSM, multicast traffic from a source is forwarded to only the receivers who have explicitly joined that multicast source. To send traffic from the source to a multicast group, PIM-SSM creates only a source-specific multicast distribution tree (no shared tree is used). PIM-SSM is best suited for one-to-many applications such as broadcast applications targeted for streaming audio and video broadcast.

Technically, PIM-SSM can use multicast addresses in the entire 224.0.0.0/4 multicast address range (i.e., address range 224.0.0.0 through 239.255.255.255). However, PIM-SSM operation is guaranteed only in the Internet Assigned Numbers Authority (IANA) assigned multicast address range 232.0.0.0/8 (i.e., 232.0.0.0 through 232.255.255.255) but with the address sub-range 232.0.0.0/24 reserved (not yet assigned).

In PIM-SSM, multicast traffic is delivered to receivers based on (S, G) channels. Multicast traffic belonging to a single PIM-SSM (S, G) channel consists of packets with a unicast IP source address S and IP destination address set to the multicast group address G. Only receivers that become members of the (S, G) channel will receive this traffic. PIM-SSM does not require any signaling from a potential source to become a multicast source in the PIM-SSM domain. However, PIM-SSM requires a receiver to subscribe or unsubscribe to an (S, G) channel to receive or not receive traffic from that particular source.

For multicast groups within the PIM-SSM multicast address range, the (S, G) channel subscription signaling process utilizes IGMPv3's INCLUDE mode membership reports. IGMPv3 allows IP hosts to signal multicast group membership with filtering capabilities that can include or exclude particular multicast sources. An IP host can (use the IGMPv3 EXCLUDE mode) to signal its desire to receive multicast traffic from all sources sending to a particular multicast group excluding some specific sources. A host can also (use the IGMPv3 INCLUDE mode) to signal its desire to receive multicast traffic only from some specific sources sending to a particular multicast group.

In PIM-SSM, SPTs rooted at the source can be created because the router closest to the receiver (that has signaled an explicit join) is informed of the unicast IP address of the multicast traffic source. The multicast source of the (S, G) channel is always known in advance, allowing PIM-SSM to efficiently build a source-based SPT multicast tree from channel receivers to the source (based on the unicast routing topology). So, PIM-SSM does not include mechanisms for establishing a connection to a Rendezvous Point through a shared distribution tree, as in PIM-SM but instead directly establishes a source-based distribution tree to the source.

Thus, in a PIM-SSM network, a host uses IGMPv3 to subscribe to an (S, G) channel by signaling a desire to join multicast group G with source S. The directly connected router which is the receiver's Designated Router, forwards an (S, G) join message to its RPF neighbor router (leading to the multicast source). Neither the receiver nor its Designated Router contacts a Rendezvous Point in this process, as would be the case in PIM-SM. The (S, G) join message initiates the creation of a source-based tree which is built hop-by-hop until it reaches the last-hop router (Designated Router) connected to the multicast source. Using the source-based tree, multicast traffic is delivered from the source to the subscribing receiver.

Also, in PIM-SSM, the receiver's Designated Router will continue to periodically transmit (S, G) join messages if it has (S, G) subscriptions on its interfaces. Therefore, as long as the Designated Router receives (S, G) subscriptions from receivers, the state of the SPT from the receivers to the source will be maintained, even if the source stops sending multicast traffic for longer periods of time.

In contrast, PIM-SM maintains the (S, G) state only if the multicast source is sending traffic and receivers are sending explicit joins to the multicast group. If a source does not send multicast traffic for more than three minutes, PIM-SM will delete the (S, G) state and only reestablish it after packets from the source are sent again through the RPT. Because PIM-SSM does not have a mechanism to notify a receiver that a source is active, the PIM-SSM network must maintain the (S, G) state as long as receivers are subscribing to that channel.

9.5.8 BIDIRECTIONAL PIM (BIDIR-PIM) TABLE ENTRIES

In BIDIR-PIM [RFC5015], multicast traffic to a multicast group is forwarded only along a bidirectional shared tree that is rooted at a Rendezvous Point. The Rendezvous Point serves as the root from which all other routers establish a loop-free spanning tree topology. Receivers signal and establish membership to the bidirectional multicast group via explicit join messages. Multicast traffic from a source is unconditionally transported along a shared tree toward the Rendezvous Point and then forwarded down another shared tree toward the receivers on each branch of the shared tree.

BIDIR-PIM is more suitable for many-to-many applications within a PIM domain. BIDIR-PIM's unconditional forwarding of traffic from a source toward the Rendezvous Point on the shared tree means there is no registering process for multicast sources (via PIM-SM Register packets over a unicast tunnel) as in PIM-SM. These changes in BIDIR-PIM allow the forwarding of multicast traffic on all routers based solely on (*, G) multicast routing entries. This also eliminates the maintenance of any source-specific state (S, G) in the routers, allowing BIDIR-PIM to scale to an arbitrary number of sources.

The use of bidirectional shared trees minimizes the amount of state information PIM routers must maintain, which is especially beneficial in PIM domains with numerous and dispersed multicast sources and receivers. Some examples of many-to-many applications include multimedia conferencing with many listeners who are also speakers, and distributed multi-player computer games. Another important many-to-many application of BIDIR-PIM is distributed inventory polling. When PIM-DM, PIM-SM, or PIM-SSM is applied to the latter many-to-many application, a multicast inventory query issued by one station will generate multicast responses from many other stations. Each multicast response from a given station will constitute communication to a separate multicast group.

Each responding station will generate a large number of (S, G) routes for each multicast group (group of receiving stations). BIDIR-PIM solves this problem by allowing the routers to maintain only a multicast group-specific (*, G) state. Thus, each router maintains only a single (*, G) route for each multicast group in order to deliver traffic to and from all the sources. BIDIR-PIM creates bidirectional shared trees that are centered at a Rendezvous Point and no SPTs are used as in PIM-SM (eliminating the need for (S, G) routes). Also, because BIDIR-PIM does not support SPTs, there is no SPT switchover (as in PIM-SM) and all traffic is always forwarded through the Rendezvous Point.

BIDIR-PIM and PIM-SM behave similarly, when packets are forwarded along a shared tree from the Rendezvous Point toward the receivers. However, BIDIR-PIM behaves differently from PIM-SM when traffic is forwarded from the sources toward the Rendezvous Point. PIM-SM cannot forward traffic in the direction pointing (upstream) toward the multicast source of the shared tree, because only traffic from one RPF interface (i.e., coming from interface leading to the source) is accepted. The RPF interface (for the shared tree) points toward the Rendezvous Point, therefore permitting multicast traffic flow only downstream (from the source).

In PIM-SM, source traffic is first encapsulated in unicast PIM-SM Register messages, which are forwarded from the source's Designated Router toward the Rendezvous Point. After the source registration process, the Rendezvous Point joins a source-based SPT (that is rooted at the multicast source). This means, in PIM-SM, traffic that originates from a source flows only toward the Rendezvous Point and not upstream on the shared tree, and also traffic sent along the source-based SPT from the source travels until it reaches the Rendezvous Point. The traffic then flows along the shared tree from the Rendezvous Point toward all receivers.

Unlike Rendezvous Points in PIM-SM, which must receive and de-encapsulate PIM Register messages (sent from a source's Designated Router in order to retrieve the source's packets), and perform other protocol-specific actions, Rendezvous Points in BIDIR-PIM implement no such specific functions. Rendezvous Points in BIDIR-PIM are simply locations in the multicast domain where both sources and receivers meet.

The above discussion therefore means that BIDIR-PIM builds a bidirectional (*, G) multicast group shared tree that carries traffic *both* upstream from multicast sources toward the Rendezvous Point, and downstream from the Rendezvous Point to receivers. The Rendezvous Point in BIDIR-PIM will never build an (S, G) entry and also the PIM routers will never construct a source-based SPT toward the source. As a result, the strict RPF-based rules employed in PIM-DM, PIM-SM, and PIM-SSM do not apply to BIDIR-PIM. Instead, BIDIR-PIM builds routes that forward multicast traffic from all hosts to and from the Rendezvous Point. This also means routers in a BIDIR-PIM network have the ability to accept multicast traffic on many incoming interfaces that flow up and down the shared tree (to and from all the hosts).

9.5.8.1 Designated Forwarder Election

To prevent multicast packets from looping, BIDIR-PIM introduces the concept of a Designated Forwarder which establishes a loop-free bidirectional shared tree centered at the Rendezvous Point. As noted earlier, the same shared tree (bidirectional tree) is used to send multicast traffic upstream from sources to the Rendezvous Point and downstream from the Rendezvous Point to the receivers.

On all shared network segments (i.e., subnets/VLANs and point-to-point links), all BIDIR-PIM routers participate in the election of the Designated Forwarder. To prevent forwarding loops, the BIDIR-PIM routers select only one router as the Designated Forwarder for each segment and for each Rendezvous Point associated with a set of bidirectional multicast groups. The Designated Forwarder is responsible for forwarding multicast traffic upstream from a network segment toward the Rendezvous Point and for forwarding multicast traffic downstream onto a segment toward the receivers.

For each Rendezvous Point, one BIDIR-PIM router on each segment is elected the Designated Forwarder and the election is usually done during the Rendezvous Points discovery process using BIDIR-PIM control messages. Also, the election of the Designated Forwarder is based on unicast routing protocol metrics and employs the same rules used by the PIM Assert processes to break ties [RFC5015].

As discussed earlier under the PIM-SM Assert mechanism, each BIDIR-PIM router attached to a common shared network segment (subnet) advertises its unicast route with a routing metric (based on an existing Interior Gateway Protocol (IGP)) to the Rendezvous Point. If the unicast routing table is populated by more than one unicast routing protocol (e.g., RIPv2, EIGRP, OSPF), then the Administrative Distance associated with the routing protocol supplying the route can be used to select the best route to the Rendezvous Point.

Each BIDIR-PIM router advertises its unicast route and routing metric in Designated Forwarder Offer, Winner, Backoff, and Pass messages. The BIDIR-PIM router with the best (lowest-cost) unicast routing metric to the Rendezvous Point is selected as the Designated Forwarder. If the routing metrics through two routers are equal, then the router with the highest IP address will be selected as the Designated Forwarder. This allows BIDIR-PIM to ensure that only one copy of a multicast packet is forwarded to the Rendezvous Point, even if there are multiple equal cost paths leading to the Rendezvous Point.

A Designated Forwarder is selected on only one interface on a point-to-point link (leading toward the Rendezvous Point). A point-to-point link is considered a network segment that interconnects two routers, and a router can only be the Designated Forwarder on one interface on that link, and, once selected, this Designated Forwarder cannot be elected on the interface at the other end of the same link. When multiple interfaces exist, the Designated Forwarder interface is the interface that has the best (lowest-cost) unicast routing metric to the Rendezvous Point. If there is a tie in the routing metrics of any two interfaces leading to the Rendezvous Point, the interface with the highest IP address wins.

Each Rendezvous Point associated with a set of bidirectional multicast groups has one Designated Forwarder selected for it on each network segment. This means that multiple BIDIR-PIM routers may be elected as Designated Forwarder on any given network segment, one (elected router) for each Rendezvous Point. Also, any particular BIDIR-PIM router in a network may be elected the Designated Forwarder (for different Rendezvous Points) on more than one attached interface.

9.5.8.2   Building the Bidirectional Group Tree and Packet Forwarding

For bidirectional multicast groups, the role of the Designated Router (as in PIM-SM) is assumed by the Designated Forwarder for the Rendezvous Point. On a network that has local multicast traffic receivers, only the elected Designated Forwarder populates its outgoing interface list (OIL) upon receiving IGMP Join messages. The receipt of IGMP and MLD (*, G) membership reports causes the BIDIR-PIM Designated Forwarder to send BIDIR-PIM (*, G) Join messages. The Designated Forwarder is responsible for sending (*, G) Join and Leave messages upstream toward the Rendezvous Point. This Designated Forwarder is the only BIDIR-PIM router on a network segment or point-to-point link allowed to send multicast traffic toward the Rendezvous Point.

The key features of BIDIR-PIM forwarding are summarized here:

- BIDIR-PIM does not use PIM Register and Register-Stop messages to register sources to the Rendezvous Point. Each multicast source directly connected to a Designated Router is able to start sending to the Rendezvous Point whenever it wants. Packets from a multicast source are picked up automatically by the directly-connected Designated Forwarder and then forwarded upstream toward the Rendezvous Point. Also, the Rendezvous Point has no way to inform the source to stop sending multicast traffic.
- When a router receives upstream traffic, it forwards the traffic only toward the Rendezvous Point if the receiving router is the Designated Forwarder on the interface on which it is received. This feature and others essentially allow BIDIR-PIM to create a bidirectional multicast shared tree between any source and the Rendezvous Point without the use of any explicit signaling. When multicast packets arrive at the Rendezvous Point, they are forwarded down the bidirectional shared tree (if there are interested receivers on the tree branches) or dropped (when no receivers have joined on any branch). It is important to note that a multicast source can also be a receiver, but this does not always have to be the case.
- When a downstream BIDIR-PIM router wishes to join the bidirectional shared distribution tree, the RPF neighbor router in the PIM Join and

Leave messages (the router sends) is always the elected Designated Forwarder for the router interface leading to the Rendezvous Point. When a Join or Leave message is received by a router that is not the elected Designated Forwarder for the interface over which the message was received, the message will be ignored. Otherwise, the router will update the bidirectional shared tree in the same way a PIM-SM would.

- All routers in a BIDIR-PIM domain support bidirectional shared trees, and can receive (S, G) Join and Leave messages. The BIDIR-PIM routers also do not need to issue PIM assert messages, since the procedure for electing a Designated Forwarder eliminates any parallel downstream paths coming from any given Rendezvous Point.
- A BIDIR-PIM router generates and maintains only (*, G) state entries for bidirectional multicast groups. The OIL associated with a (*, G) entry (in the multicast table) lists all the router interfaces on which the BIDIR-PIM router was elected Designated Forwarder and on which either an IGMP or PIM Join message has been received. If a BIDIR-PIM router is located on a tree branch that is sender-only, it will also add a (*, G) state entry, but the OIL will not list any interfaces (indicating receivers).
- If a BIDIR-PIM router receives a multicast packet from the RPF interface leading toward the Rendezvous Point, it will forward the packet downstream according to the OIL associated with the (*, G) state entry. Otherwise, only the BIDIR-PIM router that is the elected Designated Forwarder for the interface (on which the packet is received) will forward the multicast packet; the packet is discarded by all other routers.
- BIDIR-PIM Rendezvous Point addresses (and group-to-RP mappings) can be advertised by Auto-RP, PIM bootstrap router, or static RP configurations [CISCBIDIRPIM] [JUNBIDIRPIM].

9.6 MULTICAST REVERSE PATH FORWARDING (RPF)

IP routers organize the entries in their unicast routing and forwarding tables according to destination IP address prefix, next-hop IP address, and outgoing interface. Unicast forwarding then involves a router checking the destination address of a received unicast packet against a unicast forwarding table that the router maintains to determine the packet's next-hop IP address and outbound interface.

Unlike unicast forwarding, multicast forwarding involves a source transmitting traffic to an arbitrary group of interested receivers (i.e., the multicast group members) that are identified by a multicast group address. To forward traffic, the multicast router must determine in which direction the source is (i.e., the upstream direction) and which directions the receivers are (i.e., the downstream direction). If the router has receivers on multiple downstream interfaces (paths), the router replicates the multicast packet and forwards the copies out those downstream paths.

Furthermore, in multicast forwarding, a multicast router forwards a multicast packet along a distribution tree in a direction pointing away from the multicast source and also with the goal of preventing forwarding loops in the process. The multicast routers organize their multicast forwarding states (in multicast forwarding tables) to follow a logical reverse path from the multicast receiver back to the source (which can be at the root of the distribution tree) or a Rendezvous Point. The process of organizing the multicast forwarding state, forwarding multicast packets, and ensuring that multicast paths point away from the source or Rendezvous Point, is known as Reverse-Path Forwarding (RPF).

To add a branch (multicast path) to a multicast distribution tree, a multicast router performs an RPF check. Any request from an interested receiver for multicast traffic from a multicast group must pass the RPF check. The multicast router carries out an RPF check for every multicast packet received before the packet is eligible to be forwarded on any of its outbound interfaces. The RPF check is an integral part of multicast implementation in every multicast router.

When a multicast router receives IP multicast packet on an interface, it treats the source IP address in the IP multicast packet as if it is the destination address for a unicast IP packet. The unicast forwarding table the router maintains contains all known routes including that for the source IP address and its corresponding outgoing interface. Using the source IP address, the multicast router performs a lookup in its unicast forwarding table and if the outgoing interface discovered lies on the shortest path back to the source IP address of the packet and is the same router interface on which the multicast packet was received, then the multicast packet passes the RPF check. The multicast router drops packets that fail the RPF check because the incoming interface is deemed as one that is not on the shortest path back to the multicast traffic source.

9.6.1 USING THE RPF TABLE

A multicast router may maintain separate forwarding tables for performing RPF checks. A router can use the same IP forwarding table used for forwarding unicast IP packets for RPF checks or it can use a separate forwarding table created solely for multicast RPF checks. Regardless of how the table is constructed, the RPF table contains only unicast IP addresses (routes) plus their corresponding outgoing interfaces, since the RPF check is performed only on the source IP address of the multicast packet.

The main attraction in using the unicast routing/forwarding table for RPF checks is implementation simplicity. Also, maintaining a separate routing/forwarding table for RPF checks allows separate paths and routing policies to be established for unicast and multicast traffic, which further allows the (logical) multicast distribution network to be operated more independently of the unicast network.

A multicast group address must not be used in the source address field of an IP packet header and so the RPF check is not performed on the multicast group address (which is carried in the multicast packet's destination address field). RPF checks can only be performed on unicast (source) addresses because only one source sends a particular stream of multicast traffic/content to an IP multicast group address, although the same multicast content could be sent from another source (to a different multicast group).

If the router uses the same routing/forwarding table used for unicast packet forwarding also for RPF checks, then the routing/forwarding table entries can be maintained by unicast routing protocols such as RIP, OSPF, IS-IS, and BGP. If a separate multicast RPF table is used, then this table has to be populated via other means. PIM-DM RPF checks can also be performed using a special multicast RPF table populated by Multiprotocol BGP (MBGP) or Multi-Topology Routing in IS-IS (M-IS-IS). Distance Vector Multicast Routing Protocol (DVMRP) duplicates the operation of a unicast routing protocol and maintains a separate (dedicated) table for RPF checks. PIM (which is protocol independent), on the other hand, does not duplicate unicast routing protocol operations and thus must rely on some other routing protocol to populate and maintain this table.

Routing protocols such as IS-IS and BGP have extensions (using Multi-Topology Routing in IS-IS (M-IS-IS) and Multiprotocol BGP (MBGP), respectively) that allow different sets of routing information (for unicast and multicast) exchanged between routers to be differentiated. Routes learned by IS-IS can be added to the RPF table when special features such as traffic engineering are enabled. Using these routing protocols, multicast routers along multicast routes (distribution tree) can be tagged as multicast RPF routers and used by a receiving router differently than the unicast traffic routes.

The sources of information used for the RPF checks can be summarized as follows:

- **Regular Unicast Routing Table**: This contains unicast routes (static and dynamic) discovered via, for example, OSPF. These unicast routes constitute the normal source of information used for RPF checks.
- **Multicast Static Routes**: In some cases. it is not desirable to use the routes in the unicast routing table populated by unicast routing protocols. The unicast routing table may contain routes that are not suitable for multicast traffic. In such a case, a different route for multicast traffic has to be specified and static routing could be used. For example, there may be the need to avoid going over or to bypass a portion of a network that does not support multicast routing by sending multicast traffic through a tunnel (or static route). This capability is also useful when there is the need to send multicast traffic on a specific router interface without having to configure PIM on the interface.

    When a router compares multiple paths (based on longest match) for a given IP address, it gives preference to the path with the lower Administrative Distance. So, to ensure that a static route is used (in this case for transporting multicast traffic), a low Administrative Distance value must be configured for it. However, it has to be recognized that the router will still give preference to directly connected routes over all other routes (including static routes), no matter their administrative distance values.

- **MBGP Multicast Extension Routes**: MBGP [RFC4760] allows a router to maintain both unicast and multicast routing information but with each routing information type stored in a different routing table to ensure information separation. MBGP can also build different network topologies for each routing information type (different unicast and multicast topologies). MBGP allows routing policies to be defined for unicast and multicast routes. PIM can use the multicast routing information to perform its RPF lookups for multicast sources. This allows multicast traffic to be routed hop-by-hop across a multicast topology rather than over a unicast topology.

IP multicast static routes allow multicast paths to be configured that are different from those developed from unicast protocol routing tables. In PIM, a router expects to receive multicast packets on the same interface on which it sends unicast packets back to the source. This feature works well only if the unicast and multicast network topologies are congruent. However, there are cases where there is the need for unicast and multicast packets to take different paths. So as explained earlier, the most common approach to address this is to use tunneling to keep the unicast and multicast paths separate.

For example, when a path between two routers in the network does not support multicast routing, a preferred solution is to configure a tunnel between the two routers (e.g., using Generic Routing Encapsulation (GRE) tunnels). Thus, configuring static multicast routes in a network is particularly useful when the unicast and multicast topologies are different. With static multicast routes, there is no need to finds ways to make the two topologies similar.

MBGP (which supports IPv4 and IPv6) allows information describing the topology of IP multicast routes in a network to be exchanged separately (in parallel) from that describing the topology of regular IPv4 unicast routes. Thus, MBGP allows routers in the network to maintain a unicast routing topology that is different and separate from the multicast routing topology. MBGP allows inter-domain multicast routing information to be exchanged, but protocols such as PIM are still needed to construct multicast traffic distribution trees and to forward multicast traffic.

9.6.2 Data-Plane versus Control-Plane RPF Check

In the typical networking scenario, multicast routers perform RPF checks based on the contents of a unicast routing table that is populated by routing protocols like RIPv2, EIGRP, and OSPF. However, the RPF checks that multicast routers perform can be viewed from a data-plane or control-plane perspective. A router performs a data-plane RPF check when it receives a multicast packet and wants to validate if the receiving interface and upstream neighbor router sending the packet are on the shortest path to the source IP address of the packet.

On the other hand, a multicast router performs a control-plane RPF check when it originates or receives control-plane messages. Such control messages include sending PIM Join messages or receiving MSDP Source-Active TLVs from MSDP-peers (see MSDP earlier). For example, a PIM Designated Router that wants to know where to send a PIM Join message for a receiver interested in multicast traffic destined to a particular (S, G) or (*, G) group, performs an RPF lookup for the source IP address (for a source-based tree) or Rendezvous Point address (for a shared tree). The PIM RPF check influences and helps carve out the actual path (in the reversed direction toward the source or Rendezvous Point) along the multicast tree the traffic requested by the PIM Join message would take.

9.6.3 RPF CHECK

Using a multicast packet forwarding example, we describe in this section how RPF checks are performed at a multicast router. As discussed earlier when a multicast packet is received on a router interface, the router uses the unicast routing information it maintains to perform an RPF check on the packet. If the RPF check passes, the packet is forwarded out the appropriate downstream interfaces. Otherwise, the router drops the packet. Figure 9.2 illustrates a scenario of an unsuccessful RPF check while Figure 9.3 shows a successful RPF check scenario.

To forward a multicast packet from a source down the multicast distribution tree, the multicast router performs an RPF check as follows:

1. The router receives a multicast packet on interface F0, parses its source address (152.20.3.21), and performs a look up in the unicast routing table to determine if the packet has arrived on the interface that leads back to the source.

RPF Check Fails:

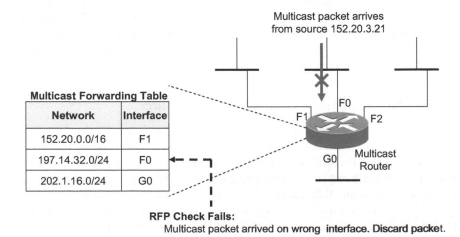

FIGURE 9.2   RPF Check Fails at a Multicast Router.

RPF Check Succeeds:

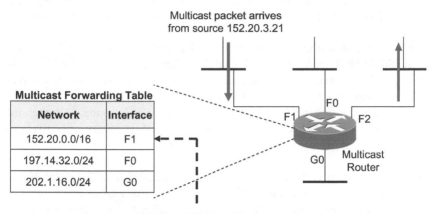

Multicast packet arrives
from source 152.20.3.21

Multicast Forwarding Table

Network	Interface
152.20.0.0/16	F1
197.14.32.0/24	F0
202.1.16.0/24	G0

RFP Check Succeeds:
Multicast packet arrived on correct interface. Accept packet.

FIGURE 9.3   RPF Check Passes at a Multicast Router.

2. The lookup reveals that the packet arrived on the wrong interface (F0). The correct interface should be F1.
3. The outcome is a failed RPF check and the packet is dropped.

If the packet had arrived on the interface leading back to the source (F1), the RPF check would have succeeded and the packet would have been forwarded. In Figure 9.3, the multicast packet arrived on interface F1. The lookup in the unicast routing table reveals that F1 is the correct interface. The RPF check succeeds, and the packet is forwarded.

9.7   MFIB COMPONENTS

In the typical switch/router or router supporting unicast forwarding, the router processor extracts routing information that is directly useable for packet forwarding from the unicast routing table or RIB (Routing Information Base), and loads it into a unicast software FIB and, possibly, one or more hardware unicast FIBs. The RIB is built and maintained by unicast routing protocols, such as RIP, EIGRP, OSPF, and BGP. When routing changes occur in the network, the route processor updates the RIB and then updates the corresponding entries in the unicast FIBs.

To forward a unicast packet in software or hardware, the forwarding engine looks up the packet's destination address in the FIB which may be implemented using a ternary content addressable memory (TCAM). The adjacency information (i.e., next-hop router IP address, outgoing interface, and if readily available, the Layer 2 address of the next hop) obtained during the lookup process from the FIB is used to rewrite the Layer 2 information in the outgoing packet. The

Layer 2 adjacency can be maintained in a combined or unified FIB or in a separate adjacency table depending on the switch/router design. The adjacency table maintains Layer 2 addresses for the next-hop routers associated with the MFIB entries.

This section describes the components that make up the MFIB architecture [CISCMFIB11] [CISCUNDERIPMUL]. These components are shown in Figure 9.4. These components and related features are not specific to any particular multicast routing protocol but instead describe collectively platform-independent properties in PIM multicast routers. On a PIM multicast router, the PIM protocols, multicast route (mroute) table, and IGMP appear collectively as single client to the MRIB:

- PIM constructs and maintains multicast (source-based and shared) distribution trees by applying RPF on a unicast routing table.
- Multicast routers use IGMP to identify multicast group members on VLANs and subnets that are directly connected to them. Hosts join and leave multicast groups using IGMP messages.
- PIM routers maintain a multicast routing (mroute) table that stores the routes used to forward multicast packets. A router also stores in the mroute table the states of incoming and outgoing router interfaces for each source and multicast group (S, G) and (*, G) address pair. The router uses this state information to discard and forward multicast packets. Each entry in the mroute table (referred to simply as an mroute in Figure 9.4) contains the following items:
  - Unicast IP address of multicast traffic source (S or *). The wildcard * indicates all sources address.
  - IP multicast group address (G)
  - Single incoming interface—Each (S, G) and (*, G) route entry has a corresponding incoming RPF interface.
  - Outgoing interface list (OIL).

Present-day switch/routers use mostly ASIC-based forwarding engines that provide Ethernet forwarding at Layer 2 and IP routing at Layer 3. The ASIC-based forwarding engines are specifically designed to forward packets at very high speeds and can sustain such speeds with high performance even when supporting QoS and security ACLs. Forwarding unicast and multicast traffic in hardware handles significantly much better high-speed interfaces with high utilization than software-based forwarding in a CPU.

Generally, the CPU is designed to handle packets with unknown destinations and exception packets. The typical switch/router supports interfaces for inter-VLAN or inter-subnet routing and switchports for Layer 2 forwarding (see discussion in *Chapter 1*). A switch/router also supports physical Layer 3 interfaces (routed interfaces) that can connect directly to the IP host and other switch/routers or routers.

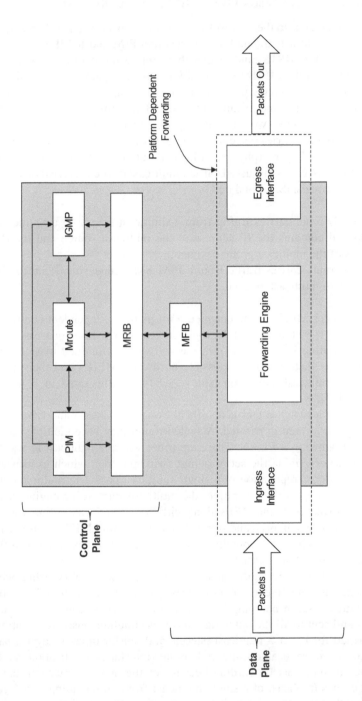

FIGURE 9.4 IPv4 MFIB Architecture.

9.7.1 Protocols and Tables Used in IP Multicast Routing

The MFIB is analogous to the unicast FIB described earlier and in other chapters. A route processor extracts the multicast routes that PIM and IGMP have created and populated in the MRIB, and distills them into a protocol-independent format that is stored in the MFIB to be used for hardware packet forwarding. The route processor removes all the protocol-specific information that is not useful for actual packet forwarding and installs in the MFIB only the essential information a packet forwarding engine would need for packet forwarding.

The MFIB contain entries that consists of (S, G) and/or (*, G) routes, with each entry having a list of Layer 3 (physical or logical) outgoing interfaces, and a single incoming RPF VLAN. As discussed earlier, multicast traffic is carried on primarily two types of routes: (S, G) and (*, G).

- An (S, G) route carries traffic from a multicast source to a multicast group and contains the IP address of the multicast source and the IP address of the multicast group destination.
- A (*, G) route carries traffic from a PIM-SM Rendezvous Point to all receivers of multicast group G.

Typically, a master MFIB is implemented with platform-dependent control and management software that runs in the route processor. The route processor loads the multicast routing information from the software-maintained master MFIB into one or more (distributed and possibly hardware) MFIBs and their associated hardware multicast expansion tables (METs) as illustrated in Figure 9.5 [CISC4500CH33].

The design of a switch/router generally allows both Layer 3 and Layer 2 forwarding to be performed in parallel. A switch/router may have multiple Layer 2 switchports attached to a VLAN. There are times where a multicast forwarding engine needs to determine the set of output switchports on which to forward a multicast packet (i.e., replication of a single multicast packet to multiple output switchports). To support this operation, the multicast forwarding engine distills the Layer 3 information in the MFIB along with the Layer 2 forwarding information (list of output switchports) and stores this in a hardware MET that is used for packet replication. The MET contains Layer 3 multicast routes along with their corresponding Layer 2 multicast entries.

Packet replication, in its most efficient form, is a mode of forwarding where instead of sending out one copy of a multicast packet at a time to each outgoing interface (within a set of outgoing interfaces), the packet is replicated into multiple copies and sent to all the outgoing interfaces simultaneously. Replication is only performed for Layer 3 multicast packets and not for unicast Layer 3 packets which are never replicated to multiple router interfaces. Replication is a key functionality in multicast forwarding because of the need, in many instances, to forward copies (replicas) of a single multicast from an incoming interface to multiple outgoing interfaces. A switch/router can perform packet replication in the following ways:

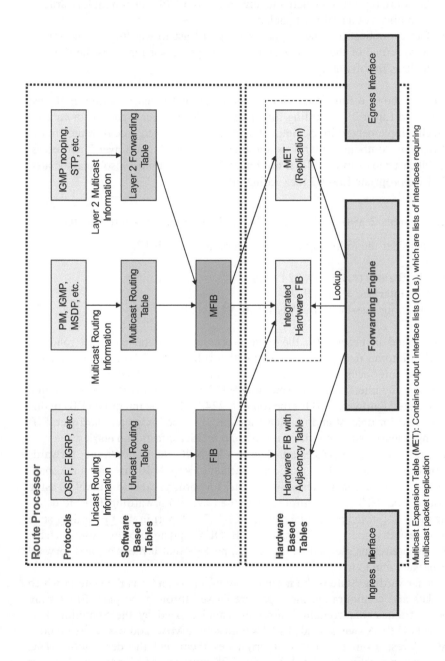

FIGURE 9.5 Protocols and Tables Used in IP Multicast Routing.

- Hardware replication where a hardware multicast forwarding engine forwards all replicas of a multicast packet.
- Software replication where the route processor CPU subsystem forwards all replicas of a multicast packet.
- Partial replication where a hardware multicast forwarding engine forwards some of the replicas and the route processor forwards the other replicas in software.

Figure 9.5 shows a functional view of the combined unicast routing, multicast routing, and Layer 2 forwarding functions used for multicast packet forwarding (typically implemented in specialized hardware). Similar to unicast routes in the FIB that have outbound interfaces and their next-hop IP and Layer 2 addresses, the multicast routes in the MFIB are Layer 3 routes that must also be associated with the appropriate Layer 2 forwarding information.

9.7.2 Layers 2 and 3 Multicast Tables Entries in a Switch/Router

Let us consider the following example of a route in an MFIB:

- MFIB entry (*, G) = (*, 224.1.6.8)
- RPF interface = VLAN 30
- Outgoing Interfaces are: VLAN 10, VLAN 20.

As illustrated in Figure 9.6, the route processor loads the multicast route (*, 224.1.6.8) into an integrated (unicast/multicast) hardware FIB table and the list of outgoing interfaces into a MET. The route processor also loads a pointer to the list of outgoing interfaces, corresponding MET index, and the RPF interface into the integrated hardware FIB for the route (*, 224.1.6.8). The integrated FIB in this case is used for unicast and multicast forwarding. The integrated hardware FIB contains unicast routes, multicast routes, and multicast fast-drop entries.

For the outgoing interfaces attached to VLAN 10, the switch/router forwards the multicast packet to all switchports attached to VLAN 10 that are in the spanning tree forwarding state. The switch/router forwards packets to VLAN 20 using the same process. The switch/router uses the Layer 2 Forwarding Table to determine the set of switchports attached to VLAN 20. A port in the forwarding state will process Bridge Protocol Data Units (BPDUs), update its MAC Address table using the addresses gleaned from Layer 2 packets that it receives, and forward user packets sent to it.

The forwarding State is the normal state of a port and it is the state in which user data and configuration messages are passed through the port. BPDUs are Layer 2 frames that contain control information used by the Spanning Tree Protocol (STP). A switch sends BPDUs with source MAC address set to a unique MAC address from the port that originates them and the destination MAC address set to a defined and well-known IEEE multicast MAC address. Switches within an extended LAN use an STP topology and exchange BPDUs. BPDUs

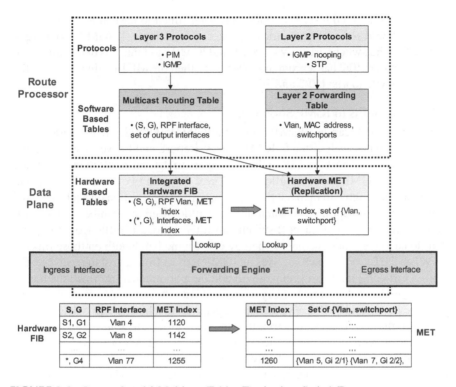

FIGURE 9.6   Layers 2 and 3 Multicast Tables Entries in a Switch/Router.

carry information on ports, MAC addresses, priorities, and costs and are used to develop loop-free (or tree) topologies in a Layer 2 broadcast domain.

When the switch/router forwards a multicast packet, in addition to forwarding it to all of the outgoing interfaces/switchports (having multicast members), it also forwards the packet to all switchports in the input VLAN that have multicast members (other than the one on which it was received). For example, assume that the input VLAN 30 has two attached switchports, Gig 30/1 and Gig 30/2. If an IP host on Gig 30/1 sends a multicast packet, a host on switchport Gig 30/2 might also be interested in receiving that packet. To enable the switch/router to forward the multicast packet to the host on switchport Gig 30/2, it must add all of the switchports attached to the input VLAN to the set of switchports that is loaded in the MET.

If VLAN 10 has switchports 10/1 and 10/2, VLAN 20 has switchports 20/1 and 20/2, and VLAN 30 has switchports 30/1 and 30/2, then the MET chain for the multicast route (*, 224.1.6.8) would list these switchports (assuming IGMP snooping [CISC4500CH23] [CISC4500CH33] [RFC4541] is enabled and the sender is on switchport 30/1): 10/1, 10/2, 20/1, 20/2, and 30/2. If IGMP snooping is enabled and VLAN 20 does not have any group members, then the multicast packet should not be forwarded to all output switchports on VLAN 20. Only switchports on which IGMP snooping has determined to have at least one group member should receive the multicast packet. For example, if IGMP snooping is enabled for the switchports in VLAN 10, and IGMP snooping has determined that only switchport 10/2 has a group member on it, then the MET chain would list the following switchports: (10/2 and 30/2).

9.7.2.1 Benefits of IGMP Snooping

A Layer 2 switch can use IGMP Snooping [CISC4500CH23] [CISC4500CH33] [RFC4541] to passively listen to IGMP Query, Report, and Leave messages transferred between IP hosts and IP multicast routers to determine IP multicast group membership. IGMP snooping allows the Layer 2 switch to examine IGMP packets passing through it to map out the multicast group registration on each port, and then maintain a mapping of switch port to multicast group membership accordingly. Through this the Layer 2 switch can filter multicast traffic from the ports that do not have group members, thereby conserving bandwidth on those links.

When the Layer 2 switch receives an IGMP Report from a host to receive traffic from a particular multicast group, it will add the port number on which the host is attached to the multicast table entry associated with the multicast group. When the switch receives an IGMP Leave Group message from a host, it will delete the port on which the host is attached from the multicast group entry in the table. IGMP snooping allows a Layer 2 switch to prevent hosts on a VLAN or subnet, or directly attached hosts who have not explicitly joined a multicast group, from receiving traffic sent to that group. It is a mechanism that allows Layer 2 switches to prune multicast traffic from switch ports/links that do not contain multicast group members.

Without IGMP Snooping, a Layer 2 switch will forward multicast packets to all of its ports in a similar fashion like broadcast traffic. A Layer 2 switch using IGMP snooping will only forward multicast traffic to the ports that have group members on. This feature is especially useful for multicast applications that are bandwidth-intensive such as IPTV that can consume a lot of port and network bandwidth.

9.7.3 MULTICAST FAST DROP

Every (S, G) and (*, G) route learned by multicast protocols such as PIM-SM and PIM-DM has associated with it an incoming or RPF interface. There are times when a multicast packet is received on an interface other than its expected RPF interface. In such cases, the packet can be forwarded to the route processor so that the PIM software can carry out special protocol processing on the packet. One example where the route processor may be called upon to perform special protocol processing is when the switch/router needs to execute the PIM Assert mechanism (see discussion earlier).

The switch/router can be configured to forward all multicast packets that arrive on non-RPF interfaces to the route processor for software processing. However, software processing is often not required for many non-RPF packets, since these packets are usually not used by the multicast routing protocols. To avoid overwhelming the route processor, some other action has to be taken to handle the non-RPF packets that potentially could have been sent to the software on the route processor.

As special action, the route processor loads fast-drop entries in the hardware forwarding engine when it receives a packet that has failed an RPF check and is not needed by the PIM protocols on the switch/router [CISCUNDERIPMUL]. A fast-drop entry is indexed by the following parameters associated with the (S, G,) route: {(S, G), incoming interface}. Any multicast packet that matches a fast-drop entry is instead Layer 2 forwarded in the ingress VLAN and is not sent to the route processor to avoid overloading it with software processing of packets that have failed the RPF check [CISCUNDERIPMUL].

Network events (that can affect multicast protocol behavior) such as those causing a change in the unicast routing table or causing a link to go down, can affect the number of packets that can be safely fast dropped. A packet could be correctly fast dropped by the hardware forwarding engine before a network change occurs but may need to be forwarded to the route processor for PIM software processing after a network topology change. The route processor therefore has to be capable of flushing fast-drop entries in response to network changes so that all the packets that have failed the RPF checks can be processed by the PIM software.

The implementation of fast-drop entries in hardware is crucial in some common network changes because these changes can cause persistent RPF check failures. Without the use of hardware fast-drop entries, the route processor would be overwhelmed by packets that have failed RPF checks that it could have avoided processing.

An alternative to installing fast-drop entries in the hardware forwarding engine is to use Dynamic Buffer Limiting (DBL) [CISCCONFIPMUL]. DBL controls the non-RPF traffic sent to the route processor so that it is not overwhelmed with too much traffic. This is a form of flow-based congestion avoidance mechanism that uses active queue management to track the queue length for each traffic flow to the route processor. This provides per-flow rate limiting of packets to the route processor. DBL drops excess packets when the queue length of a given traffic flow exceeds its configured limit.

9.7.4   USING THE MULTICAST ROUTING INFORMATION BASE (MRIB)

A PIM router maintains an MRIB which is a network topology table (map) derived from an existing unicast routing table in the router. In PIM-SM, for example, a Designated Router uses the MRIB to decide where to send PIM-SM Join/Prune messages. The router also stores in the MRIB the routing metric for each network destination address, and a router uses these routing metrics when sending and processing PIM-SM Assert messages. The MRIB maintains (S, G), (*, G) and (*, G/mask) group information that the router has discovered. The MRIB provides the next-hop router for each multicast (S, G), and (*, G) group. A receiver's Designated Router sends PIM-SM Join/Prune messages to the next-hop router on its way to the multicast source or Rendezvous Point.

The multicast control plane in a PIM router is responsible for constructing and maintaining the source-based or shared multicast distribution trees routers used to forward multicast packets to receivers. The control plane consists of various protocols such as PIM (SM, SSM, BIDIR), IGMP, and the table of mroutes, which are also all considered clients of the MRIB (Figure 9.4). The router communicates any changes, additions, and deletions made to the to the mroute table (via information provided by either PIM or IGMP) to the MRIB which is then loaded to one or more MFIBs for multicast forwarding. Any network or protocol events such as SPT switchover, PIM Asserts, liveness checking, and others related to packet delivery to multicast receivers (that require the router to send updates to the control plane) are performed through updates performed in the MRIB and MFIB.

As noted earlier, the MRIB is a protocol-independent database that stores multicast (S, G), and (*, G) route entries supplied by multicast routing protocols such as PIM and IGMP (the routing clients). The main function of the MRIB is to decouple the details and behaviors of the multicast routing protocols (PIM and IGMP) from the MFIB. It also serves as the point where the routing clients can communicate and coordinate the information needed for routing multicast traffic. Essentially, the MRIB serves as the communication channel between the routing clients [CISCIMPIPV6MUL]. The services provided by the MRIB allow the routing clients to incorporate routing entries into it, as well as read changes that other clients have made to routing entries. MRIBs can be identified by an address family to distinguish between IPv4 and IPv6 multicast routing entries [CISCMFIB11]. Each MRIB created by the multicast router can further be defined within a VRF or global context.

Routing clients communicate through the MRIB based on the setting and clearing of flags fields associated with each MRIB entry and its interface [CISCMFIB11]. Each entry in the MRIB is indexed by a source (* or S), group (G), and, possibly, a group mask (/m), and is represented as (S, G), (*, G), and (*, G/m) entries. Also, each MRIB entry has associated with it a list of interfaces and each interface in turn has flag fields that are set to describe the forwarding state of the interface. Only the MRIB clients (not the MRIB itself) interpret the entry or interface flags. The most significant entry and interface flags used in the MRIB and MFIB for IPv4 multicast are described in [CISCCONFIPMUL] [CISCUNDERIPMUL] [CISCMFIB11].

9.7.5 USING THE MULTICAST FORWARDING INFORMATION BASE (MFIB)

The Cisco MFIB architecture [CISCCONFIPMUL] [CISCUNDERIPMUL] [CISCMFIB11] was designed as a routing protocol and platform independent database for IP multicast forwarding (Figure 9.4). The MFIB provides a database with an interface through which IP multicast forwarding information and notifications can be read by multicast forwarding entities. When network topology or routing changes occur, the MRIB is updated and then the changes are copied to the MFIB. The forwarding information maintained by the MFIB has been designed to have clearly defined semantics to facilitate easy usability/portability to a wide range of platform types having their own specific hardware or software forwarding mechanisms.

The MFIB also maintains next-hop IP address plus corresponding Layer 2 address information similar to the information in the MRIB. There is a one-to-one correlation between MRIB and MFIB entries, thus, the MFIB contains all the required routing information for forwarding packets and eliminates the need for a multicast flow cache maintenance that is typically associated with flow-based forwarding schemes.

The MFIB is mainly responsible for the following [CISCMFIB11]:

- It is the database directly used by multicast forwarding engines for forwarding multicast packets. The multicast routing information in the MFIB may be formatted and added to an integrated hardware FIB and MET for multicast packet forwarding (as illustrated in Figure 9.5 and Figure 9.6).
- The MFIB is also a client that registers with the MRIB to discover the entry and interface flags set by the routing clients.
- The MFIB is used by the multicast forwarding engine to directly screen or filter out special or exception packets (received via the data-plane) and control events that must be forwarded to the control plane for special software processing.
- The MFIB may be used by the multicast forwarding engine to maintain packet counts, packet rates, and other statistics such as number of multicast data bytes received, dropped, and forwarded.

The multicast forwarding engine computes these statistics as it forwards multicast traffic. There is no need for a control plane entity to periodically poll these statistics, nor is it required for the multicast forwarding engine to periodically upload these statistics to the control plane. The MFIB may support an Application Programming Interface (API) to allow a control plane entity to query these multicast statistics counters, for example, when the network administrator requests them from a command-line interface (CLI) or when needed for MIB statistics objects.

9.7.6 Using the Distributed MFIB

A distributed MFIB (dMFIB) architecture is used in systems with multiple distributed multicast forwarding engines so that each engine can forward multicast packets locally on its own (see Figure 9.7). A dMFIB may also include some platform-specific information that allows multicast packet replication across multiple line cards. In the dMFIB architecture, the basic structure of the MFIB forwarding engines that implement the core of the multicast forwarding logic are similar in all the forwarding modules. The main functions typically implemented in a dMFIB architecture are the following [CISCMFIB11]:

- Distributes copies of a master MFIB to multiple forwarding engines including those in the line cards.
- Relays special or exception packets and protocol events captured or generated in the line cards to control entities in the route processor.

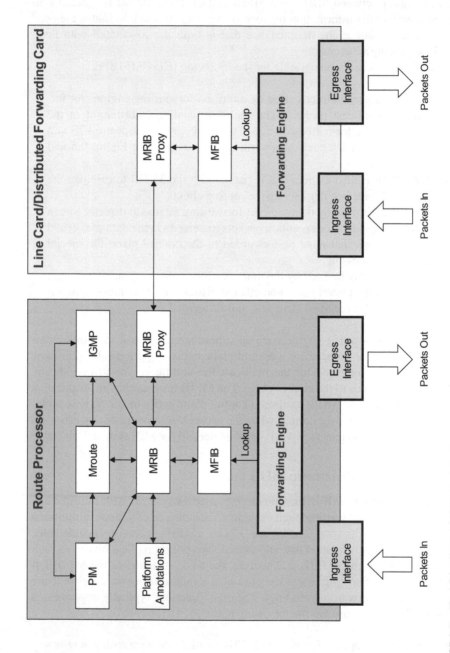

FIGURE 9.7   IPv4 Distributed MFIB Architecture.

- Provides an API so that changes to the master MFIB can be propagated to the dMFIBs, and also for platform-specific code, or code responsible for programming the distributed hardware forwarding engines, to be passed. The API may also include features to forward packets and upload traffic statistics to the route processor software (which is responsible for handling control and exception packets).
- Provides an interface to allow multicast protocol clients running on the route processor to read multicast traffic statistics on demand. To simplify the system architecture and implementation, the dMFIB is generally not designed to periodically upload traffic statistics to the route processor.

The dMFIB in conjunction with the MRIB subsystem (i.e., MRIB proxy) shown in Figure 9.7 allows the route processor to load "customized" copies of a master MFIB it maintains to each line card, plus transport, if necessary, platform-specific information related to the MFIB from the route processor to the line cards.

A distributed MFIB architecture is also very useful in switch clusters where the cluster command switch distributes a master MFIB information to the cluster member switches. In this architecture, the cluster member switches are analogous to line cards in a distributed router or switch/router architecture. The dMFIB architecture can also be used in a stacked switch architecture where the stack member switches receive MFIB information from a master stack switch.

9.8 MULTICAST PACKET FORWARDING USING THE MFIB

In this section, we discuss how a switch/router uses a unified MFIB for both process switching and fast switching of multicast traffic.

9.8.1 Process Switching

In process switching [CISCMFIB11] (also called pure software or "slow-path" forwarding), the route processor is called upon to examine, rewrite, and forward each packet that is sent to it. The packet is first received and copied into the system memory. The router then looks up the packet's multicast destination IP address in a software MFIB to find the outgoing interfaces, IP address of the next-hop routers, and, if available, their corresponding Layer 2 addresses. Each copy of the outgoing Layer 2 packet is then rewritten with the Layer 2 destination address set to the Layer 2 address of the receiving interface of its next-hop router. The route processor also computes and updates the checksum in the outgoing Layer 2 packet. The rewritten Layer 2 packet is then sent to the outgoing interface to be transmitted toward the next-hop router.

Process switching is the least efficient and scalable method for forwarding both unicast and multicast IP packets. Pure process switching is rarely used alone in modern switch/routers and routers. Process switching is often combined with fast switching as illustrated in Figure 9.8. In these architectures, process switching is applied to the first packet of a multicast flow as shown in Figure 9.8.

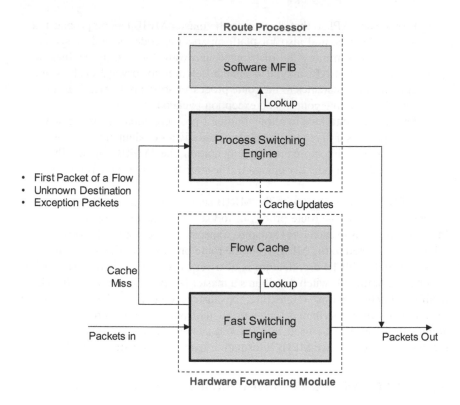

FIGURE 9.8   Process and Fast Switching of Multicast Packets.

A modern switch/router forwards a majority of multicast packets in hardware at very high-speed. However, the route processor CPU subsystem is also used to forward in software, packets with unknown destinations (i.e., destinations not in MFIB), and exception packets. In the normal mode of operation, the switch/router performs inter-VLAN forwarding (i.e., using Layer 3 forwarding or routing) in hardware.

The route processor CPU subsystem can be used to process in software, multicast traffic sent over GRE tunnels, and also when there is the need to execute the PIM Assert mechanism (see discussion earlier). In some designs, the route processor may be required to perform multicast packet replication and process non-RPF traffic [CISCUNDERIPMUL]. As noted earlier, multicast packets that fail an RPF check are called non-RPF packets. Non-RPF packets may also be filtered (i.e., persistently dropped) by a hardware forwarding engine or can be rate limited using traffic rate limiting mechanisms (such as traffic policing mechanisms).

As IP multicast applications have become very common and are now mainstream technologies, the performance requirements placed on multicast routers and switches have also become increasingly more demanding. IP multicast fast switching (also called flow cache-based or "fast-path" forwarding) allows routers to provide much higher packet forwarding performance than using strictly pure process switching.

9.8.2 FAST-PATH PROCESSING USING FLOW/ROUTE CACHING

In fast switching [CISCMFIB11], the first packet in a stream of multicast packets sent to a particular multicast group is forwarded through process switching in the route processor. After the route processor has completed the lookup operations for the first multicast packet, the results are then stored in a multicast flow or route cache. All subsequent packets for that multicast group are then forwarded through the fast switching path, which does not require the route processor to perform anymore route lookups for that multicast flow (see Figure 9.8).

The fast switching engine then rewrites the relevant fields in the outgoing Layer 2 packet (as described earlier) and the packet is sent to the outgoing interfaces. The operations for the outgoing packet include updating the Layer 2 checksum as described earlier. The Layer 2 address of the receiving interface of the next-hop router (if readily available) may be obtained from a separate or integrated adjacency table, or the switch/router may use a Layer 2 adjacency discovery protocol such as ARP to discover the address. Depending on the sophistication of the switch/router, the ARP may be implemented alongside the forwarding engine or may be handled by the route processor. In the latter case, packets requiring ARP processing will be forwarded to the route processor for software-based ARP processing.

The information maintained in the multicast flow cache is typically structured in such a fashion that it allows high-speed packet lookups and forwarding. The data structures typically used provide highly optimized lookups in hardware (using TCAMs) allowing efficient and high-speed multicast packet forwarding. For multicast fast switching, the flow cache stores just very simple information for the source (* or S), multicast group (G), and the outgoing interface lists (OILs).

In contrast, for unicast fast switching, the flow cache only needs to maintain the destination addresses along with their outgoing interfaces. Note that in unicast forwarding, a lookup may point to multiple interfaces when equal or unequal cost multipath routing is used. Both multicast and unicast flow caches may include additional fields for each entry that can be used for QoS and security processing (e.g., priority queuing, packet discard, packet tagging, packet rewrites, etc.).

9.8.3 FAST-PATH PROCESSING USING OPTIMIZED FORWARDING TABLE LOOKUP STRUCTURES (WITHOUT FLOW/ROUTE CACHING)

This method of multicast packet forwarding [CISC2TMUL11] [CISCSUP2TA11] [CISCSUP2TA14] [CISCSUP6TA16] eliminates the need for multicast flow cache maintenance typically associated with flow cache forwarding schemes as discussed earlier. For example, the Supervisor Engine 2T (and its Policy Feature Card PFC/DFC4 and compatible line cards) use an MFIB to make IP multicast forwarding decisions directly [CISC2TMUL11]. As discussed earlier, the MFIB stores a mirror image of the main forwarding information contained in the MRIB and can be used directly by a multicast forwarding engine to forward packets without relying on a multicast flow cache or process switching in the route processor.

When topology or routing changes occur in the network, both the MRIB and MFIB are updated to reflect those changes. Figure 9.9 shows a logical view of a switch/router using an MFIB for direct hardware forwarding of multicast traffic. The MFIB also maintains the most important information relevant for forwarding multicast packets: the source (* or S), multicast group (G), and multiple outgoing interfaces (OILs). The MFIB may contain additional information used for QoS and security processing.

Using specialized hardware forwarding functions geared toward high-speed packet forwarding, the PFC4/DFC4 [CISC2TMUL11] assumes multicast packet processing and forwarding functions in the Supervisor Engine 2T from the Route Processor (specifically, the Multi-Layer Switching Feature Card 5 (MSFC5)). The PFC4/DFC4 is designed to provide highly consistent forwarding performance even when packet forwarding is coupled with several IP services such as processing Access Control Lists (ACLs), address translation, QoS and security processing, flow accounting, and traffic shaping.

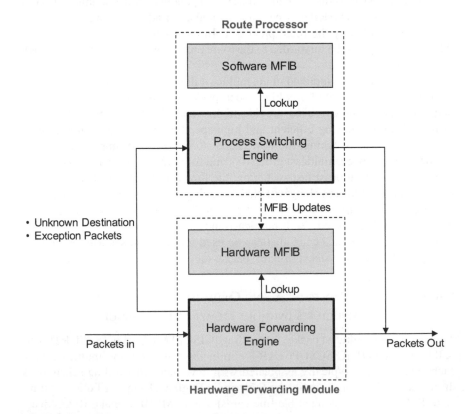

FIGURE 9.9 Direct Hardware-Based Forwarding of Multicast Packets.

The Layer 2 addresses of next-hop routers in the adjacency table are populated as the route processor discovers adjacencies. Each time an adjacency entry is created (such as through ARP), the forwarding engine may pre-assemble the Layer 2 header for that adjacency and store it in the adjacency table. Once the forwarding engine performs a lookup and determines the next hop for a multicast packet, the lookup may also point to the Layer 2 header for the next hop in the adjacency entry. This information is then used to encapsulate the outgoing IP packet before being forwarded out the interface(s).

Multicast packets received with forwarding entries in the MFIB will be forwarded directly to their outgoing interfaces by the multicast forwarding engine. Those received without forwarding entries may require the creation of new forwarding entries and so will be processed by the route processor since it normally has more information to handle such packets. In most high-performance switch/routers and routers, multicast packets are forwarded by distributed forwarding engines implemented on the line cards. This architecture reduces the load on the router processor which focuses mainly on running the control plane software as well as handling special and exception packets.

9.9 PIM-SM TUNNEL INTERFACES

PIM-SM requires multicast source to register with a Rendezvous Point and this is accomplished using a virtual tunnel from the source's Designated Router to the Rendezvous Point. The use of a virtual tunnel interface in the Catalyst 6500 that can be deployed as a source's Designated Router allows consistent handling of PIM-SM state for the PIM source registration process. The virtual tunnel interface in the Catalyst 6500 appears like any other interface listed in a PIM-SM router's OIL for the particular multicast (S, G) group during the multicast source registration process.

The Catalyst 6500 switches support PIM-SM Rendezvous Point tunnel interfaces for the multicast source registration process [CISCMFIB11] [CISC2TMUL11]. PIM-SM virtual tunnel interfaces are used in the PIM-SM Designated Router's MFIB for only the PIM-SM registration process. Two types of PIM tunnel interfaces are used by the MFIB:

- A PIM encapsulation tunnel (PIM Encap Tunnel)
- A PIM decapsulation tunnel (PIM Decap Tunnel).

A PIM-SM router dynamically creates a PIM Encap Tunnel interface whenever it discovers a multicast group-to-Rendezvous Point mapping (via Auto-RP, BSR, or Static RP configuration). The source's Designated Router uses the PIM Encap Tunnel interface to encapsulate multicast packets sent to the Rendezvous Point. Similar to the PIM Encap Tunnel, a Rendezvous Point dynamically creates a PIM Decap Tunnel interface whenever a group-to-Rendezvous Point mapping is learned. The Rendezvous Point uses the PIM Decap Tunnel interface to decapsulate PIM registration messages sent by the source's Designated Router.

In PIM-SM, the source's Designated Router receives the initial multicast packets from the attached source and encapsulates them in PIM Register messages. The source's Designated Router then unicasts the encapsulated packets over the tunnel interface to the Rendezvous Point, where the PIM Register messages are decapsulated. The PIM Encap Tunnel interface is used to encapsulate source multicast packets. If the source's Designated Router is itself the Rendezvous Point, then there is no need for the creation of a tunnel interface and consequently no need for the generation of PIM Register messages.

A Designated Router can only successfully register a multicast source with the Rendezvous Point when the tunnel interface is fully up. It is important to note that while all PIM Register messages from the source's Designated Router are sent to the Rendezvous Point via the virtual tunnels, the Rendezvous Point sends all PIM Register-Stop messages directly to the Designated Router and does not use the virtual tunnels.

REFERENCES

[CISC2TMUL11]. Building Next-Generation Multicast Networks with Supervisor 2T, Cisco Systems, White Paper, Apr. 13, 2011.
[CISC3750GUIDE]. IP Multicast Routing Configuration Guide, Cisco IOS Release 15.2(2)E (Catalyst 3750-X and 3560-X Switches), Chapter 5: Configuring Protocol Independent Multicast (PIM), 2014.
[CISC4500CH23]. Catalyst 4500 Series Switch Software Configuration Guide, 12.2(53) SG, Chapter 23, Configuring IGMP Snooping and Filtering.
[CISC4500CH33]. Catalyst 4500 Series Switch Software Configuration Guide, 12.2(53) SG, Chapter 33, Configuring IP Multicast.
[CISCBIDIRPIM]. Configuring Bidirectional PIM, Cisco IOS IP Configuration Guide, Cisco Systems.
[CISCCONFIPMUL]. Catalyst 4500 Series Switch Software Configuration Guide, IOS XE 3.9.xE and IOS 15.2(5)Ex, Chapter 38: Configuring IP Multicast, Cisco Systems.
[CISCIMPIPV6MUL]. IP Multicast Routing Configuration Guide, Cisco IOS XE Gibraltar 16.11.x (Catalyst 9500 Switches), Chapter: Implementing IPv6 Multicast, Cisco Systems.
[CISCMFIB11]. Multicast Forwarding Information Base Overview, Cisco Systems, White Paper, May 27, 2011.
[CISCMSDP12.4T]. IP Multicast: PIM Configuration Guide, Cisco IOS Release 12.4T, Chapter: Using MSDP to Interconnect Multiple PIM-SM Domains.
[CISCPIMGUIDE]. IP Multicast: PIM Configuration Guide, Cisco Systems, 2017.
[CISCSUP2TA11]. Cisco Catalyst 6500 Supervisor 2T Architecture, Cisco Systems, White Paper, 2011.
[CISCSUP2TA14]. Cisco Catalyst 6500 Supervisor 2T Architecture, Cisco Systems, White Paper, June 2014.
[CISCSUP6TA16]. Cisco Catalyst 6500/6800 Supervisor 6T Architecture, Cisco Systems, White Paper, June 2016.
[CISCUNDERIPMUL]. Catalyst 4500 Series Switch Cisco IOS Software Configuration Guide—Release 12.2(25)EW, Chapter 25: Understanding and Configuring IP Multicast, Cisco Systems.
[JUNBIDIRPIM]. Understanding Bidirectional PIM, Juniper Networks, 21 May 2018.

[JUNMULTGUID]. Multicast Protocols Feature Guide, Chapter 9 Routing Content to Larger, Sparser Groups with PIM Sparse Mode, Junos® OS, Juniper Networks.

[RFC1112]. S. Deering, "Host Extensions for IP Multicasting," IETF RFC 1112 (defines IGMP Version 1), Aug. 1989.

[RFC2117]. D. Estrin, D. Farinacci, et al., "Protocol Independent Multicast-Sparse Mode (PIM-SM): Protocol Specification," IETF RFC 2117, June 1997.

[RFC2236]. W. Fenner, "Internet Group Management Protocol, Version 2," IETF RFC 2236, Nov. 1997.

[RFC2710]. S. Deering, W. Fenner, and B. Haberman, "Multicast Listener Discovery (MLD) for IPv6," IETF RFC 2710, Oct. 1999.

[RFC3376]. B. Cain, S. Deering, I. Kouvelas, B. Fenner, and A. Thyagarajan, "Internet Group Management Protocol, Version 3," IETF RFC 3376, Oct. 2002.

[RFC3618]. B. Fenner and D. Meyer, "Multicast Source Discovery Protocol (MSDP)," IETF RFC 3618, Oct. 2003.

[RFC3810]. R. Vida and L. Costa, "Multicast Listener Discovery Version 2 (MLDv2) for IPv6," IETF RFC 3810, June 2004.

[RFC3973]. A. Adams, J. Nicholas, and W. Siadak, "Protocol Independent Multicast—Dense Mode (PIM-DM): Protocol Specification (Revised)," IETF RFC 3973, Jan. 2005.

[RFC4541]. M. Christensen, K. Kimball and F. Solensky, "Considerations for Internet Group Management Protocol (IGMP) and Multicast Listener Discovery (MLD) Snooping Switches," IETF RFC 4541, May 2006.

[RFC4601]. B. Fenner, M. Handley, H. Holbrook, and I. Kouvelas, "Protocol Independent Multicast—Sparse Mode (PIM-SM): Protocol Specification (Revised)," IETF RFC 4601, Aug. 2006.

[RFC4604]. H. Holbrook, B. Cain, and B. Haberman, "Using Internet Group Management Protocol Version 3 (IGMPv3) and Multicast Listener Discovery Protocol Version 2 (MLDv2) for Source-Specific Multicast," IETF RFC 4604, Aug. 2006.

[RFC4607]. H. Holbrook and B. Cain, "Source-Specific Multicast for IP," IETF RFC 4607, Aug. 2006.

[RFC4611]. M. McBride, J. Meylor, and D. Meyer, "Multicast Source Discovery Protocol (MSDP) Deployment Scenarios," IETF RFC 4611, Aug. 2006.

[RFC4760]. T. Bates, R. Chandra, D. Katz and Y. Rekhter, "Multiprotocol Extensions for BGP-4," IEFC RFC 4760, Jan. 2007.

[RFC5015]. M. Handley, I. Kouvelas, T. Speakman, and L. Vicisano, "Bidirectional Protocol Independent Multicast (BIDIR-PIM)," IETF RFC 5015, Oct. 2007.

[RFC7761]. B. Fenner, M. Handley, H. Holbrook, I. Kouvelas, R. Parekh, Z. Zhang, and L. Zheng, "Protocol Independent Multicast—Sparse Mode (PIM-SM): Protocol Specification (Revised)," IETF RFC 7761, Mar. 2016.

10 Unicast versus Multicast Packet Forwarding

A Case Study

10.1 INTRODUCTION

This chapter discusses the multicast forwarding mechanisms in switch/routers using the Cisco Catalyst 6500 Series as the reference architecture. The typical switch/router shares a majority of features and capabilities in this reference architecture. We start the discussion by reviewing the most important unicast forwarding features in a number of Catalyst 6500 switch/routers which we consider representative of the features found in other Cisco switch/routers and a majority of the switch/routers from other vendors. We then contrast these unicast forwarding features with the multicast forwarding features found in the Catalyst 6500 series.

Three main multicast forwarding mechanisms are used in switch/routers, namely, multicast forwarding using a centralized processor, forwarding using a flow cache, and direct multicast forwarding using a Multicast Forwarding Information Base (MFIB) [CISC2TMUL11] [CISCMFIB11] and optimized table lookup algorithms. The flow entries in the multicast flow/route cache are built by routing the first packet of a multicast flow in software, with the most relevant forwarding information used to forward the first packet added as an entry in the multicast flow cache. Subsequent multicast packets associated with the multicast flow are then forwarded using the flow cache (usually in hardware) based upon the information in the flow entry.

We discuss in greater detail multicast forwarding using a centralized processor with packet replication. The cases of ingress and egress multicast packet replications are discussed in separate sections. The scenario of centralized multicast forwarding with packet replication is chosen because it involves relatively more complex processing steps when compared to the other two multicast forwarding methods mentioned earlier.

10.2 UNICAST FORWARDING TABLE AND TCAM LOOKUP ARCHITECTURE

The Ternary Content Addressable Memory (TCAM) is used extensively in switch/routers and routers for storing and looking up forwarding tables and instructions. In the Catalyst 6500 the FIBs, QoS and security Access Control lists (ACLs), and NetFlow accounting tables all utilize TCAMs. The TCAM allows entries to be accessed in parallel and provides fixed lookup performance independent of the number of entries contained. A TCAM is typically structured as groups of values or patterns with each group associated with a mask. The mask associated with a group is used to "wildcard" a portion of a value in the group.

Figure 10.1 and Figure 10.2 illustrate the use of TCAMs for IPv4 lookup in a routing device. IPv4 address prefix entries in the unicast FIB TCAM are logically arranged from most specific to least specific prefix (/32 prefix to 0/0 address). The 0.0.0.0 address (0/0) is the default address and is the entry that terminates all unicast address entries in the FIB. The IPv4 lookup process in a generic unicast forwarding TCAM can be described by the following steps:

1. The unicast destination IP address is parsed from the received IP packet.
2. The destination IP address is used to create a lookup key.
3. The lookup key is compared to the value entries in the TCAM with the associated group mask applied to each entry as it is compared.
4. The longest matching prefix among the TCAM entries (called a "hit") returns an adjacency pointer or index as well as the adjacency or number of adjacencies involved if load-sharing is required.
5. The adjacency index and packet field data applicable to the load-sharing scheme are fed to a load-sharing hash function.
6. The load-sharing hash function returns an adjacency pointer offset value that is used to determine a number of forwarding parameters for the next hop(s) from the indexed adjacency table (shown in Figure 10.1 and Figure 10.2) such as rewrite MAC, VLAN, and encapsulation information.

The direct FIB based forwarding engines allow very high-speed and high-throughput packet forwarding. This is supported in most of the Cisco routing devices with forwarding modules such as the Supervisor Engines 2, 32, 720, 2T and 6T. These modules together with the local line card forwarding engines support hardware-based forwarding with extended features. In the Catalyst 6500, the FIB contains the destination network IP addresses (IP prefixes), outgoing interfaces, and next-hop router IP addresses, while the adjacency table (Figure 10.1 and Figure 10.2) contains the next-hop IP addresses and their corresponding Layer 2 addresses.

The use of an FIB allows the control plane operations to be decoupled from the data plane operations. The control plane builds a master FIB which is then downloaded to the hardware FIBs used for packet forwarding (data plane operations). The lookups in the FIB are based on longest prefix matching using the destination address prefix carried in the IP packet. A "hit" in the FIB returns an adjacency index which points to memory location that contains the rewrite information for the adjacency (next hop), plus, possibly, other information that includes those for processing QoS and security ACL, NetFlow lookups, etc. These additional processing requirements are done in parallel in the Catalyst 6500 forwarding modules.

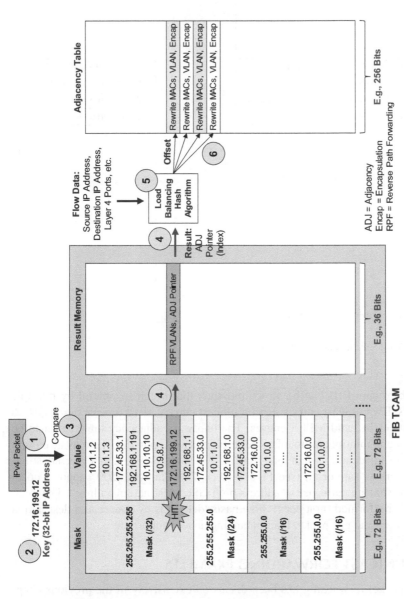

FIGURE 10.1 IPv4 FIB TCAM and Adjacencies—TCAM Lookup.

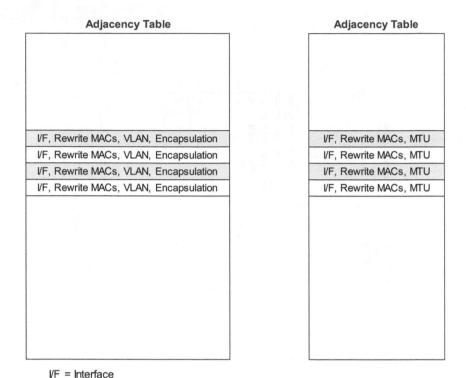

Adjacency Table

| I/F, Rewrite MACs, VLAN, Encapsulation |
| I/F, Rewrite MACs, VLAN, Encapsulation |
| I/F, Rewrite MACs, VLAN, Encapsulation |
| I/F, Rewrite MACs, VLAN, Encapsulation |

Adjacency Table

| I/F, Rewrite MACs, MTU |
| I/F, Rewrite MACs, MTU |
| I/F, Rewrite MACs, MTU |
| I/F, Rewrite MACs, MTU |

I/F = Interface
MTU = Maximum Transmission Unit

FIGURE 10.2   Adjacency Table Types.

The hardware FIB can be structured such that it can be shared by multiple protocols: IPv4 unicast entries, IPv4 multicast entries, IPv6 unicast entries, IPv6 multicast entries, and MPLS entries. The hardware adjacency table can also be shared among multiple protocols. The result of a lookup in the FIB may also point to multiple adjacencies when load sharing over multiple paths to a given destination network is supported (see Figure 10.1). The Catalyst 6500 supports up to eight load-sharing paths per IP address prefix (i.e., destination address). The load-sharing is performed on a per-IP flow basis (default is by source and destination IP addresses) and per-packet load-balancing is not supported.

10.3   UNICAST FORWARDING EXAMPLES

Unicast packet forwarding has been discussed extensively in the previous chapters. In this chapter, we use select Catalyst 6500 designs to highlight the most important features related to unicast packet forwarding. This discussion sets the tone for us to show the main differences between unicast and multicast packet forwarding in the typical switch/router architecture such as the Catalyst 6500.

10.3.1 CATALYST 6500 SUPERVISOR ENGINE 2

As discussed in *Chapter 4*, the Supervisor Engine 2 supports a Policy Feature Card 2 (PFC2) daughter card, Switch Processor, optional Multilayer Switch Feature Card 2 (MSFC2) daughter card that contains the Route Processor, in addition to a number of internal DRAM and bootflash modules. The PFC2 contains the Layer 2 and Layer 3 forwarding engines, each having memory (CAM and TCAM) modules that store the relevant forwarding tables and instructions.

The Supervisor Engine 2 supports 2 x 1 Gigabit Ethernet GBIC uplink ports and an interface to which an optional external 256 Gb/s crossbar Switch Fabric Module (SFM) can be connected. The Supervisor Engine 2 also supports a separate 32 Gb/s shared switching bus. The optional external 256 Gb/s crossbar SFM works with the Supervisor Engine 2 and the CEF256 and dCEF256 line cards. The fabric channels to the SFM run at full duplex 8 Gb/s (8 Gb/s in and 8 Gb/s out the SFM.). The CEF256 line cards support connectivity to the crossbar switch fabric and the 32 Gb/s shared switching bus at the same time. The Classic line cards (see *Chapter 4*) can connect only to the 32 Gb/s shared bus and rely solely on the Supervisor Engine for packet forwarding.

The MSFC2 Route Processor is responsible for running the Layer 3 protocols, maintaining Layer 3 routing information, and generating the forwarding information that is to be downloaded to the forwarding engines. The Switch Processor is responsible for running the Layer 2 protocols, downloading the forwarding tables to the forwarding engine hardware, and monitoring the router interfaces and system environmental status. A Protocol Redirection Logic located on the PFC2 is responsible for capturing IGMP/MLD messages and redirecting them to the Route Processor for multicast group membership information to be learned and recorded.

The PFC supports the key components that enable high-speed hardware packet forwarding. The PFC2 and PFC3 (discussed later) support Layer 2 forwarding, IPv4 unicast forwarding, IPv4 multicast forwarding, QoS and security ACLs, traffic policing, and NetFlow accounting. PFC3 has extended features and also supports IPv6 unicast and multicast forwarding, MPLS/VRF-lite, BIDIR-PIM, NAT/PAT, GRE/IPv6 tunnels, and control plane policing.

Figure 10.3 shows the processing steps involved in centralized unicast forwarding in a Catalyst 6500 with Supervisor Engine 2 and a CEF256 line card (without the optional Distributed Forwarding Card (DFC)). In this forwarding architecture, a single, centralized forwarding engine, the PFC2, performs all forwarding operations for the system—Layer 2, Layer 3, QoS and security ACLs, etc. The overall system packet forwarding performance is limited by the performance of the PFC2.

10.3.2 SUPERVISOR ENGINE 32

The Supervisor Engine 32 shown in Figure 10.4 and described in [AWEYA1BK18] [CISCSUPENG32], supports a PFC3B daughter card, Switch Processor, and

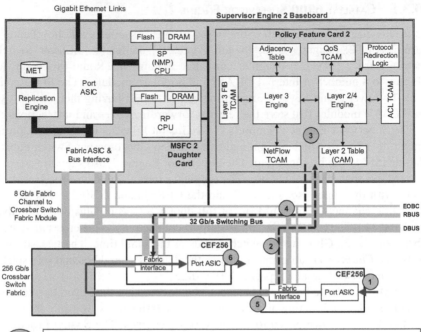

FIGURE 10.3   Catalyst 6500 Supervisor Engine 2—Centralized Unicast Forwarding.

MSFC2a daughter card that contains the Route Processor, in addition to a number of internal DRAM and bootflash modules. The PFC3b contains the Layer 2 and Layer 3 forwarding engines, each having memory (CAM and TCAM) modules that store the relevant forwarding tables and instructions.

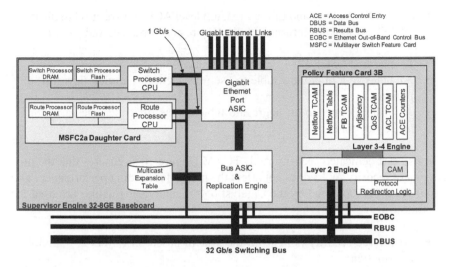

FIGURE 10.4   Supervisor Engine 32 Architecture.

Component	Description
Route Processor	This runs the Layer 3 protocols, maintains Layer 3 routes and state, and generates the forwarding information for download to the forwarding engines
Switch Processor	This runs the Layer 2 protocols, downloads the forwarding tables to the forwarding hardware, and monitors interfaces and environmental status
FIB TCAM	This contains IPv4/IPv6 address prefix entries and their corresponding next-hops and egress ports used for Layer 3 forwarding
Layer 2 CAM	This contains Layer 2 (MAC) address to port mappings used for Layer 2 forwarding
Adjacency Table	This contains IP next-hop to Layer 2 (MAC) address mappings used for rewrites in outgoing packet
QoS TCAM	This contains ACL entries used for QoS processing and filtering
ACL TCAM	This contains ACL entries used for security processing and filtering. The ACE counters are hardware for maintaining ACL TCAM counters
NetFlow TCAM	This contains statistics and NetFlow features
Fabric and Bus Interface	This ASIC provides interfaces to the crossbar switch fabric and 32 Gb/s shared switching bus
Multicast Expansion Table (MET)	This contains Outgoing Interface Lists (OILs) requiring multicast packet replication.
Replication Engine	This provides packet replications services for multicast traffic and Switched Port Analyzer (SPAN)
Protocol Redirection Logic	This captures IGMP/MLD packets and redirects them for multicast group membership information to be recorded

The Supervisor Engine 32 supports only a 32 Gb/s shared bus. It supports neither an optional external nor integrated crossbar SFM. This Supervisor Engine is discussed here to allow us to cover the different unicast forwarding features supported by the Catalyst 6500 Series. The CEF256 and CEF720 line cards support connectivity to a crossbar switch fabric and the 32 Gb/s shared switching bus at the same time. The Classic line cards (see *Chapter 4*) can connect only to the 32 Gb/s shared switching bus. This means the Supervisor Engine 32 can support the Classic, CEF256, and CEF720 line cards over the 32 Gb/s shared switching bus.

QoS ACLs are stored in QoS TCAM (Figure 10.4) and are used to classify traffic for marking, QoS tagging, and policing. The TCAMs support standard ACLs and extended IPv4, IPv6, and Layer 2 (MAC) level ACLs for traffic classification. The QoS TCAM lookups return the following results for a received packet:

- A remarked DSCP/IPv4 Precedence value to use
- An index to a microflow table to use (that identifies a microflow traffic policer)
- An index/pointer to an aggregate table to use (that identifies a traffic aggregate policer).

The use of a dedicated security ACL TCAM (Figure 10.4) ensures that the processing of security ACLs does not affect the packet forwarding performance. The Security ACLs supported by the Catalyst 6500 Supervisor Engines are used for the following:

- To enforce security policies in the system based on Layers 2, 3, and 4 information
- Router ACL (RACL): These ACLs are used to process all traffic crossing a Layer 3 interface (routed interface) in a specified direction (inbound or outbound traffic). The ACLs are used to permit/deny the transfer of traffic between IP subnets or VLANs.
- VLAN ACLs (VACLs): These ACLs are used to process (permit/deny) inbound or outbound traffic belonging to a VLAN.
- Port ACLs (PACLs): These ACLs are used to process all traffic on a Layer 2 interface (switchport interface).

Figure 10.5 shows the processing steps involved in centralized unicast forwarding in a Catalyst 6500 with Supervisor Engine 32 and a Classic or CEF256 (without DFC) line card. Note that the Classic, CEF256 and CEF720 line cards all support connectivity to the 32 Gb/s shared switching bus. The CEF256 and CEF720 line cards also support connectivity to a crossbar switch fabric.

In distributed forwarding, each line card has a local packet forwarding engine module (called a Distributed Forwarding Card (DFC)). This allows the central forwarding engine in the PFC and distributed forwarding engines in the line cards to perform IP packet address lookups and forwarding independently and simultaneously. The packet forwarding implementation is fully distributed with forwarding decisions made at the line card or PFC module level. The PFC and line card DFC have similar hardware forwarding components and both support full Layer 2 and Layer 3 forwarding, QoS and security ACLs, etc.

The FIB and other forwarding tables and instructions are downloaded from the Supervisor Engine to each DFC in the system. The FIBs in all forwarding engines are synchronized with the master FIB in the route processor to allow consistent forwarding decisions to be made. This means the hardware FIBs are always all identical to the software master FIB. The hardware FIBs are also always updated as network topology changes occur. The control plane

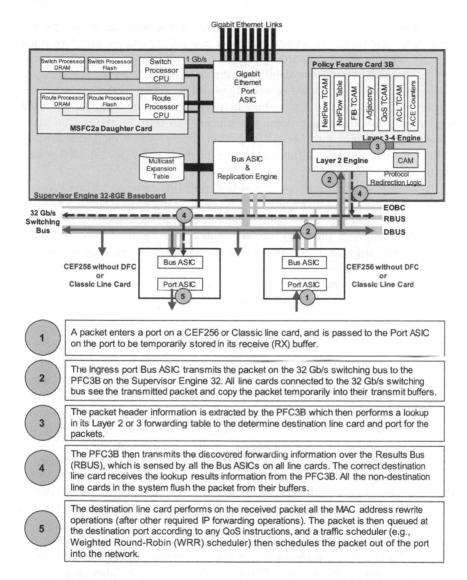

FIGURE 10.5 Catalyst 6500 Supervisor Engine 32 Architecture—Centralized Unicast Forwarding.

unencumbered by actual traffic forwarding focuses solely on control plane tasks such running the routing protocols, ARP, spanning tree, etc. The overall system packet forwarding performance in this architecture is equal to the aggregate performance of all the forwarding engines. Scalability here is dependent on the number and performance of the forwarding engines. This is the architecture used in high-performance routing devices and systems that seek to achieve very high packet forwarding rates.

In contrast, with flow cache-based forwarding, the first packet of a flow is forwarded in software by a route processor and subsequent packets forwarded directly in hardware by forwarding engines in the PFC or line cards using lookups in a local flow cache. Scalability in this case depends on the performance of the route processor: How fast new flows can be set up in the hardware forwarding engines and flow cache, how network topology changes are managed (e.g., route flaps, etc.), the processing demands and tasks on the control plane (running the routing protocols, ARP, spanning tree protocol, etc.), and stability of the critical control plane functions while the route processor establishes new flows.

In distributed forwarding, an ingress DFC on a line card receives packets and performs all lookups locally. Once the packets are fully processed, they are sent directly to the destination line card without passing through the PFC or MSFC. Figure 10.6 describes the steps involved in distributed unicast forwarding in a CEF256 line card with a DFC in the Catalyst 6500 with Supervisor Engine 32. Distributed forwarding, unlike flow cache-based forwarding is deterministic, highly scalable, and enables high throughput packet forwarding. The DFC3 is an optional daughter card in the CEF256 line cards.

10.3.3 CATALYST 6500 SUPERVISOR ENGINE 720

As discussed in *Chapter 8*, the Supervisor Engine 720 supports a PFC3 daughter card and an MSFC3 daughter card that integrates both the Switch Processor and Route Processor, each with a number of internal DRAM and bootflash modules. The PFC3 also contains the Layer 2 and Layer 3 forwarding engines, each having memory (CAM and TCAM) modules that store the relevant forwarding tables and instructions. The Supervisor Engine 720 supports the following PFC3 types: PFC3A, PFC3B, and PFC3BXL. Unlike the Supervisor Engine 2 which can support an optional external 256 Gb/s SFM, the Supervisor Engine 720 supports a built-in 720 Gb/s crossbar Switch Fabric Module (SFM). The Supervisor Engine 720 also supports a separate 32 Gb/s shared bus.

The 720 Gb/s crossbar switch fabric is integrated on Supervisor Engine 720 baseboard and has fabric channels that run at 20 Gb/s full duplex (20 Gb/s in and 20 Gb/s out). As discussed in *Chapter 8*, the 720 Gb/s crossbar switch fabric works with all fabric-enabled and fabric-only line cards. The speed of the fabric channels is auto-sync (8 Gb/s or 20 Gb/s) on a per-slot basis to allow connectivity to either 8 Gb/s line cards (CEF256 and dCEF256) or 20 Gb/s line cards (CEF720 or dCEF720). The CEF256 and CEF720 line cards support connectivity to the 720 Gb/s crossbar switch fabric and the 32 Gb/s shared at the same time. The Classic line cards (see *Chapter 4*) can connect only to the 32 Gb/s shared bus. Similar to the CEF256 line cards, the DFC3 is also an optional daughter card in the CEF720 line cards.

Figure 10.7 shows the processing steps involved in centralized unicast forwarding in a Catalyst 6500 with Supervisor Engine 720 and a CEF256 line

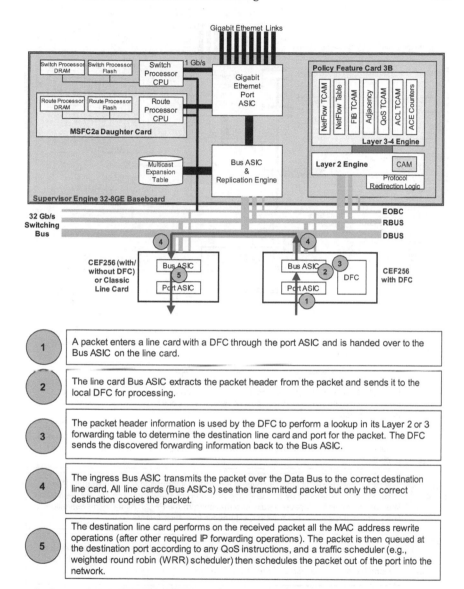

FIGURE 10.6 Catalyst 6500 Supervisor Engine 32 Architecture—Distributed Unicast Forwarding.

card (without a DFC). The steps involved in centralized unicast forwarding in a Catalyst 6500 with a CEF720 line card (without DFC) are shown in Figure 10.8. Figure 10.9 describes the steps involved in distributed unicast forwarding in the Catalyst 6500 with Supervisor Engine 720 (with dCEF256 line cards, dCEF720 line cards, or line cards with DFC (CEF256 and CEF720)).

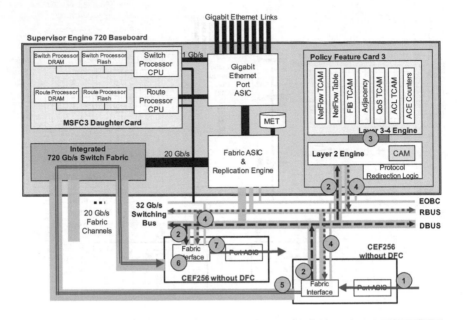

1 A packet enters a line card through the port ASIC and is handed over to the Fabric ASIC on the line card.

2 The ingress port Fabric ASIC transmits the packet header on the 32 Gb/s switching bus to the PFC3 on the Supervisor Engine 720. All line cards connected to the 32 Gb/s switching bus see the transmitted packet header and copy it temporarily into their transmit buffers.

3 The packet header information is extracted by the PFC3 which then performs a lookup in its Layer 2 or 3 forwarding table to the determine destination line card and port for the packet.

4 The PFC3 then transmits the discovered forwarding information over the Results Bus (RBUS), which is sensed by all the Fabric ASICs on all line cards. The correct destination line card receives the lookup results information from the PFC3. All the non-destination line cards in the system flush the packet header from their buffers.

5 As soon as the ingress line card receives the lookup results, it transmits the packet data payload over the crossbar switch fabric to the destination line card. The payload is not transmitted over the 32 Gb/s shared switching bus.

6 The Fabric ASIC on the destination line card receives the packet data payload from the crossbar switch and combines this with its corresponding packet header received earlier on over the 32 Gb/s shared switching bus.

7 The destination line card performs on the received packet all the MAC address rewrite operations (after other required IP forwarding operations). The packet is then queued at the destination port according to any QoS instructions, and a traffic scheduler (e.g., Weighted Round-Robin (WRR) scheduler) then schedules the packet out of the port into the network.

FIGURE 10.7   Catalyst 6500 Supervisor Engine 720 Architecture—Centralized Unicast Forwarding with CEF256 Line Cards.

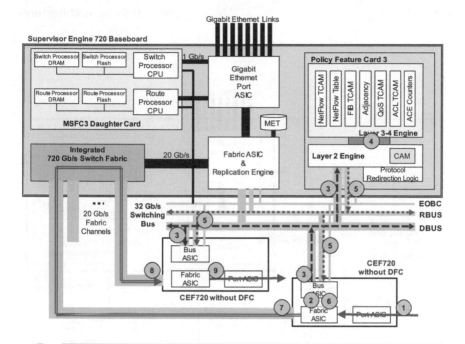

1	A packet enters a line card through the port ASIC and is handed over to the Fabric ASIC on the line card.
2	The Fabric ASIC extracts the packet header and hands it over to the Bus ASIC on the line card.
3	The Bus ASIC transmits the packet header on the 32 Gb/s switching bus (Data Bus (DBUS)) to the PFC3 on the Supervisor Engine 720. All line cards connected to the 32 Gb/s switching bus also see the transmitted packet header.
4	The packet header information is extracted by the PFC3 which then performs a lookup in its Layer 2 or 3 forwarding table to determine the destination line card and port for the packet.
5	The PFC3 then transmits the discovered forwarding information over the Results Bus (RBUS), which is sensed by all the Bus ASICs on all line cards.
6	As soon as the ingress line card Bus ASIC receives the lookup results, it passes them to the Fabric ASIC.
7	As soon as the Fabric ASIC receives the lookup results, it transmits the packet over the crossbar switch fabric to the destination line card. The packet is not transmitted over the 32 Gb/s shared switching bus.
8	The Fabric ASIC on the destination line card receives the packet from the crossbar switch fabric.
9	The destination line card performs on the received packet all the MAC address rewrite operations (after other required IP forwarding operations). The packet is then queued at the destination port according to any QoS instructions, and a traffic scheduler (e.g., Weighted Round-Robin (WRR) scheduler) then schedules the packet out of the port into the network.

FIGURE 10.8   Catalyst 6500 Supervisor Engine 720 Architecture—Centralized Unicast Forwarding with CEF720 Line Cards.

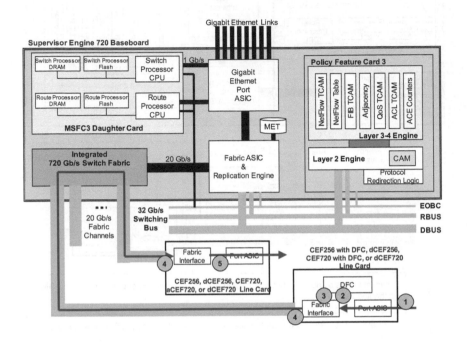

1. A packet enters a line card with a DFC through the port ASIC and is handed over to the Fabric ASIC on the line card.

2. The line card Fabric ASIC extracts the packet header from the packet and sends it to the local DFC for processing.

3. The packet header information is used by the DFC to perform a lookup in its Layer 2 or 3 forwarding table to determine the destination line card and port for the packet. The DFC sends the discovered forwarding information back to the Fabric ASIC.

4. The ingress line card, through its Fabric ASIC, prepends an internal switching tag to the packet (which specifies the destination line card), and transmits the packet into the switch fabric module (SFM). The SFM, using the internal switching tag, switches the packet to the specified destination line card.

5. The destination line card performs on the received packet all the MAC address rewrite operations (after other required IP forwarding operations). The packet is then queued at the destination port according to any QoS instructions, and a traffic scheduler (e.g., Weighted Round-Robin (WRR) scheduler) then schedules the packet out of the port into the network.

FIGURE 10.9   Catalyst 6500 Supervisor Engine 720 Architecture—Distributed Unicast Forwarding.

10.4   MULTICAST FORWARDING TABLES AND TCAM LOOKUP ARCHITECTURE

Figure 10.10 shows the TCAM based data structures used for multicast packet lookups and forwarding. The MFIB contains IPv4 multicast entries that are arranged logically from most specific to least specific address pairs. The adjacency table in this case has a different format from that used for unicast forwarding and with the key piece of information being the MET index. The MET contains the outgoing interface lists (OILs) for each multicast group (Figure 10.11).

Unlike IPv4 and IPv6 unicast forwarding which require only one destination address per entry, IPv4 and IPv6 multicast forwarding require two addresses per entry (S, G) or (*, G) as shown in Figure 10.10. Every valid IP packet that arrives at a Catalyst 6500 is sent to a forwarding engine on the line card DFC (if one exists) or the PFC on the Supervisor Engine. The forwarding engine makes the forwarding decision to determine the next-hop router and outgoing interface or whether to drop the packet. The forwarding decision includes a destination Local Target Logic (LTL) index which is a destination index (to a data structure) that the router uses to select the physical port(s) on which the packet should be forwarded (Figure 10.11). The MET index is another important part of the forwarding decision also shown in Figure 10.11.

The multicast lookup process in the FIB TCAM can be described by the following steps (Figure 10.12 and Figure 10.13):

1. The source and multicast group IP addresses are read from multicast packet.
2. A lookup key is created based on the parsed source and multicast group IP addresses.
3. The lookup key is used to compare the entries in the TCAM with the associated mask applied. For all (S, G) entries, all the bits in the pair are compared.
4. The longest matching address pair entry returns a reverse path forwarding (RPF) interface and an adjacency index to the adjacency entry.
5. A lookup using the adjacency index in the adjacency table returns an entry that contains adjacency information such as rewrite MACs and encapsulation information, as well as a MET index.
6. Any replication engine in the system uses the MET index to access the indexed MET and replicates packets to specified interfaces in the OIL. Multicast packet replication is the process of creating one or more copies of a multicast packet.

10.5   MULTICAST PACKET REPLICATION

Packet replication forms an important part of multicast packet forwarding. Packet replication is the process by which a network device makes multiple copies of a particular packet and sends each copy out an interface toward a receiver. What differentiates the different replication methods is where the replication is

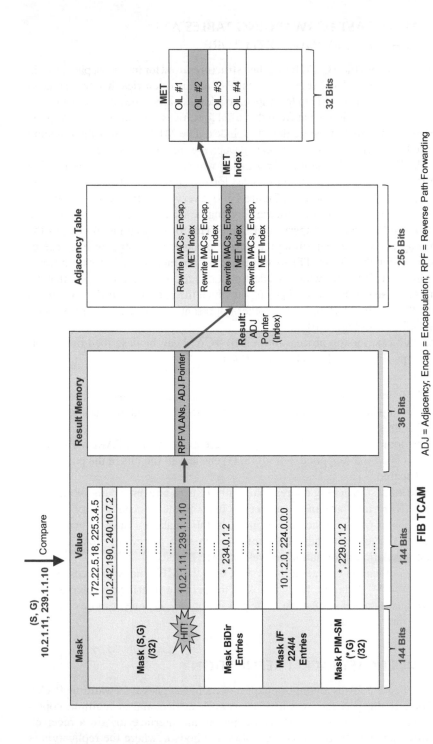

FIGURE 10.10   IPv4 Multicast FIB TCAM, Adjacencies, and MET.

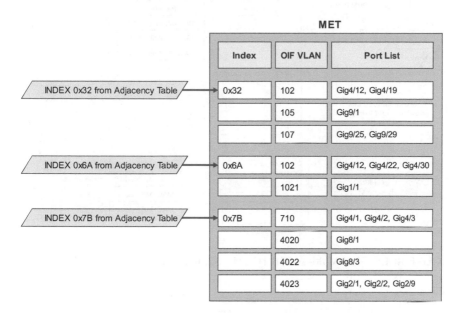

OIF = Outgoing Interface

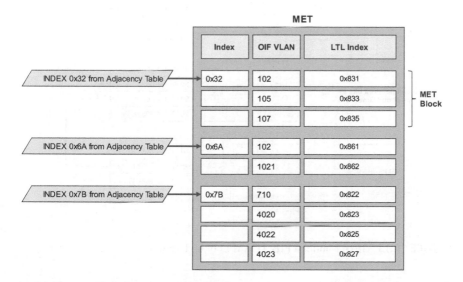

FIGURE 10.11   MET Structure Examples.

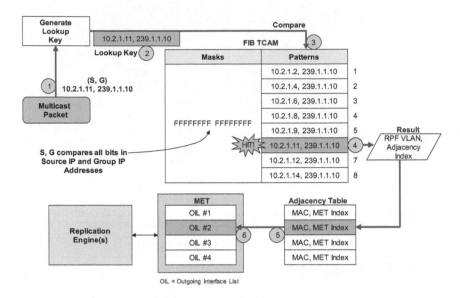

FIGURE 10.12   IPv4 Multicast FIB TCAM Lookup Example.

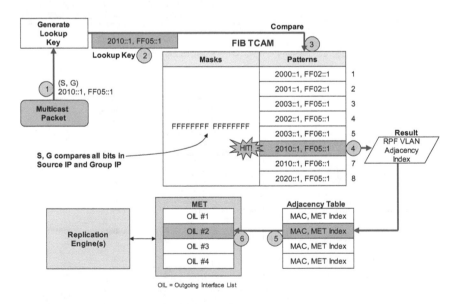

FIGURE 10.13   IPv6 Multicast FIB TCAM Lookup Example.

performed. Some routers perform replication in a centralized processor. Other routers with distributed processing use specialized hardware to perform packet replication in the line cards. Advanced systems with crossbar switch fabrics use sophisticated scheduling algorithms plus the inherent packet replication capabilities of the switch fabric to replicate and forward multicast traffic (see *Chapter 2*).

In the Catalyst 6500, the multicast packet replication modes of a system refer to the location in the multicast router at which multicast replication is performed. Depending on the system architecture, the packet replication load in the Catalyst 6500 can be distributed between the Supervisor Engine and the line cards. The Supervisor Engine always has its own local replication engine. The fabric-enabled and fabric-only line cards also have their own local replication engines. For Supervisor Engines and line cards without a DFC, address lookups are performed by the PFC on the Supervisor Engine.

10.5.1 Centralized Packet Replication

In a majority of low-end platforms, incoming multicast packets are forwarded to a central processing module for replication. That module may perform special processing on the packet, replicate it, and then send it to the line cards for forwarding to other external devices. In the centralized replication model, the replication process may have to compete for processing and memory resources with other important processes used for packet forwarding. Depending on the number of packets requiring replication, the centralized resources can be oversubscribed, resulting in serious performance problems for the most important control plane processes and traffic.

In the Catalyst 6500 Classic line cards (see **Chapter 4**), packet replication is always carried out centrally on the Supervisor Engine. The packet replication in this line card type is performed as follows:

* The Supervisor Engine performs all multicast packet replication for all line cards in the system.
* All arriving multicast packets are transferred over the 32 Gb/s shared switching bus to the Supervisor Engine.
* All replicated packets also pass over the 32 Gb/s shared switching bus to the egress line cards.
* The PFC performs lookups for all arriving packets and then replicate the packets.
* There exists only one MET in the system which is the MET used by the replication engine on the Supervisor Engine.

10.5.2 Packet Replication in the Line Cards

In modern switches and routers, the need for high-speed packet forwarding requires the use of specialized ASICs. So, distributed forwarding systems use ASICs to push forwarding decisions as close as possible to the line cards or interfaces.

The Catalyst 6500 fabric-enabled and fabric-only line cards (see also **Chapter 4**), support two packet replication modes:

* Ingress multicast packet replication
* Egress multicast packet replication.

10.5.2.1   Ingress Multicast Packet Replication

Some distributed forwarding systems use replication engine ASICs associated with the ingress line card or interface to perform replication. In this method, the ingress line card or interface replicates the multicast packet and forwards copies over the switch fabric to the egress line cards and interfaces. Ingress replication distributes processing and memory resource demands across multiple line cards or interfaces but may occasionally require forwarding by the central processor depending on the processing needs of the received packet. Ingress replication mode in the Catalyst 6500 has the following features:

- This mode of packet replication requires the use of a crossbar switch fabric and replication-capable line cards (fabric-enabled and fabric-only line cards).
- The replication engine on the ingress line card performs multicast packet replication to the outgoing interfaces (OIFs). One copy of a multicast packet is forwarded across the switch fabric to each of the egress line cards having outgoing interfaces (OIFs). If a multicast packet is destined to three egress line cards, the ingress line card will send three copies of the packet across the switch fabric, one separate copy to each egress line card at a time.
- In ingress replication mode, address lookups are performed in the ingress DFC or PFC for arriving multicast packets and replicated packets.
- All replicated packets are forwarded over the switch fabric to the egress line cards.
- The architecture supports multiple METs with each replication engine having its own local MET. The contents of all METs are synchronized.
- The system auto-detects the default replication mode, but this setting can be changed.

10.5.2.2   Egress Multicast Packet Replication

In some designs, the replication engine ASICs associated with the egress line cards or interfaces can also perform replication. Although replicating only at the egress line card or interface could lead to a loss in efficiency in some instances, the egress line cards in many platforms may be required to terminate some encapsulated multicast packets destined to certain domains. This may make the egress line card a more ideal point for packet replication because that particular line card has many interfaces leading to downstream multicast receivers. Egress replication mode in the Catalyst 6500 has the following features:

- This mode of packet replication is supported on the Supervisor Engine 720 with only certain line card types (e.g., CEF720).
- All the line cards on the chassis must be capable of egress packet replication.
- Egress packet replication is not optimized unless the line cards have DFCs installed.

- Lookups for arriving packets are performed on the ingress DFC.
- Lookups for packets replicated by the egress replication engine are performed on the egress DFC.
- For outgoing interfaces that are on the ingress line card, the local replication engine performs the packet replication.
- For outgoing interfaces that are on other line cards, the ingress replication engine sends a single copy of the multicast packet over the switch fabric to all egress line cards. If a multicast packet is destined to three egress line cards, the ingress line card will send only a single copy of the packet across the switch fabric (and not multiple copies).
- The replication engine on the egress line card performs packet replication for all local outgoing interfaces.
- The METs on different line cards can be asymmetric i.e., different.

10.5.3 Combined Replication Methods

A system may implement a distributed replication architecture that has a combination of centralized, ingress, and egress replication. An ingress line card may perform one level of replication and then forward one copy of the packet to each egress line card. Each egress line card in turn can create copies of the received replicated packet, to be sent to each of its local interfaces. This combined method of replication also distributes processing and memory resource demands across as many modules as possible. A system may use distributed replication where replication is performed on both the ingress line card and the egress line card. This is the replication model mostly used in the Catalyst 6500 Series.

10.5.4 Packet Replication at Layer 3 versus Layer 2

Layer 3 replication involves creating one or more copies of a multicast packet to be forwarded on each of the interfaces in an outgoing interface list (OIL). For IP (Layer 3) multicast packet forwarding and replication between (one or multiple) router interfaces, the Replication Engine is responsible for the replication. Layer 2 replication involves creating copies of a multicast packet to be forwarded within a single IP subnet or VLAN. If Layer 2 multicast replication is required when Layer 2 forwarding is done between ports on the same line card, the Port ASIC on the line card is responsible for the replication. If multicast packet replication is required when forwarding between ports on different line cards over the crossbar switch fabric, the Fabric ASIC performs the replication.

In the Catalyst 6500, multicast packets arriving on a line card without a replication engine (as in the Classic line cards) will be replicated by the replication engine on the Supervisor Engine. All fabric-enabled line cards are capable of operating in the ingress replication mode. The system will default to ingress replication mode when at least one line card in the system is not capable of egress replication.

10.5.5   PACKET REPLICATION IN THE SWITCH FABRIC: PREFERRED METHOD

Most switch fabrics (shared-bus, shared-memory, crossbar switches, etc.) have inherent or in-built multicast and broadcast features that allow a single input interface to send a single packet to multiple output interfaces simultaneously. An input interface is able to send a packet to multiple output interfaces without having to send a copy of the packet to each output interface one at a time (N output interfaces will require N separate copies to be sent). As discussed in **Chapter 2**, crossbar switches with well-designed scheduling algorithms are capable of transferring and replicating multicast traffic efficiently from an input port to multiple output ports.

Even with such capabilities, a crossbar switch may still require the use of egress replication to allow an output port to replicate packets to one or more outgoing interfaces that have receivers interested in the multicast traffic. This means the multicast-capable crossbar switch fabric will not require ingress replication but may use egress replication. Research in the development of more efficient multicast scheduling algorithms for crossbar switch fabrics is still ongoing, but **Chapter 2** provides some insight into the main issues involved in multicast traffic scheduling.

10.6   MULTICAST FORWARDING ARCHITECTURE EXAMPLE: CATALYST 6500 SUPERVISOR ENGINE 720

The Route Processor on the MSFC (Figure 10.14) is responsible for the following multicast control plane functions:

- Running the control plane protocols such as PIM, IGMP, MLD, Auto-RP, Bootstrap Router (BSR), Multicast Source Discovery Protocol (MSDP), unicast routing protocols, etc.
- Managing the IP multicast routes in the MRIB
- Calculating the RPF interfaces for multicast traffic
- Downloading IP MRIB entries (maintained by the Route Processor) to the Switch Processor for installation in the PFC and DFC hardware forwarding engines.

The Switch Processor (Figure 10.14) is responsible for the following multicast control plane functions:

- Managing and maintaining the hardware FIBs in the PFC and DFC
- Processing IGMP packet resulting from IGMP snooping
- Processing PIM snooping packets
- Performing the IGMP Querier function
- Performing Statistics Collection and Reporting.

With PIM snooping, a Layer 2 switch limits multicast packets to a multicast group to only those switch interfaces/ports that have downstream receivers that have joined that group. By listening to PIM Join and Prune messages, PIM Hello messages, and election messages sent by a BIDIR-PIM Designated Forwarder, the

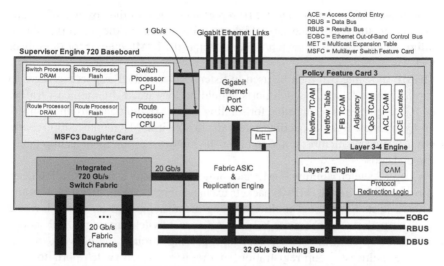

FIGURE 10.14 Supervisor Engine 720 Multicast Architecture.

Component	Description
Route Processor	RP runs the multicast routing protocols and builds the mroute tables, while the SP handles the download/programming of these tables into appropriate forwarding hardware.
Switch Processor	RP downloads the mroutes (FIB), adjacency tables, and MET to the SP, and then SP then installs these tables in the appropriate forwarding hardware. Multicast FIB and adjacency tables are copied to the PFC/DFC hardware, while the MET are copied and installed in the replication engines. The SP also performs IGMP and PIM snooping and maintains the Layer 2 (MAC) addressed table for IGMP snooping.
Multicast FIB TCAM	This contains the multicast routes (mroutes). This consists of (S,G) and (*,G) multicast route entries, and RPF VLAN.
Layer 2 CAM	This contains multicast MAC address entries and their corresponding interfaces.
Adjacency Table	This contains the Layer 2 rewrite information (MAC addresses) for multicast packets and indexes into the MET.
QoS TCAM	This contains ACL entries used for QoS processing and filtering.
ACL TCAM	This contains ACL entries used for security processing and filtering.
NetFlow TCAM	This contains statistics and NetFlow features.
Fabric and Bus Interface	This ASIC provides interfaces to the crossbar switch fabric and 32 Gb/s shared switching bus.
Multicast Expansion Table (MET)	This contains Outgoing Interface Lists (OILs) for multicast routes (i.e., list of interfaces requiring multicast packet replication).
Replication Engine	This provides packet replications services for multicast traffic and Switched Port Analyzer (SPAN).
Protocol Redirection Logic	This captures IGMP/MLD packets and redirects them for multicast group membership information to be recorded.

switch is able to learn which interfaces on which it should send the multicast traffic within a specific subnet or VLAN.

In order for IGMP and IGMP snooping [CISC4500CH23] [CISC4500CH33] [RFC4541] to function, there must be a multicast router on the subnet or VLAN that generates IGMP queries. When a subnet or VLAN does not have a multicast router to originate IGMP queries, then an IGMP querier must be used to send multicast group membership queries. The IGMP querier sends out periodic IGMP queries that trigger the hosts in the subnet or VLAN that want to receive

IP multicast traffic to send out IGMP report messages. In the absence of a multicast router, the IGMP querier (which must be present in the network) can be configured on a switch or switch/router to act as the IGMP querier for the subnet or VLAN.

IGMP snooping can then be used to listen to these IGMP report messages to establish which Layer 2 switch ports should be forwarded the multicast traffic. The IGMP querier is responsible for sending out IGMP multicast group membership Query messages at specified intervals, to solicit IGMP membership reports from active group members, and to allow the multicast group membership tables to be updated.

A Layer 2 switch running IGMP snooping can passively listen to IGMP Query, Report, and Leave (in IGMPv2) packets exchanged between multicast routers and multicast hosts to map out multicast group membership and on which Layer 2 switch ports these members are located. A Layer 2 switch running IGMP snooping listens and examines IGMP messages passing through the network, recognizes the multicast group registration, and registers which switch ports to send the multicast traffic accordingly. The switch forwards multicast traffic only to the ports that have multicast group members.

IPv4 multicast forwarding in the Catalyst 6500 can be done on central forwarding engines or on distributed multicast hardware forwarding engines. Some line cards support distributed multicast packet replication using on-board replication engines. In the Catalyst 6500, PIM-SSM and PIM-SM forwarding are also carried out in hardware while BIDIR-PIM forwarding is done in hardware only in some modules. The Catalyst 6500 off-loads a majority of forwarding tasks from the Route Processor to the distributed forwarding modules. The key functions are described as follows. The Route Processor on the Supervisor Engine 720 (Figure 10.14) derives the following key data structures from the MRIB:

- **Multicast FIB**: This contains the (S, G) and (*, G) entries, and their RPF subnets or VLANs
- **Adjacency Table**: This contains rewrite information for multicast adjacencies such as the Layer 2 addresses and MET index (to a separate MET)
- **Multicast Expansion Table (MET)**: This table (also called the Replication Expansion Table (RET)) contains the output interface lists (OILs), that is, lists of router interfaces having ((S, G) and (*, G)) group members and requiring multicast packet replication. The MET stores the {VLAN, switchport} replication information for Layer 2 multicast/broadcast/flooding associated with IP multicast forwarding. Each Replication Engine in the system has its own local MET. The contents of the MET (Figure 10.11) are read using the MET index obtained from the adjacency table (Figure 10.10). MET contains the list of outgoing interfaces and their corresponding destination LTL index (as shown in Figure 10.11).

The Route Processor downloads the earlier tables to the Switch Processor which then installs them in appropriate hardware tables in the forwarding modules:

- The MFIB and adjacency tables are copied to the PFC and DFC hardware forwarding engines.
- The MET is copied to the replication engines in the system.

The MET memory is located on the replication engines and not on the PFC or DFC. The Switch Processor is also responsible for entering the results obtained from IGMP snooping into the Layer 2 tables (Figure 10.14). IGMP snooping is used to limit the flooding of multicast traffic on Layer 2 switch ports that do not have multicast group members.

To facilitate IGMP snooping and multicast packet filtering, the Protocol Redirection Logic on the PFC (Figure 10.14) recognizes IGMP packets and redirects them to the Switch Processor on the MSFC. The Switch Processor then installs the active Layer 2 ports having multicast group members in the Layer 2 table. Multicast packets are only forwarded to the ports in the Layer 2 table having group members. The Protocol Redirection Logic on the PFC focuses on intercepting and redirecting only IGMP and PIM packets (Figure 10.15).

With PIM snooping, a Layer switch is able to constrain multicast "flooding" to only the Layer 2 ports that have multicast group members. PIM snooping is mainly used in a Layer 2 core that has PIM-connected receivers and works as follows in the Catalyst 6500:

- The PFC or DFC Layer 2 forwarding ASICs (via the Protocol Redirection Logic) listen to the Layer 3 contents of PIM packets.
- The Layer 2 forwarding ASICs (via the Protocol Redirection Logic) recognize PIM packets and redirects them to Switch Processor on the Supervisor Engine.
- The Switch Processor installs/removes Layer 2 forwarding entries in the Layer 2 tables for switch interfaces which send PIM Join/Prune messages.
- The switch/router forwards multicast traffic to the Layer 2 interfaces according to the multicast entries learned via PIM snooping (per VLAN).

Note that the PFC and the DFC have essentially the same packet processing and forwarding components including the Protocol Redirection Logic.

We discussed in *Chapter 4* that the Catalyst 6500 switch/routers support three types of line cards: Classic, fabric-enabled, and fabric-only line cards. The Classic line cards connect only to the 32 Gb/s shared switching bus and rely on the centralized forwarding engine on the PFC for packet forwarding. In a Catalyst 6500 switch/router using the Classic line card, the entire packet payload is always transmitted on the 32 Gb/s shared bus.

The fabric-enabled line cards connect to both a crossbar switch fabric and the 32 Gb/s shared bus. This line card when not equipped with the optional DFC uses the centralized forwarding engine on the PFC for packet forwarding. In a Catalyst

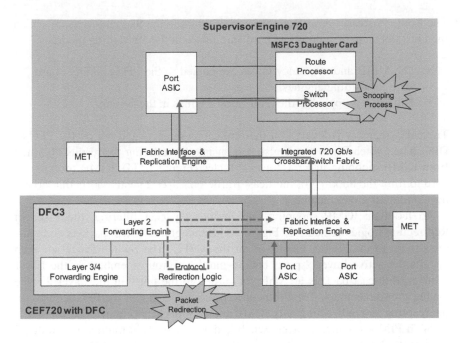

FIGURE 10.15   Illustrating IGMP Snooping/PIM Snooping in the Catalyst 6500.

6500 switch/router using the fabric-enabled line card, only packet headers are transmitted on the 32 Gb/s shared bus for lookup in the centralized forwarding engine in the PFC—the packet payload is always transmitted over the crossbar switch fabric.

The fabric-only line cards connect only to crossbar switch fabric and use a distributed forwarding engine on an onboard DFC for packet forwarding. These line cards are not designed to support the 32 Gb/s shared bus, so after ingress lookups locally on the DFC, the packets are always transmitted over the crossbar switch fabric to the destination module.

The CEF256 is a fabric-enabled line card (Figure 10.16) and connects to both a crossbar switch fabric (256 Gb/s in Supervisor Engine 2 or 720 Gb/s in Supervisor Engine 720) and the 32 Gb/s shared bus. Without a DFC, it uses the centralized packet forwarding services provided by the PFC. Figure 10.16 shows the multicast related components in the CEF256 line card. The dCEF256 line cards are fabric-only line cards (Figure 10.17) and connect only to a 256 Gb/s or 720 Gb/s crossbar switch fabric. This line card uses the distributed forwarding engine on the line card's DFC for packet forwarding. Figure 10.17 also shows the multicast related components in the dCEF256 line card.

The CEF720 line cards are also fabric-enabled line cards but are designed to take full advantage of the higher bandwidth provided by the 720 Gb/s crossbar switch fabric (Figure 10.18). These line cards use the centralized forwarding

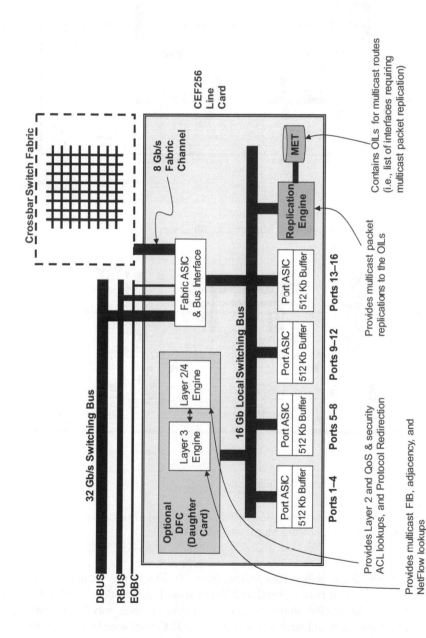

FIGURE 10.16 CEF256 Line Card Multicast Architecture.

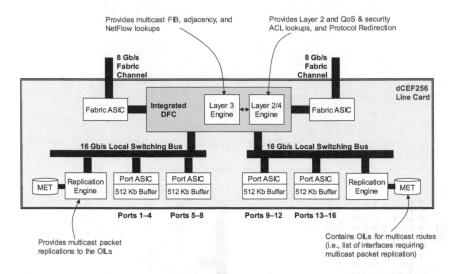

FIGURE 10.17   dCEF256 Line Card Multicast Architecture.

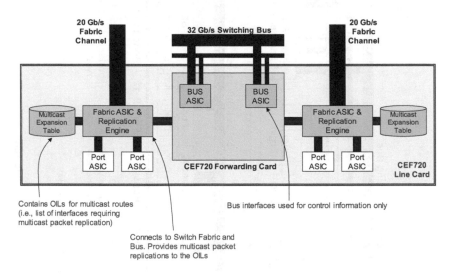

FIGURE 10.18   CEF720 Line Card Multicast Architecture.

engine on the PFC3 for packet forwarding. Each 20 Gb/s fabric channel on the CEF256 line card has a Fabric ASIC and Replication Engine and a local MET. The Bus ASIC to the 32 Gb/s shared bus in this line card is used only for transferring control information and not end-user data. The 32 Gb/s shared bus is used for lookups in the PFC3—the payload is always transmitted over the crossbar switch fabric. However, if a DFC3 is present on the line card, then the ingress lookups are always performed locally on the card—the 32 Gb/s shared bus is not used.

The dCEF720 line cards connect only to the 720 Gb/s crossbar switch fabric. These line cards use the distributed forwarding engine on the DFC3 for packet forwarding. This line card is capable of processing arriving packets and forwarding them directly to the destination line cards. These line cards are designed not to support the 32 Gb/s shared bus, thus, ingress lookups are always performed locally on the card, and the entire packet is always transmitted over the crossbar switch fabric.

The aCEF720 line cards (see **Chapter 8**) also take full advantage of the bandwidth in the 720 Gb/s crossbar switch fabric but use a flow cache-based forwarding engine for packet forwarding (called accelerated CEF (aCEF) in Cisco terminology). Using the aCEF720 line card, the centralized forwarding engine on PFC3 performs the first lookup for the first packet of a given flow. Then the ingress aCEF (or flow cache-based) forwarding engine in the aCEF720 line card performs lookups for subsequent packets of that flow locally. The packet forwarding performance of this architecture varies depending on the traffic mix, but it works well mostly when the traffic consists of long flows where the first packet arrivals are not random.

10.6.1 INGRESS PACKET REPLICATION MODE EXAMPLE: CATALYST 6500 SUPERVISOR ENGINE 720

In this section and the next, we focus on centralized multicast forwarding because it involves relatively more complex processing than distributed multicast forwarding in line cards with DFCs. Multicast forwarding in a system with line cards having DFCs is very similar in complexity to unicast forwarding with line cards with DFCs other than the use of MFIBs and the need for packet replication in the former. We use the Supervisor Engine 720 and the CEF720 line cards as the reference architecture for our discussion.

In the ingress multicast packet replication mode, the ingress line cards perform the replication for the outgoing interfaces on all line cards. Figure 10.20 and Figure 10.21 describe centralized multicast forwarding in the Catalyst 6500 Supervisor Engine 720 with CEF720 line cards using ingress packet replication. In the network scenario, a single Catalyst 6500 is used to interconnect end users in four VLANs: VLAN "Pentagon" (PEN), VLAN "Semi-Circle" (CIR), VLAN "Triangle" (TRI), and VLAN "Square" (SQU).

Figure 10.20 and Figure 10.21 show the port assignment to the four VLANs:

- Two ports on line card 1 and one port on line card 2 connect to hosts on VLAN PEN.
- The multicast source is a host on VLAN PEN and is reachable through one of the two ports on line card 1 connected to VLAN PEN.
- One port on line card 1 connects to hosts on VLAN CIR.
- One port on line card 2 and one port on the Gigabit Ethernet Port ASIC on the Supervisor Engine 720 connect to hosts on VLAN SQU.
- One port on the Gigabit Ethernet Port ASIC on the Supervisor Engine 720 connects to hosts on VLAN TRI.

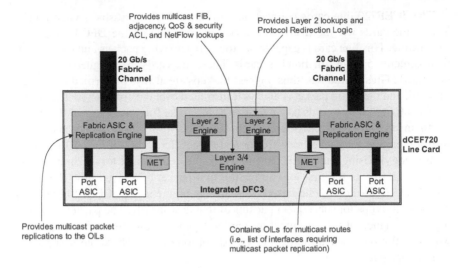

FIGURE 10.19   dCEF720 Line Card Multicast Architecture.

- The multicast source on VLAN PEN and connected to a port on line
  card 1 sends traffic to hosts on VLANs PEN, CIR, TRI, and SQU.

Figure 10.20 and Figure 10.21 describe in detail the steps involved in sending multicast traffic from the source to the receivers in the four VLANs using ingress replication. In these figures, the abbreviation FPOE refers to Fabric Port of Exit [CISCLANSW04]. In Cisco switch/routers that employ crossbar switch Fabric ASICs, each fabric channel to/from the crossbar switch fabric connects directly to a set of physical ports. Hence, for each unique physical port on the system with a unique index (also called a port of exit (POE) index) there is also a corresponding unique FPOE index. For multicast forwarding, each outgoing interface associated with an mroute is mapped to one or more unique POE/FPOE indices, and with each POE associated with a {MAC address, VLAN} pair.

The POEs are associated with physical ports on the switch/router to which external devices/networks can be connected while the FPOE are the ports on the switch fabric to which the line cards and other system modules (including the Supervisor Engine) can be connected. So, an FPOE index identifies a specific fabric channel on the switch fabric while a POE index identifies a specific physical port in the system.

The interface between the switch fabric and a system module (which may have POEs) is the Fabric ASIC. The FPOE is provided as part of the result received from the forwarding engine lookup operations (in the PFC or DFC) and is used by the Fabric ASIC for data forwarding across the switch fabric. The FPOE is a value carried in an 18-bit field (or tag) attached to the packet header. The packet is forwarded across the switch fabric to the correct FPOE as identified by the FPOE index on the packet.

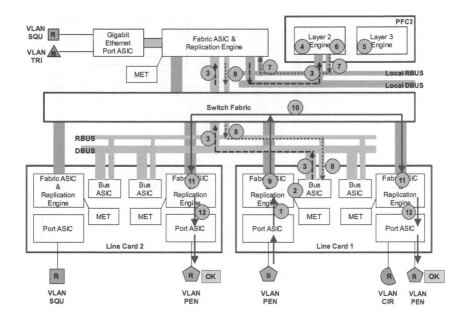

VLANs: "Pentagon" = PEN; Semi Circle" = CIR; Triangle" = TRI; "Square" = SQU.

1. A multicast packet from source S in VLAN PEN enters a line card through the port ASIC and is handed over to the Fabric ASIC on the line card.
2. The Fabric ASIC extracts the packet header and hands it over to the Bus ASIC on the line card.
3. The Bus ASIC transmits the packet header on the 32 Gb/s switching bus (DBUS) to the PFC3 on the Supervisor Engine 720.

Replication and Forwarding to VLAN PEN:

4. Layer 2 engine in PFC3 performs Layer 2 lookup in the *ingress* VLAN (PEN) and then forwards the packet header to the Layer 3 engine.
5. Layer 3 engine performs lookup in its multicast FIB using the packet header information. Layer 3 engine also performs a RPF check and any required *ingress* VLAN ACL, VACL and QoS lookup.
6. Layer 3 engine returns lookup result to Layer 2 engine. Result contains LTL index for multicast packet forwarding in the *ingress* VLAN (PEN) as well as indices for lookup in the MET.
7. Layer 2 engine sends final result to Fabric ASIC on the Supervisor Engine 720 over an internal (local) RBUS.
8. Fabric ASIC on Supervisor Engine 720 then forwards result over RBUS to the originating Bus ASIC which accepts the result. All other Bus ASICs discard it.
9. Fabric ASIC on ingress line card (1) rewrites the packet according to the received result, constructs a Switch Fabric packet containing the rewritten packet and forwards it to the Switch Fabric.
10. Using the FPOE in the fabric packet, the Switch Fabric forwards it only to switch fabric channels that have receivers or mrouters in the ingress VLAN (VLAN PEN).
11. Fabric ASIC on line card 2 (i.e., egress line card) receives fabric packet from the Switch Fabric and forwards it to the Port ASIC.
12. Port ASIC receives the rewritten packet and forwards it to receiver (R) in the ingress VLAN PEN.

FIGURE 10.20 Catalyst 6500 Supervisor Engine 720 Architecture—Centralized Multicast Forwarding with CEF720 Line Cards—Ingress Packet Replication Mode (Steps 1 to 12).

10.6.2 Egress Packet Replication Mode Example: Catalyst 6500 Supervisor Engine 720

In the egress multicast packet replication mode, the ingress multicast traffic is distributed over the fabric to the egress line cards which perform the packet replication for the outgoing interfaces. Figure 10.22 to Figure 10.26 describe centralized

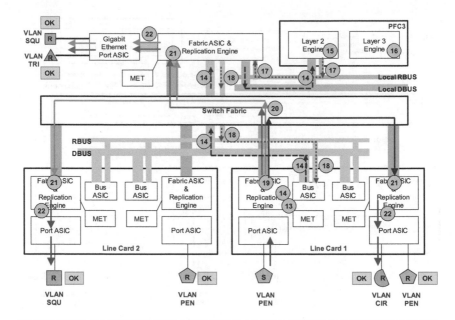

FIGURE 10.21 Catalyst 6500 Supervisor Engine 720 Architecture—Centralized Multicast Forwarding with CEF720 Line Cards—Ingress Packet Replication Mode (Steps 13 to 22).

Replication and Forwarding to VLAN CIR, SQU and TRI:
13. Using the MET indices contained in the result received in Step 6, ingress Replication Engine (RE) on line card (1) performs a lookup in its MET to obtain all the OIFs in the OIL.
14. RE makes one copy of the original multicast packet, for each of the OIFs in the OIL, and transmits a corresponding packet over the DBUS to the PFC3 (each copy is processed as follows):
15. Layer 2 engine in PFC3 does not perform a lookup and forwards appropriate packet headers to Layer 3 engine.
16. Layer 3 engine receives packet headers from the Layer 2 engine and performs egress ACL, VACL and QoS lookups.
17. Layer 3 engine forwards result to Layer 2 engine which forwards result over an internal RBUS to the Fabric ASIC on the Supervisor Engine 720.
18. Fabric ASIC on Supervisor Engine 720 forwards result over RBUS to originating Bus ASIC which accepts the result. All other Bus ASICs discard it.
19. Fabric ASIC on ingress line card (1) rewrites the packets according to the results, constructs a Switch Fabric packet containing the rewritten packet, and forwards it to the Switch Fabric.
20. Using the FPOE in the fabric packet, Switch Fabric forwards packet only to channels that have receivers or mrouters in the egress VLANs (CIR, SQU, and TRI).
21. Fabric ASICs on egress line cards (1 and 2) receive fabric packet from the Switch Fabric and forward it to Port ASICs.
22. Port ASIC receives the rewritten packet and forwards it to receiver (R) in the egress VLAN (CIR, SQU and TRI).

multicast forwarding in the Catalyst 6500 Supervisor Engine 720 with CEF720 line cards using egress packet replication. We assume the same networking scenario as the ingress replication case described earlier where a single Catalyst 6500 is used to interconnect end users in four VLANs: VLAN "Pentagon" (PEN), VLAN "Semi-Circle" (CIR), VLAN "Triangle" (TRI). and VLAN "Square" (SQU).

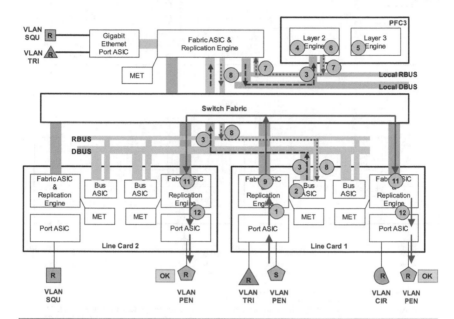

1. A multicast packet from source S in VLAN PEN enters a line card through the port ASIC and is handed over to the Fabric ASIC on the line card.
2. The Fabric ASIC extracts the packet header and hands it over to the Bus ASIC on the line card.
3. The Bus ASIC transmits the packet header on the 32 Gb/s switching bus (DBUS) to the PFC3 on the Supervisor Engine 720.

Replication and Forwarding to VLAN PEN:
4. Layer 2 engine in PFC3 performs Layer 2 lookup in the *ingress* VLAN (PEN) and then forwards the packet header to the Layer 3 engine.
5. Layer 3 engine performs lookup in its multicast FIB using the packet header information. Layer 3 engine also performs a RPF check and any required *ingress* VLAN ACL, VACL, and QoS lookup.
6. Layer 3 engine returns lookup result to Layer 2 engine. Result contains LTL index for multicast packet forwarding in the *ingress* VLAN (PEN) as well as indices for lookup in the MET.
7. Layer 2 engine sends final result to Fabric ASIC on the Supervisor Engine 720 over an internal RBUS.
8. Fabric ASIC on Supervisor Engine 720 then forwards result over RBUS to the originating Bus ASIC which accepts the result. All other Bus ASICs discard it.
9. Fabric ASIC on ingress line card (1) rewrites the packet according to the received result, constructs a Switch Fabric packet containing the rewritten packet, and forwards it to the switch fabric.
10. Using the FPOE in the fabric packet, the Switch Fabric forwards it only to Switch Fabric channels that have receivers or mrouters in the ingress VLAN (VLAN PEN).
11. Fabric ASIC on line card 2 (i.e., egress line card) receives fabric packet from the Switch Fabric and forwards it to the Port ASIC.
12. Port ASIC receives the rewritten packet and forwards it to receiver (R) in the ingress VLAN PEN.

FIGURE 10.22 Catalyst 6500 Supervisor Engine 720 Architecture—Centralized Multicast Forwarding with CEF720 Line Cards—Egress Packet Replication Mode (Steps 1 to 12).

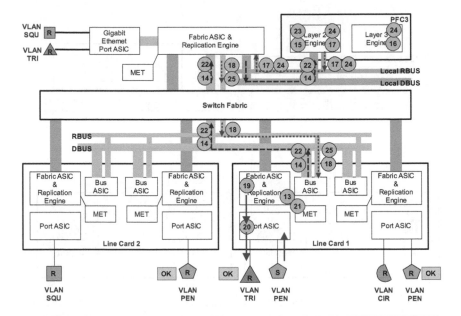

Replication and Forwarding to VLAN TRI on Line Card 1:

13. Using the MET index contained in the result received in Step 6, ingress RE performs a lookup in its MET to obtain all the OIFs in the OIL that are local to this RE. There is one multicast receiver in VLAN TRI local to this RE.
14. RE makes a copy of the original multicast packet to be sent to VLAN TRI and Fabric ASIC transmits a corresponding packet over the DBUS to the PFC3 for egress processing.
15. Layer 2 engine in PFC3 does not perform a lookup and forwards appropriate packet headers to Layer 3 engine.
16. Layer 3 engine receives packet headers from the Layer 2 engine and performs egress ACL, VACL, and QoS lookup for VLAN TRI.
17. Layer 3 engine forwards result to Layer 2 engine which then forwards it to Fabric ASIC on Supervisor Engine 720.
18. Fabric ASIC on Supervisor Engine 720 forwards result over RBUS to originating Bus ASIC which accepts the result. All other Bus ASICs discard it.
19. Fabric ASIC on ingress line card (1) receives result and forwards copy of multicast packet to Port ASIC.
20. Port ASIC forwards multicast packet to receiver in VLAN TRI based on destination index in the received result.

Replication and Forwarding to VLAN CIR on Line Card 1:

21. RE performs a second lookup in the MET using the MET index in the previous result. This lookup yields an egress replication VLAN ID and a destination index.
22. RE copies the multicast packet to the (internal) egress replication VLAN (of switch/router) and Fabric ASIC. RE transmits a corresponding packet over DBUS to the PFC3.
23. Layer 2 engine lookup indicates Layer 2 forwarding (bridging) to all other line cards with multicast receivers and engine flags the multicast packet so that it is replicated by the receiving line card.
24. Layer 3 engine performs no RACL, VACL or QoS lookups on this packet. Result is forwarded to Layer 2 engine which then forwards it to Fabric ASIC of the Supervisor Engine.
25. Fabric ASIC transmits result over the RBUS and is received by Fabric ASIC on the line card 1. All other line cards discard result.

FIGURE 10.23   Catalyst 6500 Supervisor Engine 720 Architecture—Centralized Multicast Forwarding with CEF720 Line Cards—Egress Packet Replication Mode (Steps 13 to 25).

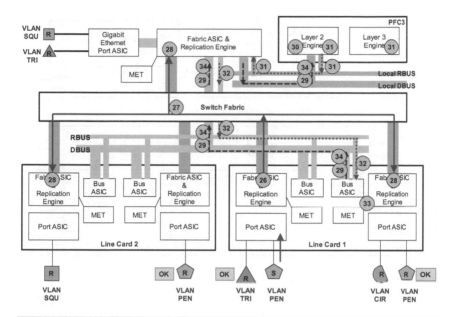

26. Fabric ASIC constructs FPOE to forward multicast packet to all line cards with local receivers or mrouters in the egress VLANs and forwards the packet to the switch fabric in the egress replication VLAN.
27. Using the FPOE in the fabric packet, switch fabric forwards packet only to channels that have local receivers or mrouters on any OIF.
28. Fabric ASICs on egress line cards receive the packet on the internal replication VLAN (of the switch/router) and hand it over to the RE.
29. Fabric ASIC that received the multicast packet on the internal replication VLAN forwards the packet to the PFC3 for lookup.
30. Layer 2 engine in PFC3 recognizes packet is flagged for egress replication and forwards packet headers to Layer 3 engine.
31. Layer 3 engine performs multicast FIB lookup using secondary entry which yields MET index for replication to all local OIFs. Layer 3 engine forwards result to the Layer 2 engine which then forwards it to the Fabric ASIC on Supervisor Engine.

Note: Steps 29 – 31 are repeated for each of the line card fabric ASICs that received the multicast packet on the internal replication VLAN. Each Fabric ASIC needs the result of the FIB lookup (i.e., the index for the MET lookup to obtain the OIL for all the local multicast receivers and mrouters)

32. Fabric ASIC on Supervisor Engine forwards result which is received by fabric ASIC on line card 1. All other line cards discard result.
33. RE performs a MET lookup using the MET index contained in the result and replicates packet onto VLAN CIR.
34. Multicast packet is forwarded over the DBUS to the PFC3 for an egress lookup.

FIGURE 10.24 Catalyst 6500 Supervisor Engine 720 Architecture—Centralized Multicast Forwarding with CEF720 Line Cards—Egress Packet Replication Mode (Steps 26 to 34).

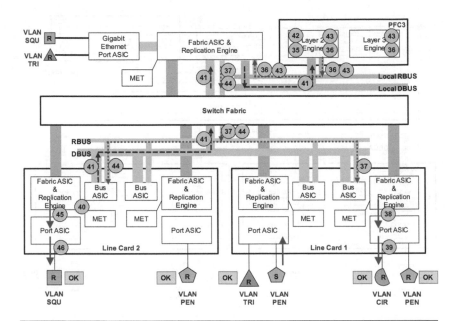

35. Layer 2 engine on PFC3 performs Layer 2 lookup in egress VLAN (VLAN CIR) and forwards packet headers to Layer 3 engine.
36. Layer 3 engine performs egress VLAN RACL, VACL and QoS lookups for and forwards result to Layer 2 engine which then forwards it to the Fabric ASIC on Supervisor Engine.
37. Fabric ASIC on Supervisor Engine forwards result which is received by Fabric ASIC on line card 1. All other line cards discard result.
38. Fabric ASIC forwards a copy of multicast packet to Port ASIC.
39. Port ASIC forwards packet to multicast receiver in VLAN CIR based on destination index in the result.

Replication Forwarding and to VLAN SQU on Line Card 2:
40. RE on line card 2 performs a lookup in its MET using the MET index contained in the result and replicates the packet onto VLAN SQU.
41. Multicast packet is sent to the PFC3 over the DBUS for an egress lookup.
42. Layer 2 engine in PFC3 performs Layer 2 lookup in egress VLAN (VLAN SQU) and forwards packet headers to Layer 3 engine.
43. Layer 3 engine performs egress VLAN RACL, VACL and QoS lookups and forwards result to Layer 2 engine which then forwards it to the Fabric ASIC on Supervisor Engine.
44. Fabric ASIC on Supervisor Engine forwards result which is received by Fabric ASIC on line card 1. All other line cards discard result.
45. Fabric ASIC forwards a copy of multicast packet to Port ASIC.
46. Port ASIC forwards packet to multicast receiver in VLAN SQU based on destination index in the result.

FIGURE 10.25 Catalyst 6500 Supervisor Engine 720 Architecture—Centralized Multicast Forwarding with CEF720 Line Cards—Egress Packet Replication Mode (Steps 35 to 46).

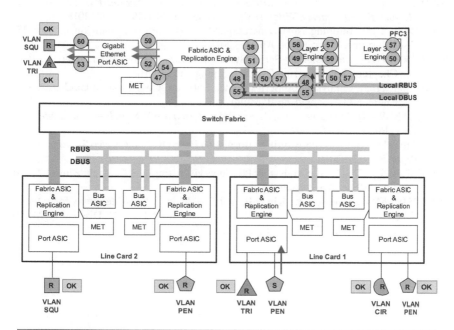

Replication and Forwarding to VLAN TRI on Gigabit Ethernet Port ASIC:

47. RE on Supervisor Engine performs a MET lookup using the MET index contained in the result and replicates packet to be sent to VLAN TRI.
48. Multicast packet is forwarded over an internal DBUS on the Supervisor Engine to the PFC3 for an egress lookup.
49. Layer 2 engine on the PFC3 performs Layer 2 lookup in egress VLAN (VLAN TRI) and forwards packet headers to Layer 3 engine.
50. Layer 3 engine performs egress VLAN RACL, VACL, and QoS lookups and forwards result to Layer 2 engine which then forwards it to the Fabric ASIC on Supervisor Engine.
51. Result received by Fabric ASIC on the Supervisor Engine but is not sent over the external RBUS.
52. Fabric ASIC on the Supervisor Engine forwards a copy of packet to Port ASIC.
53. Port ASIC (on Supervisor Engine) forwards packet to receiver in VLAN TRI based on destination index in the result.

Replication and Forwarding to VLAN SQU on Gigabit Ethernet Port ASIC:

54. RE on Supervisor Engine performs a MET lookup using the MET index obtained in the result and replicates packet to be sent to VLAN SQU.
55. Multicast packet is forwarded over the internal DBUS to the PFC3 for an egress lookup.
56. Layer 2 engine on PFC3 performs Layer 2 lookup in egress VLAN (VLAN SQU) and forwards packet headers to Layer 3 engine.
57. Layer 3 engine performs egress VLAN RACL, VACL, and QoS lookups and forwards result to Layer 2 engine which then forwards it to the Fabric ASIC on Supervisor Engine.
58. Result received by fabric ASIC on the Supervisor Engine but is not sent over the external RBUS.
59. Fabric ASIC forwards a copy of multicast packet to Port ASIC.
60. Port ASIC forwards packet to multicast receiver in VLAN SQU based on destination index in the result.

FIGURE 10.26　Catalyst 6500 Supervisor Engine 720 Architecture—Centralized Multicast Forwarding with CEF720 Line Cards—Egress Packet Replication Mode (Steps 47 to 60).

REFERENCES

[AWEYA1BK18]. J. Aweya, *Switch/Router Architectures: Shared-Bus and Shared-Memory Based Systems*, Wiley-IEEE Press, ISBN 9781119486152, 2018.

[CISC2TMUL11]. Building Next-Generation Multicast Networks with Supervisor 2T, Cisco Systems, White Paper, Apr. 13, 2011.

[CISC4500CH23]. Catalyst 4500 Series Switch Software Configuration Guide, 12.2(53) SG, Chapter 23, Configuring IGMP Snooping and Filtering.

[CISC4500CH33]. Catalyst 4500 Series Switch Software Configuration Guide, 12.2(53) SG, Chapter 33, Configuring IP Multicast.

[CISCLANSW04]. D. Barnes and B. Sakandar, *Cisco LAN Switching Fundamentals*, Cisco Press, July 15, 2004.

[CISCMFIB11]. Multicast Forwarding Information Base Overview, Cisco Systems, White Paper, May 27, 2011.

[CISCSUPENG32]. Cisco Catalyst 6500 Supervisor Engine 32 Architecture, Cisco Systems, White Paper, 2006.

[RFC4541]. M. Christensen, K. Kimball, and F. Solensky, "Considerations for Internet Group Management Protocol (IGMP) and Multicast Listener Discovery (MLD) Snooping Switches," IETF RFC 4541, May 2006.

Index